panama

NATIONAL GEOGRAPHIC
TRAVELER

panama

by Christopher P. Baker
photography by Gilles Mingasson

National Geographic
Washington, D.C.

CONTENTS

**Pages 2–3: A day on the beach at Cayo Zapatillo Uno in Bocas del Toro
Opposite: Fireworks over Iglesia San Pedro, Isla Taboga**

TRAVELING WITH EYES OPEN

Alert travelers go with a purpose and leave with a benefit. If you travel responsibly, you can help support wildlife conservation, historic preservation, and cultural enrichment in the places you visit. You can enrich your own travel experience as well.

To be a geo-savvy traveler:

- Recognize that your presence has an impact on the places you visit.

- Spend your time and money in ways that sustain local character. (Besides, it's more interesting that way.)

- Value the destination's natural and cultural heritage.

- Respect the local customs and traditions.

- Express appreciation to local people about things you find interesting and unique to the place: its nature and scenery, music and food, historic villages and buildings.

- Vote with your wallet: Support the people who support the place, patronizing businesses that make an effort to celebrate and protect what's special there. Seek out local shops, restaurants, and inns. Use tour operators who love their home—who love taking care of it and showing it off. Avoid businesses that detract from the character of the place.

- Enrich yourself, taking home memories and stories to tell, knowing that you have contributed to the preservation and enhancement of the destination.

That is the type of travel now called geotourism, defined as "tourism that sustains or enhances the geographical character of a place—its environment, culture, aesthetics, heritage, and the well-being of its residents." To learn more, visit National Geographic's Center for Sustainable Destinations at *nationalgeographic.com/travel/sustainable.*

panama

ABOUT THE AUTHOR & PHOTOGRAPHER

After studying geography at the University of London and Latin American Studies at the University of Liverpool, author **Christopher P. Baker** settled in California and established a career as a travel writer, photographer, and lecturer. He has written for more than 200 leading international publications as well as more than 20 books, including *National Geographic Traveler* guidebooks to Colombia, Costa Rica, Cuba, and the Dominican Republic, and *Mi Moto Fidel: Motorcycling through Castro's Cuba.* A two-time national book award winner, Baker is also a National Geographic Resident Expert, and escorts cruise tours of Costa Rica and Panama plus tours and photo expeditions to Cuba and Colombia for National Geographic Expeditions. In 2008, he won the prestigious Lowell Thomas Award for Travel Journalist of the Year.

Photographer **Gilles Mingasson** grew up in Grenoble, France, before moving to Paris to pursue a career in photojournalism. After being sent to the United States on assignment, he made Los Angeles his base. In 1990 Mingasson spent six months bicycling 7,500 miles (12,070 km) across the Soviet Union with two cameras (and a serious saddle rash). On the eve of profound changes that few had yet grasped, he photographed ordinary people who had lived their entire lives under the Soviet state. Today, Mingasson works on feature and travel stories for clients including *Newsweek, Fortune, Reader's Digest, Scholastic, Sky, Le Nouvel Observateur, L'Equipe, Reppublica Delle Donne, Espresso, Elle,* and *Le Figaro.* Some of his projects have included NASCAR Dads, global warming in an Eskimo village, and a documentary on Latinos in the United States. Assignments have taken him to Asia, Australia, Latin America, Europe, India, and North Africa.

Charting Your Trip

Grandiose, dramatic, spanning an entire continent: The huge Panama Canal is synonymous with the country it bisects. But the canal's importance should not overshadow the country's other treasures. Wildlife wonders, pristine beaches, and the modern delights of Panama City await visitors to Panama.

Holding a pivotal position at the juncture of two great continents and seas, Panama is a meeting point for the flora and fauna of each. The oceans, mountains, and forests teem with colorful animals and birds. And Panama City is one of the world's great financial centers and a cosmopolitan capital with a rich and turbulent history as well.

How to Visit

Most visitors reach this slender country by air (typically arriving at Tocumen International Airport near Panama City) or boat (many cruise lines make Panama a stop). Cars are the best way to get around the countryside, but if you are traveling to more remote areas, a four-wheel-drive vehicle is necessary. Islands can be reached via boat or small plane.

A shorter visit should concentrate on Panama City, the nearby canal, and perhaps a short hop by air to one of the more remote regions for an experience of tropical nature and indigenous culture. Longer visits can take in the coffee culture of the highlands and the magnificent surfing beaches along the Caribbean.

If You Have One Week

Don't let the wealth of options confound you. It's easy to plan an itinerary that condenses the best that there is to see and do. A weeklong visit should begin in **Panama City,** the capital, where rental cars, buses, and planes are all readily available for your touring needs. Here, you can explore the ruins of Panamá Viejo and Casco Antiguo—the recently restored and vibrant, museum-packed colonial heart. Be sure to visit the Museo del Canal Interoceánico, Catedral Metropolitano, and Plaza de Francia. Factor in time for a walking tour of Balboa to include the Panama Canal Administration Building; and leave time as well for the Biomuseo. Panama City's modern districts are packed with world-class hotels, restaurants, and nightclubs. The city's key sites can all be seen in two days.

Panama City makes a great base for visiting the nearby canal, best experienced at the **Miraflores Locks Visitor Center,** 30 minutes from the city, and on a boat excursion through the locks booked through local tour operators.

Visitor Information

Panama's central tourist organization is **Autoridad de Turismo Panama** (ATP; *Edificio BICSA, Ave. Balboa at Aquilino de la Guardia, Panama City, tel 526-7000 or 800/231-0568 in the U.S., visit panama.com*). ATP has bureaus throughout the country; see regional listings at *atp.gob.pa*. Panama's environmental agency, **Autoridad Nacional del Ambiente** (ANAM; *tel 500-0898; anam .gob.pa*), administers national parks and other protected areas.

The **Chagres** watershed is great for birding, perhaps at the Canopy Tower or at Gamboa Rainforest Resort, where an aerial tram gives you a great perspective, and for white-water rafting on the Río Chagres. Twenty-eight miles (45 km) east of Colón, the Caribbean port of **Portobelo** has fortresses recalling Spanish wealth and the wicked deeds of pirates past. While here, you can dive amid coral reefs and the wrecks of Spanish treasure galleons. Even the farthest point can be reached in three hours by car from Panama City. Allow two days for the canal and Caribbean.

Next, hop a plane for the short ride to **El Porvenir** in the San Blas Islands. Buy *molas*—fabric art made with a reverse-appliqué technique—on Wichub Huala and hire a boat for the ride to **Isla de los Perros,** where you can snorkel in turquoise waters and sun on irresistibly white sands. After an overnight stay for a real taste of indigenous culture, fly back to Panama City and board a flight to **Darién** for birding and hiking in the largest intact rain forest swathe in Central America. Ancon Expeditions *(tel 269-9415, anconexpeditions.com)* can make arrangements for a two-day visit to either **Cana,** at 1,500 feet (457 m) elevation within Parque Nacional Darién, or to **Reserva Natural Punta Patiño**—two incomparable venues for spying harpy eagles, macaws, monkeys, and a plethora of other exotic wildlife. With luck, you may even see capybaras, tapirs, and—fingers crossed!—an elusive big cat.

> **NOT TO BE MISSED:**
>
> A walking tour of Casco Antiguo **68–70**
>
> Birding at the Canopy Tower in Gamboa **99**
>
> A cruise through the Panama Canal **102–103**
>
> Lazing on a beach in the Archipiélago de las Perlas **113**
>
> Buying *molas* in Kuna Yala **126**
>
> Snorkeling at Isla Granito de Oro **163**
>
> Whale-watching in the Gulf of Panama **164–165**
>
> Sampling fresh-grown coffee in Boquete **196–197**
>
> A hike in the cloud forests of Volcán Barú **198–199**

If You Have More Time

Panama offers amazing diversity, including sensational beaches. Some of the best line the shores of the **Archipiélago de las Perlas,** well worth the flight to Isla Contadora. Or, head west by car to **Playa Blanca** (popular with Panama's middle class), stopping en route for at least one night in **El Valle de Antón**—a Shangri-la mountain valley good for hiking, horseback riding, and an adrenalin-charged ride on the Canopy Adventure zipline. Don't miss a gourmet dinner, too, at La Casa de Lourdes.

The world is suddenly waking up to the allure of the **Azuero Peninsula.** Studded with colonial towns, this heartland of Panama's

Blue-and-gold macaws are a treat for birders in the lowlands of eastern Panama.

Tipping Tips

In Panama, tipping is used to reward good service; tips are not given automatically. Most restaurants add a 10 percent service charge to the bill; there's no need to pay extra except for extraordinary service. On group tours, tip guides $1 per person per day; $5 daily per person is an appropriate fee for private tour guides. Tip bellboys $0.50 per bag. Chambermaids are often overlooked—$1 per day is plenty. Taxi drivers don't normally expect tips.

folkloric traditions also boasts excellent birding in coastal wetland reserves; do take the short boat ride out to **Isla Iguana** to view the frigate bird colonies and perhaps even encounter whales. Surfing here is superb. And nowhere else in the country will you find such a hive of festival activity. Take your pick, from the Festival de la Pollera to Las Tablas's bacchanalian Carnaval.

Sportfishers and scuba divers never had it so good as in the waters off **Isla Coiba,** reached via a three-hour boat ride from the surfing paradise of Playa Santa Catalina. Inland, birders and hikers can take short drives off the Interamerican Highway to pick from a medley of options: **Parque Nacional Omar Torrijos** and **Parque Nacional Santa Fé de Veraguas.** Heading south, you can take in pre-Columbian sites around **Natá.**

Those craving cooler weather and highland birds might spend some time around the resort town of **Boquete.** In the heart of coffee country, it is a base for hiking **Volcán Barú;** the slopes are also accessible from the alpine hamlet of **Cerro Punta,** at the very edge of Parque Internacional La Amistad. For a tropical beach experience, head to **Bocas del Toro.** This offbeat archipelago where everyone gets around by water taxi is fast going mainstream. But its top-ranked surfing beaches, coral reefs, and wildlife-rich forests combine with over-the-water hotels, restaurants, and bars infused with Afro-Caribbean charms.

Active Pursuits

Panama is finally getting late-in-the-day praise as a surfers' paradise for its diamond-dust beaches and thrilling breakers. Beaches along the shores of both

Wet or Dry? Best Times to Visit

The nation has distinct wet (May–Nov.) and dry (Dec.–April) seasons and weather is fairly predictable throughout the year. Dry season is considered the best time for touring, as sunny skies and lack of rain are the norm. It's also high season, when many hotels are full, rental cars book up, and rates for both are raised. However, Panama also has numerous distinct climatic zones, with many microclimates and regional variations. Along the Caribbean coast and Darién, there is a good chance of rainfall year-round. And while temperatures throughout the country

vary little from season to season, the relatively dry Azuero region can broil throughout summer. The lowlands are perpetually humid.

Wet season sees a fall in visitors and in hotel and car rental rates. This time of year has its benefits. Vegetation is lush from all the rains. And in much of the country, rainfall is typically an afternoon affair, often limited to short-lived downpours. However, heavy, prolonged rain is possible anywhere, and the Caribbean and Darién regions, in particular, often see day after day of heavy rains.

Children play soccer on the narrow side streets of Casco Viejo, Panama City.

the Pacific and Caribbean have great surfing, including surf camps that offer instruction for newbies. **Playa Santa Catalina** and **Bocas del Toro** are the big-league locales.

Panama has fabulous coral reefs, especially around **Isla Coiba,** the **Archipiélago de las Perlas,** and off the eastern Caribbean shore. Although no diving is allowed in Kuna Yala, the former treasure port of **Portobelo,** on the Caribbean coast, is a major center. Large pelagic creatures (including manta rays and sharks) are the big draw to **Parque Nacional Marino Golfo de Chiriquí** (accessed from Boca Chica), where sportfishers find their own raptures of the deep. **Lago Gatún** is stocked with bass that give anglers a rod-bending fight to remember. And sportfishing vessels set out from Tropic Star Lodge, on the Darién coast, to wrestle marlin at the Hannibal Banks.

White-water rafting is also top-shelf here, with rivers such as the **Chagres,** near Panama City, and the Chiriquí, near Boquete, drawing thrill seekers with its roller-coaster rides. ∎

Renting a Car

Renting a car is a fabulous way to get around Panama, but it comes with some warnings.

Although roads throughout most of the country are in good condition, local drivers can be reckless. Don't leave anything in your car for fear of theft. Don't pay tickets on the spot; take care of them with the rental company.

Insurance is mandatory. Most rental companies (see Travelwise pp. 229–230) will honor insurance issued abroad if you can prove that you are specifically covered for Panama. Drive the speed limit, be on your guard, and you should be fine.

History & Culture

Monumento Homenaje a la Democracía, Panama City
Opposite: Palm trees and hats provide shade from the intense tropical sun; the *guayabera* shirt is a Panamanian icon.

Panama Today

In Panama, a slim-waisted tropical nation about the same size as South Carolina, you can find rain forests teeming with exotic animals, cloud forests atop rugged mountains, and vibrant indigenous cultures. Bisecting it all is the Panama Canal, the world's most concentrated highway of commerce. Cosmopolitan Panama City basks in wealth brought by the canal's liquid power.

Tourism has come late to Panama, partly because of a recent history tarred by the excesses of a notorious dictator. The lingering perception of the country as a banana republic is now outdated. Gen. Manuel Antonio Noriega (1938–) is long gone, following a U.S. military invasion in 1989, and democracy is soundly established. True,

Rascacielos—skyscrapers—scratch the night sky in Bella Vista, Panama City.

Panama still has political and economic problems, but this is usually nothing more than a footnote for tourists, many of whom thrill to a fascinating history tracing back to a distant pirate past.

The ancient fortresses of Portobelo and San Lorenzo still echo with the clash of cutlasses and the roar of cannon. The ruins of Panamá Viejo provide mute testimony to the ferocity of pirate Henry Morgan's (1635–1688) ruthless attack. And cobbled remnants of the Camino Real and Camino de Cruces treasure trails, which once linked Panamá Viejo and Portobelo, still peek forth from the jungled terrain. Walking the mossy pathways, it is easy to imagine you hear the braying of mules laden with bullion destined for Spanish galleons.

Panama City—a modern metropolis pinned by glittering skyscrapers—equally prizes its past, especially as seen in the colonial jewel of Casco Antiguo. This old neighborhood is full of museums, cathedrals, trendy restaurants and jazz clubs,

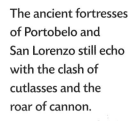

The ancient fortresses of Portobelo and San Lorenzo still echo with the clash of cutlasses and the roar of cannon.

and quaint mansions painted in soft impressionist colors: lemon yellow, tangerine, guava green. Still, the thoroughly 21st-century city has recently gained a state-of-the-art subway system.

Contrasts abound in this sultry nation. The Canal Zone—the green beltway that surrounds the canal—is a seamless blend of moisture-laden forests merging southward into Darién, a vast rain forest that is home to jaguars, monkeys, poison dart frogs, and other wildlife species of every stripe, spot, and hue. In the Península de Azuero, the tapestry changes to dusty tan; cowboys trotting through rustic colonial-era hamlets add quaint notes to the lyrical landscape. The Chiriquí highlands comprise rugged mountains flanked by rows of glossy green coffee bushes. Shading them are mist-shrouded forests that shelter the resplendent quetzal, a bird known for its astounding beauty. The Caribbean Sea—embroidered with offshore coral reefs and cays licked by calm waters the color of jade—offers the appeal of distinctive cultures: one rooted in an Afro-Caribbean heritage, the other deriving from the indigenous Kuna peoples, whose women are garbed as flamboyantly as the most exotic of scarlet macaws.

Ah, yes . . . the birds! Visitors always speak rapturously of phenomenal birding. Panama—a crossroads between two continents and two oceans—has many more species than Costa Rica, the neighbor whose spot in the ecotourism limelight has forced Panama to wait unrecognized in the wings. But birders are finally flocking to the country—as are surfers rushing to catch Panama's rising wave.

Sportfishers are also being lured by seas filled with trophy contenders—dorado, blue marlin, yellowfin, even peacock bass—lining up for the hook. Hikers take in the mountain highs in Parque Nacional Volcán Barú and Parque Internacional La Amistad. The scuba diving is astounding. You can take your pick of two dozen beaches where you can see marine turtles nesting and even top off your adventure tour by whale-watching off the Archipiélago de las Perlas. And no visit to Panama is complete, of course, without a boat trip through the gargantuan locks of the canal.

The Panamanians

If ever a country were a melting pot, Panama—whose population tops 3.6 million—is it, with every ethnicity thrown into the *sancocho* stew. Elaborately costumed Kuna Indians. Barely costumed Emberá-Wounaan Indians. Afro-Caribbeans. Hindu merchants. Chinese supermarket owners. "Pure-blood" Spanish elites sipping cocktails at Panama City's exclusive Club Unión. Beyond Panama City, the country is predominantly mixed-blood mestizo.

Courtesy in Panama

You can smooth your visit to Panama by avoiding a few of these cultural faux pas:

- Don't grip too tightly when shaking hands.
- Don't disparage Panamanian culture. Panamanians are proud of their country and are especially touchy about past U.S. imperialism.
- Don't act like a know-it-all. Modesty is appreciated.
- Don't use *piropos,* impolite "compliments" meant to woo women.

The early Spanish colonists who came in search of gold encountered thriving indigenous cultures. Many quickly succumbed to European disease and the ruthlessness of 16th-century Spanish conquistadores, though eight pure-blood indigenous groups survive today. The mixing of native Indian and Spanish blood produced an exotic mestizo population (today comprising 70 percent of the nation), while French, Dutch, and English merchants and pirates added their singular contributions. These foreign groups were quickly assimilated into the mainstream Spanish-speaking culture, as were large numbers of African slaves imported to Panama throughout the 16th and 17th centuries. Many slaves, however, escaped to remote jungle hideouts and established communities whose occupants today proudly wear their badge as descendants of *cimarrones* (runaways). Their unions with indigenous peoples resulting in mixed-blood *mulatos* added further spice to the pot.

Thousands of North Americans moved through Panama during the 1840s en route to or from the California gold rush. To ease their passage, Chinese and Indian indentured laborers were brought in to lay the Panama Railroad—a daunting endeavor for which thousands paid with their lives (many Chinese laborers committed suicide en masse). The ultimately ill-fated French effort to build a canal, initiated in 1881, elevated the cosmopolitan nature of Panamanian society to a new level with an influx of French immigrants. But Ferdinand de Lesseps's *grande enterprise* employed laborers from around the globe, while prostitutes were in such demand that *"langoustes arrivées"* ("lobsters coming") was telegraphed down the line whenever a new shipload docked. Meanwhile, other European immigrants—mostly Swiss and central European farmers—settled the Chiriquí highlands, where they established coffee fields and market gardens.

Then came the 20th century and with it the United States' epic, century-long involvement in Panama. During the ten years of canal construction, from 1904 to 1914, U.S. engineers commanded nearly 60,000 workers from around the world, most from the Caribbean islands. Many stayed, alongside the families of almost 10,000 U.S. workers ("Zonians," who ran the canal) and an even greater number of U.S. military personnel who arrived to stitch North American customs into the cultural quilt of the nation. Recent decades have witnessed a new influx of North Americans and Europeans seeking to retire in the sun, principally around Boquete and Bocas del Toro.

National Identity

Panamanians, or *panameños,* have mixed feelings about their complex relationship with the United States. Panama was wrested from Colombia by the first-ever display of U.S. gunboat diplomacy. In 1903, French national Philippe Bunau-Varilla (then minister pleni-potentiary to the U.S.) signed the Hay-Bunau-Varilla Treaty, guaranteeing Panamanian independence only on a short leash. The 10-mile-wide (16 km) Panama Canal Zone spanning the waterway's entire 50-mile (80 km) length became U.S. territory, and more than a dozen military bases were maintained there (Zonians were a privileged class, liv-ing rent free), rankling Panamanian sensibilities. In 1964, simmering resentments boiled over in deadly riots. The subsequent success of Omar Torrijos Herrera (1929–1981) in negotiating the Panama Canal Treaty—which gave the canal back to Panama—resulted

The Río Caldera carves a gorge into the slopes of Boquete, an area farmed for coffee.

Diablos (devils) dance in Los Santos during the Corpus Christi festival.

in a rush of *soberanía,* sovereignty fever. Since 1999, Panamanians have been on their own. Few people feel nostalgia for the days when the U.S. military directly employed thousands of local civilians (at preferential wages) and pumped 350 million dollars into Panama's economy every year.

About 75 percent of the population is urban: One in every three citizens lives in Panama City. Except for Colón and David, most other towns are relatively small agricultural and commercial centers. The majority of rural folk live a simple life, tending coffee and farms in the highlands and cattle on the lowlands. There, everyday life evokes the cowboy spirit—notably in the Azuero Peninsula, heartland of Panama's folkloric traditions.

Standards of Living

Panamanians' life expectancy is on a par with that of developed nations, although infant mortality is double that of the United States. The population enjoys free public education and decent public health care, although some regional disparities exist. The financial and service sectors are advanced, as are telecommunications. Panama City is a leading international banking center with a large middle class.

While Panama's per capita income of $16,500 is high for Central America, its society is far from egalitarian. Panama's prosperity is evident. Yet there is no avoiding the impoverishment

found nationwide: Almost 26 percent of the population lives in poverty (17 percent in extreme poverty), many in urban slums marked by unemployment and crime. Thousands of impoverished *colonos* (non-Indian migrant farmers) continue to practice subsistence slash-and-burn agriculture, felling precious forests for cattle. And some critics believe that Panama City's wealthy elite, secluded in deluxe high-rise condos, are out of touch with the plight of impoverished Ngöbe-Buglé Indians or Dariénitas (inhabitants of Darién Province, many of them descendants of African slaves).

An unofficial racial pecking order exists, closely related to socioeconomic status; the country's indigenous people and black population continue to face discrimination. Family trumps most other considerations in business and politics. Dynasties are evident in the government, where blood connections open doors. And many trades are monopolized by single groups: Throughout Panama, for example, Chinese merchants own a majority of supermarkets and corner stores—known colloquially as *chinitos.*

Indigenous Peoples Today

Panama has about 300,000 indigenous people, about 6 percent of the total population. Most live within five autonomous districts *(comarcas)* where indigenous groups are guaranteed rights to self-government. Politically disempowered on a national level, these groups remain suspicious of outsiders. Despite the passage of well-intentioned laws intended to safeguard their heritage, the government continues to issue rights to powerful mining and logging entities that whittle away at the Native Americans' lands.

Panama's most numerous indigenous people are the Ngöbe-Buglé (pop. 188,000), who live a reclusive existence in the western highlands. The arrival in the 1930s of transnational banana corporations and cattle ranchers forced the Ngöbe from many of their traditional coastal habitats; caught in a cycle of poverty, they practice slash-and-burn agriculture while others migrate to work seasonally as coffee-pickers or plantation workers. In October 1996, several hundred Ngöbe-Buglé demonstrators marched to Panama City to demand their own comarca, which was established the following year. Covering almost one-tenth of Panama's surface area, it spans Bocas del Toro, Chiriquí, and Veraguas Provinces.

The majority of rural folk live a simple life, tending coffee and farms in the highlands and cattle on the lowlands.

The Kuna (pop. 65,000) inhabit the southern Caribbean zone and San Blas Archipelago, which they have occupied for only a few hundred years. During the early 20th century, the newly formed Panamanian government tried to suppress Kuna traditions and forcibly Westernize the culture. Following a violent revolt in 1925, the Kuna were granted cultural and political autonomy. These people, who have traditionally lived from fishing and harvesting coconuts for sale, passionately protect their land. Nevertheless, declining fish stocks have

Ngöbe-Buglé Phrase Book

The Guaymí people of western Panama and eastern Costa Rica comprise several distinct tribes. Most numerous are the Ngöbe, who have intermingled with the Buglé to jointly number 156,000 and live in a *comarca* (autonomous reservation) divided into seven districts spanning Chiriquí, Bocas del Toro, and Veraguas Provinces and covering about 9 percent of Panama's territory. They speak Ngabere (a phonetic form of the Chibcha language), with an alphabet of 18 consonants and 8 vowels. One-quarter of the Ngöbe-Buglé people speak only Ngabere. Here are a few phonetic terms to know:

> *yan-tera dego*, **good morning**
> *yan-tera dere*, **good afternoon**
> *yan-tera day-oo*, **good evening**
> *ma bone-yo*, **hello**
> *ma cone-yo*, **what is your name?**
> *ti go . . .* , **I am/my name is . . .**
> *atwai hederre*, **see you later**
> *coing*, **thank you**

forced the Kuna to look to tourism to bolster their fortunes, while increasing numbers have migrated to Panama City and other towns.

The rain forest–dwelling Emberá-Wounaan (pop. 30,000) of Darién are a gentle and friendly people culturally related to Amazonian tribes. Though referred to jointly, the two groups are ethnically and linguistically separate. They live by fishing, farming, and hunting, using blow darts tipped with the deadly skin secretions of frogs. Though traditionally nomadic and lacking tribal organization, in recent years they have coalesced to form permanent villages, encouraged by the Panamanian government. They lack the political clout of the more numerous and organized Kuna; the influence of missionaries and other Westerners continues to dilute traditional practice.

Government & Politics

Panama is defined by the constitution of 1972 as a democratic republic run by an elected president (assisted by two vice presidents) and a 12-member cabinet. Presidents serve a single five-year term and may not serve consecutive terms. Power resides in the unicameral Asamblea Nacional (National Assembly), which makes legislation and is comprised of 71 elected members representing the nation's provinces plus the Kuna Yala and Ngöbe-Buglé comarcas. Members serve five-year terms and sit in the high-rise Palacio Legislativo overlooking Parque Legislativo in Panama City. The Supreme Court comprises nine appointed judges who serve ten-year terms. Elections are overseen by an electoral tribunal.

Panama is divided into nine provinces—Bocas del Toro, Chiriquí, Coclé, Colón, Darién, Herrera, Los Santos, Panamá, and Veraguas—each overseen by an appointed governor. In addition, two of the five autonomous indigenous regions have representation in the central government.

Political Parties & Personalities

Between 1968 and 1989, when the United States overthrew Manuel Noriega, the president and Legislative Assembly were under the sway of military dictators. Political parties were relatively weak. Even now, Panamanian parties still revolve around the personalities of their leaders, rather than emphasizing a clear philosophy.

President Juan Carlos Varela (1963–), of the nationalistic Panameñísta Party, was elected to office in May 2014, replacing Ricardo Martinelli Berrocal (1952–). Martinelli represented the Cambio Democrático (CD, Democratic Change) party, founded in 1998. The main rival is the Partido Revolucionario Democrático (PRD), founded in 1978 by supporters of Omar

Torrijos to give his military rule legitimacy. It draws its strongest support from labor unions and the urban middle class. The PD is closely allied with the third main party, the Partido Pan-ameñista, founded in 1936 by Arnulfo Arias Madrid (1901–1988). This centrist party gains its main support from the provinces and is strongly nationalistic. Arias's widow, Mireya Moscoso de Gruber (1946–), headed the party in the 1990s and in 1999 became Panama's first female president. The Partido Popular has a defined ideology espousing concern for social welfare.

The government is known for corruption, and public cynicism is rife. Nevertheless, President Martín Torrijos espoused "zero tolerance" for corruption and enacted laws to make government more transparent. President Martinelli campaigned on an anticorruption platform, but he himself has been mired by charges of corruption and authoritarianism. In 2014 his vice president, Juan Carlos Varela, won the presidential election on his own promise to clean up government and reduce poverty.

Following the U.S. invasion to topple Noriega in December 1989, his Panamanian Defense Force disbanded; the country today has no armed forces. An armed police force looks after national security, while the U.S. military reserves the right to intervene to protect the canal. ■

Ship passages at Gatún Lock have played out seamlessly for a century.

Food & Drink

Panama has long been a cultural crossroads for the world, and the fusion of international flavors is reflected in the restaurant scene. Every town has its Chinese restaurant, South American *parrillada* (steak house), and pizzeria. Thai and Japanese restaurants, even Indian and Middle Eastern cuisine, abound in Panama City, which competes with international cities around the world for the variety and quality of its cuisines.

Maize (corn) is a staple of many Panamanian country kitchens.

Panama's uniquely flavorful native cuisine melds indigenous, Spanish, and African influences into a mouthwatering mélange. The dish most associated with the country is *sancocho*, a soup that comes in regional variations and may contain corn, yucca, and any number of other vegetables.

Panamanians are big on meats. They're fond of roast pork (especially at fiesta time) and *patacón con puerco*, pork with plantain. *Pollo asado* (roast chicken) is a staple of *comida criolla*. *Bistec* (steak) is also popular. *Arroz con pollo* (rice and chicken) is another favorite, often seasoned with onions and garlic or served topped with peas or even crumbled hard-boiled egg yolk at breakfast.

More often, Panama's *desayuno típico* (typical breakfast) includes thick corn tortillas with fresh cheese, roast meats, and eggs. Among the urban middle class, however, American dining habits have ousted the Panamanian tradition of rice and beans.

The name Panama is an indigenous word for "abundance of fishes." No wonder, then, that seafood also abounds on local menus. Almost every seafood restaurant worth its salt features *ceviche*, raw fish marinated with chopped onions and peppers. The fish of choice are tilapia and *corvina* (sea bass), often served with *ajo* (garlic), while dorado (mahi mahi) and *pargo* (snapper) are also favored. Peruvian seafood restaurants add their own distinct flavors. The Caribbean coast simmers its lobster, shrimp, and other seafood in unique spices and coconut milk, and trout is a local delicacy in Boquete.

Panamanians' use of corn reflects indigenous traditions, as in a *tamal*—cornmeal pastry stuffed with stewed chicken or pork, peppers, garlic, and onions, then wrapped in a banana leaf and boiled. *Chiricanos,* typical of the Azuero Peninsula, are baked pastries made of ground corn and shredded coconut sweetened with sugarcane juice and honey. Panamanians have a weakness for *dulces* (sweets) made of coconut and sugar, as in *cocadas,* sold by the roadside.

Other dishes to try include:

Plátano en tentación, a popular side dish consisting of baked plantain sweetened with molasses and cinnamon.

Carimañolas, mashed boiled yuccas stuffed with beef and then deep fried.

Chicheme, a drink of ground corn and milk flavored with cinnamon and vanilla.

Tamal de olla, oven-baked corn tamales stuffed with meat and vegetables, plus raisins.

Comida corriente at lunchtime, inexpensive set meals containing a combination of local dishes (see sidebar below).

Regional markets are cornucopias of tropical fruits, such as mangoes, melons, papayas, pineapples, and strawberries fresh from the Chiriquí highlands. These and local favorites such as *marañón* (cashew fruit) and *guanábana* find their way into *batidos,* delicious iced shakes made with water or

Puerco frito con patacones—fried pork and plantains—is a Panamanian culinary favorite.

milk. *Agua de pipa*—water from a green coconut—is drunk as the perfect pick-me-up on hot days. Panama's local lager-style brews (e.g., Soberana and Balboa) are also perfectly suited to the tropical climate when served chilled, *bien fría.*

The urban workingman's drink is *seco,* a harsh sugarcane liquor often drunk with milk; his country cousins favor *vino de palma,* a rough alcohol made from palm sap. The country's prized Carta Vieja rum is light bodied and smooth in flavor. Wine is popular with the middle classes.

Panama's light-roast *arabica* coffee is also world class, and individual labels regularly make the top-ten list of international coffee critics, but the most prized beans usually are exported. Coffee in Panama is typically drunk American style or thick and heavily sugared, espresso style.

EXPERIENCE: Dining Like a Local

There's no shortage of good restaurants in Panama serving international cuisines, from French to Chinese and nouvelle fusion. The country's history as a crossroads of cultures has infused Panama with globe-spanning menus that have little in common with native traditions. But you'll come to appreciate the country more, and save money, if you adopt local habits when dining.

Look for **bocas,** savory snacks such as chicken wings served at most self-respecting bars. **Sodas** are small family-run roadside or market eateries found nationwide. Distinctly no-frills, they offer the chance to dine with working-class locals. They serve simple local fare, including **casados** (or *comida corriente*), inexpensive set meals of different dishes—a salad, a starch, a main course—served on one plate. These workers' lunches (*casado* means "marriage") have either beef, chicken, or fish served with a combination of beans and rice or potatoes, plus vegetables, fried yucca, and perhaps fresh cheese, plus the salad.

Panamanian History

When on August 15, 1914, the Panama Canal was officially opened with the passage of the S.S. *Ancón,* it marked the culmination of a dream dating back five centuries. Panama has always been a path between seas, from the time of pre-Columbian Indians, who followed a trail across the country, to today's era of massive container ships.

First Peoples

People migrating south may have occupied the region we know today as Panama as early as 12,000 years ago. Nearly a million indigenous people are thought to have inhabited the region by the time of the Spanish conquest in the 1500s. Several dozen diverse tribes, distinguished by their distinct ceramics and artifacts, were divided into three cultural zones in west, east, and central Panama. Most succumbed to the brutality of Spanish occupation and to European diseases, and only eight indigenous tribes exist today.

The country is speckled with rocks bearing mysterious petroglyphs. Dozens of archaeological sites have also been uncovered throughout the region, though no massive pyramids or even towns have been unearthed, and most sites date back no more than two thousand years. Although trade links existed between the cultural groups and with more advanced cultures to the north and south, the Panamanian peoples seem not to have evolved the complex sociopolitical structures of societies elsewhere in the Americas. Panama's peoples never unified to form a kingdom but remained under chieftains *(caciques)* who ruled over competing areas. The names of these leaders were adopted by the Spanish for each tribe and the regions they inhabited.

> **Panama's peoples never unified to form a kingdom but remained under chieftains *(caciques)* who ruled over competing areas.**

Western Cultures

The Barriles culture is considered Panama's earliest major civilization. It originated in today's Costa Rica and moved into Panama about 500 B.C., when the group settled the Chiriquí highlands around a ceremonial site on the slopes of Volcán Barú. Eventually the culture extended to the Caribbean and Pacific coasts. It evolved from simple agricultural communities based on cultivation of corn and beans to ranked societies, reaching a zenith about A.D. 500 before being abruptly destroyed when Volcán Barú erupted.

The Barriles left behind monochrome pottery, *metates* (three-legged stone corn-grinding tables), and life-size stone statues showing men (often clutching severed heads in their hands) being borne on the shoulders of slaves. In time, the Barriles were replaced by the Coclé and the classic Chiriquí and Veraguas cultures who left behind elaborate earthenware, including ceramics and gold pieces made with the lost-wax technique.

Central Cultures

The most important (and oldest) archaeological sites thus far discovered are in the Pacific lowlands, centered on the current provinces of Coclé, Herrera, and Veraguas.

Groups that settled along the Pacific coast introduced agriculture about 3000 B.C. By A.D. 500, complex societies had evolved based on intensive slash-and-burn agriculture, although they also relied upon fishing and commercial trade with other groups throughout Mesoamerica. Headed by powerful caciques, they also warred with other tribes for control of the most productive land.

The largest site, Sitio Conte, near the current town of Penonomé, served as an important pre-Columbian burial site for at least 200 years. It was discovered in the

Pre-Columbian carvings cover the Piedra Pintada (Painted Stone) near El Valle.

Spanish explorer Vasco Núñez de Balboa sees the Pacific Ocean in 1513.

1930s when the Río Grande changed course and exposed fabulous burial treasures, most of which now reside in museums around the world.

Gold objects—and the lost-wax metallurgical technique employed to make them—were introduced from Peru around 2,000 years ago. Metallurgy was quickly adopted by local tribes, who shaped animal figurines and decorative body items, such as bracelets, pendants, and chest plates, reserved for caciques. When they died, caciques were buried with their wives, servants, and possessions, including ceramics such as vases and pedestals painted with elaborate zoomorphic designs.

Parque Arqueológico El Caño, near the town of Natá, dates from around A.D. 1100 and, like Sitio Conte, features geometrically aligned stone columns, some carved into the shapes of animals and humans. Most of the stones were removed at the time of discovery.

Eastern Cultures

The eastern cultures were the first to experience the brutality of early Spanish conquistadores, who enacted a policy of extermination. Little is known about these peoples, not least due to the rugged inaccessibility of much of the terrain and their near-total destruction at the hands of the Spanish. These hunter-gatherers spoke a Chibcha language and were related to Amazonian tribes. (The Choco tribe—known as the Emberá-Wounaan Indians—inhabit the area today. The Choco migrated from Amazonian regions around the 18th century.)

The eastern peoples lived in circular huts constructed on pole frames with walls of cane and roofs of thatched palm, similar to those in which many of their descendants live today. Spanish conquistadores reported that caciques lived in the largest huts, which contained the smoked bodies of ancestors wearing gold masks. The ceramics of these groups were comparatively crude, although they were skilled at using stone tools to fashion sleek canoes from logs hollowed by fire.

First Europeans

The first European to sight Panama was Spanish explorer Rodrigo de Bastidas (1460–1527), who sailed along the Caribbean shore of Darién in 1501. The region's indigenous peoples greeted the newcomers while adorned in their finest gold bracelets, earrings, and chest plates. The following year, Christopher Columbus (1451–1506) arrived during his fourth and final voyage to the New World; he explored the shoreline between Bocas del Toro and Darién and established an ill-fated settlement near the mouth of the Río Belén. He named the region Veraguas after a local tribe.

In 1513, Spanish explorer and regional governor Vasco Núñez de Balboa crossed the isthmus and claimed the Pacific Ocean for Spain (see sidebar below). His administration was succeeded by that of the more rapacious Pedro Arias de Ávila, who founded Nuestra Señora de la Asunción de Panama (Panama City) as the first Spanish settlement on the Pacific and relocated the capital there. Balboa's even-handed treatment of the

Vasco Núñez de Balboa

In 1510, Vasco Núñez de Balboa (1475–1519)—a former member of Rodrigo de Bastidas's crew—stowed away aboard a merchant vessel to escape his creditors. He ended up in Darién as an early settler of Santa María la Antigua del Darién, the first successful town constituted in the isthmus by the Spanish crown. Balboa quickly rose to become governor of the region. Three years later, he crossed the isthmus and, on September 25, 1513, became the first European in the Americas to see the Pacific Ocean. Clad in armor, Balboa famously waded into the ocean (which he named Mar del Sur, Southern Sea) to claim it for Spain. The discovery positioned Panama as a staging point for the conquest of the Pacific coast.

Balboa's discovery of the Pacific and the pearl-rich Archipiélago de las Perlas fueled the jealousy of rival conquistador Pedro Arias de Ávila (1440–1531), alias Pedrarias Dávila, who connived to have himself named as Balboa's successor. In 1519, the new governor had Balboa tried for treason on trumped-up charges and put to death.

A captured Spaniard bows before Sir Henry Morgan during the Welsh privateer's sacking of the city of Panama in the 1670s.

indigenous peoples was replaced by brutal tyranny and exploitation. Entire communities were put to the sword, while others were enslaved to extract gold from the Darién jungles. By the mid-16th century the indigenous peoples had christened the Spaniards *guacci-guacci* after a kind of predatory mammal. Whole tribes withered and died under the intolerable hardships of forced labor. European diseases such as smallpox, measles, and tuberculosis, against which they had no resistance, hastened their demise. Groups such as the Buglé fought long bitter struggles against the Spanish but gradually retreated into the thickly forested mountains of the Cordillera Central and the Caribbean coastal plains of Veraguas.

Treasure Routes

After the conquest of Virú (today's Peru) by Francisco Pizarro (1478–1541) in 1532, the plundered wealth of the Inca began filling the vaults of Panama City—capital of the province then known as Castillo de Oro, an ever changing district that also included much of today's Nicaragua and Costa Rica—as down payment on a glittering future. The settlement grew swiftly as the chief entrepôt for the wealth of the New World being transferred to Spain. Unimaginable quantities of silver, gold, emeralds, pearls, and other treasures were transported by mule across the

isthmus in a one-week journey for shipment to Spain.

In 1516, conquistador Gaspar de Espinosa (1484–1537) began construction of the Camino Real, a road connecting Panama to the Caribbean port of Nombre de Dios (founded in 1510). The harbor at Nombre de Dios was ill chosen, however, due to its exposure to hurricanes. Thus, in 1585, the terminus was switched to San Felipe de Portobelo, named in honor of the king. A royal decree ordered construction of a second mule trail, the Camino de Cruces, a far easier route that connected Panama City with the town of Cruces on the Chagres River; passage continued via boat to the Caribbean.

The treasure-laden mule trains that followed the trails were timed to coincide with the annual arrival of the Spanish *flota* (fleet) bearing the products of the Old World. The fleet reached Cartagena following a ten-week journey from Spain and split into two fleets, bound separately for Mexico and Panama, while couriers were sent ahead to inform the king's agents and merchants of the ships' impending arrival. Hundreds of vessels converged on Nombre de Dios and, later, Portobelo. The annual fairs (in which silver and raw materials were traded for manufactured goods) drew thousands of Spanish merchants, soldiers, clerics, merchants, and scribes. Nombre de Dios and Portobelo grew from sleepy *pueblos* to bustling treasure ports. By law one-fifth (the *quinto*) of New World treasure had to go to the king of Spain, whose own galleons got priority in the treasure ports of the Spanish Main. More than 200,000 tons (181,400 metric tons) of silver were shipped to Spain through Portobelo from 1550 to 1650. (Spain's debts were so great, however, that much of it was shipped directly to European bankers in Venice.) So much silver was shipped aboard bulging merchantmen that mountains of bullion were left behind in the street.

The vast wealth drew the larcenous attention of pirates: cold-hearted cutthroats capable of astoundingly inhumane deeds. English slave-trader-turned-pirate Sir Francis Drake (1540–1596) attacked Nombre de Dios in 1572; the following year he successfully waylaid a mule train laden with treasure. The Spanish developed a flotilla system to guard the creaking treasure ships, with one galleon for every ten merchant vessels. They also built fortifications to guard Portobelo and the mouth of the Río Chagres. In 1595, Drake and John Hawkins (1532–1595) set out with 26 ships and an audacious plan to sack Nombre de Dios and Panama City. Hawkins died en route, while Drake fell ill and on January 27, 1596, died and was buried at sea near the mouth of Portobelo. Pirate William Parker (1587–1617) successfully sacked Portobelo in 1602, and in 1668 Welsh pirate Henry Morgan sacked the town and held the occupants for ransom. In 1671,

> **By the mid-16th century the indigenous peoples had christened the Spaniards *guacci-guacci* after a kind of predatory mammal.**

Morgan even used the mule trails to attack Panama City, which he burned to the ground. After the sacking, the residents reestablished their city a few miles west at a more defensible position—today's Casco Antiguo. Panama and Portobelo suffered so many depredations that Spain finally permitted passage of ships around Cape Horn, ending the golden age of Portobelo as the "richest little city in the Indies."

Colonial Era

Spain's monopoly on the isthmus was challenged in 1698 when the Company of Scotland was founded to establish a colony of Scots on the Caribbean coast of Darién. The colony of New Edinburgh was a fiasco (most of the 1,200 settlers soon perished from starvation or disease) and the financial fallout forced Scotland to give up all notion of independence from England.

During the early 18th century, archenemies England and Spain settled into a period of more or less peaceful coexistence. In 1731, however, English sea trader Robert Jenkins, sailing in the West Indies, was arrested by Spanish coast guards, who cut off his ear. Seven years passed before Jenkins told his story—and showed his shriveled ear—to the House of Commons. The aroused parliamentarians voted for war (now sometimes known as the War of Jenkins' Ear), and reserve naval officer Sir Edward Vernon (1684–1757) set off for the Caribbean in command of six warships. On November 20, 1739, he arrived off Portobelo, which, notwithstanding its formidable fortifications, surrendered after a short resistance. The fortresses were promptly blown up. The Spanish lost no time in building larger, more modern defenses.

> ## Company of Scotland
>
> **William Paterson, a Scot who founded the Bank of England in 1694, made a fortune through trade. In 1695, he initiated the Company of Scotland Trading to Africa and the Indies. Thousands of Scots invested money to establish an ill-fated colony in Panama's Darién. When the rival East India Company forced the English Parliament to withdraw support from Paterson's venture, the Scottish economy was virtually bankrupted, causing the dissolution of the Scottish Parliament.**

The Spanish imperial age was waning, however, ushering in a period of stagnation for Central America. Panama was relegated to backwater status. Occasionally, civil wars inspired by growing nationalist sentiments spilled into the province as independence sentiments swept through Spain's weakened Latin American empire. On November 10, 1821, the residents of La Villa de los Santos township petitioned Latin American liberator Simón Bolívar (1783–1830) for independence in a letter, the *Primer Grito de Independencia* (First Call for Independence). Eighteen days later, Panama broke from Spain and joined Gran Colombia, a union that initially included Colombia, Ecuador, Peru, and Venezuela. In 1826, Bolívar initiated an ultimately unsuccessful congress (hosted in Panama City's Casco Antiguo) to create a union of all the republics. In 1830, Gran Colombia fractured. Panama proclaimed independence, but neighboring Colombia forced it to reunite, with Panama becoming one among Colombia's many provinces. Panama's union with Colombia was uneasy, however, and many rebellious incidents were violently suppressed.

Canal Fever

In 1848 the outpost province of Colombia was thrust back onto the world stage by the discovery of gold in California. No railroad yet spanned the United States.

Adventurers from around the world landed in Panama to cross the isthmus via the old Camino de Cruces. Bandits preyed upon the gold seekers as they stumbled along the grueling weeklong trail. Thousands succumbed to yellow fever, malaria, and other diseases. Demand for mule transport fostered exorbitant prices. Future Civil War hero and U.S. president Capt. Ulysses S. Grant (1822–1885) was forced to use his own money to meet the extortionate fee charged for mules to transport the cholera-stricken U.S. Fourth Infantry across the peninsula en route to San Francisco. Then came William Henry Aspinwall (1807–1875), an entrepreneur who founded the Pacific Mail Steamship Company and the Panama Railroad, completed in 1855 at a cost of some 6,000 lives. Between 1848 and 1869, about 375,000 argonauts crossed the isthmus via mule and, eventually, rail.

The success of the Panama Railroad sparked notions of something grander. Step in French engineer Count Ferdinand de Lesseps (1805–1894), who had just succeeded in building the Suez Canal and now set his eyes on building a sea-level canal through the Isthmus of Panama. His Compagnie Universelle du Canal Interocéanique de Panamá was launched in 1880; de Lesseps purchased (from Colombia) the exclusive right to build a canal, and stock was issued to finance the effort. The stubborn Frenchman resisted all entreaties to abandon the ill-conceived sea-level idea and adopt a dam-and-lock system until it was too late. The cost and difficulties of digging La Grande Tranché (Great Trench) through mountains and taming the Río Chagres and devastating tropical diseases were simply too great. About 22,000 laborers died (most were Caribbean islanders felled by malaria and yellow fever) before the company foundered in 1889, bringing financial ruin to investors. The French government also collapsed in the fallout as financial frauds, political bribes, and influence peddling were revealed; eventually, de Lesseps and his son Charles were each sentenced to five years in prison.

> **Adventurers from around the world landed in Panama to cross the isthmus via the old Camino de Cruces.**

A brief and bloody interlude—the Prestán Uprising—occurred in 1885 after Rafael Aizpuru (1843–1919), former president of the department of Panama, seized power. Colombian troops were dispatched from the Caribbean port of Colón. Pedro Prestán, a rabble-rousing Haitian, took advantage of the troops' absence to seize control of Colón. Prestán demanded that the captain of a boatload of armaments hand over the goods. When the captain refused, Prestán took five Americans hostage and threatened to kill them if the captain of the U.S. gunboat *Galena* (which was anchored offshore) landed troops. Having been promised the arms, Prestán released the hostages, but the *Galena* swiftly towed the arms-bearing ship beyond reach. Colombian troops returned to Colón and routed Prestán and his mob, but not before the rebel put the town to the torch. The wooden town was almost entirely destroyed. Prestán was captured and hanged while Aizpuru was deposed by U.S. marines.

The Canal & Independence

Meanwhile, the United States had decided that a shortcut between the seas was crucial to its evolving naval power and had grown determined to build a canal, with Nicaragua the most likely route. That Panama was eventually chosen is due largely to the indefatigable efforts of one man: Philippe Bunau-Varilla (1859–1940), former chief engineer of the Compagnie Universelle du Canal Interocéanique de Panamá.

In 1894, Bunau-Varilla had organized the Compagnie Nouvelle, which acquired the French rights to build a canal; in 1904, he sold the rights to the United States for 40 million dollars. This one-man whirlwind pursued a relentless, brilliant, and ultimately successful campaign to influence the U.S. Congress and President Theodore Roosevelt (1858–1919) on behalf of the Panama route. Once the decision was made, the United States was determined to bully the Colombian government into negotiating a canal treaty on dictated terms.

When Colombia refused to agree to the U.S. terms, a plot was hatched to sever the province of Panamá. Prompted by Bunau-Varilla, prominent and ambitious Panamanian citizens conspired with Panama Railroad officials. On November 3, 1903, they declared independence from Colombia (Bunau-Varilla's wife had even stitched together the first flag of Panama).

The United States instantly recognized the breakaway republic. Meanwhile, the ever wily and prescient Bunau-Varilla had gotten himself named Panama's ambassador to the United States. Preempting the arrival in Washington of an official Panamanian delegation to negotiate the terms of a new canal treaty, the Frenchman negotiated the Hay-Bunau-Varilla Treaty committing the United States to build a canal across the Isthmus of Panama on terms highly preferential to the U.S.

The treaty granted the United States sovereignty of the canal and a 10-mile-wide (16 km) Canal Zone that would be governed exclusively by the United States in perpetuity; the U.S. government paid the new Panamanian government ten million dollars, plus an annual payment of $250,000. Panama's constitution was written by Bunau-Varilla in a New York hotel room and rigged to let the United States meddle whenever it pleased. The Hay-Bunau-Varilla Treaty—a fait accompli delivered to a stupefied and livid official Panamanian delegation—became a bone of contention between the two nations for decades.

On May 4, 1904, the French-owned assets in Panama were handed over to the United States, and the Stars and Stripes were raised.

Left Behind

When Panamanians declared independence from Colombia in 1903, U.S. president Roosevelt sent the gunboat *Nashville* to Panama to prevent Colombian troops from landing to suppress the insurrection. As the Colombian troops already ashore were rushed from Colón to Panama City, swift-thinking Panama Railroad officials insisted that the Colombian officers ride in the front of the train as a matter of protocol; they then uncoupled the rear carriages, leaving the troops behind. Upon arrival in Panama City, the Colombian officers were arrested by their own soldiers, who had been bought off by the conspirators.

The Greatest Engineering Feat of All Time

U.S. engineers understood, where the French had not, that a sea-level canal was out of the question. The U.S. plan called for damming the Chagres, the principal river in the canal's path, to create a massive lake 85 feet (30 m) above sea level, with three lock chambers at each end of the lake to raise and lower ships to sea level: The isthmus would be bridged, not severed. Cuban doctor Carlos Finlay's (1833–1915) irrefutable proof that yellow fever was transmitted by mosquitoes was another key element in the canal's success. An all-out and ultimately successful effort was made to eradicate

Massive metal gates at Gatún Locks dwarf workers in 1910, during construction of the canal.

the *Aëdes aegypti* and *Anopheles* mosquitoes (transmitters of yellow fever and malaria, respectively) under farsighted medical officer Col. William C. Gorgas (1854–1920). Meanwhile, Chief Engineer John F. Stevens (1853–1943) set up a flatbed train system that would be essential for hauling out rock as the canal was blasted through the Culebra Cut, 9 miles (14 km) of mountains forming the continental divide. In 1907, Stevens resigned and was replaced by Col. George W. Goethals (1858–1928), an efficient military engineer who saw the effort by the U.S. Army Corps of Engineers to fruition.

When completed after ten years of grueling effort, the canal extended some 50 miles (80 km) from Limon Bay on the Atlantic Ocean to Panama Bay on the Pacific. On January 7, 1914, an old French crane boat, the *Alexandre La Valle*, made the first complete passage of the waterway, although the canal wasn't officially opened until August 15, 1914, when the S.S. *Ancón* transited. On August 3, 1914, the same day that the dark clouds of World War I broke over Europe, the first oceangoing vessel—the *Cristobal*—passed through the canal. Theodore Roosevelt's Big Ditch had chopped 9,000 miles (14,484 km) off the journey for ships sailing from New York to San Francisco.

Flag Riots

Arnulfo Arias Madrid's anti-U.S. rhetoric was shared by much of the populace, who resented the overbearing presence of the United States and its repeated interference in Panama's domestic affairs. The first serious riots occurred in 1947, when Panama's national legislature met to consider extending rights for the U.S. military to use bases outside the Canal Zone. The simmering resentment boiled over in the so-called Flag Riots that erupted on January 9, 1964.

The Kennedy Administration had agreed to fly the Panamanian flag next to the Stars and Stripes in the Canal Zone. When Kennedy's successor Lyndon Johnson announced plans to reduce the number of flags flown in the Zone, many Zonians (U.S. residents of the Zone) took offense. A flag-raising initiative was organized. When students at Balboa High School raised an American flag in defiance of the governor's orders, Panamanian students from the Instituto Nacional set out to raise their national flag alongside. Their flag was torn down. Tempers flared and before long full-scale riots broke out. Panamanians from all walks of life were drawn into the maelstrom, which left 27 dead, the majority Panamanians shot by U.S. troops. The Flag Riots were a seminal moment in Panama's history, marking a turning point in U.S.–Latin American relations.

Shaping Panama

The years following completion of the canal witnessed marked economic progress in Panama as roads, telephones, and other elements of modern infrastructure were installed throughout the nation. Democracy, however, was slow to take hold. Turbulent politics caused the United States to intervene militarily in Panama's domestic affairs in 1908, 1912, and 1918, and again in 1925 when the Panamanian government's forced suppression of Kuna culture provoked a violent revolt in San Blas. Led by Nele Kantule and Cimral Colman, the Kuna declared independence and established their own nation, the Republic of Tule. The United States intervened, but not before 22 policemen and 20 tribesmen had been killed. Self-rule was granted to the Kuna in 1938.

In 1936, the right of U.S. intervention was revoked when the Hull Alfaro Treaty replaced the Hay-Bunau-Varilla Treaty. The treaty was named for Arnulfo Arias Madrid (1901–1988), leader of Acción Comunal, a radical group that in 1931 violently overthrew the government of Florencio Harmodio Arosemena (1872–1945). After a short interlude, Arias's brother was installed as president. A charismatic populist, Arias espoused *panameñismo,* a vehemently racist, fascistic, and anti-U.S. nationalism. His popularity among the poor was such, however, that he was elected president three times between 1940 and 1984; each time he was deposed by the police, who evolved a virulent enmity for *arnulfistas.* Nonetheless, Arias is credited with having established Panama's social security system.

Arias's chief nemesis was José Antonio Remón Cantera (1908–1955), commander of the National Police. Elected to the presidency in 1952, he initiated progressive reforms before being assassinated in a machine-gun attack at the horse-racing track that now bears his name. In 1968, Arnulfo Arias was elected for a third time. Immediately he called for the canal to be turned over to Panama. However, he was toppled by the military only 11 days into his term. In the resulting chaos, a handsome, charismatic National Guard colonel, Omar Torrijos Herrera, seized power, initiating a 21-year spell of military rule. After swiftly overcoming a countercoup, Torrijos established himself as a popular leader who engaged the state more actively in the economy and instituted sweeping and progressive reforms. Panama's health service was expanded. An agrarian reform distributed land to impoverished peasants. And a modernization program invested millions of dollars in Panama City. However, the constitution was suspended, the press was censored, and many political opponents were murdered.

Torrijos (who is remembered fondly by Panamanians to this day) consolidated his popularity with the Torrijos-Carter Treaty. Signed by Torrijos and President Jimmy Carter in Washington on September 7, 1977, the treaty called for the increasing involvement of Panamanians in canal operations, the eventual transfer of the canal to the Republic of Panama, and the closure after a 20-year term of all U.S. military bases. Torrijos's triumph was greeted with a rush of *soberanía*—sovereignty fever. A digital clock was even set up outside the canal administration building, where it ticked down the seconds until the canal finally passed fully into Panama's hands in 1999.

The Noriega Years

On July 31, 1981, Torrijos was killed when his small plane mysteriously crashed into a mountain. His untimely death left a vacuum in which a series of military figures jostled for power. Torrijos had named one of his supporters, Lt. Col. Manuel Antonio Noriega (1938–), as head of military intelligence. Noriega soon gained control of the National Guard (which he renamed the Fuerza de Defensa de Panama—Panamanian Defense Force) and the country, which he proceeded to rule through fear and intimidation

Antigovernment demonstrators take to the streets of Panama City on March 14, 1988.

while a constitutional president and fraudulent elections maintained the sham of democratic proceedings.

In September 1985, Torrijos's protégé and vocal Noriega opponent Dr. Hugo Spadafora (1940–1985) was seized while returning to Panama from exile in Costa Rica. Discovery of his decapitated and brutally tortured corpse catalyzed growing disgust with Noriega's corrupt, thuggish rule, which used paramilitary "Dignity Battalions" to terrorize and murder opponents. Nonetheless, Noriega, who had been on the CIA payroll since the early 1970s (then CIA director George H. W. Bush had authorized an annual payment of $110,000 to Noriega), continued to receive tacit U.S. support. The U.S. government turned a blind eye to Noriega's involvement in drug trafficking and money laundering hand in hand with Colombia's Medellín cartel. In 1987, former Noriega supporter Col. Roberto Díaz Herrera went public with claims that Noriega was responsible for the deaths of Torrijos and Spadafora. The public outcry resulted in a "Civic Crusade" in which Panama's middle class took to the streets calling for Noriega to step down. Noriega responded by organizing his own demonstrations from among his base, the urban (mostly nonwhite) underclass.

> On December 20, 1989, President George H. W. Bush ordered a military invasion—Operation Just Cause—to capture Noriega.

Noriega's political opponents rallied to support Guillermo Endara Galimany (1936–2009) in the May 1989 elections against Noriega's handpicked candidate, Carlos Duque. When it was clear that Duque had lost by a wide margin, Noriega canceled the election he had shamelessly attempted to rig. Former president Jimmy Carter, in Panama as an observer, denounced Noriega, who unleashed his paramilitaries to suppress demonstrations. Endara and his two vice presidential running mates were seen on television being beaten by Noriega goons wielding steel pipes.

Washington's mood had now shifted. The U.S. had imposed economic sanctions in March 1988, halted all canal payments, and encouraged a coup (which it declined to support at the vital moment). The coup occurred on October 3, 1989. Noriega, however, managed to rally his most loyal troops and the coup failed. Bloody reprisals were enacted as the increasingly paranoid Panamanian leader began to rely on his vicious paramilitary units. Meanwhile, clashes between Noriega's forces and U.S. troops stationed in Panama escalated and came to a head on December 17, when a U.S. marine in civilian clothes was shot dead.

On December 20, 1989, President George H. W. Bush ordered a military invasion—Operation Just Cause—to capture Noriega. The dictator took refuge in the Vatican Embassy. After ten days of psychological warfare (rock music was blasted day and night), Noriega surrendered and was extradited to the United States, where in 1992 he was sentenced to a 30-year prison term for racketeering, drug trafficking, and money laundering. With deductions from that time for good behavior, he completed his sentence in September 2007 and was sent to France, where he was jailed for seven years for money laundering.

In 1995, Panama sentenced Noriega to 20 years in absentia for murder. In December 2011, he returned to Panama where he was imprisoned. Although only 23 U.S. soldiers were killed during the invasion, as many as 4,000 Panamanian civilians may have died, and thousands more were rendered homeless after U.S. forces attacked El Chorrillo, a poor district of Panama City and the setting for Noriega's command center.

Juan Carlos Varela was elected president in 2014.

New Democracy

Following Noriega's ouster, the Panamanian Defense Force was disbanded and Guillermo Endara Galimany was sworn in as president. Despite the difficulties of trying to reestablish democracy in the wake of a military invasion, Endara's term is considered a success. In 1999, Panamanians elected their first female president, Mireya Moscoso, widow of former president Arnulfo Arias. Her administration became mired by corruption charges. That same year, Enrique Garrido, a Kuna legislator, became the first indigenous person to head the nation's Legislative Assembly.

At noon on December 31, 1999, the Republic of Panama assumed full responsibility for the canal under the control of the Autoridad del Canal de Panama (ACP). All 11,000 U.S. troops departed, and 14 major military bases and dozens of "Small Town, U.S.A." townships were turned over to the Panamanian government. America's century in Panama was over, although a bilateral treaty gives Uncle Sam the right to return if the canal's security is threatened. The ACP has since operated the canal as a profitable business (the U.S.-run Panama Canal Commission was a break-even entity). In 2006, a national plebiscite approved ACP plans to expand the canal and build a new megaport at the Pacific entrance, both capable of handling mammoth ships of a size never dreamed of when the canal was built (see feature pp. 94–97).

In May 2004, Martín Torrijos (1963–), son of Omar Torrijos, was elected president. Elected in 2009, Ricardo Martinelli and his administration made significant reforms aimed at luring visitors from abroad. The past decade has witnessed a boom in tourism, which grew an average of 12 percent from 2004 to 2014. In May 2014, Martinelli was replaced by Juan Carlos Varela, an engineer whose family owns Panama's biggest liquor producer. Varela's anti-corruption message resonated with voters. Although visitors topped 2.2 million in 2013, the country's potential has barely been tapped. The canal expansion, scheduled for completion in 2015, promises to further boost the nation's economy, which is today the second most competitive in Latin America. Panama's future looks bright. ■

Land & Landscape

A tenuous land bridge barely separating two great oceans and two American continents vastly different in character, Panama is sculpted to show off the full potential of the tropics. The terrain varies from rain forest as lush as the biblical Garden of Eden to cloud forest steeped in swirling mists on Volcán Barú's slopes. To either side, forested hills rise to a backbone of mountains.

Elongated and shaped in a gentle S-curve aligned roughly east–west, the isthmus is between 30 and 120 miles (48–193 km) wide and narrowest at its tendril-thin waistline, where the Panama Canal cuts through. The land we see today began to rise from the sea barely three million years ago, the product of geological upheavals caused by the jostling of three tectonic plates.

Despite Panama's location entirely within the tropics, extremes of elevation and relief spawn a profusion of microclimates. The arid flatlands of Azuero and the sodden coastal plains of Colón could belong to different worlds. Though temperatures in any one place scarcely vary year-round, the smothering heat of the lowlands contrasts markedly with the crisp cool of the highlands. And despite the narrowness of the isthmus, the climate differs sharply between Pacific and Caribbean sides: The latter receives the moisture-laden trade winds and considerably more rainfall.

There are only two seasons: wet (May–Nov.) and dry (Dec.–April), though in many parts of the country the seasons might more correctly be termed "wet" and "less wet." The humidity is less oppressive on the Pacific side, although heavy enough to cling like a damp shawl in wet season, when the cooling breezes die, gray cascades of rain pour down in torrents, and the forests of trees and skyscrapers vanish behind a thick silver veil.

> **Despite Panama's location entirely within the tropics, extremes of elevation and relief spawn a profusion of microclimates.**

Up to 35 percent of the nation is sheltered in some 16 national parks and 48 other protected areas, some 1,300 square miles (3,367 sq km) of it in seven national parks bordering the Panama Canal in a 10-mile-wide (16 km) forested watershed. Marine parks protect some of the more than 1,500 islands close to shore. Many of these isles are ringed by coral reefs, while the country hosts America's largest mangrove estuaries.

The Panamanian government has long been an advocate of ecological preservation, at least on paper. Nonetheless, during the past century, much of Panama was denuded by cattle ranching and slash-and-burn agriculture. Much of the Azuero Peninsula and the foothills of the Cordillera Central have been virtually deforested. More recently, the extension of the Interamerican Highway into western Darién has been calamitous for forests. And the past decade (2000–2008) saw a further 3 percent decline in primary forest, although the nation is gaining in overall forest cover due to forestry schemes.

From semidesert to rain forest paradise, Panama's range of terrains reflects the full diversity of the tropics, and each region is as distinct as a thumbprint.

An untouched jungle-like mountain forest in Parque Internacional La Amistad

Overwater bungalows, Bocas del Toro, lapped by the Caribbean Sea

Western Highlands

Dominating the landscape of far western Panama, dauntingly rugged mountains rise dramatically from the coastal plains, separating the Caribbean and the Pacific like a great wall. Rising to 11,400 feet (3,475 m) atop Volcán Barú, near the border with Costa Rica, these great *cerros,* or peaks, are folded in serrated pleats—the Cerro Trinidad, Cordillera de Tabasará, and Cordillera Central—cut by deep valleys.

Moisture-bearing winds from the Caribbean dump their liquid cargo on the soggy eastern slopes, feeding lush rain forests profusely smothered in bromeliads and delicate orchids. Clouds swirl about windswept summits, where mosses and ferns thrive in the mists haunted by the whistles of resplendent quetzals. Much of this velveteen jungle is protected within Parque Internacional La Amistad, a refuge for endangered wildlife. Volcán Barú rises amid these mountains and last erupted in the 16th century. Bubbling hot springs and steaming fumaroles attest to its latent power.

Central Panama

About two-thirds of Panama's population lives in a belt spanning the isthmus at its narrowest and lowest point. Fully one-third of Panamanians live in Panama City, a sprawling coastal metropolis at the southern entrance to the Panama Canal (because the isthmus runs east–west between the oceans, the canal runs more or less north–south). The rest of the populace is concentrated west of the city in provincial towns and dusty agricultural villages in a belt stretching along the foothills of the Cordillera Central and linked by the Interamerican Highway. The expansion of population eastward is a recent phenomenon, and most settlements are small and inconsequential. The country is effectively divided in two, metaphorically and literally, by the canal.

At the canal's southern end, the nation's cosmopolitan capital, Panama City, faces the Golfo de Panamá. Nearby Isla Taboga draws day-trippers by ferry, while farther out, the

Archipiélago de las Perlas offers tantalizing beaches and superlative snorkeling and diving. The capital city seeps eastward along the Interamerican Highway, unspooling through spongy, half-drowned coastal lowlands filled with brackish swamps. Westward the highway grants access to a string of beaches popular with city dwellers on weekends. The Altos de Campana rise inland, a partially deforested mountain range comprised of isolated, sheer-sided craggy mounds and rugged vales traversed by marked trails. One broad vale, El Valle de Antón, stands out for its exquisite beauty and springlike climate. Colón, a down-at-the-heels Caribbean port city, commands the canal's northern gateway. Spanish fortresses still guard the mouth of the Chagres and the entrance to the ancient treasure port of Portobelo.

Eastern Caribbean

Arcing southeast for 142 miles (230 km), this enticingly beautiful coastline is decorated with the San Blas Islands, more than 350 coral-based isles in jade-colored waters a short distance offshore. Hemming in the coast, a backdrop of lush green mountains forms a spine separating the Caribbean from Darién Province. Comprising the autonomous Kuna Yala *comarca* (district), this is purely Kuna Indian terrain. No non-Kuna live here, ensuring that the indigenous culture remains one of the most intact native communities in the world. The Kuna population is concentrated on about one dozen densely packed islands. Many isles have humble facilities for tourists. Simple watercraft are the main mode of travel, permitting access to uninhabited islands fringed by soft sand beaches and warm tropical waters perfect for snorkeling. The reef peters out to the east, ending its protection. The coastal plain is farmed with coconut groves although mainland settlements are few, and none exist in the thickly forested Serranía de San Blas and Serranía de Darién mountains, accessible only in the Área Silvestre Protegida de Narganá.

The Darién Isthmus

Panama's vast, sparsely populated southeast quarter broadens eastward, framed to the north by the Serranía de San Blas and Serranía de Darién mountains and to the south by mountain chains that rear above the Pacific. The mountains cup a basin some 155 miles long (250 km), drained westward through the broad Golfo de San

Río Chagres

The Panama Canal forms a great trench through Panama's low-lying center, flanked to each side by mountains cloaked in a dozen shades of tropical green. Broken into peaks and troughs like a tormented sea, these lushly forested heights span a half dozen or so national parks protecting the water sources—not least the mighty Río Chagres—that feed the canal, and thereby the country's economy.

The Chagres drains a basin the size of Rhode Island. Home to Emberá Indians,

and a source for exhilarating white-water river trips, the Chagres region harbors a mind-boggling array of bird and wildlife species, including large populations of monkeys, jaguars, and harpy eagles. The tempestuous Chagres feeds west into Gatún Lake, which flooded 164 square miles (425 sq km) of forest when the river was dammed in 1906. The lake is still littered with half-drowned trees and studded with islands where wildlife thrives.

Miguel. Prodigious rainfall pummels the region. The rivers form liquid highways for isolated communities of Emberá-Wounaan Indians and Afro-Antillean peoples.

Construction of the Interamerican Highway in the 1970s opened the intermontane valley to loggers and farmers. Much of the rain forest that carpeted the region has since disappeared. The highway ends at Yaviza, beyond which fully half of Darién is still smothered by the Western Hemisphere's second largest rain forest. In the spongy heat of Parque Nacional Darién, a UNESCO World Heritage site, the vegetation is as luxuriant as anywhere on Earth. Giant cedro trees tower 100 feet (30 m) in the air, orchid species are counted in their hundreds, and you can almost sense the vegetation growing around you. Much of the park is mountainous, reaching 6,152 feet (1,875 m) atop Cerro Tacarcuna. East of the Golfo de San Miguel, the lonesome shoreline unfurls ruler straight, lined with black-sand beaches.

Western Pacific

The southern foothills of the western highlands ease onto broad, rolling coastal plains that curve around the Golfo de Chiriquí. The *llanura* (plain) narrows eastward, and westward curls around the Bahía de Charco Azul to the long, slender tip of Punta Burica. The western flatlands are smothered in banana plantations to the Costa Rica border.

Panama's largest island was once a penal colony; today it is a nature reserve occupied mostly by monkeys, iguanas, and birds.

The deeply indented, irregular Pacific shore stretches in total for 767 miles (1,234 km). The Pacific Ocean tides are tremendous—rising and falling by as much as 20 feet (6.1 m). Beaches like ribbons of silver lamé unspool along the claw-like Burica Peninsula and along the gulf's wild eastern shoreline, washed by rugged waves favored by surfers. The waters along the central shore are thick with mangroves forming a braided maze that comprises the Manglares de David, the largest such complex in Panama. The riparian system teems with birds, while marine turtles crawl onto lonesome beaches to lay their eggs.

Offshore, Parque Nacional Marino Golfo de Chiriquí protects warm waters thronged by marine life: sharks, manta rays, marlin, and smaller fry amid the coral reefs. Farther out lies uninhabited Isla Coiba, the centerpiece of Parque Nacional Coiba, a UNESCO World Heritage site. Panama's largest island was once a penal colony; today it is a nature reserve occupied mostly by monkeys, iguanas, and birds such as scarlet macaws. Sportfishers and scuba divers rate these waters as world class. The city of David sits square in the center of the region and can be stiflingly hot, the air often still as an oppressive stone.

Azuero Peninsula

This oblong region jutting south into the Pacific Ocean is Panama's dry quarter. Cacti thrust up from the parched earth that culminates in the Saharan landscapes of Parque Nacional Sarigua. A rugged mountain chain to the west files eastward to a featureless, honey-colored plain. The lowlands have long been cleared of forests to make room for ranches and, later, sugarcane. Cattle rest in the shade of trees spreading their gnarled branches to the ground. In spring and summer, yellow bark, purple jacaranda, and bright orange flame-of-the-forest speckle Azuero, and the hot, heavy air is redolent with

Sunshine drenches the palm-studded isles of San Blas.

fragrance. Time-warp colonial towns, where Panama's folkloric traditions run deep, color the main highway running inland of the eastern shore. Remarkably, few tourists know of Azuero's relaxed charms. Surfers are drawn to the waves rolling onto broad slivers of taupe sand. Thousands of shorebirds flock to the flats. Offshore, Refugio de Vida Silvestre Isla Iguana, a rookery for frigate birds, dots the warm waters that nourish coral reefs and draw humpback whales to breed. This refuge, as well as the nearby Refugio de Vida Silvestre Isla de Cañas, are also vital nesting sites for marine turtles.

Western Caribbean

The relatively smooth Caribbean shore is 477 miles (768 km) long. Its western portion extends southeast from the Río Sixaola and the Costa Rica border, a broad coastal plain forming a vast sea of banana trees separated from the sea by a complex of mangroves and swamps. The dusty service center of Changuinola is choked with truck traffic linking the *fincas* (plantations) of international fruit companies to the port of Almirante, a funky gateway (by water taxi) to the Archipiélago de Bocas del Toro. The island chain draws adventure seekers to the charming, colorful Afro-Caribbean–flavored center of Bocas Town. The reef-combed and mangrove-lined isles enfold the tranquil Laguna de Chiriquí, where dolphins cavort in the bay of Bocatorito. Parque Nacional Marino Isla Bastimentos, famous for its strawberry-colored poison dart frogs, protects a mosaic of mangroves, towering rain forest, and pristine coral reefs.

To the east, the Península Valiente hooks around the lagoon, beyond which the Caribbean coast curves along the Golfo de los Mosquitos—a remote, sparsely inhabited world where the air smells of fecundity. Hard-pressed Ngöbe-Buglé and Teribe communities speckle the region; many welcome visitors as they turn to ecotourism as an alternative to slash-and-burn agriculture. ■

Flora & Fauna

Panama, a pivotal region at the juncture of the Americas, is a meeting point for the biota of each. Profuse in wildlife, the environment is a veritable tropical Eden, a cornucopia of biodiversity that was reflected in the words President Theodore Roosevelt wrote to his daughter in 1906: "It is a real tropic forest, palms and bananas, breadfruit trees, bamboos, lofty ceibas, and gorgeous butterflies and brilliant colored birds fluttering among the orchids."

Luxuriant Greenhouse

This diversity of plants and animals exists despite the fact that the country lies wholly within the tropics, between 7 and 9 degrees north of the Equator. Panama boasts ten distinct ecological zones, from coastal mangrove forests and swampy wetlands to cloud forests. These forests, shrouded in ethereal mists, are found atop the higher peaks. The colorful canvas even has its dun patches, pockets of dry deciduous forest merged into the parched savannas of Azuero.

On the whole, though Panama is steeped in humidity and near-constant high temperatures, with the sun passing almost directly overhead throughout the year. Combined with profuse rainfall that tops a drenching 200 inches (500 cm) in many places, the heat fuels luxuriant growth. The bountiful country hosts more than 10,000 known plant species, including more than 1,500 varieties of trees and at least 678 fern species, some 13 feet tall (4 m) with fiddlehead fronds that could grace titanic cellos.

> Panama boasts ten distinct ecological zones, from coastal mangrove forests and swampy wetlands to cloud forests.

Orchids & Other Flowers

Panama is singularly rich in orchids: About 1,200 orchid species have been identified so far, including the Flor del Espíritu Santo, or Holy Ghost orchid, the beautiful white national flower. Thriving on moisture, these exquisite plants are found at every elevation, from sea level to the upper slopes of Volcán Barú. At any time of year, dozens of species are in bloom, ranging from the pinhead-size *Platystele jungermanniodes* to the sinister beauty of the Dracula species, such as *Dracula vampira,* with black tapering leaves up to 12 inches long (30 cm).

Most orchid species are epiphytes (Greek for "air plants"), arboreal nesters that root on other plants, drawing their moisture through spongelike roots direct from the air. Other epiphytes include bromeliads, whose thick, tightly whorled spiky leaves form cisterns that trap water and falling detritus whose decay sustains the plants. Many tropical forests resemble vast galleries, so dense are the colonies of air plants thriving in the compost atop massive boughs.

The landscapes flare with color: orange and purple angel trumpet vines; anthuriums in whites, reds, and pinks; begonias; heliconias (more than 30 species); carnal red passionflowers; and *labios ardientes* (hot lips) looking like Marilyn Monroe's kiss-me pout. Even the rare tropical dry broadleaf deciduous forests of Azuero explode in vivid colors in dry winter months, when *corteza amarilla* (yellow bark), purple jacaranda, and flame red *Spathodea,* or African flame-of-the-forest, brighten the landscape before dropping their petals like colored confetti.

Mangroves & Wetlands

Panama's shorelines are home to five species of *manglares* (mangroves). These halophytic plants—terrestrial species able to survive with their roots in salt water—thrive in

Mist shrouds the forested heights of Volcán Barú, feeding luxuriant growth.

alluvium washed down to the coast. Vast forests of mangroves grow along the estuarine shoreline, especially along the Golfo de Chiriquí, Bahía de Panama, and Golfo de San Miguel. Standing over the dark waters, their interlocking stilt roots forming a tangle among the braided channels, mangroves rinse silt from the slow-flowing rivers to form new land by the shore. Thus, they fight tidal erosion and trap nutrients that nourish a profligate world. Migratory waterfowl, wading birds, and small mammals abound, thriving on amphipods, crabs, mussels, and other tiny creatures that inhabit the watery sloughs—vital nurseries, too, for fish species and marine invertebrates.

Water hyacinths crowd Lago Gatún and Lago Bayano in the center of the country. Other grassy wetlands, swamp forests, and freshwater pools concentrate inland of the Bahía de Panama, drawing migratory shorebirds. The marshes of Área Protegida Ciénaga de las Macana and Refugio de Vida Silvestre Cenegón del Mangle, a manatee habitat on the Pacific coast, as well as those of San San Pond Sak, on the Caribbean coast, flood in rainy season, when they are flush with fulvous whistling-ducks and other waterfowl.

Selecting a Wilderness Guide

When it comes to spotting wildlife and learning about Panama's flora and fauna, a naturalist guide is essential (see Travelwise p. 263). Countless visitors to the country report that their guides were the highlight of their trips. The amazing ability of the finest guides includes an eagle's-eye ability to spot and identify wildlife that the untrained eye will surely miss. The best guides have had a lifetime of experience in the field and have built solid reputations. Many are specialists in birds, botany, or herpetology. Most are freelancers and can be hired through such companies as **Ancon Expeditions** (tel 269-9415, anconexpeditions.com).

Rain Forests

Crown jewels of neotropical life, rain forests are among the most complex ecosystems on Earth. Biologists recognize at least 13 types of rain forest, ranging from lowland jungle to high-mountain cloud forest at elevations around 4,000 feet (1,220 m), where branches drip with mosses and epiphytes thrive in the mists. Different forests stem from differences in altitude, rainfall, and soil. Thus the same latitude may be marked by tropical evergreen rain forest on the Caribbean coast and seasonally dry semideciduous forest on the Pacific coast. All rain forests receive more than 100 inches (250 cm) of rainfall per year. The true lowland rain forests that smother the *llanuras* (flatlands) of the Caribbean plains and Darién may receive up to 300 inches (750 cm).

The lowland rain forest is a multilayered riot of green. Trees of Gothic proportion grow to 100 feet (30 m) or more before merging like giant umbrellas, forming a solid canopy. Some species with trunks like great Corinthian columns, such as the mahoganies and ceiba or silk cotton, soar past their neighbors. The hundreds of tree species are festooned with bromeliads, parasitic plants, and creepers.

In the hot, humid tropics, plants grow year-round. Dead leaves decompose quickly and nutrients are recycled into the forest canopy. Thus, tropical soils are thin, and the massive hardwood trees spread their great roots wide, like giant serpents; the huge trees are flanged at their bases, like rockets, to prevent their toppling over.

Only about 10 percent of the sunlight reaches the cool, dank forest floor, where plants such as the "poor man's umbrella" (*sombrilla de pobre*) put out broad leaves to soak up the subaqueous light. The lack of sunlight precludes growth so that the saplings of many

EXPERIENCE: Birding at Its Best

Wherever you are in the country, the birding is sure to astound. With so many distinct ecological zones, you're spoiled for choice. Hosting a wide network of specialized tour guides, Panama is a favorite destination for birders.

Many visitors come specifically to spot the resplendent quetzal—a kind of Holy Grail that is easily seen in the highlands around Volcán Barú. The Pacific's coastal wetlands draw waterbirds in their millions. And the varied habitats of Darién are unsurpassed for checking off an A to Z of avian species, from aracarias and antpittas to the harpy eagle.

A perfect tour would visit several habitats, perhaps combining montane cloud forest, lowland rain forest, mangroves, coastal wetland, and offshore islands.

Still, some specific locales offer birding par excellence. Here are a few of the best places to tick off from the checklist of more than 960 species.

Resplendent quetzals live in mountainous forests.

Birding Hot Spots

Cana Field Station (see pp. 134–135), at 1,600 feet (500 m) on the flank of Cerro Pirre, in Darién, is renowned for king vultures, macaws, and great curassows. Contact **Ancon Expeditions** (tel 269-9415, anconexpeditions.com).

Pipeline Road (see p. 101), which leads from the Gamboa Highway into Parque Nacional Soberanía, is Panama's preeminent birding trail. More bird species have been counted here in a 24-hour period than anywhere else in the world.

Sendero los Quetzales (see p. 199) is named for the resplendent quetzal, which is abundant in the cloud forests around this trail connecting the highland town of Boquete with Cerro Punta, to east and west sides, respectively, of Volcán Barú.

Birding Tour Guides

Birding Panamá (tel 392-5663, birdingpanama.com) uses the best local guides in the business. Its website includes descriptions of best birding sites.

Cheeseman's Ecology Safaris (tel 408/741-5330, cheesemans.com) offers springtime tours that include such world-renowned birding sites as Parque Nacional Soberanía and Sendero los Quetzales.

Panamá Audubon Society (tel 232-5977, audubonpanama.org) offers more than 20 birding field trips each year.

high-canopy species stop growing once they reach about 10 feet (3 m), then wait until a tree falls, opening a patch of light, before erupting into explosive growth. Much of the life of the forest takes place in the sunlit upper canopy, which resounds with the calls of birds and unseen creatures.

Bountiful Ark

Panama is home to almost 1,000 bird, 225 mammal, 214 reptile, and 155 amphibian species, including 104 species of frogs and toads. Insect species number in the tens of thousands and countless marine species swim and crawl out at sea. Over the eons, life-forms from the north and south have migrated through the narrow land bridge and diversified remarkably. The sheer range of adaptation to the varied local relief and climate is quite wonderful.

Birds: Ornithologists' hearts take flight in Panama, which despite its comparatively tiny size boasts an astounding 978 or so species of birds, 12 of them found only here. Some 150 species are migrants—the isthmus is a bottleneck for birds migrating between the Americas. Panama's coastal wetlands are particularly rich in migratory shorebirds, such as sandpipers, willets, and whimbrels, often seen in tens of thousands. White ibises, spoonbills, and herons pick for morsels down by the shore, where coastal mangroves prove ideal nesting sites for pelicans, frigate birds, and even boobies, which can be seen on Isla de los Pájaros (Swan's Cay) and on islands of the Golfo de Panamá and Golfo de Chiriquí.

> **Over the eons, life-forms from the north and south have migrated through the narrow land bridge and diversified remarkably.**

The forests are alive with the squawks and screeches of parrots barreling overhead in jet-fighter formation. Panama has 18 species, from the diminutive Panama Amazon to the giant blue-and-gold macaw, one of six endangered macaw species found here. Large flocks of scarlet macaws can be seen on Isla Coiba, plunging between the treetops like flying rainbows.

Keel-billed and chestnut-mandibled toucans, with their bananalike beaks, are common throughout the country. So, too, are cattle egrets, easily seen in pastures. And quetzals, the emerald jewels of the cloud forest, are more numerous here than anywhere else in Central America. They're a dime a dozen around Volcán Barú, especially in springtime when the ardent males are given to wooing their prospective mates with daring soar-and-swoop displays. Visitors should listen for the quetzal's mournful two-note whistle.

The country also hosts dozens of species of tanagers and trogons and doves, plus bellbirds, umbrellabirds, and antbirds scavenging on insects and lizards flushed out by columns of army ants. The list goes on and on.

Panama's national bird is the massive harpy eagle, largest by far of the nation's 50 or so raptor species. It nests atop the tallest trees, keeping a sharp eye out for monkeys and other potential snacks that it will snatch up on the wing. Although the bird is endangered throughout its range, the Fondo Peregrino-Panama has a successful breed-and-release program.

Mammals: Almost half of Panama's 218 mammal species are bats, ranging from fruit-eaters and vampires (feeding mainly on the blood of sleeping cattle) to hawk-size fishing bats with large claws adapted for snatching fish on the fly. Most mammal species are shy and not easily seen by visitors, as with the country's six species of elusive and well-camouflaged tropical cats.

Far more easily viewed are Panama's seven species of monkeys, from the tiny endemic Geoffrey's tamarin, the omnivorous white-faced capuchins, and the black-headed spider monkey to herbivorous mantled howlers. Male howlers are heard as often as seen; the forests vibrate to their stentorian roars. Two- and three-toed sloths *(perezosos)* are commonly seen snoozing in treetops (see sidebar p. 50). And

A mantled howler monkey relaxes in Azuero Province.

capybaras, the world's largest rodents, inhabit sloughs at the northernmost end of their range.

On the ground, the adorable raccoonlike brown coati *(pizote)* is ubiquitous. Herds of potentially aggressive white-lipped and collared peccaries are sometimes encountered deep in the rain forests. Baird's tapirs—trunk-nosed distant cousins of elephants—inhabit both lowland and montane forests. Agoutis (large rodents), anteaters, and armadillos are other common mammals. And otters swim in the rivers of Parque Nacional Chagres.

Amphibians & Reptiles: Amphibians and reptiles thrive in the hot, damp tropics. Snakes, of which Panama has more than 120 species, are everywhere, although usually well camouflaged and not easily seen. A swaying vine turns out to be an eyelash pit viper, so green as to be almost iridescent, curled in sensuous coils on a branch. Boas up to 10 feet long (3 m) are often spotted along riverbanks. Most snake species are small, preying on small birds, lizards, and rodents. Fewer than 10 percent are venomous.

The viper family includes the much-feared, burnished brown fer-de-lance (locally called equis—meaning "X"—for the marks on its back), an aggressive giant that accounts for most of the fatal snakebites in Panama. Brightly banded coral snakes account for many of the others. Fortunately, there are no known occurrences of humans being bitten by the highly venomous black-and-orange sea snake often seen in swarms in the Bahía de Panama.

Frogs abound, including red-eyed tree frogs and gaily colored poison dart frogs hopping about the forest floors, secure in the Day-Glo liveries meant to warn off predators. In recent decades, a deadly fungus has killed off many frog and toad species and threatens Panama's endangered and earless golden frog *(Atelopus zateki)*, a national symbol revered for its ability to communicate by a kind of semaphore.

Sloths

Sloths *(perozosos)* are commonly seen moving in treetops at a pace close to rigor mortis, using their powerful arms and curved claws. Panama has two species: the three-toed sloth and the smaller nocturnal Hoffman's two-toed sloth. These leaf-eaters have huge stomachs to process large quantities of fairly indigestible food, which can remain in their stomach for up to one week. Their metabolic rate is correspondingly slow; the animal even garners heat from direct sunlight, much like cold-blooded reptiles. Sloths typically spend 18 hours a day sleeping and digesting their meals. They do not wash much, and their shaggy fur is tinted green by algae and inhabited by bugs.

American crocodiles *(cocodrilos)*, which reach lengths of up to 15 feet (4.5 m), infest the river estuaries and lowland waterways, including Lago Gatún. Their diminutive cousins, caimans, rarely grow beyond 6 feet (1.8 m). The tree-dwelling iguana inhabits both wet and dry lowland forests and can grow to 3 feet (0.9 m); its population has been greatly reduced by *campesinos* for its tasty meat. A highlight among the dozens of smaller reptiles is the basilisk lizard, a lowland dweller nicknamed the "Jesus Christ lizard" for its ability to run across water on its hind legs.

Five species of marine turtles come ashore to lay their eggs at beaches on both the Caribbean and Pacific coasts. The most exhilarating sight is the synchronized mass nestings of olive Ridley turtles that takes place at Refugio de Vida Silvestre Isla de Cañas during full moons in autumn.

Panama boasts a number of colorful amphibians, including the red-eyed tree frog.

Marine Life: The warm waters off Panama's coasts are thickly populated by fish and marine mammals. Manatees, endangered marine herbivores, inhabit the watery seclusion of San San Pond Sak. The waters of the Golfo de Chiriquí and Golfo de Panamá teem with game fish, luring anglers seeking dorado, tuna, and marlin. Humpback whales, minke whales, false killer whales, and even sperm whales and orcas gather to mate and give birth in the nutrient-rich gulf waters.

Harmless manta rays, whale sharks, octopuses, crabs, and spiny lobsters the size of house cats: These and other creatures thrill scuba divers in Panama's Pacific waters. On the Caribbean side of the isthmus, a kaleidoscopic array of fish plays tag in the coral-laced waters of the San Blas Islands and Bocas del Toro, where dolphins perform like a circus troupe.

Insects: Incalculably rich in insect fauna, Panama resounds to a cacophonous buzz. The country is thought to have more than 18,600 insect species per acre (46,000 per ha), from microscopic flower mites that hitch rides inside the nostrils of hummingbirds to the 3-inch-long (7.5 cm) rhinoceros beetle.

Tiny Isla Barro Colorado alone has more than 200 ant species, from vast swarms of army ants to the less aggressive leaf-cutters scurrying along well-worn pathways with shards of scissored leaves above their heads. Some 1,600 species of butterflies flit about the country, including the vivid electric-blue morpho butterflies. ∎

> **Five species of marine turtles come ashore to lay their eggs at beaches on both the Caribbean and Pacific coasts.**

Culture

Panameños are extremely proud of their vibrant cultural scene. The country is incomparably rich in folkloric tradition, and the visual arts have shed prescriptive straightjackets to arouse the admiration of the world. Classical and contemporary music are avatars of the nation's lively cultural spirit, recalling rich indigenous traditions that predate the Spanish arrival.

Visual Arts

Panama has an artistic tradition dating back 10,000 years, to a time when pre-Columbian peoples adorned their ceremonial bowls and other ceramics with stylized red, black, and ocher motifs. During the colonial period, most artistic expression was relegated to religious art. Post-independence Panamanian art is associated above all with Roberto Lewis (1874–1949), whose allegorical, romantic murals, inspired by the belle époque of France, adorn the Palacio Presidencial and Teatro Nacional. Lewis became director of Panama's first art academy, the Escuela Nacional de Pintura, in 1939, and influenced an entire generation of artists. Manuel E. Amador's (1869–1952) modernism led the way for more abstract art, typified by Eudoro Silvera (1917–), Alfredo Sinclair (1915–2014), and Guillermo Trujillo (1927–), known for his distinctive works that fuse love of country with the mythology of its indigenous people.

Panama's eclectic fine-arts scene—long overshadowed by the U.S. presence—has lacked a recognizable national theme. An exception is the work of acclaimed artist Brooke Alfaro (1949–), who in 2000 moved from working on canvas to video art to create portraits of the life of Panama's marginalized underclass. Meanwhile, inspired by the works of Cuba's Wilfredo Lam (1902–1982), Colón native Arturo Lindsay (1946–) has concentrated on exploring African spiritual and aesthetic traditions.

The nation's largest collection of works by Panamanian artists is found in permanent and revolving exhibitions in Panama City's Museo de Arte Contemporáneo. The museum hosts weekly workshops and every two years hosts the Bienal de Arte.

Earning international recognition for their photography are Iraida Icaza (1952–) and Sandra Eleta (1942–), known for her book, *Portobelo: Fotografías de Panamá,* and her recent photo-documentaries of the Emberá-Wounaan, who decorate their bodies with patterns etched with the juice of the jagua.

Ngöbe-Buglé *Chácaras*

Ngöbe-Buglé indigenous people use *chácaras* (or *kra* in the native tongue) for transporting everything from babies to market goods. Woven from the fiber of wild pita and cabuya plants, these bags come in various sizes, and every adult owns several. Medium-size chácaras are carried on the shoulder. Larger bags rest on the back and are supported by a strap around the forehead. The plant fibers are dyed in the absence of men under a new moon (to produce more intensity) in a palette of colors. Each design is imbued with symbolism and tells a fable, or mimics a landscape or the skin and colors of particular animals.

Panamanian art at the Instituto Nacional de Cultura

Sculpture

The sculptural landscape is undistinguished, notwithstanding a strong heritage of ritualistic sculptures associated with pre-Columbian cultures. Creation of the Instituto de Artes in 1907 spawned a school of sculptors (mostly Europeans) working in neoclassical style. In the 1940s, José Mora Noli (1923–1981) emerged as the first contemporary Panamanian sculptor. Today's preeminent sculptor is Isabel de Obaldía (1957–), who works predominantly with glass.

Crafts

Panama has a lively theater scene, with everything from the classics to experimental pieces performed in venues large and small.

On the crafts front, Panama is famed for its stitched appliqué *molas* exclusive to the Kuna people, for elaborately embroidered white lace *pollera* dresses, and for grotesque papier-mâché devil masks from the towns of Azuero. The popular masks are collector's items from the hands of such master maskmakers as Darío López and Iván de León.

Market stalls are brimful with straw hats, available in a variety of styles (though the famous "Panama hats" are actually made in Ecuador). Some of the highest quality weaves and designs are achieved by the Ngöbe-Buglé people, who normally wear straw hats for celebrations, when they adorn their hats with feathers. Most hats derive from the provinces of Coclé and Herrera, where weaving is a true cottage industry in Azuero hamlets such as Ocú and Pedregosa. The very best hats are made in the early morning or late at night. The rest of the day the sweat builds up on the weaver's fingers, and atmospheric conditions are too variable for the absolute continuity necessary in a *fino*.

Tourism has stimulated the production of indigenous crafts whose secrets are passed down through generations. The Emberá-Wounaan are acclaimed for tightly woven flat basketry adorned with animal motifs, and for their skill as carvers who turn tagua palm nuts into small animal figurines. The Ngöbe-Buglé are known for their unique *chácaras,* bags hand-knitted from the fibers of the cabuya and pita plant (see sidebar p. 52). Common design elements in all Ngöbe-Buglé art are the triangle, representing both mountain and valley of the culture's home environment, and snake designs *(culebrakrays)* that reflect the importance of snakes in Ngöbe-Buglé mythology. These peoples excel, too, in the beauty of their *chaquiras*—exquisite glass bead necklaces up to 12 inches wide (30 cm).

Literature

Panama was slow to evolve a literary culture or writers of distinction. The early exceptions were novelist and dramatist Víctor de la Guardia (1772–1823), poet Dario Herrera (1870–1914), and nationalist poet Amelia Denis de Icaza (1836–1911), best known for her patriotic poem, "Al Cerro Ancón," about Ancón Hill. The nation found its most vital expression in the mid-20th century through the pens of such novelists as avant-garde Guillermo Sánchez Borbón (1924–2005), who wrote under the pseudonym Tristán Solarte, and Ricardo Miró (1883–1940), who wrote the poem "Patria," a homeland homage.

Despite a high literacy rate, Panamanians as a whole are dispassionate about literature. Inward looking, and intensely focused on themes of daily life on the isthmus, local authors still produce mostly poems and short stories that tend toward the prosaic. Latter-day standouts include poet Joaquín Beleño (1922–1988), known for his novels *Luna Verde* and *Gamboa Road Gang,* nationalistic works about injustices of the Panama Canal, and Carlos Francisco Changmarín (1922–2012), who wrote mostly on countryside themes. Prominent among contemporary authors, Enrique Jaramillo Levi (1944–) also edits Panama's literary review, *Maga.*

Theater

Panama has a lively theater scene, with everything from the classics to experimental pieces performed in venues large and small. Noted Panamanian-born stage director José Benjamin Quintero (1924–1999) pioneered the off-Broadway movement of the 1950s and was a cofounder of New York's legendary Circle in the Square Theatre. The Theater Guild of Ancón performs in English at the art deco Teatro Balboa in Panama City. The nation's leading theater is the Teatro Nacional.

Music & Dance

Panama today swings to a salsa beat. Nonetheless, Panama's folkloric tradition runs deep, although *música folclórica* (often referred to as *típico* or *pindín*) is performed today mostly in festivals and stage presentations. Panama's típico music fuses the sound of the five-string *mejorana* guitar with *tambores* (African bongo drums) and pre-Columbian musical instruments such as tagua seedpods and *churucas* (gourd rattles). Dances are typified by the *punto,* the mejorana, the *tamborito* (Panama's national dance), and similar stomps for couples dressed in traditional clothing: the *montuño* hat and white shirt for men and the ankle-length, frilled lace *pollera* for women. Traditional dancing is based on the stylized Spanish *paseo,* with men and women alternately circling each other, accompanied by much "yip-yipping"—in Panama the shouts are called *saloma*—and tossing of scarves and straw hats.

EXPERIENCE: Partying at Local Fiestas

Panama's year is a whirligig of fiestas. Almost every town has a patron saint's day *(fiestas patronales),* typically featuring a rodeo and *tope* (display of horse-riding skills), fireworks, a beauty pageant, and traditional music and dance. Religious *feriados* (holidays) and processions are held during Holy Week, while more bacchanalian Carnavales take place around Lent. The nation's indigenous communities hold their own unique and colorful festivals. The Autoridad de Turismo Panamá website *(visitpanama.com)* has a listing. Here are some key fiestas:

Feria de las Flores y el Café *(Jan., Boquete)* draws thousands of gawkers to *ooh!* and *aah!* at the glorious displays of flowers.

Carnaval *(March, Las Tablas)* is considered Panama's most colorful street bash. Folkloric dancing, beauty contests, live street bands, carnival floats, and plenty of partying alfresco.

Festival de la Pollera *(July, Las Tablas)* pays homage to Panamanian traditions—notably the national dress—with competitions to crown La Reina de la Pollera, the National Pollera Queen.

Festival Nacional de la Mejorana *(Sept., Guararé)* features an ox-cart parade plus traditional guitar music. It's Panama's main folkloric festival.

Grammy-winning musician Rubén Blades once served as Panama's minister of tourism.

Every week a folkloric festival seems to be taking place somewhere in the Azuero, the heartland of Panamanian music and dance. None is more colorful than the Corpus Christi festival, highlighted by devil dancers in masks and elaborate costumes. The Ngöbe-Buglé, Emberá-Wounaan, and Kuna communities also enjoy demonstrating their centuries-old dances, performed to the accompaniment of drums and Pan-style flutes.

Many típico dances, such as *los enanos* (the dwarfs) and *el zaracundé,* are derived from African culture and performed during festivals by dancers dressed in dry banana leaves. Colón Province is known for its *congos,* performances featuring drama, music, and dance that recount the history of Panama's Afro-colonial people. Contemporary island tunes also infuse the culture: The Bastimentos Beach Boys, from Bocas del Toro, are legendary exponents of Calypso.

On the classical front, the national symphony orchestra was created in 1941 under the baton of celebrated Spanish composer Alberto Galimany (1889–1973). The Ballet Nacional de Panamá was founded in 1970. The popularity of the classical genres among urbanites was boosted when British ballerina Dame Margot Fonteyn (1919–1991) settled in Panama. Panama hosts the Festival Nacional de Ballet each October. Today classical music is sponsored by the private Asociación Nacional de Conciertos, founded by Panamanian pianist Jaime Ingram (1928–).

The capital's cosmopolitan jazz scene finds its major outlet in the annual Panama City Jazz Festival each January. The festival's founder is Panama's well-known jazz composer, pianist, and Grammy-winner Danilo Pérez (1965–), a cultural ambassador for Panama.

The younger generation has forsaken traditional forms of music and dance for hip-hop, rock, and Latin rhythms—salsa, *cumbia,* and hip-swiveling merengue. Panama City's nightclubs throb on weekends to the *vida loca* vibe. Hot performers include the Latin rock band Los Rabanes and top-selling cumbia artists Samy and Sandra Sandoval. Panama's undisputed ambassador of contemporary sound is salsa superstar (and politician) Rubén Blades (1948–). Born into an artistic family, Blades attained national hero status for his lyrics on social and nationalist themes. ■

A vibrant financial capital teeming with cosmopolitan restaurants, hotels, and nightlife, while nature and the canal are never far away

Panama City

The seawall at Plaza de Francia

Panama City

Cosmopolitan, compact, and steamy, Panama's capital city spreads along the shore of a broad Pacific bay at the southern entrance to the canal. Its hot maritime climate at times feels like a Turkish sauna. Hotter still is the city's cool Latin vibe. At once colonial and contemporary, this city of around 1.3 million people (Panamanians know it simply as "Panama") is the most sophisticated metropolis between Miami and Maracaibo.

A crossroads between two continents and two oceans, the city has been motivated by commerce for 500 years. Founded in 1519 at the mouth of the Río Abajo, the ancient city prospered as the Pacific marshaling point for treasures bound for Spain via the Camino Real. In 1671, cutthroat pirate Henry Morgan ravaged the city, leaving charred ruins in his wake. A fresh start was made on a promontory known as San Felipe. Safe behind thick fortress walls, the new city evolved fine mansions in Spanish colonial style. The city's fortunes were also boosted by the mid-19th-century California gold rush and construction of the Panama Railroad, with its terminus in Panama City, while the arrival of the Compagnie Universelle du Canal Interocéanique in the 1880s added Parisian flavors to the quarter now known as Casco Viejo or Casco Antiguo.

Independence in 1903 and canal construction thrust the city headfirst into the 20th century. Entire new districts—Ancón, Balboa, Quarry Heights—went up overnight alongside U.S. military bases. For eight decades, Zonians (U.S. residents of the Canal Zone) lived a pampered colonial lifestyle with their own schools, hospitals, commissaries, and clubs. Though the U.S. bases have closed, the tidy neighborhoods of white bungalows and town houses surrounded by shade trees retain their charm.

Positioned by the canal as a once distant outpost of international commerce, the city has since evolved into a sprawling metropolis.

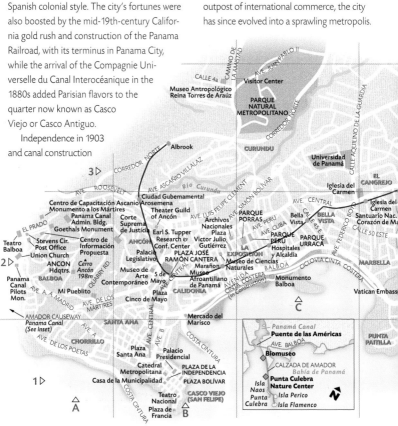

Today, Panama City is a major international banking center humming with modernity. The glass-and-marble towers of the banking district, the high-rise condominiums of Punta Paitilla, and the teeming commercial district of El Cangrejo are all a far cry from the UNESCO World Heritage site encompassing the ancient ruins of Panamá Viejo and the cobbled streets of Casco Viejo.

A quilt of loosely defined neighborhoods and multiple ethnicities, the city offers startling contrasts. The middle- and upper-class districts of Bella Vista, El Cangrejo, and Marbella, boasting boutique hotels and sophisticated restaurants, are in the midst of a high-rise building boom. The expansion has failed to engulf the ancient quarter, still rich in colonial-era allure. Brimming with scenic plazas, museums, and ecclesiastical treasures, Casco Viejo is on the upswing as investors turn ugly ducklings into gracefully remodeled mansions, hip restaurants, and trendy cafés.

NOT TO BE MISSED:

**Museo del Canal Interoceánico
63–64**

**Attending a concert at the Teatro
Nacional 67**

**A walking tour of Casco
Viejo 68–70**

**Hiking in Parque Natural
Metropolitano 71**

**Having a shirt made by the real
"Tailor of Panama" 78–79**

Much of Panama City, however, is more Mean Street than Main Street. English-speaking guides are available on Casco Viejo's crowded sidewalks, where a strong police presence helps keep crime at bay. However, some parts of Casco Viejo are best avoided, as are the neighboring labyrinthine streets of Santa Ana, Salsipuedes, and El Chorrillo, which are lined with crime-ridden tenements. ∎

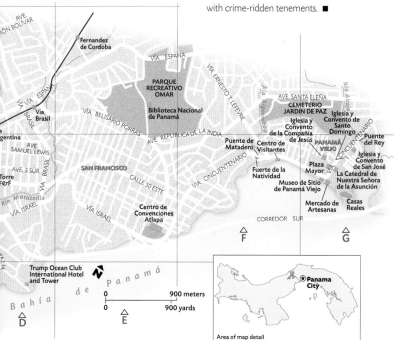

Casco Viejo

Founded in 1673 following the sacking of Panamá Viejo, the Old Quarter is the most colorful and intriguing part of the city. Though now lacking fortified walls and decrepit in parts, this timeworn living museum is full of historic buildings, quaint plazas, and charming sidewalk cafés. Declared a UNESCO World Heritage site in 1997, this quarter known colloquially as San Felipe is a world apart from the 21st-century metropolis of modern Panama City.

Charming gardens and Spanish colonial architecture make Casco Viejo a fine place for a stroll.

Casco Viejo

🗺 58 B1

Visitor Information

✉ Oficina de la
Casco Viejo
Ave. A & Calle 3,
Casco Viejo

☎ 209-6300

cascoantiguo.gob.pa

The new city was much smaller (40 acres / 16 ha) than its precursor, Panamá Viejo, which covered 124 acres (50 ha). The buildings were owned by wealthy and powerful families, who rented out their lower floors and mezzanines to artisans and storekeepers.

The original walls, with bastions and a moat with counterscarp to guard the land approach, restricted development within the city. The settlements that sprang up extramurally–beyond the city walls–housed African slaves and poorer elements of the population.

In 1878, a devastating fire—the worst in a series of destructive blazes—razed one-third of the ancient city. Many of the buildings that remained declined quickly in the punishing tropical climate. An ambitious restoration project was begun in 1997 to restore Casco Viejo to its former grandeur. Almost two decades later, the area—resembling New Orleans's French Quarter—has regained its vitality as well as a new luster. Even the poorest streets have a lingering dignity beneath the grime baked in by centuries of tropical heat.

The neighborhoods seem to spring from the pages of history books as you roam the narrow brick-paved streets, lined with gaily painted colonial confections in stone. Wrought-iron balconies drip with giddily colorful flowers, while walls of variegated tropical pastels smolder gold in the late afternoon sunlight. In the evening, it is a pleasure to sit beneath the streetlamps illuminating fashionable restaurants and bars.

Here you'll find some of the city's most alluring sites: Iglesia de San José, Plaza de la Independencia, Plaza Bolívar, Palacio de las Garzas, and—a good place to begin your visit—Plaza de Francia.

Although gentrification is ongoing, pockets of depression remain, and caution is required at night. Even by day avoid the Chorrillo area immediately west of Casco Viejo. An elevated causeway over the ocean—the Costa Cintura—was initiated in 2013 and will eventually ring Casco Viejo.

Plaza de Francia

This plaza opens to the sea air at the tip of the peninsula, where Casco Viejo meets the bottle green bay. Originally it supported a fort that was torn down at the turn of the 20th century. At that time, it was renamed in honor of the French and their pioneering attempt to construct the canal.

Shaded by jacaranda and palms, the plaza is dominated by a pencil-thin obelisk crowned by a Gallic cockerel and guarded at its base by bronze busts of Ferdinand de Lesseps and four other figures prominent in the French effort to build a canal. The story of the canal's construction and of the 22,000 workers who gave their lives is visible on stone tableaus engraved in the walls of a half-moon gallery beneath the **Paseo Esteban Huertas** esplanade. Also honored by a plaque is Carlos J. Finlay, the Cuban physician who discovered the link between the *Aëdes aegypti* mosquito and yellow fever.

In rough weather, waves crash against the eastern seawall; in Spanish colonial days, condemned convicts were chained to this wall

INSIDER TIP:

Casco Viejo is once again the cultural center of Panama City. New restaurants and art galleries pop up every month.

—BEN HIRSCH
*National Geographic
field researcher*

and drowned. Today nine vaults built into the wall—**Las Bóvedas—** house an art gallery plus Restaurant Las Bóvedas, hosting jazz on Friday nights. Immediately north is the gleaming white, triple-tiered **Instituto Nacional de Cultura** (National Institute of Culture), the government agency responsible for the nation's museums and other cultural institutions. The building

Plaza de Francia
🅰 58 B1, 69

Instituto Nacional de Cultura
✉ Plaza de Francia
☎ 501-4000 or 211-4034
🕐 Closed Sat.–Sun.
inac.gob.pa

Commonsense Precautions in the City

Panama City, like most urban centers, has its share of opportunistic thieves, who seek easy targets. Here are a few sensible guidelines that can help you avoid the quick hands of a pickpocket.

- Wear your shirt over your fanny pack, and make sure that the clasp isn't exposed.
- Leave your jewelry at home and your valuables in the hotel safe.

- Carry money and documents in a money belt worn inside your skirt or pants.
- Make photocopies of your important documents. Leave the originals in the hotel safe.
- Don't carry your camera lose on your shoulder; sling it around your neck.
- Use a zippable purse; keep it locked, and wear it over your neck.

Museo de Arte Religioso Colonial

- ✉ Ave. A at Calle 3
- ☎ 208-2897
- 🕐 Closed Sun.–Mon.
- 💲 $

Plaza de la Independencia

- Ⓜ 58 B1, 69

also holds the tiny **Teatro Anita Villalaz** *(tel 501-4020)*.

Facing onto the plaza on the north side is the robin's-egg blue **French Embassy** *(Calle 1 at Plaza de Francia, tel 211-6200)*, admired from its east side by a life-size bronze effigy of Pablo Arosemena (1836–1920), principal negotiator with the U.S. government of the canal treaty and later president of the Republic of Panama (1910–1912 and 1920). Each July 14, the embassy hosts an outdoor party complete with fireworks.

Near the Plaza: The ruins two blocks northwest of the plaza are those of the **Iglesia y Convento de Santo Domingo** *(Ave. A at Calle 3)*, built by Dominicans in 1756 on the site of earlier churches destroyed by fire. The adjacent **Museo de Arte Religioso Colonial** is a trove of religious artworks dating back to the 16th century, including the convent's original baroque altar.

Plaza de la Independencia

Formerly called Plaza de la

Catedral, the largest and the most important of the Old Quarter's squares is ringed by colonial-era buildings and has an octagonal pergola at its heart. The Spanish classicism of aristocratic homes blends with 19th-century French rococo, with the humble and haughty side by side. In dry season, the park explodes in a bouquet of colors: canary-bright yellow bark, delicate pink poui, and flame-red royal poinciana ignite the square.

Dominating the square on the west side is the **Catedral Metropolitana** *(Calle 7 Este at Ave. Central; see pp. 64–65)*, begun in 1688 and completed in 1796. The city's colonial ecclesiastical masterpiece presents a striking facade, with a centerpiece—part Moorish, part rippling baroque—built with stones from the ruins of the Convento de la Merced in Panamá Viejo. It is flanked to each side by triple-tiered bell towers, inlaid with mother-of-pearl and dazzlingly white in the phosphorescent light of midday. The cathedral played host to the signing of the declaration of independence from

Colombia on November 3, 1903. A reliquary toward the front of the church contains the skeleton of Santo Aurelio, hidden behind a painting of Jesus.

Diagonally across from the cathedral, on the square's southwest corner, is the **Casa de la Municipalidad** *(tel 506-5705)*, dating from 1910 and designed in beaux arts style by Italian architect Gennaro Nicola Ruggieri. On the second floor, the tiny, two-room **Museo de História de Panamá** *(Casa de la Municipalidad, Plaza de la Independencia, tel 501-4128, closed Sat. & Sun., $)* traces the nation's history from the arrival of Balboa until 1977. Exhibits include armaments, scale models of ancient fortresses, old maps, and documents. Signs are in Spanish only.

Built in quintessential French colonial fashion, the grand three-story edifice with mansard roof on the square's southeast side is the splendid **Museo del Canal Interoceánico**, which opened in 1997 in the former headquarters of the Compagnie Universelle du Canal Interocéanique. The building began life as the Grand Hotel (where Ferdinand de Lesseps was fêted with a banquet in 1879) and later housed the U.S. Canal Commission from 1904 to 1912.

The eclectic exhibits recalling the Herculean canal-building efforts are laid out chronologically and include mementos of the California forty-niners, an informative section on the building of the Panama Railroad, and model ships that include the S.S. *Ancón,* the steamer that made the first official Panama Canal transit. The upstairs *sala* exhibits coins and

Museo del Canal Interoceánico

🅰 69

✉ Plaza de la Independencia

☎ 211-1649

🕐 Closed Mon.

💲 $

museodelcanal.com

Hemmed by twin campaniles, the baroque Catedral Metropolitana faces Plaza de la Independencia.

Inside Catedral Metropolitana

stamps, including Canal Zone stamps, plus a copy of the Torrijos-Carter Treaty of 1977 that committed the United States to handing over the canal to Panama. Other exhibits include pre-Columbian gold, Spanish armor and weaponry, and the desk at which Panama's declaration of independence was signed. The labels are solely in Spanish, although English-speaking guides are available with advance notice. Audio tours are offered for a fee.

Belfry

In the Vicinity

The former **Iglesia y Convento de la Compañia de Jesús** *(Calle 7 Oeste)*, just south of the plaza, is now but a shell with a baroque facade and columns; its innards are in ruins. It was founded by Jesuit bishop Francisco Javier de Luna in 1749 and enjoyed a brief life as a university—the Universidad Javeriana—before being destroyed by fire in 1781 (the Jesuit order had already

Catedral Metropolitana

Nave

Altar

Front doors

Facade

Palacio Presidencial

⬛ 58 B1

✉ Ave. Eloy Alfaro, bet. Calles 6 Este & 7 Este

☎ 527-9600

🕐 Tours Tues.–Fri. 1 week's written notice required (no shorts, jeans, T-shirts, or sandals)

presidencia.gob.pa

been expelled from the country in 1767).

Reputedly the oldest house in Casco Viejo, the simple two-story **Casa Góngora** (*Ave. Central at Calle 4 Oeste, tel 212-0338, closed Sat. & Sun.*), one block east of the plaza, was built for a Spanish pearl merchant in 1756. It survived the ravages of three fires and today functions as an art space and concert hall. Tours are in Spanish only.

The official residence of the Panamanian president, the **Palacio Presidencial** occupies an entire block one block north of the plaza. Visits are by prior request only. Erected in 1673 and rebuilt in 1921 in Moorish style, the palace is colloquially called the Palacio de las Garzas (Palace of the Herons) for the herons that strut around the Patio Andaluz, the marble-floored lobby centered on a fountain inlaid with mother-of-pearl. Highlights include a gallery of life-size bronze statues representing the virtues and the elaborate Salón Amarillo and Salón Los Tamarindos, adorned with beautiful murals by Roberto Lewis. Visitors are also shown the Salón de Gabinete, where the president's weekly cabinet meetings are held (the president doesn't actually live here).

Plaza Bolívar

With its neatly clipped trees and colorful buildings, this delightful plaza is the most intimate of Casco Viejo's squares. The plaza is enlivened by chic bars and cafés and vibrates with guitar music in the voluptuous heat of the night. It is named for Simón Bolívar (1783–1830), the Latin American "Liberator" who led the fight for independence from Spain.

Royal palms shade a dramatic **monument of Bolívar,** who in 1826 organized a congress (the Congreso Anfictiónico) here for the cause of Latin American union. Though Bolívar never attended, the meeting convened in a convent schoolhouse on the park's northeast corner. Today the **Palacio Bolívar** (alias the Antiguo Instituto Bolívar) houses the Ministerio de Relaciones Exteriores, or Foreign Ministry.

Simón Bolívar

Adored throughout South America as El Libertador (The Liberator), Simón Bolívar (1783–1830) is considered the George Washington of South America and was the military-political leader who freed much of the continent from Spanish colonial rule. Born in Caracas, he was bequeathed a fortune when his parents died while he was still a child. Bolívar joined the independence cause in 1810 and, in 1813, captured Caracas as head of a nationalist army, the first of a chain of victories that led to a union of independent nations—Gran Colombia—in Latin America, in 1819.

Bolívar drew up the constitution and became Gran Colombia's first president. Bolívar's union, however, split apart due to regional dissent and revolt. On April 27, 1830, he resigned as president and died on December 7 in Quinta de San Pedro Alejandro, in Santa Marta, where he was buried in the cathedral. In 1842 his body was moved to Caracas, where he slumbers in the National Pantheon of Venezuela.

Expect to pay $60 and up for a fine, tight-woven Panama hat in one of Casco Viejo's many shops.

—DAVID KENNEDY
National Geographic contributor

Beyond the carved wooden portal, the inner courtyard—the Plaza de Los Libertadores—is adorned with the coats of arms of the republics that participated in the congress; on its east side a bronze bust of Bolívar gazes down on an excavated portion of the original convent. The mosaic floor inset with a huge compass is protected by a vast skylight.

The *palacio's* courtyard can be explored during business hours, as can the twin-room **Sala Bolívar.** The Sala Capitular (Meeting Room) where the congress was held contains a copy of Bolívar's gold ceremonial sword encrusted with 1,374 diamonds; an upstairs room displays the original documents of the congress.

The adjoining Romanesque **Iglesia y Convento de San Francisco de Asís** *(Calle 3 Este at Ave. B)* dates from 1761 and has a see-through belfry and a fairly austere interior. Permission to climb the campanile can be obtained at the office to the rear of the church. Feeling like Quasimodo staring from between the bells, you gain a fine vantage over Casco Viejo, including the recently renovated **Iglesia San Felipe de Neri** *(Ave. B at Calle 4),* built in 1688

and thereby one of the oldest structures in Panama. Its bell tower is adorned with mother-of-pearl.

Spectacular after a recent renovation, the **Teatro Nacional** *(Ave. B at Calle 3 Este, tel 262-3525, teatrodepanama.com, $),* on the plaza's southeast corner, was inaugurated in 1908 with a performance of *Aida.* A mini La Scala in the tropics, it was designed by Gennaro Nicola Ruggieri in Italianate style and is decadently adorned in rococo fashion.

The theater's horseshoe-shaped, three-tier auditorium still has the original gilt-and-red-velvet seats and is capped by a dome with masterful, patriotically themed murals by Panamanian artist Roberto Lewis. Lewis's bust occupies the lobby alongside that of Dame Margot Fonteyn, the beloved British ballerina and long-term Panama resident, who performed here.

This busy venue presents an eclectic range of productions throughout the year, from serious theatrical works to lighter fare such as *High School Musical.* ■

Plaza Bolívar
🅰 58 B1, 69

Palacio Bolívar
🅰 69
✉ Antiguo Instituto Bolívar, Plaza Bolívar, Calle 3
☎ 511-4100
🕐 Closed Sat.

Simón Bolívar looks over Casco Viejo from his pedestal in Plaza Bolívar.

A Walk Around Casco Viejo

This walk explores the nation's most complete colonial region: an architectural trove of exquisite historic buildings, from early 17th-century fortress ruins to French-style, 19th-century mansions and even early 20th-century art deco treasures. Concentrated around four main plazas, the region includes much of the city's finest architecture.

Blossoms of a flame-of-the-forest emblazon Plaza de Francia.

An ongoing renaissance backed by conscientious investors has saved much of this historic area from demolition while turning the near-ruins into neighborhoods of chic restaurants, boutiques, and bars. Walking the main streets, tiled with red bricks, is quite safe due to a heavy police presence and the availability of *asistentes de turismo* (licensed guides). Nonetheless, Casco Viejo poses risks for anyone venturing off this beaten track.

Begin the walk at the **Oficina del Casco Antiguo/Casco Viejo ❶** (*OCA, Calle 3 &*

NOT TO BE MISSED:

- **Museo del Canal Interoceánico**
- **Catedral Metropolitana**
- **Palacio Presidencial • Teatro Nacional • Plaza de Francia**

Ave. A, tel 209-6300, cascoantiguo.gob.pa), a government information office, and walk north along Calle 4 to Avenida Central. Turn left.

Plaza de la Independencia

One block brings you to **Plaza de la Independencia ❷** (see pp. 62–64). Stroll about the square clockwise, stopping in at the fascinating **Museo del Canal Interoceánico** (see pp. 63–64) and, next door, the motley **Museo de História de Panamá** (see p. 63). After exploring the **Catedral Metropolitana** (see pp. 62–63) on the west side of the plaza, follow Calle 7 Oeste south one block and turn right onto Avenida A. After one block you reach **Iglesia de San José** (Ave. A bet. Calles 8 & 9), a diminutive church whose simple exterior belies the gorgeous baroque altar within. According to legend, the gold altar originally graced the Iglesia de San José in Panamá Viejo. Painted black on the eve of Henry Morgan's sack of that city, it survived the pirate's predation and was later moved to its current location.

Stepping from the church, head one block west to **Parque Herrera ❸**, a run-down plaza with a life-size bronze statue of Gen. Tomás Herrera on horseback. Continue west 50 yards (46 m) to the **Baluarte Mano de Tigre,** a watchtower and sole remnant of the colonial city wall. Retrace your steps to the park and follow Calle 9 Oeste one block north to the **Iglesia de la Merced,** boasting an exquisite baroque west facade. The handsome neo-classical building diagonally across, on the west

---

- 🅜 See also area map pp. 58–59
- ➤ Oficina del Casco Antiguo/ Casco Viejo
- 🕓 4 hours
- ⬛ 1.5 miles (2.4 km)
- ➤ Museo de Arte Religioso Colonial

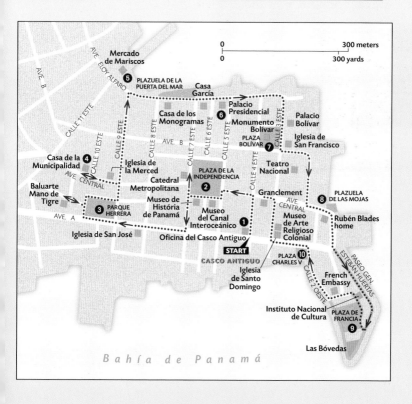

A baroque altar draws visitors to the Iglesia de San José.

side of Casa 10 Este, is the **Casa de la Munici-palidad** ❹, headquarters of the city government. Return to Calle 9 Este and turn left. At Avenida Eloy Alfaro, turn left for **Plazuela de la Puerta del Mar,** a tiny triangular plaza giddy with bougainvillea. Pause here to admire the sepia facade of the **Casa de los Monogramas,** which began life as a convent in 1743 and is graced by wooden balustrades. Take time also to follow your nose to the seafood stalls at **Mercado de Mariscos** ❺, 100 yards (92 m) west. Now walk 100 yards east to the police guard post *(Calle 7 Este)*. After being searched, you pass into the secure zone of the presidential palace. Immediately on your right, note the **Casa García,** and beyond, the ornate

gleaming white Moorish-influenced **Palacio Presidencial** ❻ (see p. 66); herons can be seen strutting around in the courtyard.

Follow Avenida Eloy Alfaro east to Calle 3 Oeste. Turn right and walk 50 yards (46 m) to the entrance of the **Palacio Bolívar** (see pp. 66–67). After visiting the **Sala Bolívar,** exit the former convent. If your timing is good, the bell tower of the **Iglesia de San Francisco** (see p. 67) will be open for you to ascend to take in the fine view over **Plaza Bolívar** ❼ (see pp. 66–67). Back at ground level, look for the steps that lead up to the **Monumento Bolívar.** The exquisite Moorish-inspired three-story building on the north side is an apartment complex with restaurants on the ground floor.

Plazuela de las Mojas

Cross to the southeast corner to enter and explore the **Teatro Nacional** (see p. 67), then follow Avenida B around to **Plazuela de las Mojas** ❽. The beautifully restored three-story colonial building on the south side is the private **home of Rubén Blades,** world-famous salsa singer and onetime minister of tourism. Fifty yards (46 m) beyond, ascend the steps to follow **Paseo General Esteban Huertas,** a waterfront ramp that leads to **Plaza de Francia** ❾ (see pp. 61–62), with its busts and plaques honoring the French effort at building the Panama Canal. Passing **Las Bóvedas** and the **Instituto Nacional de Cultura** on the east, and the handsome **French Embassy** (see p. 62) on the north side, follow Calle 2 Oeste its 50-yard (46 m) length to tiny **Plaza Charles V** ❿, with a bust of the Holy Roman emperor (1500–1558).

Turn left onto Avenida A, passing the ruins of **Iglesia de Santo Domingo** (see p. 62) on your right. Call in at the adjoining **Museo de Arte Religioso Colonial** (see p. 62), containing religious icons. Then follow Calle 2 Oeste north one block to Avenida Central. Turn left to finish with a well-earned reward at **Granclément** (see Travelwise p. 239), serving delicious gelato ice creams.

Parque Natural Metropolitano

Tropical America's only fully fledged wildlife refuge and forest environment within city limits, this park teems with animals and birds and protects one of the last vestiges of Pacific seasonally dry forest in Central America. City dwellers flock here for outdoor recreation.

Established in 1985, the 655-acre (265 ha) Metropolitan Nature Park is only a ten-minute drive north of the city center and is reached via Corredor Norte, which runs along the park's eastern edge. Covering the hills on the city's north side, this rare remnant of lowland semideciduous Pacific dry forest forms a biological corridor linked to Camino de Cruces and Soberanía National Parks. The forests explode in riotous color during dry season, when the trees drop their leaves and wildlife is more easily seen.

More than 250 bird species flit about the forest, including blue-crowned motmots, keel-billed toucans, oropendolas, lance-tailed manakins, and Baltimore orioles. Iguanas and boa constrictors are among the 36 reptile species. Turtles scuttle about in the Río Curundu, where caimans keep a hungry eye out for fish. Sloths creep along the branches, Geoffrey's tamarins cavort in the treetops, and coatis are sometimes seen at ground level. An early morning visit is best for wildlife viewing.

Begin at the **visitor center** *(tel 232-5516)* at the park entrance near the junction of Camino de la Amistad and Avenida Juan Pablo II. The center has maps and displays on local flora and fauna. Orchids blossom in the *orquideario* outside. Well-signed paths begin here and weave through the park, although hiking alone isn't advised for safety reasons. The 0.4-mile (0.6 km) **Sendero La Momótides**, being flat, provides a short introductory walk. The interpretative **Sendero La Cienaguita** nature trail is best for wildlife viewing (buy a self-guided booklet at the visitor center) and forms a loop with the **Camino del Mono Tití**, which claws its way up through the forest to the **Cerro Cedro** mirador (observation platform). At 492 feet (150 m), it grants sweeping vistas over the city and Miraflores Locks. Even more spectacular views can be enjoyed atop the 138-foot (42 m) **Smithsonian Canopy Crane,** *(reservations only via Ancon Expeditions, tel 269-9415, anconexpeditions.com).* ■

Parque Natural Metropolitano

- 58 C3
- Ave. Juan Pablo II
- 232-5552
- Visitor center closed Sun.; guided hikes by appt.
- $

parquemetro politano.org

Keel-Billed Toucans

Large, vocal, and vivid, the keel-billed toucan is a must-see for visitors to Panama. Averaging about 20 inches (51 cm) long, the yellow-breasted bird is unmistakable, with a multicolored bill about a third of its length. The birds move through the trees in flocks, uttering their croaking calls and gathering up fruit, berries, and insects, swallowing them with a quick flick of the bill.

Calidonia & La Exposición

Flanked by the city's two main arteries—Avenida Balboa and Vía España—these twin districts clasped between Casco Viejo and Parque Natural Metropolitano play host to most of the city's museums, as well as to many of the city's budget-oriented and mid-range hotels.

A colorful *diablo rojo* (red devil) bus threads its way through the congested streets of Calidonia.

**Calidonia &
La Exposición**
🅰 58 B2 & C2

Avenida Central

Connecting Casco Viejo to Calidonia, this broad street is worth the stroll to gain an intimate impression of life in the city. A suitable starting point is **Plaza Santa Ana,** where **Café Coca Cola** *(tel 228-7687)*—supposedly the oldest coffeehouse in the country and a local institution—is good for a fortifying espresso.

Avenida Central north of the plaza is brick paved and pedestrian only. Lined with budget hotels and discount shops, the boulevard is a whirlwind of color and motion. Here you will see Kuna women gorgeously costumed in flashes of tropical hues; street vendors selling *guarapo* (sugarcane juice); and local youth dolled up in the latest fashions, jiving to brassy salsa tunes.

Stick to the pedestrian boulevard. The hardscrabble Santa Ana area and the Salsipuedes district east of Plaza Santa Ana are run-down and require caution, especially by night. The Salsipuedes area includes **Barrio Chino,** a tiny Chinatown centered on Calle 15 Este.

Plaza Cinco de Mayo

The pedestrian precinct leads north to the maelstrom of triangular Plaza Cinco de Mayo, centered on a small fountain that doubles as the **Monumento a los Caídos** (Monument to the Fallen), or firefighters' monument. The memorial honors six *bomberos* (firefighters) killed on May 5, 1914, when the blaze they were fighting ignited an adjacent fireworks factory. Every November 27 the plaza is the setting for a torch-lit parade by the nation's Cuerpo de Bomberos, who don their spiffy dress uniforms and march through town.

On the plaza's east side is the erstwhile Pacific Railroad station, an imposing neoclassical edifice erected in 1912 with a facade graced by great Doric columns. Today it is the Estación 5 de Mayo on the Metro Bus and Metro system. To the rear of the building and worth a browse is the open-air **Mercado de Buhonería** (crafts market; *Ave. 4 Sur at Calle 23 Este*). One block north, a *plazuela* contains a **statue of Mahatma Gandhi** (*Ave. Central & Calle L*) usually garlanded in flowers placed by members of the city's large Hindu population.

The **Museo Afroantillano de Panamá** (West Indian Museum of Panama) recalls the back-breaking contribution of West Indian laborers in the construction of the Panama Railroad and the Panama Canal. Housed in a wooden structure that was once a Christian mission church, this humble gem displays photographs and paintings, plus quilts and other exhibits of fine needlework alongside period furnishings and personal belongings.

Vicinity of Parque Legislativo

The nation's Asamblea Legislativa (Legislative Assembly) performs its duties in the **Palacio Legislativo** (*tel 512-8300*), to the northwest of Plaza Cinco de Mayo. The building stands

in **Plaza José Remón Cantera.** Soaring over this raised plaza is a black granite monument, **Friso Alegórico a la Justicia** (Allegorical Frieze to Justice), by Peruvian sculptor Joaquín Roca Rey (1923–2004). It was erected in memory of assassinated president José Antonio Remón Cantera (1908–1955). The plinth bears his words: "Neither alms, nor millions, we want justice."

INSIDER TIP:

The sinuous pathway alongside the Cinta Costera is the city's best place to stroll and take in the cityscape and ocean airs.

—TOM O'NEILL
National Geographic magazine writer

On the north side of Avenida de los Mártires, the **Monumento a los Patriotas** (Monument to the Patriots) features three human figures clambering up a flagpole, an homage to the nationalists who died during the Flag Riots of January 1964 (see sidebar p. 34). Only 100 yards (91 m) north is the Smithsonian Tropical Research Institute's **Earl S. Tupper Research & Conference Center** (*Tupper Bldg., Ave. Roosevelt 401, tel 212-8000*). The center's splendid bookstore and research library are open to the public, and a 176-seat auditorium and exhibit hall host free science-related seminars every Tuesday from 4 to 5 p.m.

Museo Afroantillano de Panamá

⚑ 58 B2

✉ Ave. Justo Arosemena & Calle 24

☎ 501-4130

💲 $

samaap.org

Museo de Ciencias Naturales

- ⓜ 58 B2
- ✉ Ave. Cuba at Calles 29 Este & 30 Este
- ☎ 225-0645
- ⏰ Closed Sun.–Mon.
- 💲 $

Plaza Victor Julio Gutiérrez

Laid out in a grid, La Exposición extends northeast of Calidonia and has three small parks at its heart. The roofed Plaza Víctor Julio Gutiérrez (Aves. Perú & Cuba at Calles 31 Este & 32 Este) is the setting for the drawing of the national lottery (see sidebar below) at the **Edificio de la Lotería** (Ave. Cuba & Calles 31 & 32), the Lottery Building, on the east side of the concrete plaza.

The main draw nearby is the **Museo de Ciencias Naturales** (Museum of Natural Sciences), one block west of the plaza. It has four rooms dedicated to entomology and marine biology, geology and paleontology, vertebrates, and foreign fauna. Albeit modest in scope, it summarizes the animals you might

hope to see in the wild, as well as some from beyond the Americas.

Note the magnificent building in neoclassical style, circa 1924, on the square's north side. It houses the **Archivos Nacionales** (Ave. Perú at Calles 31 & 32, tel 501-6151), the national archives.

Parque Belisario Porras

This rather formal park (Calles 33 Este & 34 Este at Aves. Peru & Cuba) surrounded by Spanish colonial centenary buildings is the unlikely setting for the city's premier annual event: Carnival! Down its center median come the comparsas (processions) graced by girls in polleras and, on the final day, others in sequined G-strings and gaudy feathers, gyrating like the most exotic and excited of tropical birds. Pinning the park is

La Lotería

Panamanians love a good bet, but it's the national lottery that commands the entire country's attention, with all eyes on the twice-weekly drawing.

Large crowds pack into Parque Víctor Julio Gutiérrez—headquarters of La Lotería Nacional de Beneficia (tel 507-6800, lnb.gob.pa)—for the fiesta-like drawings, which are broadcast live on radio and TV. Lasting several hours, each drawing is preceded by music and dances with beauty queens adorned in polleras. In a tradition dating back to the lottery's founding in 1919, a globular metal cage is used as a receptacle. Lottery balls, each containing a single number, are placed in the cage, which is spun . . . and spun . . . and spun by a spindled handle. After an interminable number of revolutions, the globe is stopped and one of four specially

chosen children nervously steps forward to choose a ball. The ball is opened with solemnity to reveal the hidden number.

The process is repeated three times to generate the winning combination, good for a $2,000 first prize in the regular lottery. Two sets of four numbers are also chosen to produce the second ($600) and third ($300) prizes. Tickets cost as little as 25 cents for two-number tickets that pay out smaller winnings if the numbers correspond to the last two digits of the winning combination. On the last Friday of every month, Panamanians wait breathlessly for the results of a special drawing called Gordito del Zodiaco (Little Fattie of the Zodiac), named, one supposes, for the stars that align for the winner of the grand prize, which can top one million dollars.

Now framed by towers, the Vasco Núñez de Balboa Monument still dominates the Coastal Beltway.

Monumento Belisario Porras, by Spanish sculptor Víctor Macho (1887–1966), commemorating Belisario Porras (1856–1942), a founding father of the nation. The Romanesque **Iglesia de Don Bosco** *(Ave. Central at Calle 34),* one block to the northwest, was built in the 1950s with a minaret-like tower.

One block east of the park is leafy **Parque Perú,** marked by a bust of Francisco Arias Paredes (1886–1946), who led the 1931 coup that toppled corrupt U.S.-backed president Florencio Arosemena. Numismatists and philatelists on a busman's holiday should head to the nearby **Casa Museo del Banco Nacional** in a charming little upper-class home dating from 1925. The museum boasts a collection of coins and stamps dating back to the conquistadores.

Cinta Costera

Curving along Panama Bay in the shape of a shepherd's crook, this broad beltway-boulevard was laid out from 2007 to 2009 parallel to Avenida Balboa, linking Casco Viejo to ritzy Punta Paitilla. Some 74 acres (30 ha) were reclaimed from the sea along 1.6 miles (2.6 km) of shoreline, and attractively landscaped with a *malecón* (promenade), bicycle path, various parks, an amphitheater, and fountains. Traffic now flows eastbound along a new three-lane highway and westbound on Avenida Balboa.

Midway along the malecón is a small park with the marble **Monumento Balboa** *(bet. Calles 35 & 36).* Gaily painted fishing boats unload their catch at the wharves at the southern end of Balboa, where fresh seafood is sold at **Mercado del Marisco** *(Calle 23 Este).* ■

Casa Museo del Banco Nacional

✉ Ave. Cuba at Calle 34 Este
☎ 225-0640
🕐 Closed Sat.–Sun.

EXPERIENCE: Learn Spanish in Panama

Panama is renowned as a center for Spanish language instruction. There are dozens of schools to choose from in Panama City, Boquete, and Bocas del Toro, and others are sprinkled around the country. You can choose from a wide range of options, from one-week quickie immersion class to monthlong (or longer) intensives.

The country offers so much to see and do when class is out. Spanish language courses are also a tremendous way to immerse yourself in the local culture, not least because most schools room their students with local families.

Panamanian Spanish

It helps that Panamanians have very clear diction. Nonetheless, each Latin American country speaks its own dialect, with regional variants that can leave even Spanish speakers scratching their heads.

Christopher Howard's *Official Guide to Panamanian Spanish* is a handy travel guide that provides Panama-specific guidance, including Panamanian slang and idioms. Here are a few Panamanian colloquialisms to know:

¡Alla la Máquina! Holy cow!

Con el huevo encima. Someone who's slow.

¡No frieges! You're joking!

¡Que wecha la tuya! That's rude!

Se cree la gran vaina. He/she thinks she's the greatest.

Spanish Language Schools

Many schools combine education with classes in local dance and cultural

mores. Some combine excursions. Rarely do classes take up more than 20 hours a week; 4 hours daily, Monday through Friday, is the norm. Check to ensure that classes are small so you can receive personal attention. If you seek one-on-one instruction, make sure it's available before signing up. Here are a few reputable schools:

Casco Viejo Spanish School is ideally located in the heart of Panama City's Casco Viejo. It has classes for everyone from travelers to businesspeople. Contact: Calle 4A & Ave. A, Casco Viejo, Panama City, tel 228-3258, *cascospanish.com*

Habla Ya Panama Spanish School, in the highland resort town of Boquete and also at Bocas del Toro, offers

Spanish courses for various needs and abilities. Groups are limited to four students per classroom, allowing you to benefit from unique personalized attention. Contact: Los Establos Plaza 20, Boquete, tel 730-8344, *hablayapanama.com*

ILERI Language Institute, in Altos del Chase, a mere 20-minute drive from downtown Panama City, places its emphasis on conversation. Its Spanish Immersion Program and more advanced courses are limited to four people, taught by bilingual Panamanians. It also has evening business classes and a Children's Spanish Immersion Program that places student families with a Panamanian family. Contact: Calle 17 C Norte #20H, Altos de Betania, tel 392-4086, *ileripanama.com*

Spanish Panama, located in the business district of El Cangrejo in the heart of Panama City, earns rave reviews for its one-on-one classes and weeklong crash course in Panamanian Spanish conversation, including a Latin dance class. It also offers sightseeing tours and homestay options. Contact: Vía Argentina & Ave. 4B Norte, Panama City, tel 213-3121, *spanishpanama.com*

El Cangrejo & Bella Vista

A forest of mirrored skyscrapers towers over the ritzy neighborhoods at the trendsetting, commercial heart of the modern city. El Cangrejo is known for its casinos, Bella Vista for fine restaurants and a sizzling night scene. The banks of Marbella glitter in the evening sunlight alongside the condominiums of the residential Punta Pacifica and Punta Paitilla peninsula.

Sites of interest are few here. An exception is **Parque Urracá** (*Ave. Balboa at Calle 45 Este*) in Bella Vista. The park is the starting point for the annual Christmas Parade and the Parade of Torches, held each November 2, when firefighters march the first flag of the Republic to Plaza de la Independencia. Avenida Federico Boyd leads north from the park to busy Vía España. Rising over the junction is the white-and-gray neo-Gothic facade of **Iglesia del Carmen** (*Vía España at Ave. Manuel E. Bautista*). A twin-spired medieval inspiration built in 1947, it features a Byzantine altar.

The sprawling **Universidad de Panamá** (*Ave. Manuel E. Bautista, tel 523-500*), the national university, is one block north, in El Cangrejo. The campus hosts the **Instituto Geográfico Nacional Tommy Guardia** (*Calle 57 Oeste at Ave. 6a Norte, tel 507-9684*), a source for maps of Panama.

Despite its seeming antiquity, the **Santuario Nacional del Corazón de María** was dedicated in 1949. The interior has fine stained glass, and a side entrance opens to a courtyard with a fountain and peacocks. Its facade—part Romanesque, part Spanish colonial style—is at odds with the sea of modernity, including the spiral-shaped **Torre F&F** (*Calle 50 at*

The Santuario Nacional del Corazón de María in Bella Vista

Calle 56), auguring through the heart of El Cangrejo.

The city's ritziest area, **Punta Paitilla**, at the eastern end of Avenida Balboa in Marbella, is a veritable Manhattan in the tropics, its glass-and-marble towers crowned by the sail-like **Trump Ocean Club** (*Calle Punta Colón*). Nestled in their shadow is the **Vatican Embassy** (*Ave. Balboa at Ave. de Italia*), where Gen. Manuel Noriega famously sought asylum. ∎

Santuario Nacional del Corazón de María

⧉ 59 D2
✉ Calle 53 Este & Aves. 2a Sur & 3a Sur
☎ 263-9833
www.santuario nacional.net

The Real Tailor of Panama

A fine suit speaks volumes in Panama, and when it comes to sophisticated duds for the country's elite, the universal choice is a Savile Row–style boutique straight from the pages of novelist John le Carré's thriller *The Tailor of Panama*.

Skilled tailors work under the watchful instruction of José Abadi and his son Adán (above).

"La Fortuna, since 1925" it reads in elegant letters on the *rótulo* (sign) outside the Orión commercial building on Vía España, 100 yards (91 m) east of Vía Argentina. Loosely portrayed as Pendel & Braithwaite Limitada in John le Carré's thoughtfully textured spy thriller, this establishment *(tel 263-6487, closed Sun., lafortunapanama.com)* is known to *panameños* of discernment as the real "tailor of Panama."

In le Carré's satire, anybody of importance in Central America passes through Harry Pendel's doors. He dresses everyone from crooks and spies to the Panamanian president. His fitting room hears more confidences than a priest's confessional. While le Carré's tale of a tailor reluctantly engaged as a tattletale for a British agent was fictional, there is more than a kernel of truth to the notion of a Panamanian tailor being privy to everyone's secrets. La Fortuna has long been the *sastre* (tailor) of choice for presidents, ambassadors, generals, and members of Panama's Asamblea. Omar Torrijos, the late dictator, once joked that La Fortuna's owner, José Abadi, was the only man for whom he would drop his trousers. José even made suits for actors Pierce Brosnan and Geoffrey Rush when they came to Panama in 2000 to film the screen version of le Carré's novel.

Cut From the Same Cloth

José Abadi (1926–2008) ran with pride the company his father founded in 1925 to cater to a select clientele. Today his son Adán Abadi oversees a cadre of 17 highly skilled tailors. The junior Abadi is now the family presence on the premises, fussing over the cut of a suit and happy to regale you with his father's old tales of the visits by former Panamanian president Martín Torrijos Espino and by actors Rush, Brosnan, and Jamie Lee Curtis. You'll leave the store wondering just what *real* secrets the late José gleaned in his years in the business.

The shop walls are lined with racks of precisely cut chiffon shirts and inky blue suits of thin silk cashmere. A fitted hand-stitched shirt can be made for you in as little as two days. A custom-tailored suit takes at least ten days and requires two fittings. The workers can craft a suit to match any photograph you bring in, whether you want to evoke scholar, urban warrior, or business bigwig. A double-breasted

Fabric waits to be transformed into custom suits at La Fortuna.

herringbone or a trimly fit monochrome suit of Armani, Ferré, or Versace cloth can be had for around $500, complete with a personalized panel sewn inside the jacket denoting that the suit was made exclusively for you at the original shop of the Real Tailor of Panama.

Sombreros Montuños

Panama hats—the sartorial splendors worn by FDR, Winston Churchill, and stars of the silver screen—don't come from Panama. Surprisingly, the overwhelming majority are made in Ecuador. Nonetheless, the men of Panama do wear handwoven *sombreros de paja toquilla,* hats of native straw. Known as *sombreros montuños,* they hail mainly from the villages of Ocú and La Pintada. The *ocueño* features a turned-up brim with a single black or brown line, with a braided cord unique to the village; the *pintado* has a straight brim decorated with black patterns, often in multiple rings.

The hats, which take between two weeks and a month to produce, respectively, are made from the white fibers of a plant called *bellota.* The fibers are stripped from the leaves, boiled, and then sun-dried until they are bleached a creamy white. The same fibers are used for the pattern rings and derive their coloration (anywhere from rust red to black) from being boiled.

Ecuadorian hats lack the black trim characteristic of the Panamanian version and are woven crown to brim as a single unit. Panama's hats, however, are woven in half-inch strips that are wound around a wooden form and sewn together. The highest quality montuños are so finely woven that not even water can pass between the threads.

Amador Causeway

With gorgeous views toward Panama City on one side and the Bridge of the Americas and busy canal channel on the other, the breakwater known as Calzada de Amador is one of the city's most appealing recreational areas. In recent years, the causeway has become a trendy venue for hip youth and, following major investment, a hub for international visitors.

Multicolored, multifaceted, and multimedia: Panama City's Biomuseo is an instant icon.

Amador Causeway

🅰 58 A1–A2

The palm-lined *calzada* (causeway) is fringed by a recreational path popular with joggers, bicyclists, and city dwellers walking their dogs. You can rent bicycles and in-line skates at Bicicletas Ralí (*tel 223-8054, bicicletasrali.com*). Walking the calzada is especially pleasurable at dawn and dusk. While beloved of locals, the tempting sands of **Isla Naos** can't be recommended due to sewage washing in off the bay.

Connecting Balboa to the islands of Naos, Culebra, Perico, and Flamenco, the causeway was constructed of rock removed during construction of the canal. It extends 3 miles (4.5 km) across tidal mud flats to block silt-bearing currents that might clog the canal's southern entrance. After its completion in 1913, the entire causeway became a mighty U.S. military complex— Fort Grant (later Fort Amador)— established to guard the approaches. Two formidable 14-inch (36 cm) cannon were mounted there on railway carriages and could be transported across the isthmus to protect either approach to the canal.

During World War II, **Isla**

Flamenco was a bombproof strategic command center. Today it is the setting for the **Fuerte Amador Resort & Marina** *(tel 314-1980),* with a cruise ship terminal, major shopping mall, and marina full of sleek yachts straight out of a James Bond movie. You can charter boats at the Flamenco Yacht Club *(reservaciones@fuerteamador.com).* By night, Fuerte Amador's two dozen or so cosmopolitan restaurants, bars, and nightclubs thrum to a South Beach–style *vida loca* vibe.

Close to the marina, **Panamá Canal Village** *(tel 314-1414)* holds the neo-colonial–styled **Figali Convention Center,** a venue for many of the city's biggest concerts, from classical to rock. A new convention center in the shape of a harpy eagle is to take flight here. Nearby, **Parque Torrijos-Carter** contains the Monumento Histórico Mausoleo del General Omar Torrijos Herrera, beneath which the former de facto leader slumbers.

Punta Culebra Nature Center

Sharks, turtles, and crabs! The Smithsonian Tropical Research Institute has a marine research station that occupies former military bunkers atop rocky Punta Culebra. Visitors are welcome at the marine exhibitions center, an open-air museum with six aquariums dedicated to marine coastal environments. One aquarium displays species of the Pacific, while Caribbean species inhabit another. Children will especially enjoy the sharks and turtles and the pond where they can touch sea stars and other marine invertebrates.

Two trails meander through a rare patch of Pacific tropical dry forest, a Central American ecosystem that is almost extinct today. Sloths can be seen feeding languidly or snoozing. Iguanas abound. And the forest is a refuge for armadillos and birds of all kinds: cormorants, frigate birds, and even the rare blue-footed booby. A sheltered sandy beach is fringed by white mangrove forest.

Waves crash against the tip of the peninsula, causing crabs to scurry back and forth. Here, a viewing veranda has a telescope and educational profiles on various types of vessels, permitting visitors to identify many of the ships nearby. ∎

Punta Culebra Nature Center

✉ Calzada de Amador

☎ 212-8793

🕐 Closed Mon.

💲 $

stri.org

Biomuseo

Panama City's Biomuseo (see sidebar p. 88) finally opened in 2014 as a joint effort of the Smithsonian Tropical Research Institute, the University of Panama, and the Interoceanic Regional Authority. Designed by Frank Gehry (1929–), creator of the futuristic Guggenheim Museum in Bilbao, Spain, the museum is being touted as an icon for Panama, much as the Opera House is for Sydney. Located at the entrance to the causeway, the gaudily painted structure is faceted like quartz crystals and topped by a roof with a twisting silhouette meant to evoke the forces of nature. Its eight halls feature multimedia exhibitions showcasing Panama's astonishing biodiversity, from its oceans to its cloud forests. The museum is surrounded by a "biopark" showcasing Panama's flora.

Balboa & Ancón

Spiraling around Cerro Ancón, the city's highest point, are three contiguous communities laid out a century ago as the "capital" of the former Canal Zone and U.S. military command. Stately royal palms rise like silver Corinthian columns here; broad-canopied mango trees and jacarandas cast pools of cool shadow on streets lined with buildings from grandiose to quaint, all in tropical vernacular style with red-tile roofs and broad eaves.

Murals in the Panama Canal Administration Building depict the monumental canal-building effort.

Balboa

Occupying the sloping land immediately east of the Pacific terminus of the canal, Balboa, between Cerro Ancón and the east side of Cerro Sosa, still houses the operating head-quarters for the Panama Canal. The town was named for Vasco Núñez de Balboa, the first Span-iard to see the Pacific Ocean.

The monumental E-shaped **Panama Canal Administration Building,** at the northwest-ern foot of Cerro Ancón, was inaugurated on July 15, 1914, on a hilltop overlooking Balboa township. Visitors are welcome to enter on weekdays to admire the high-domed rotunda, with its stately marble columns (the eight columns were accidentally installed upside down) and alcoves containing busts of Ferdinand de Lesseps, Theodore Roosevelt, and Emperor Charles V. Draw-ing your eyes upward is a cupola framed by Panama Canal murals. Graphic in detail, enormous in scope, the murals, painted by

New York artist William B. Van Ingen (1858–1955), record the monumental achievement in four main scenes depicting the Gaillard Cut, the building of the Gatún Dam spillway, construction of a lock miter gate, and the Miraflores Locks. The mahogany and Tennessee marble staircase leads up to an art gallery of canal-related paintings by U.S. artist Al Sprague and, above, relief maps from the construction era.

To the rear (west) of the building, a flight of 110 steps leads down to **El Prado** (formerly Avenida 9 de Enero), a palm-lined boulevard with a grassy median built to the exact dimensions of a lock chamber (110 feet/34 m wide by 1,000 feet/305 m long). Concerts are held on the lawns near the steps on Tuesday and Thursday evenings in dry season. At the base of the steps stands the **Goethals Monument,** a gray marble monolith erected to honor George W. Goethals, chief engineer of the canal project from 1907 to 1914. Approximately 100 yards (91 m) west, across Avenida Roosevelt, a 95-ton (86 metric ton) **Bucyrus steam shovel** (one of dozens employed during the construction of the canal) is exhibited at the roadside.

Between the monument and shovel stands the former Balboa High School, now the **Centro de Capacitación Ascanio Arosemena** (Edificio 704, tel 272-9249, closed Sat.–Sun.), the training center for canal employees. The breezeway entrance hosts the **Monumento a los Mártires,** with an eternal flame dedicated to the 21 Panamanians killed during the January 9, 1964,

Flag Riots, known in Panama as the "Day of the Martyrs" (see sidebar p. 34). The names of those killed are inscribed on 21 slender pillars surrounding the location of the original flagpole—long gone—that inspired the fatal riots. Inside, hallways exhibit memorabilia relating to the canal construction.

Stevens Circle, at El Prado's south end, is a small rotunda with a monument to John Stevens (chief engineer 1905–1907). To your left, note the single-story **Balboa Post Office** and, ahead, the **Teatro Balboa** (tel 228-0327),

INSIDER TIP:

The Theatre Guild of Ancón [anconguild .com] promotes English language plays, keeping alive a Zonian tradition spanning more than half a century.

—KENNY LING
National Geographic contributor

an art deco jewel built in 1946 as the Electric Theater movie house and still functioning as a concert hall. The voluptuously adorned lobby gleams with mosaic tilework. **Niko's Café** (see Travelwise p. 239), in a former bowling alley on the northeast side of Stevens Circle, has black-and-white period photos of old Panama.

Avenida Arnulfo Arias Madrid (formerly Balboa Road) leads east from the circle past the ecumenical **Union Church** (tel 314-1004), a

Balboa & Ancón
🅜 58 A2 & B2

Panama Canal Administration Building
🅜 58 A2
✉ 101 Heights Rd., Balboa
☎ 272-1111
🕐 Closed Sat.–Sun.
pancanal.com

soaring Gothic-style edifice dating from 1917. Immediately beyond is the rather incredible **Monumento a la Democracia,** featuring a circular fountain pierced by a long, spearlike sliver of bronze. The sculpture by Colombian artist Hector Lombana (1930–2008) was dedicated in 2002 and honors three-time Panamanian president

Mi Pueblito

Comprising three stereotypical villages, **My Little Village** (*Ave. de los Martires, closed Mon., $*), at the eastern foot of Cerro Ancón, serves as a museum of Panamanian culture and traditions. The main exhibit replicates a colonial-era country village; around its cobbled plaza are a mission-style Spanish church, mayor's office, telegraph office, and a museum dedicated to the colorful national costume, the *pollera*. The Antillean–West Indian village, with its gaily painted wooden structures, includes La Casa del Café, offering dozens of coffee brands. Set against the forested hills, the Indian village represents indigenous cultures, with thatched huts and artifacts honoring the Kuna, Emberá, and Wounaan ways of life. There are restaurants and souvenir stores. Folkloric groups perform on Friday and Saturday evenings.

Arnulfo Arias Madrid (1901–1988), who is shown standing at the pointy tip and waving at Panamanian people rushing to greet him.

On the monument's north side, the **Panama Canal Pilots headquarters** (*tel 228-4868*) displays a 9-foot-long (3 m) scale model of the M/V *John Constantine* four-masted barque in the boardroom. The receptionist may let you in to see it. Facing the monument from the

east is the former **Centro Artesanal, Antiguo** craft market.

Quarry Heights

Quarry Heights, northeast of Balboa, was headquarters of the U.S. Southern Command and of the U.S. military in Panama from 1916 to 1999. Noted for their architectural significance, the homes of this leafy district (today renamed Altos de Ancón) were built on two terraces quarried from Cerro Ancón and were mostly occupied by military officers and by doctors who practiced at nearby Gorgas Hospital. Lined with mahogany trees, bamboo, and palms, the beauty of its bucolic streets recalls the days when the atmosphere within the Zone was that of an affluent country club.

The two-story **Administrator's House** (*107 Heights Rd.*), standing at the junction of Heights Road and Quarry Road, was the palatial quarters of the chief engineer during construction. It originally overlooked Culebra Cut so that the administrator could keep an eye on the excavation; in 1914, the house was loaded onto a train and rebuilt at its present site. Today it is used as a guesthouse for foreign dignitaries.

Quarry Road grants access to forested 654-foot-high (198 m) **Cerro Ancón,** once topped by fortified guns but today marked by a flagstaff from which flutters a giant Panamanian flag. Panamanian poet Amelia Denis de Icaza (1836–1911), sitting in bronze effigy beneath the flag, gazes serenely over the views of the city. The woodsy hill is today a nature reserve teeming with monkeys, agoutis, and sloths.

It's a stiff 20-minute hike to the summit along the asphalt road that gains 323 feet (98 m) as it coils upward from the headquarters of the **Asociación Nacional para la Conservación de la Naturaleza** (ANCON; *Bldg. 153, Calle Amelia Denis de Icaza, tel 314-0052, ancon .org*). Police are usually present at the summit, where muggings have been reported; it is best not to hike alone. There are plans to erect a museum at the top of the hill.

East of ANCON, as you begin to ascend Cerro Ancón, you look down upon **Montague Hall** *(Bldg. 88, Andrews Rd.)*, a nondescript concrete oblong building that was until 1999 the unlikely headquarters of the entire U.S. Southern Command. Inset in the rock face is the entrance to a bombproof 40-room command post tunneled deep inside Cerro Ancón in 1942. It still serves as a center for the Strategic Plan of National Security, and is off-limits to visitors.

Ancón

The hill's northeast side was the setting for the original French settlement, centered on Ancón Hospital, founded in 1881 as L'Hôpital Notre Dame du Canal. By 1907 Ancón Hospital had 96 buildings. In 1928, the main building—fronted by a two-story neoclassical portico and topped by green copper domes—was renamed **Gorgas Hospital** after the chief sanitary officer who conquered yellow fever and malaria. Part of the sprawling hillside facility today houses the **Corte Suprema de Justicia** *(Gorgas Rd., tel 212-7300)*, Panama's Supreme Court.

At the base of Gorgas Road, the Romanesque **Catedral San Lucas** *(tel 262-1280)*, fronted by a row of Corinthian columns, dates back to 1923. The cathedral hosts musical events, when choral groups send bats fluttering from the rafters. Another church—**Parroquia Sagrado Corazón de Jesús** *(Ancon Blvd. at Chame St.)*—in Spanish colonial vernacular is 200 yards (183 m) to the northwest.

Culture vultures may thrill to the nearby **Museo de Arte Contemporáneo,** occupying a former Masonic hall from the 1930s. Privately owned and relying on donations by working artists, the twin-tier

Museo de Arte Contemporaneo

- 58 B2
- San Blas Pl., Ancón
- 262-3380
- Closed Mon.
- $
- macpanama.org

Theatre Guild of Ancón

- Calle DIJ
- 212-0060
- anconguild.com

INSIDER TIP:

Boxing fans should dine at La Tasca de Durán *[Calle Alberto Navarro, tel 213-0100]*, where owner Roberto Durán often stops to tell tales of his fights with "Sugar" Ray Leonard and others.

—JUSTIN KAVANAGH
National Geographic Travel Books editor

museum displays more than 400 contemporary ceramics, paintings, photographs, and sculptures by prominent artists from Panama and around the world. The museum hosts art and serigraphy classes, informal lectures, and music recitals. Tucked amid palms to the northwest, the **Theatre Guild of Ancón** performs regularly in a quaint Caribbean-style wooden structure. ∎

ná Viejo

gust 15, 1519, as the first city along the Pacific shore, Panamá Viejo today is a rld Heritage site, a national monument, and an archaeological treasure. Parts of the enclave have been restored, allowing visitors to appreciate what was once one of the wealthiest cities of its time.

Built atop a pre-Columbian burial ground on a promontory overlooking the sea, the original city prospered for a century and a half as a clearinghouse and marshaling point for the Camino Real treasure trail. Panama became a city of more than 5,000 houses, but most buildings were consumed in the conflagration of 1671 that followed pirate Henry Morgan's attack; the city was then abandoned.

In recent decades, slums have arisen atop much of the former city. The site was named a national monument in 1976 and a restoration project begun under the auspices of the Patronato Panamá Viejo, which has administered Panamá Viejo since 1995. The busy Vía Cincuentenario highway cuts through the heart of the old city. A walking tour should take about two hours.

West Side

The entrance to the old city in colonial times was the still-extant **Puente de Matadero** (Bridge of the Slaughterhouse), a stone bridge spanning the Río Algarrobo. It was guarded by the **Fuerte de la Natividad** (Nativity Fort), its gun emplacements now covered with creeping vines. Immediately east is the modern **Centro de Visitantes de Panamá Viejo** (visitor center). The center's excellent **Museo de Sitio de Panamá Viejo** displays musket balls, coins, surgical knives, and other pieces unearthed at the site.

A walking trail shaded by widespreading trees leads from the

Newly restored, the bell tower of La Catedral de Nuestra Señora de la Asunción provides a glimpse into the past.

visitor center to a series of historical sites, beginning with the **Iglesia y Convento la Merced.** This church was spared during Morgan's attack and was thereafter disassembled and reconstituted in the new city. Beyond stood the **Iglesia y Convento de San Francisco,** completed by the Franciscans in 1603, and the **Hospital de San Juan Dios,** erected in 1521. Only remnants of these sites remain.

Among the best preserved structures is the **Iglesia y Convento de las Monjas de la Concepción,** built by Concepción nuns. It retains its bell tower and a well. Adjoining it to the east, the **Iglesia y Convento de la Compañía de Jesús** was completed in 1582.

East Side

The city's ancient heart was the **Plaza Mayor,** the main square, today a grassy swathe. To its east stood the two-story **Cabildo de la Ciudad,** the city hall, and the **Casas Reales,** guarded by a moat. This center of power housed the governor and nobles, plus the court and city dungeons.

Rising over Panamá Viejo, the enormous bell tower of **La Catedral de Nuestra Señora de la Asunción** (built between 1619 and 1626) gives the best impression of the city's former glory. Restoration was completed in 2006. The 90-foot (27 m) tower contains a modern staircase that you can ascend for views from the lookout. The rest of the cathedral remains in ruins. To the north are the skeletons of the **Casa del Obispo** (Bishop's House) and

Casas Terrín, built about 1640 for a nobleman. The Dominicans' **Iglesia y Convento de Santo Domingo,** founded in 1571 farther north, stood within earshot of slaves being brought ashore at the wharfside **Casa de los Genoveses** to the east.

The famous Altar de Oro originally graced the **Iglesia y Convento de San José** at the extreme north end of Panamá Viejo. The altar was later relocated to the new city (see p. 62); the Augustine church. The northern entrance to the city and gateway to the Camino Real was the **Puente del Rey** (King's Bridge), completed in 1634 and arching over the Río Abajo.

After exploring the ruins, you might browse the **Mercado Nacional de Artesanías** (Crafts Market), south of Plaza Mayor, where indigenous peoples sell their wares. ∎

EXPERIENCE:
Volunteer to Unearth the Past

Panamá Viejo is an active archaeological site and offers travelers the option of supporting a deserving cause. The **Patronato Panamá Viejo** *(P.O. 0823-05096, Panama, tel 226-8915, patronato@panamaviejo .org)* has ongoing research and conservation projects and seeks volunteers to help in such tasks as cleaning archaeological materials, classifying artifacts, organizing collections, and taking measurements and pictures in the field. Students (especially those majoring in archaeology, anthropology, or history) are preferred. The cost is $1,000 monthly, including lunch daily (accommodation and other meals are not included).

Panamá Viejo
🅰 59 G2
Visitor Information
✉ Vía Cincuentenario
☎ 226-8915
panamaviejo.org

Museo de Sitio de Panamá Viejo
🅰 59 G2
✉ 4 miles (6.4 km) NE of downtown
☎ 226-8915
🕐 Closed Mon.
💲 $
panamaviejo.org

More Places to Visit in Panama City

Museo Antropológico Reina Torres de Araúz

Celebrating the nation's pre-Columbian heritage, this museum is to be expanded into the nation's foremost art center. Only a small selection of its 14,000-piece collection is on view, including stone *metates* (curved ceremonial tables), grinding tools, and stone figurines. Most exhibits relate to the Barriles culture. Glittering under spotlights are gold figures, amulets, half-moon-shaped nosepieces, and other ancient treasure—collectively called *huacas*—excavated from the tombs of *caciques*. Guided tours are given in Spanish.

⚠ 58 B3 ✉ Calle 4 Este & Ave. Ascanio Villalaz, Llanos de Curundú ☎ 501-4731 🕐 Closed Mon. 💲 $

Parque Recreativo Omar

An oasis of tranquility on the city's northeast side, Omar Recreation Park is Panama City's second largest metropolitan park. This green swathe, in the middle-class San Francisco district, is considered one of the city's best venues for picnics. Originally Panama's first golf course, it was renamed to honor Gen. Omar Torrijos, who ruled Panama from 1968 to 1981; his bust stands by the main gate. Facilities include a jogging trail, a swimming pool, and children's play areas, plus baseball, soccer, and tennis courts. The park is also home to the country's largest library, **Biblioteca Nacional de Panamá** *(tel 224-9466, binal.ac.pa, closed Sun.).* ⚠ 59 E3 ✉ Ave. Belisario Porras & Calle 74

Puente de las Américas

The cantilevered Bridge of the Americas was completed in 1962 at a cost of 20 million dollars as the first bridge spanning the canal, replacing a ferry that had been the sole means of crossing the waterway at this point. It rises 384 feet high (118 m) and is 5,425 feet long (1,654 m) in 14 spans. You can take the pedestrian sidewalks to the bridge's western side, where a lookout station offers a fine, albeit foreshortened, perspective.

⚠ 58 inset ✉ Via Interamerican Hwy., 0.5 mile (1 km) W of Calle Amador

---

EXPERIENCE: Enjoy Fun-filled Family Activities

To keep the kids happy in Panama City, these four venues should do the trick: **Panama Marine Adventures** *(tel 226-8917, pmatours.net)* invites you to hop aboard a Segway for a unique and fun way to explore Panama City. The company has three itineraries, including Casco Viejo and Panamá Viejo, aboard these eco-friendly two-wheelers. Children must be at least ten years old. The **Biomuseo** *(Calzada de Amador, tel 830-6700, biomuseopanama.org; see p. 81)* opened in 2014. This Frank Gehry–designed museum has state-of-the-art exhibits on biodiversity and the natural world.

Take the kids hiking through **Parque Natural Metropolitano** *(Ave. Juan Pablo II, tel 232-5552, parque metropolitano.org; see p. 71)* in search of monkeys, sloths, agoutis, and deer in this rain forest park on the edge of the city. **Punta Culebra Nature Center** *(Isla Naos, Calzada de Amador, tel 212-8793, stri.org/english/visit_us/culebra; see p. 81)* is a Smithsonian Tropical Research Institute research station and a wonderful venue for learning about marine ecology. The Nature Center includes shark, fish, and marine turtle tanks; an array of exhibits; and trails through coastal forest.

Richly forested, offering world-class birding, not to mention excursions on the canal

Central Caribbean & the Canal

Tropical fish at Miraflores Locks
Visitor Center

Central Caribbean & the Canal

The route that changed the world, the Panama Canal is the nation's most visible symbol. Extending from Colón on the Caribbean Sea to Panama City on the Pacific Ocean, this 51-mile-long (80 km) umbilical cord linking two oceans is both a feat of engineering and Panama's main tourist draw. The lush hinterlands swarm with wildlife, while fortress ruins recall the days when Sir Francis Drake wreaked havoc along the Spanish Main.

Sleepy San Pedro, on Isla Taboga, offers a calming contrast to bustling Panama City.

Topping every visitor's list of things to see, the canal is both grand and tourist friendly. Viewing the passage of enormous cruise ships and cargo vessels is easy at the Miraflores and Gatún Locks, where spectator stands provide an intimate perspective. The Miraflores Locks Visitor Center even features world-class exhibition halls, as does the new Panama Canal Expansion Observation Center. Nor do you need to book yourself on a cruise ship to experience the thrill of a canal passage: Excursion vessels operate weekly.

This narrow isthmus separating two oceans has served for centuries as a commercial route between the Old and New Worlds. Four centuries before the canal was built, millions of pounds of silver and gold were transported across the isthmus via the Camino Real and, later, the Camino de Cruces. Built by Indian slaves, the ancient trails are

remarkably well preserved and today are popular as hiking trails, delving into cathedral-like naves beneath branches draped with air plants.

The former Canal Zone that extends 10 miles (16 km) to either side of the canal serves as a biological corridor of astonishing wealth. The need to guarantee a water supply for the canal has ensured that the forests have been protected. The watershed is enshrined within national parks whose lush rain forests provide hikers and birders with rewards aplenty (pick up a copy of *The Panamá Canal Birding Trail* map and guide, published by USAID and the Panama Audubon Society). Just minutes from Panama City, visitors can park by the highway and view wildlife with ease. Parque Nacional Soberanía, Parque Nacional Chagres, and Parque Natural Summit Panama are linked by smaller enclaves of primeval forest to form La Ruta Ecológica entre dos Océanos—the Ecological Route between Two Oceans. Capybaras, monkeys, ocelots, kinkajous, sloths, and an encyclopedic assortment of feathered friends call these forests home.

The Emberá Indians also live deep in the mountainous interior, where effervescent rivers provide white-water thrills. Welcoming visitors with ceremonial dances, the Emberá villages are easily accessed by boat or on package excursions from Panama City. By contrast, the Caribbean communities of Colón, Portobelo, and Nombre de Dios murmur with an Afro-Antillean beat. The cuisine and clapboard houses of the coast known as the Costa Arriba hint at a Caribbean potpourri. Portobelo's fortress ruins echo to the footsteps of marauding pirates, while the town flickers to life every October during the Black Christ Festival.

On the Pacific side, Isla Taboga lies a mere 30-minute boat ride from Panama City. A century ago, this Pacific Ocean isle was a favored idyll for day-trippers (among them Paul Gauguin) escaping the mainland heat and humidity. It still lures city dwellers who come for beach time with ocean breezes. Farther out, the Archipiélago de las Perlas studs the aquamarine seas like coral jewels. The isles' white-hot blazing beaches are stunners, shelving gently into shimmering waters. Only two islands have resort facilities (a third—Isla Viveros—is slated for major touristic development). The rest of the archipelago is left to nature and the fishing and pearl-diving communities. ■

NOT TO BE MISSED:

A day trip to Isla Taboga 92

Touring Miraflores Locks Visitor Center 93

Hiking a portion of the Camino Real trail 101

An exciting boat ride through the Panama Canal locks 102

A walking tour of Portobelo 110–112

The Archipiélago de las Perlas 113

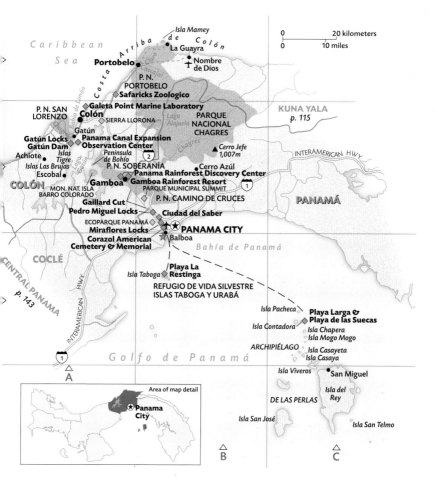

Isla Taboga

Nicknamed the "island of flowers" for the hibiscus, bougainvillea, jasmine, and Taboga roses that bloom in riotous abundance, this laid-back island is almost Mediterranean in flavor and understandably popular with day-trippers escaping the heat and bustle of Panama City.

Isla Taboga

🅜 91 B2

Visitor Information

taboga.panamanow .com

Refugio de Vida Silvestre Islas Taboga y Urabá

🅜 91 B2

✉ Ranger station, 1 mile (1.6 km) S of Iglesia San Pedro

☎ 250-2082 or 500-0855

anam.gob.pa

Cooler and less rainy than its neighbor Panama City, the 568-acre (230 ha) isle, 11 miles (18 km) south of the city, was first settled by the Spanish in 1524 and later served as a base for Francisco Pizarro's conquest of the Inca Empire as well as for piratical predations on Spanish shipping.

The quaint village of **San Pedro,** tucked in a horseshoe cove between forested hills and sheltered beach, surrounds tiny whitewashed **Iglesia San Pedro,** founded in 1524 and acclaimed as the one of the oldest churches in the Western Hemisphere. The adjacent flower-filled plaza is

---

Gauguin & Isla Taboga

Painter Paul Gauguin (1848–1903) first escaped Europe in 1887 with plans to buy some land on Isla Taboga and live "on fish and fruit for nothing . . . without anxiety for the day or for the morrow." Alas, the land was priced beyond his reach. Penniless, he ended up laboring as a tropical tramp on the French canal project before sailing off for the island of Martinique and, eventually, for Tahiti.

---

marked by a statue of Nuestra Señora del Carmen, the island's patron saint.

Colorful fishing boats bob at anchor off **Playa La Restinga,** a handsome little beach that sparkles on sunny days; avoid the crowds on weekends. Aqua-bikes and kayaks can be rented, and at low tide you can walk across a sand bar to **Isla El Morro.** Local fishermen can take you to good snorkeling spots.

The narrow main street leads along the waterfront and ascends through forest past abandoned **World War II bunkers** and the ruins of a Spanish cannon embrasure. The trail ends atop **Cerro de la Cruz,** where you can survey the isle and the gulf.

Covering the entire western fringe of Isla Taboga, **Refugio de Vida Silvestre Islas Taboga y Urabá** protects the site where as many as 100,000 brown pelicans nest from January to July. To visit, get permission from ANAM (Autoridad Nacional del Ambiente, Panama's national environmental authority) beside the ferry dock. The short ferry ride to the island aboard the *Calypso Queen* (tel 314-1730, $$), departing from La Playita de Amador, is a treat. Keep your eye out for whales as you cross the glassy bay. ∎

Miraflores Locks

The closest set of canal locks to Panama City and in many ways the most impressive, these twin-flight locks at the Pacific entrance to the canal are an engineering marvel and justifiably the most visited site in the country.

Stretching for more than a mile (1.6 km) including the approach channel, the scale of the locks is humbling, reducing your perspective to an ant's as cruise ships and supertankers the height of ten-story buildings ease past at fingertip distance. While the lift of the other two locks is fixed, the lift at Miraflores varies between 43 feet (13 m) and 64.5 feet (19 m) due to the tides of the Pacific Ocean. Completed in May 1913, Miraflores, with only two flights linking the Pacific Ocean with Miraflores Lake, has the deepest chamber and tallest gates of the three locks.

An 1887 Belgian locomotive abandoned during creation of Gatún Lake is displayed near the steps to the visitor center. Outside, the **Culebra Cut Rock**—dedicated "to the builders of the canal"—is inset with a plaque quoting President Theodore Roosevelt.

Miraflores Locks Visitor Center

The state-of-the-art visitor center opened in December 2003 on the east side of the locks. Overlooking the locks and control tower, the four-story edifice has viewing verandas on three levels. Bilingual guides offer running commentaries as up to four vessels transit the locks simultaneously.

Tethered by taut steel cables, a Panamax cargo ship is guided through Miraflores Locks by locomotive *mulas* (mules).

The center has a 182-seat theater, plus four exhibition halls with dioramas, interactive displays, and video presentations. Displays cover the history and ecology of the canal; the third floor features a scale model and a pilot-training simulator. After touring the center, you can dine alfresco on the third-floor restaurant terrace.

The visitor center is off Gaillard Highway, a 30-minute drive from the city. Metro Buses serve Miraflores from the SACA terminal at Plaza Cinco de Mayo. ∎

Miraflores Locks Visitor Center

🅰 91 B3

✉ 5 miles (8 km) NW of Balboa via Ave. Omar Torrijos Herrera (Gaillard Hwy.)

☎ 276-8325

💲 $$

pancanal.com

Panama Canal

Simple in conception, monumental in scale, and a work of genius in design and construction, the Panama Canal is a supreme triumph of humanity over nature. The largest and most costly human endeavor ever mounted to its day, the canal fulfilled a dream dating back to Balboa's first sighting of the Pacific in 1513, and is about to be expanded.

After its expansion, the Panama Canal will handle ships even larger than this Panamax-size vessel.

History

The canal's completion cut ten days off the sea passage around the Horn and elevated the country to a position of supreme strategic importance. Today ships of all shapes transit 24/7, maintaining a passage that has operated flawlessly for a century.

The canal's construction eventually gave birth to the Republic of Panama. A testament to U.S. engineering ingenuity and economic will, it also heralded the arrival on the world stage of the United States' unbridled power. Construction from 1906 to 1914 cost an unprecedented 375 million dollars. A truly unimaginable 500 lives (mostly black laborers) were lost per mile (1.6 km) of canal.

Cut through the narrowest and lowest saddle of the Central American isthmus, the canal runs through Panama north to south, connecting the Caribbean Sea (north) and Pacific Ocean (south). Approximately 50 miles

(80 km) long, it features three sets of *esclusas* (locks), each with twin chambers side by side. Each chamber measures 1,000 feet (305 m) long by 110 feet (34 m) wide. Upper chambers have double layers of paired miter gates to prevent catastrophic flooding if the first pair is breached. Every captain must relinquish control of his or her vessel to a pilot for the duration of every transit, which averages eight hours. Currently, northbound ships transit between midnight and noon, and southbound ships between noon and midnight (the canal has operated around the clock since 1963, when the lighting system was installed along the Gaillard Cut).

Administration

After completion of the canal in 1914, responsibility for canal administration was vested in various U.S. government agencies. Following the Torrijos-Carter Treaty

INSIDER TIP:

The Miraflores Locks Visitor Center and the Panama Canal Expansion Observation Center [see p. 106] give travelers a sense of the history of the canal and the incredible scale of the engineering achievement.

—NEIL SHEA
National Geographic *magazine writer*

in 1977, Panama gained jurisdiction of the former Canal Zone and on December 31, 1999, the ACP, or Panama Canal Authority, assumed responsibility for the canal and its 2,134-square-mile (552,761 ha) watershed.

Since taking over operations in 1999, the ACP has invested more than $1 billion in improvements, increasing canal capacity and improving average transit time by 20 percent. More than 14,000 ships pass through the canal every year, generating $2 billion in annual revenue. The highest toll was (U.S.) $375,600, paid in 2011 by the *Norwegian Pearl* cruise ship; the lowest fee—36 cents—was paid in 1928 by English adventurer Richard Halliburton, who swam the canal in ten days.

Previously, the largest vessels allowed on the canal—called Panamax ships—were 106 feet (32 m) wide and 965 feet (294 m) long. This meant that due to its inability to handle today's mega-size ("post-Panamax") ships, the canal has been losing market share to the Suez Canal.

To stop this loss to the country's economy, the Panama Expansion Project (Ampliación del Canal), or Third Set of Locks, was overwhelmingly approved by a public referendum in 2006 with an anticipated budget of $5.25 billion.

The mammoth *ampliación* (expansion) project will create a separate lock system large enough for 150,000-ton (136,000 metric tons) post-Panamax vessels, three times the size of Panamax vessels. This will also facilitate two-way

traffic of the world's largest tankers and container ships around the clock, easing passage through Panama with new, updated locks to compliment the current set.

How the Original Locks Work

A ship transiting from the Caribbean to the Pacific Ocean enters the channel at the Bay of Limón and sails 6 miles (10 km) to Gatún Locks (see p. 98). This triple-lock system raises ships 85 feet (26 m) to the level of Gatún Lake. The 27-mile (37.8 km) passage across the lake ends at the north end of the 8.5-mile-long (13.7 km) Gaillard Cut, named for Col. David Gaillard, the engineer in charge of excavating this passage through the continental divide. After passage, ships enter the single-step lock at Pedro Miguel and are lowered to Miraflores Lake. At Miraflores Locks (see p. 93), ships are lowered two more flights to the level of the Pacific Ocean.

Navigational markers help guide the ships through the channels and lake. Once in the locks, vessels move under their own propulsion but are tethered to electric locomotives called *mulas* (mules), working in tandem on narrow-gauge tracks to keep the ships tautly aligned. With every ship's passage, 52 million gallons (197

EXPERIENCE:
Transit the Canal

To gain a feel for the canal, including the incomparable experience of lifting and dropping through the locks, try a "partial transit." Two companies provide these trips on the canal aboard small cruise ships, with lunch included. **Canal & Bay Tours** (*tel* 209-2009, canalandbaytours.com, $$$$$) offers trips every Saturday year-round from the Muelle de Amador dock. **Panama Marine Adventures** (*tel* 226-8917, pmatours.net, $$$$$) has similar trips aboard the *Pacific Queen* departing Flamenco Marina every Saturday, plus Thursdays in January through April.

million l) of fresh water are flushed out to sea: The canal accounts for some 60 percent of the nation's use of fresh water.

The entire system is powered by nothing more than the flow of fresh water. Water from either Gatún Lake or Miraflores Lake fills the locks and raises the ships; water flowing from one chamber to the next or to the sea-level channels empties the locks and lowers the ships.

Water surges through three giant culverts (each up to 22 feet/6.7 m wide) embedded in the center wall dividing the chambers and in each of the outer side walls. Valves at each end of the culverts control the ingress and egress of water. No pumps are involved. Sliding up and down on roller bearings like windows in a frame, the valves at the upper end of the chamber are opened while the valves at the lower end are closed to flood a lock. Water pours down the main culvert

and through 20 smaller cross-culverts that run beneath the floor of each lock perpendicular to the main culverts. The water then boils up into the chambers through 70 well-like culverts. The large number of wells, distributed evenly across the chamber floors, minimizes turbulence while permitting each chamber to be filled or emptied of 52 million gallons (197 million l) of water in as little as eight minutes. To empty a chamber, the valves at the upper end are closed and those at the lower end are opened.

The canal's enormous metal gates (the heaviest, the lower chamber gates at Mira-flores, weighing 745 tons/676 metric tons) are opened and closed with hydraulic struts. The entire system was designed to operate electrically, with a water spillway at Gatún Dam generating the power for the 1,500 electric motors. Each set of locks is controlled from a

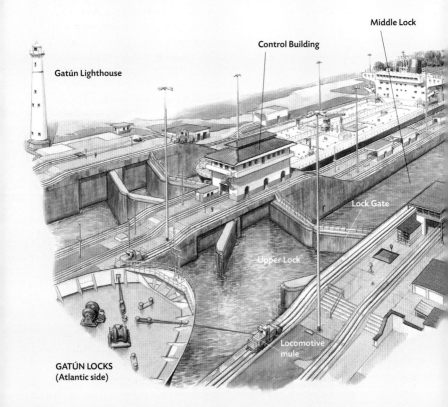

Gatún Lighthouse

Control Building

Middle Lock

Lock Gate

Upper Lock

Locomotive mule

GATÚN LOCKS
(Atlantic side)

Panama's mammoth expansion project is a $5.25 billion bet on the country's economic future.

Lower Lock

central room resembling an airport control tower. In recent years, a computer-based control system using fiber-optic cable has replaced the original electrome-chanical system, while the original hydraulic valves are now computer-controlled.

How the New Locks Work

The Panama Expansion Project (Ampliación del Canal), or Third Set of Locks, features two new lock systems parallel to the existing locks to accommodate the post-Panamax vessels of modern shipping: The Pacific chambers will be southwest of the Miraflores Locks, and the Atlantic chambers will be east of the existing Gatún Locks. The new locks utilize the partially excavated paths of an unfinished set of locks initiated in 1939 by the United States (these were suspended in 1942 with the outbreak of World War II).

They are linked to the Atlantic and Pacific entrance channels by new approach lanes, including a 3.8-mile (6.1 km) channel connecting the new Miraflores Locks to the Culebra Cut. Each new lock system will have three 60-foot-deep (18.3 m) consecutive chambers measuring 1,400 feet (426.7 m) long and 180 feet (54.8 m) wide. Like the old system, no pumps are involved; water will flow by gravity. However, to conserve water each chamber will have three parallel "reutilization basins," or reservoirs (for a total of nine basins per lock and 18 basins in total), tiered to permit 60 percent of water to be recycled. Unlike the old miter-gate system, the new locks' mammoth roller gates will slide horizontally, while tugboats will replace mules to tether the behemoth ships and keep them on course in the chambers.

To accommodate post-Panamax vessels—and the extra fresh water required to fill the new locks—Gatún Lake was dredged to raise it by 1.5 feet (0.45 m) to a maximum operating level of 89 feet (27.1 m). Combined with the deepening and widening of the navigation channels, this will increase freshwater capacity by 165 million gallons (more than 624 million liters)—good for an additional 1,100 lockages annually.

Lago Gatún & Around

An integral part of the canal, this 166-square-mile (423 sq km) freshwater lake provides the billions of gallons of water necessary to operate the locks. Nearby are communities and parks that offer spectacular opportunities for birding and wildlife observation.

Mighty Gatún Lake feeds the locks and provides electric power for the Panama Canal system.

Lago Gatún

91 A3

First conceived by French engineer Godin de Lépinay (1821–1898) in 1879, Gatún Lake was formed by damming the Río Chagres at Gatún, near the river's mouth, to create a body of water to bridge the isthmus. Flooding took four years (1910–1914) to bring the lake to its full depth, with the surface now 85 feet (26 m) above sea level.

At the time of its creation, Gatún Lake was the world's largest artificial lake. The water inundated much of the Panama Railroad (a new railroad had to be built on higher ground) and dozens of villages and impoverished local communities, few of whose occupants received compensation. Giant

trees that could form submerged hazards to shipping were cut down and the trunks dynamited. Gnarled trunks still protrude from the cobalt waters like witches' fingers. Ships follow the course of the now submerged riverbed—the deepest part of the lake—traveling 23 miles (37 km) between the Gatún Locks and Gaillard Cut. The navigational channel is currently being deepened to permit the passage of vessels of greater draft and to increase water storage capacity, providing enough water for the new locks being built (see p. 97).

Nature tours of the lake by canopied boat are offered by Aventuras 2000 (tel 227-2000, aventuras2000.com, $$$$). Expect to see snail kites, Panama flycatchers, anhingas, monkeys, and sloths. Jungle Land Panama (see Travelwise p. 241) offers kayak and fishing trips. Anglers rave about the lake's feisty peacock bass (known locally as *sargento*), an Amazonian species that was introduced to Gatún Lake decades ago and has since proliferated, to the benefit of the crocodiles. Panama Fishing & Fun Time *(tel 203-3363, letsfishpanama.com)* also offers fishing trips.

Gamboa & Around

Midway along the canal, graced by colorful duplex wooden houses in U.S. colonial style, the small community of Gamboa provides a fine base for exploring the surrounding tropical forests. Several nearby sites are five-star venues for superb wildlife viewing.

Gamboa: Gamboa, 20 miles (32 km) northwest of Panama City, was built in the early 1930s and nuzzles up to forested hills where the Río Chagres pours into the Panama Canal. Madden Road ends a short distance beyond, where begins Pipeline Road (see p. 101) for the ultimate birding experience.

Inducing ornithological exhilaration in birding visitors, the 12-sided metal **Canopy Tower** (see Travelwise p. 241), is a former U.S. military radar station converted into an ecolodge. Poking up over the forest from atop Semaphore Hill, the observation deck over Parque Nacional Soberanía (see pp. 100–101, 104) is just the ticket for birders

eager to spy motmots, whitewhiskered puffbirds, olivaceous flatbills, and other dazzling species. Howler and tamarin monkeys frolic nearby, and agoutis, anteaters, and coatis are commonly seen on Semaphore Hill Road. Day visitors are welcome, but an overnight stay is recommended.

Parque Municipal Summit: Considered Panama's national botanical garden and zoo, this city-owned park has more than 150 species of trees, palms, and shrubs from around the world

shading sprawling lawns good for picnicking and relaxing. Fenced exhibits enclose such elusive creatures as margays, ocelots, peccaries, and magnificent jaguars. For birders, a highlight is the large harpy eagle breeding enclosure.

Gamboa

▲ 91 A3

Parque Municipal Summit

▲ 91 B3

✉ Madden Rd., 6 miles (10 km) NW of Miraflores

☎ 232-4854

💲 $

municipio.gob.pa/?p=466

Monkey Islands

More than 7,000 simians—white-faced capuchins, mantled howlers, black-handed spider monkeys, rufous-naped tamarins, and night monkeys—inhabit the group of 42 islands collectively called Islas Tigre and Islas Las Brujas. The monkeys were all once captive (either as pets or for the illegal monkey trade) and were released here to prepare them for reintroduction into the wild. Begun in 1982, the Primate Refuge and Sanctuary of Panama (PRSP) grew to become the world's second largest primate sanctuary, with a mission of caring for and rehabilitating the mammals. The refuge is now closed as part of security efforts around Gatún Lake. Visits are no longer allowed, but the monkeys still frolic.

Gamboa Rainforest Resort

⛰ 91 A3

✉ Gamboa,
12 miles (20 km)
NW of Panama
City

☎ 314-5000

🕐 Rainforest Aerial
Tram: 9:15 a.m.,
10:30 a.m.,
2 p.m., &
3:30 p.m.
Tues.–Fri.;
7:30 a.m.,
9:15 a.m.,
10:30 a.m.,
& 3 p.m.
weekends;
closed Mon.

💲 $$–$$$$$
(depending
on activity)

gamboaresort.com

Gamboa Rainforest Resort:

Welcoming day visitors, this luxury hotel and spa enjoys an incredible setting overlooking the Río Chagres. It specializes in nature-themed activities, including wildlife safaris by boat and guided birding hikes. Go-it-aloners can follow the resort's easily hiked **Sendero de la Laguna,** a gravel-lined mile-long (1.6 km) trail.

To learn about rain forests, take a guided tour at the **Interpretative Park,** 250 acres (101 ha) of lowland tropical forest and marsh. Also here: an orchid nursery, a butterfly exhibit, a model Emberá village, and a serpentarium. A resort highlight is a ride on the **Rainforest Aerial Tram,** with 18 carriages that rise 367 feet (112 m) to a mirador (lookout) offering superlative 360-degree vistas.

Parque Nacional Soberanía:

With a remarkable diversity of wildlife close to the capital, this rain forest park *(Gaillard Hwy., 16 mi/25 km NW of Panama City, tel 500-0855, $)* protects much of the Panama Canal watershed and teems with animals. Birds ranging from red-lored Amazons to harpy eagles have earned Parque Nacional Soberanía a reputation for some of Central America's finest birding.

Created in 1980 to preserve 54,597 acres (22,104 ha) of forest cover, Soberanía National Park extends south from the eastern shores of Gatún Lake to a few miles south of the Río Chagres. The terrain undulates gently like a great swelling sea and rises to 279 feet (85 m) atop **Cerro Calabaza.** Silk cotton trees, giant mahoganies, and smooth gray cuipo trees

Visitors on the Rainforest Aerial Tram gain insights into tropical ecology.

Treasure Trails

The wealth plundered from the Inca Empire crossed the isthmus en route to Spain via two trails built by slave labor. Begun in 1516, the **Camino Real** linked Panama City to Nombre de Dios (and later to Portobelo). Traversing the continental divide, it was "eighteen leagues of misery and curses" in which mules laden with silver ingots often sank in quagmires or plunged down the mountainside. The **Camino de Cruces**—a far easier route—was begun in 1527 and linked Panama City to the port of Venta de Cruces on the Río Chagres. Its paving stones were laid in the form of the Christian cross: hence Trail of Crosses. To begin hiking the Cruces trail, park by Km marker 6.3 on Madden Road.

like silvery columns of light form a lush canopy over the forest, home to more than 100 mammal, 79 reptile, and 55 amphibian species.

The park also has birds: crested eagles, keel-billed toucans, white-bellied antbirds, violaceous trogons. Renowned for its phenomenal birding, Soberanía vibrates with squawks, chirps,

INSIDER TIP:

Check out the hummingbird show in the Parque Nacional Soberanía visitor center; the nearby tower offers great views of the rain forest canopy.

—JUSTIN KAVANAGH
*National Geographic
Travel Books editor*

and screeches. Serious birders take to the 10-mile-long (16 km) Camino del Oleoducto, more famously known as **Pipeline Road** and considered among the best birding trails in the world: More species of birds have been sighted there in a single day than anywhere else on Earth! The road leads to the **Panama Rainforest Discovery Center,** with a 130-foot-tall (40 m) observation tower and trails. Only 25 visitors are allowed before 10 a.m.—the early bird gets the worm!

Capybaras, the world's largest rodents, are frequently seen in early morning in the swampy area near the entrance to the trail. Opportunities also abound for sighting other mammals, such as anteaters, coatimundis, kinkajous, and howler monkeys.

The broad 4-mile-long (6.4 km) **Plantation Road** also offers spectacular birding. With luck you might spot an army ant swarm attended by bicolored, ocellated, and spotted antbirds. The short **Sendero El Charco** trail begins roadside and leads to a small waterfall and refreshing pool, while **Sendero Camino de Cruces** follows the 16th-century Camino de Cruces (see sidebar above). A section of cobbles has been reclaimed from the jungle and restored. In places you can detect hoof hollows etched by the metronomic march of many mules.

The trail eventually leads to the Río Chagres—a five-hour venture for intrepid hikers—where *(continued on p. 104)*

Panama Rainforest Discovery Center

✉ Pipeline Rd.
☎ 6588-0697
💲 $$–$$$$

pipelineroad.org

A Waterborne Excursion Through the Canal Locks

A passage through the canal is the dream of almost every visitor to Panama. The experience of transiting the locks, as opposed to merely viewing them from the sidelines, is one of the country's most thrilling and rewarding journeys. Small cruise vessels that operate "partial transits" offer the opportunity to feel the surge of water filling and emptying the locks; running narratives enhance the journey.

The *Pacific Queen* provides a thrilling excursion from its berth at Amador Causeway.

The trip described here is for a northbound passage from **Muelle de Amador.** Apply plenty of sunscreen and have patience, as skippers must take on an ACP pilot before entering canal waters. (See sidebar p. 95 for cruise operators.)

Once under way, it is a five-hour journey to Gamboa. Arching over the canal entrance, the **Bridge of the Americas ❶** (see p. 88) looms overhead as your vessel slides beneath its broad span. Within minutes, you pass the bustling commercial port of **Balboa** on the eastern shore, beyond which the banks are cloaked in deep verdure. Crocodiles can often be seen on sunny days hauled out on the banks.

About 2 miles (3 km) from the bridge, you pass on your left construction of the

NOT TO BE MISSED:

Bridge of the Americas
• Miraflores Locks • Gaillard
Cut • Centennial Bridge

Ampliación del Canal (Panama Expansion Project; see p. 97) at a site known as the **Third Cut,** an unfinished canal that was dug in the 1930s to permit the passage of U.S. battleships. As you approach the entrance to **Miraflores Locks ❷** (see p. 93), you pass the former Fort Clayton U.S. military base on the east bank. Today the enclave is the **Ciudad del Saber** (see p. 114).

After bucking the current as the first lock is drained, the huge lock gates sweep open, your vessel eases into the chamber, the gates close, and the lock fills with swirling water. With the vessel tethered securely, you can touch the massive walls. In less than eight minutes the lock has filled and you look *down* upon the walls. The metal gates to the fore open, and you move into the second chamber, where the process is repeated. Larger vessels in adjoining locks levitate or fall around you as the electric trains called *mulas* guide them through.

Entering **Lago Miraflores,** you approach **Pedro Miguel Locks ❸** for the third and final lock passage. Beyond, the canal narrows through the **Gaillard Cut ❹,** spanned by the graceful twin-towered **Centennial Bridge,** opened in 2004 and linking Panama City to the town of Arraiján. Passing beneath this high-strung harp (illuminated at night), the stepped rock face of **Gold Hill** looms on your right, with

Contractor's Hill on your left. Nature then closes in. With luck you might spot toucans and parrots bursting from the bottle green forests that line the 8.5-mile (14 km) Gaillard Cut. Excavators continue to gnaw at the cut, which today averages 630 feet (192 m) wide to permit the passage of ever larger ships.

Some 7.5 miles (12 km) beyond the bridge, the **Río Chagres** pours into the cut beneath a metal bridge. Note the black-painted **lighthouse** atop the north bank; dating from 1914, it has been supplanted by modern navigational markers. Another 400 yards (366 m) brings you to the wharf at **Gamboa ❺** and the end of your journey, where return transfers await.

🅜 See also area map p. 91
▶ Muelle de Amador
🕒 5 hours
↔ 15 miles (24 km)
▶ Flamenco Marina, Gamboa

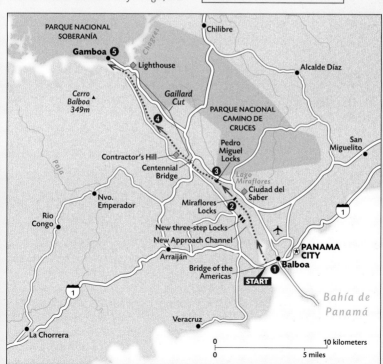

**Monumento
Natural Isla
Barro Colorado**

🅰 91 A3

✉ Southern Gatún
Lake

☎ 212-8951 for
reservations

🕐 Boat departures
from Gamboa
7:15 a.m. Mon.–
Fri.; 8 a.m.
Sat.–Sun.

💲 $$$$

stri.org

**Comunidad Wounaan San
Antonio** (tel 507/6637-9503) and
Comunidad Emberá Ella Purú
(tel 507/6537-7223) welcome visitors interested in an immersion in
one of Panama's indigenous
cultures. **Emberá Village Tours**
(tel 848/4072-9503, emberavillage
tours.com) arranges tours.

    The ANAM office at the park
entrance has maps and issues
hiking and camping permits.
Tour companies offer trips from
Panama City and can arrange birding guides. Robberies have been
reported; don't hike alone.

A kinkajou (a member of the raccoon family)

**Monumento Natural Isla
Barro Colorado:** Isla Barro
Colorado rises from the waters
of southern Gatún Lake. The
largest island in the canal system, it is also the centerpiece
of the namesake 13,800-acre
(5,600 ha) nature monument
incorporating the 4,000-acre
(1,500 ha) island, plus five surrounding mainland peninsulas
(Bohío, Buena Vista, Frijoles,
Gigante, and Peña Blanca).
The area was established as a

biological reserve in 1923 and
today functions as an open-air
laboratory for scientists from
around the world. Since 1946,
it has been managed by the
Smithsonian Tropical Research
Institute (STRI), which operates
an intensive study program of
tropical ecosystems.

    Smothered in lowland tropical
moist forest, the island is home
to 115 mammal species (including
ocelots, peccaries, five monkey
species, and 74 species of bats),
plus 381 kinds of birds and innu-
merable insect species that include
more than 200 varieties of ants.
More than 35 miles (56 km) of
trails lace the island, although visitors are restricted to a smaller network of nature trails that weaves
beneath massive strangler figs,
palms, and ceibas.

    The island is open to daytime
visitors by arrangement through
STRI or approved tour operators,
with 45-minute transfers aboard
the STRI launch from Gamboa.
Ashore, guided two-hour hikes
along the interpretative nature
trails lead through soaring forest
and end at the visitor center in the
Field Research Station. Make reservations well in advance; no children under ten are permitted. ∎

Colón & Around

Birthed with the Panama Railroad in 1850, the country's third largest city is inextricably linked to the quests of trans-isthmian passage. Despite its size and moments of illustrious history, Colón (pronounced ko LOAN) is only now emerging from a long spell of depression and should be explored only with a guide or organized tour. Beyond the city await an ancient fortress, prime birding sites, and A-list coastal vistas.

Panoramic vistas are a highlight of the rail journey linking Panama City with Colón.

Colón

The sultry port city of Colón (pop. 78,000) was built by the Pacific Railroad Company on Isla Manzanillo at the Bahía de Limón's eastern tip. Most of the original structures were destroyed by a fire on March 31, 1885.

Avenida Central, the tree-shaded central boulevard colloquially called El Paseo, makes a pleasant stroll. Among its many statues and monuments are the monument of John Stevens (at Calle 16), the statue of Ferdinand de Lesseps (bet. Calles 3 & 4), and the Columbus monument (bet. Calles 2 & 3). Caribbean clapboard houses in faded tropical pastels line the boulevard. A sturdy contrast, the

New Washington Hotel (see Travelwise p. 240) boasts a Moorish facade and a surfeit of marble. The grand dame, established in 1913, counted presidents William Howard Taft and Warren Harding among its guests.

Cruise ships dock at **Colón 2000 wharf** (Paseo Gorgas), close to the **Zona Libre** (Ave. Roosevelt, Calle 13, tel 475-9500, colonfree tradezone.com), the world's second largest free-trade zone after Hong Kong. Trading principally with international wholesalers, the zone generates about ten billion dollars annually.

Outskirts of Colón

Avenida Bolívar leads west from Colón past the old hilltop **Cementerio Monte de**

Colón
◪ 91 A3
Visitor Information
✉ ATP office, Comercial Colón 2000, Paseo Gorgas & Calle 11
☎ 475-2301

Panama Canal Expansion Observation Center

✉ 5 miles (8 km) S of Colón

☎ 276-8325

💲 $$

visitcanaldepanama.com

Safarick's Zoologico

✉ Maria Chiquita, 10 miles (16 km) east of Colón

☎ 435-6900

💲 $$$$

safarickszoo.com

Parque Nacional San Lorenzo

🅰 91 A3

Visitor Information

✉ Centro El Tucán, Achiote

☎ 226-6602

Esperanza (formerly Mount Hope cemetery), dating from 1908, with a section for U.S. servicemen. Signs point the way to the **Panama Canal Expansion Observation Center,** where a mirador (lookout deck) grants a lofty perspective over the new esclusas (locks) at Gatún. An amphitheater shows documentaries, and a café and alfresco restaurant offer fine lake views.

At Gatún Locks, a spectacular stand allows an eagle's-eye view of ships passing through the three-stage locks. Crossing under the huge mitered gates via a one-lane swing bridge, you arrive at the **Gatún Dam.** Completed in 1913 and damming the Río Chagres about 6 miles (10 km) from its mouth, the dam measures 1.4 miles (2.3 km) along the top and 2,100 feet (640 m) thick at

the base. Fourteen gates top its curvilinear spillway.

East of town, **Safarick's Zoologico** gets you up close to capybaras, howler monkeys, and other rarely seen creatures. Highlights include a walk-through aviary and butterfly enclosures.

Parque Nacional San Lorenzo

Created in 1997, San Lorenzo National Park spreads over 23,852 acres (9,653 ha) of coastal wetlands, cativo forests, and semideciduous forest where U.S. forces and astronauts once learned jungle survival. The former Fort Sherman Jungle Operations Training Center (JOTC) has served nature lovers since 1999; you need to present your passport to enter. An astounding 430 bird species have been identified here, as well as 81 mammals, including jaguars and tapirs. Birders flock like breeding macaws to **El Camino de Achiote** and the **Sendero El Trogón** trail. Guides can be hired at the Centro El Tucán visitor center, in Achiote.

The park's highlight is **Castillo de San Lorenzo el Real de Chagres,** a fort looming magnificently over the mouth of the Río Chagres. Dating from 1597, its rusted cannon and timeworn walls recall the day in 1671 when Henry Morgan and his pirates stormed the ramparts. Today a UNESCO World Heritage site, it has excellent signage in English.

Nearby, the U.S. Army's School of the Americas has been transformed into a luxury hotel, the Meliá Panamá Canal (see Travelwise p. 241). ∎

EXPERIENCE: Explore the Forest Canopy

Ninety percent of the rain forest biota lives in the canopy. To discover it take a trip for a monkey's-eye view.

Boquete Tree Trek (tel 202-6843, aventurist.com), on the slopes of Volcán Barú (see pp. 198–199), has ziplines slung between trees. You'll ride attached to the cable in a secure harness.

Panama Outdoor Adventures (tel 6605-8171 panamaoutdooradventures.com), between Colón and Portobelo, lets you whiz between treetops on nine cables—the longest is 722 feet (220 m) long.

Gamboa Rainforest Aerial Tram (tel 314-5000, gamboaresort.com), at the Gamboa Rainforest Resort (see p. 100), let's you ride in an open-air tram, accompanied by a naturalist guide.

Parque Nacional Chagres

Created in 1985, Chagres National Park is named for a legendary Indian chief who ruled the region at the time of the conquistadores. Encompassing 500 square miles (1,295 sq km), the park protects the watershed of Río Chagres Basin and is a veritable Noah's ark of animals and birds.

The Chagres and its tributaries drain 1,300 square miles (3,367 sq km) and provide much of the drinking water for Panama City, as well as water for the canal. The upper reaches cascade in a violent torrent that spills onto lowland and slows to big lazy loops. Before construction of the Gatún Dam, the river flowed unimpeded into the Caribbean. Tamed, today it feeds Gatún Lake.

The terrain ranges from 200 feet (60 m) above sea level to 3,303 feet (1007 m) atop **Cerro Jefe** in the southeast. Giant cedro trees tower more than 100 feet (30 m) above the lowland tropical moist forest. The park boasts more than 500 bird species, including the rare Tacarcuna bush tanager. Crocodiles and otters swim in the rivers and five species of monkeys swing from the trees. Cerro Jefe and neighboring 2,529-foot (771 m) **Cerro Azul** are known for their birdlife; they are most easily accessed from the Km 40 marker on the Interamerican Highway, 24 miles (39 km) east of Panama City (a four-wheel-drive vehicle is required).

Río Chagres was dammed in 1935 to form **Lago Alajuela,** which offers excellent fishing. Boats cross Lake Alajuela to **Comunidad de Emberá Parará**

Two Oceans

At 3,303 feet (1,007 m), Cerro Jefe in Parque Nacional Chagres may not rank among the world's highest peaks, but when you reach its summit, you may still feel that you're standing on top of the world. Below you is the old Camino Real, the Panama Canal, and, on a clear day, views of both the Atlantic and Pacific Oceans.

Puru, a friendly Emberá Indian community that provides an opportunity to learn about native lore. The **Emberá Drua community** *(tel 333-2850 or 6709-1233, trail2.com/embera/tourism.htm)* is farther inland.

Hikers can try out the old **Camino Real treasure trail** (see sidebar p. 101), a narrow, overgrown, and rugged jungle path that follows the valleys of the Ríos Boquerón and Nombre de Dios. A guide is essential. The rocky upper Chagres provides a thrilling white-water run.

You can camp at Cerro Azul ranger station *($)*, and there are several simple hostels and inns near Cerro Jefe. Bring insect repellent, and keep a wary eye out for venomous snakes. ∎

Parque Nacional Chagres

🗺 91 B3

✉ Lago Alajuela: Carretera Transístmica & Carretera Calzada Larga; Cerro Azul: 16 miles (25 km) N of Tocumen via Interamerican Hwy.

☎ 350-7521 or 6711-8512

💲 $

anam.gob.pa

Pillage & Plunder

Pirates color Panama's chromatic past. Swashbuckling a blazing trail through the Indies, cutthroat privateers and pirates were the terrorists of their day, entirely lacking in compassion and scruples. For almost two centuries, these wild and ruthless sea rovers plundered the Spanish Main, the Spanish-controlled coastline running from Panama to the Orinoco River.

Don Pedro de Valdés, admiral of the Spanish flagship *Nuestra Señora del Rosario*, surrenders his sword to Sir Francis Drake in 1588, following the defeat of the Spanish Armada.

No Spanish strongholds were as tempting as the ports of Nombre de Díos and Portobelo, the New World's main gateways for great galleons laden with treasure en route to Spain. From the earliest days of Spain's discovery of the Americas, Panama served as the chief conduit for the continent's wealth. From pearls of the Archipiélago de las Perlas to Colombian emeralds and silver and gold pillaged from the Inca of Peru, treasure in mind-boggling quantities passed through the isthmus to await transshipment to Spain.

Panama was a plum ripe for picking. Daring foreigners seized Spanish galleons at will, often with the official sanction of Spain's sworn enemies: England, France, and Holland licensed captains as privateers to attack Spanish ships and cities in the New World.

Sir Francis Drake

The most notorious privateer was Sir Francis Drake (1540–1596), who first sailed to the New World in 1567 with his cousin John Hawkins and a cargo of African slaves. Their fleet was attacked by the Spanish, filling Drake—a devout Protestant—with anti-papist hatred. In 1572 he returned and ransacked Nombre de Dios, captured several Spanish vessels, and waylaid a mule train on the Camino de Cruces. Drake sailed for England with the ships' holds groaning with treasure.

Sanctioned by Queen Elizabeth I, in 1577 Drake set out again with five vessels and the purpose of plunder. After pillaging the Pacific coast of South America, the pirate—reduced to one vessel, the *Golden Hind*—captured the *Nuestra Señora de la Concepción* treasure ship and returned to England in 1580 after circumnavigating the world. Drake (who was now so feared that the Spanish used the name *El Draque* to frighten children) returned to Panama in 1596 with a fleet of 26 ships. He died on his ship of dysentery, following an attack on Portobelo, and was buried at sea.

In the mid-17th century, a new breed of cutthroats appeared. The "buccaneers" began life as a motley group of seafaring miscreants of all creeds and nations who had coalesced off Hispaniola, where they hunted wild boar and raised livestock for sale to passing ships (the dried meat was called *boucan*). The Spanish resented their presence, however, and drove them to sea. They formed the Brethren of the Coast and turned to piracy against the Spanish. Success swelled their numbers and eventually they were officially welcomed to Port Royal, Jamaica, which became their base.

Henry Morgan

Chief among them was Henry Morgan (1635–1688), a ruthless Welshman: When Morgan sacked Portobelo in 1688, he used nuns and monks as human shields against Spanish fire. Morgan's ruinous rape of the Spanish Main was crowned in 1671 by the sacking and destruction of Panama City (in the chaos, the city burned down, denying Morgan much of his loot). Spain and England had just signed a peace treaty, however. Although Morgan was recalled to England to stand trial, he was exonerated, then knighted and even named governor of Jamaica. In 1697, Spain and England made peace and embarked on a crusade to suppress piracy.

The Rise and Fall of Pre-Columbian Gold

The people of the Americas began to master goldsmithing as early as 2000 B.C. In time, the Mesoamerican cultures crafted some of the finest gold sculptures ever produced. Weighted with symbolism and religious significance, their glittering masterpieces—headdresses, pendants, face masks, and figurines—reflected an appreciation for gold far exceeding mere wealth.

The polytheistic pre-Columbian cultures revered gold as the sweat or tears of the sun, the supreme deity. They fashioned items in an abundance of anthropomorphic and zoomorphic figures, produced for ceremonial or religious functions, including funerary and other face masks. Jaguars, bats, frogs, and crocodiles were prevalent. Other items were produced as symbols of status or purely for aesthetic value.

The arrival of the conquistadores, colonists, and pirates in the 16th century witnessed the demise of indigenous gold production and artistry as well as the decimation of almost three millennia of cultural achievement. Vast quantities of gold treasure were seized, melted down, and shipped to Spain aboard treasure ships.

The mines of Darién and Veraguas eventually fell into disuse, although *oreros* (prospectors) still work Panama's streams and hillsides seeking the eternally elusive nugget that will land them on Easy Street.

Parque Nacional Portobelo

This park, covering 139 square miles (360 sq km), is a triptych protecting forested coastal mountains, 44 miles (70 km) of shoreline, and Caribbean waters that sustain precious mangroves and coral reefs. It encloses Spanish colonial ruins dating back five centuries to when the town of Portobelo was the most important treasure port in the Americas.

Pointing toward a colorful past, the cannon of Fuerte Santiago still stand guard at Portobelo.

Parque Nacional Portobelo

🗺 91 B4

Visitor Information

✉ Calle Principal Frente at la Alcaldía

☎ 448-2165

💲 $

Portobelo and the wild and beautiful surrounding Caribbean region known as the Costa Arriba de Colón has seen only limited development since its 16th-century colonial heyday.

Portobelo

This somnolent town, 28 miles (45 km) east of Colón, lives up to the name—Beautiful Port—given to the setting by Christopher Columbus, when his worm-eaten ships limped into the bay on November 2, 1502, during the explorer's final voyage to the New World. Nestled

within gently folded hills, the town enjoys an exquisite setting when seen from the sea.

Founded in 1597 following Sir Francis Drake's sacking of Nombre de Dios, Portobelo became the departure point for the treasure fleets carrying the plundered wealth of South America back to Spain. Although the town had a permanent population of fewer than 1,000 people, more than 10,000 traders flocked in every year for the trade fair that coincided with the arrival of the Spanish fleet. Although Portobelo remained unwalled, castles went up and Portobelo, with Havana and Veracruz, was the most heavily fortified town in the Americas. The first two fortresses, Fortaleza Santiago de la Gloria and Todo Fierro (Iron Castle), were completed in 1620 but destroyed in 1738 by English naval commander Admiral Edward Vernon.

The 18th-century fortress ruins seen today are second generation and smaller than their precursors, since they protected a port that had lost its importance as trade waned. Built into the rugged hills on each side of the bay, their *baluartes* (watchtowers) peek out from between palms atop walls slowly yielding to the encroaching jungle.

Entering town, you pass the **Batería de Santiago,** with cannon in embrasures; a stepped trail that begins on the right-hand side of the road leads uphill to another battery offering spectacular views. The former Castillo de Santiago de la Gloria, 150 yards (137 m) farther along, is now built over, but steps on the right lead up to the **Mirador El Perú** lookout. Across the harbor, the twin batteries of the **Fuerte de San Fernando** were intended to catch invaders in a cross fire.

Castillo de San Jerónimo guards the harbor in the center of town and points its rusting cannon toward the ghosts of pirates past. On its south side, the recently restored twin-story **Real Aduana** (tel 448-2024, $), the customhouse, hosts a small museum welcoming you with an excellent English-language video on the history of Portobelo, an illuminated map of the treasure fleet routes, plus cannonballs and 3-D models of the castles.

A stone's throw east, the **Iglesia de San Felipe** features a two-tier campanile rising over the town. Birds swoop around the simple altar of gilt mahogany and statue of the Black Christ. Time your visit for the last Sunday of the month, when a special 11 a.m.

Black Christ Festival

Every October 21, as many as 40,000 people throng Portobelo for the Festival del Nazareno, which honors the life-size wooden figure of a black Christ thought to have answered Portobelo's prayers for salvation from a cholera epidemic. Pilgrims petition favors, while others are drawn to the colorful spectacle. Each *peregrino* **(pilgrim) wears an ankle-length velvet toga of deepest claret edged with lace and aglitter with faux jewels, gold braid, and sequins. Secular tokens are often pinned to the toga. At night the effigy is borne from the church atop a litter carried by as many as 40 men** robed in purple. **Barefoot and with heads freshly shaved, they snake through Portobelo—three steps forward, two steps back—swaying side to side in time with lively music. The penitents follow, some crawling on their knees. At midnight, the litter is returned to the church, pilgrims cast off their robes, and Portobelo explodes in an irreligious bacchanal. At any time of year watch for performances by Agropaciones de Congo** *(Casa Artesenal, Calle Principal, tel 66693-5690),* **which keeps alive traditional slave-era music and dance under the direction of "Mama Ari"—Aristela Blanca.**

Mass incorporates African-based Congo traditions. Tucked away to the rear of the church, the tiny former church-hospital of **San Juan de Dios** contains the **Museo del Cristo Negro de Portobelo,** displaying colorful festival robes.

Twin islands stand guard at the entrance to the deepwater bay. Supposedly the pirate Sir Francis Drake was buried off **Isla Drake** (1 mile/1.6 km W of Portobello) on January 28, 1596, after he died in these waters following an attack on Portobelo.

Natural Highs

The rivers that rise inland of Portobelo snake down to Portobelo Bay in long, lazy loops perfect for boating tours into

INSIDER TIP:

Portobelo hosts a festival (Feb. or March) **in which demonic dancers in fantastic costumes perform "devil dances."**

—CHRISTIAN ZIEGLER
National Geographic photographer

the mangroves and lowland moist forest. You can hire a local boatman to take you on a wildlife safari along the **Río Cascajal** and **Río Claro.** Sloths, howler monkeys, river otters, and even crocodiles and caimans are possible wildlife treats.

The wrecks of Spanish galleons will tempt divers near **Arrecife**

Salmedina, a fine coral reef also blessed with the remains of a Beech C-45 warplane 75 feet (23 m) down. Panama Divers (see Travelwise p. 264) offers trips.

Isla Grande, 3 miles (5 km) northeast of Portobelo, is a popular weekend retreat for urbanites from Panama City. Lilting reggae rhythms drift down the frost white sand, and surf washes over a coral reef a short distance beyond calm turquoise shallows. A lighthouse built by the French in 1893 tops the isle. Nearby **Isla Mamey** is also good for snorkeling. Water taxis for Isla Grande and Isla Mamey depart the waterfront village of La Guayra, 13 miles (21 km) east of Portobelo.

Farther along, the serpentine coast road provides a roller-coaster ride through picturesque countryside framed by the mountains of Parque Nacional Chagres (see p. 107). Some 15 miles (25 km) east of Portobelo, you arrive at **Nombre de Dios,** a funky fishing village spanning a river of the same name. First settled in 1509, the town served as the treasure port of the isthmus for 77 years. However, the harbor proved unsafe in storms (in 1525 an entire fleet was sunk) and was superseded by Portobelo.

Great excitement surrounded the discovery of a wreck in 1998 off Playa Damas. Thought to be Columbus's *Vizcaína,* which sank hereabouts in 1502, the ship was declared a national monument, although the wreck still lies in archaeological limbo five fathoms beneath the surface. ∎

Archipiélago de las Perlas

Comprising more than 200 islands and cays just a two-hour boat ride or 20-minute plane trip from Panama City, these emerald jewels are made complete by their exquisite setting in waters of mesmerizing blues and greens. Humpback whales and other whale species frequent the warm waters in winter and can even be seen from shore.

The island group, between 40 miles (65 km) and 68 miles (110 km) southeast of Panama City, is named for the pearls found there. After wiping out the indigenous population, the early Spanish set up a pearl trade. Communities on **Isla Casaya** and neighboring **Isla Casayeta** still live on the profits of pearl diving.

Episodes of the TV series *Survivor* were filmed on unin-habited **Isla Mogo Mogo** and **Isla Chapera,** whose charms are typical. They feature beaches with sands like pulverized sugar, coral reefs patrolled by a kaleidoscope of fish, and lush forests roamed by anteaters, iguanas, and peccaries.

Tiny **Isla Contadora** is the most developed isle and is served by an airstrip. Multimillion-dollar vacation houses are nestled along Conta-dora's 11 gorgeous beaches. Even the largest and most developed of the beaches, **Playa Larga,** however, excels in wildlife viewing. Nearby **Playa de las Suecas** offers good snorkeling. Golfers can get into the swing on a nine-hole course, and **Las Perlas Sailing** *(tel 314-1800, lasperlassailing.com)* offers diving, fishing, and whale-watching.

The largest isle, 93-square-mile (240 sq km) **Isla del Rey,** has the sole town, San Miguel. The clear waters around the island offer some of Panama's best sportfishing, scuba diving, and

The white-sand beaches of Isla Contadora are launching pads for latter-day pearl hunters.

whale-watching. To the west, **Isla San José** hosts the island's most upscale hotel, the **Hacienda del Mar** (see Travelwise p. 239), which offers ATV tours, kayaking, and other activities. ∎

La Peregrina

The plump, pear-shaped "Peregrina Pearl," weighing more than .03 ounce (10 g), was discovered in the archipelago in the 16th century. Vasco Núñez de Balboa presented it to King Ferdinand V of Spain. It was later given as a gift to Mary Tudor (daughter of Henry VIII). In 1969 actor Richard Burton bought it for $37,000 for his beloved Elizabeth Taylor.

Archipiélago de las Perlas

🗺 91 C1 & C2

Visitor Information

✉ Contadora Welcome Center, Playa Galeon, Isla Contadora

☎ 250-4081

contadorapanama .com

More Places to Visit in Central Caribbean & the Canal

Ciudad del Saber

Spanning 297 acres (120 ha) of the former Fort Clayton U.S. Army base, the City of Knowledge comprises a broad-ranging number of Panamanian and international institutions dedicated to research. Initiated in 1999, the site today hosts such entities as the Smithsonian Tropical Research Institute, the Meteorological Center of Panama, and the Organization of American States. The former residence of the Commander-in-Chief of the Clayton base now serves as an interpretive center *(Bldg. 173, Gonzalo Crance St.)*, with exhibits on the history of the U.S. military in Panama.
cdspanama.org 🄰 91 B3 ✉ Clayton, 5 miles (8 km) NW of Balboa ☎ 306-3700

Corozal American Cemetery & Memorial

This beautifully landscaped 16-acre (6.5 ha) military cemetery, just off Avenida Omar Torrijos Herrera, in Clayton, near the Miraflores Locks, is cared for by the American Battle Monuments Commission. A paved path leads uphill from the visitor center to a memorial in the form of a rectangular granite obelisk under the Panamanian and U.S flags. Interred beneath rows of identical tombstones are the remains of 5,364 U.S. veterans and civilians associated with construction and/or operation of the canal. The oldest grave dates back to 1790.
abmc.gov/cemeteries-memorials 🄰 91 B3 ✉ Calle Rynicki, Clayton, 3 miles (5 km) NW of Balboa ☎ 317-6034

Galeta Point Marine Laboratory

The Smithsonian Institution operates Galeta Point Marine Laboratory, a science and marine education center created in 1997 on the site of a U.S. Navy satellite communications system. The facility has a visitor center where exhibits include a whale skeleton. Aquariums and marine pools display moray eels, sea stars, stingrays, and turtles. A boardwalk leads into the mangroves, where long-billed shorebirds pick for tasty morsels in the mudflats.
stri.org 🄰 91 A3 ✉ Isla Galeta, 3 miles (5 km) NE of Colón ☎ 212-8191 🕐 Closed Sat.–Sun. 💲 $$

Parque Nacional Camino de Cruces

Established in 1992, the 18-square-mile (46 sq km) national park connects Parque Nacional Soberanía (see pp. 100–101, 104) to the north and Parque Natural Metropolitano (see p. 71) to the south. Predominantly moist tropical forest, it also preserves portions of the eponymous treasure trail (see sidebar p. 101), which awaits excavation. The park hosts many of the same species as its neighbors, including slaty-tailed trogons.
anam.gob.pa 🄰 91 B3 ✉ Pedro Miguel, 7 miles (14 km) N of Balboa ☎ 500-0839

Sierra Llorona

Popular with birders, this 494-acre (200 ha) tropical forest reserve is centered on a modern ecolodge offering cozy accommodations (see Travelwise p. 240). More than 210 bird species have been spotted here along 2.5 miles (4 km) of trails that wind through the lowland and mid-elevation rain forest, as well as poison dart frogs, kinkajous, and various monkeys. Pre-dawn birding tours are offered. Observation platforms offer bird's-eye views of the canopy. A four-wheel-drive or high-chassis vehicle is essential for the bumpy, muddy road.
sierrallorona.com 🄰 91 A3 ✉ 2.8 miles (4.5 km) N of La Sabanita, 9 miles (14.5 km) SE of Colón ☎ 202-3166 💲 $$$

A glimpse into indigenous life in the Caribbean islands of the Archipiélago de San Blas

Kuna Yala

Detail of a reverse-appliqué *mola*, a Kuna specialty

Kuna Yala

The beautiful Archipiélago de San Blas is a seagirt wilderness of sandy coral islands that stretches for almost 140 miles (226 km) along Panama's Caribbean coast. Together, the island chain and a narrow mainland strip compose the Comarca de Kuna Yala, a district exclusively populated by Kuna people. Most Kuna live in 40 communities on palm-fringed islands—the majority no more than dots on a map—spread throughout the archipelago.

Kuna children enjoy simple pleasures at play on Isla Corbisky.

The *comarca* covers 2,151 square miles (5,570 sq km), extending from the ridgeline of the continental divide to the continental shelf offshore. The pencil-thin district stretches almost from Punta Cocoye in the west to Cabo Tiburón and the Colombian border. Close to half is marine territory speckled with coral cays and lush isles protected by an offshore coral reef.

The narrow mainland coastal strip is farmed with coconut palms and provides a hunting and agricultural ground for Kuna, who conscientiously preserve the virgin forests that shawl the Serranía de San Blas and Serranía del Darién mountains inland. In all these miles, only one road—a treacherous affair suitable only for the most rugged vehicles—penetrates the mountains to link the comarca to the rest of Panama. The Kuna wish to keep it that way and have

named the entire western mainland comarca a nature reserve.

These self-governing people protect their cultural identity and bloodlines with vigor. Foreigners are subject to Kuna local law, and

visitation by tourists is strictly regulated. Kuna even restrict who may fish in their waters, as well as what may be caught. Despite the beauty of the reefs, scuba diving is not permitted. The snorkeling, however, is unsurpassed.

The reception offered to tourists varies from isle to isle: welcoming and open on some, but reticent and wary on others. Visitors are expected to show respect for Kuna culture. Dress modestly away from the beach. Most villages are tightly packed warrens of humble bamboo-walled huts. Their sole appeal is the chance to experience an indigenous lifestyle close at hand and to photograph the exuberantly costumed women (the men dress Western fashion). The populated isles tend to be polluted with trash, and over-the-water toilets make swimming here a risky business. Still, you can paddle out in dugout canoes (*ulus*) to any of dozens of uninhabited private islands. Always, you'll be accompanied by one or more Kuna custodians, who will usually be happy to make you a meal of fresh fish.

Access requires boat or air travel. Air Panama (see Travelwise p. 229) serves airstrips throughout the archipelago with light aircraft; reserve well in advance. Boats can whisk you to smaller islands farther afield. With long distances between each island cluster, it is best to concentrate on one area. The few hotels that exist are rustic (extremely so, in most cases) and, like all businesses in the comarca, are

owned and operated exclusively by Kuna, who serve simple meals. There are few freestanding restaurants. A registration fee (*usually $3–$5*) is charged for each island visit (yachters must also pay a $5 anchorage fee at each isle). If traveling independently, you will need your passport, which must be presented immediately to local Kuna police.

Travel is made easier by booking travel and accommodations in advance through a tour operator in Panama City. Day trips are available. Kuna Yala is a cash-only society (there is only one bank in the comarca).

Yachters, take heed: These waters are tricky—easterly waters can be exceedingly rough—and drug-trafficking is common. A copy of *Cruising Guide to the Isthmus of Panama* by Nancy and Tom Schwalbe Zydler is a must. ■

NOT TO BE MISSED:

Snorkeling at Isla de los Perros 119

Dining with villagers at Bungalows Eco-Lodge La Chunga 123

Witnessing a *congreso* 124

Photographing the Kuna's rarely seen way of life 125

Bargaining for *molas* 126

Diving in the pristine waters of Bahía de Escribano 126

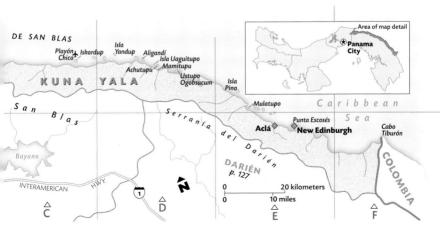

El Porvenir & Western Isles

With dozens of easily accessed islands to choose from, visitors typically pick the western group speckling the Golfo de San Blas. Cruise ships disgorge passengers en masse around the two hot spots of El Porvenir and Cartí. Each cluster offers fantastic snorkeling, while the Cayos Holandeses even boasts a number of wrecks.

Silken waters ring the picture-perfect isles of San Blas, such as Isla Pelícana.

Around El Porvenir

Lying about 1 mile (1.6 km) east of Punta de San Blas, the small island of **El Porvenir** (known to the Kuna as Gaigirgordup) is the main gateway to the western islands, as well as capital of the entire *comarca,* despite its minimal populace and facilities. The isle hosts an airstrip (unused at press time), a few bamboo-walled houses, a police station, a Kuna administrative post, and the **Museo de la Nación Kuna.** The small, two-story museum exhibits ceramics, kitchen utensils, musical instruments, baskets, and an example of a Kuna grave. Several nearby islands are within a few minutes' travel by boat.

Nearby **Wichub Huala** is one of the most popular islands. Large cruise ships often anchor offshore and disgorge as many as 1,000 passengers into the narrow village streets extending from one end of this tiny isle to the other. Almost every square inch seems taken up by Kuna women hawking exquisite *molas* (see sidebar p. 126).

Barely a stone's throw north of Wichub Huala, **Ukuptupu** is a rocky speck of an isle with a warren of wooden boardwalks connecting a hodgepodge of simple houses and a hotel that until 1998 served as a Smithsonian Tropical Research Institute facility.

Completing this small island grouping, beachless **Nalunega,** immediately southwest of El Porvenir, is cleaner and more endearing than neighboring and heavily polluted Wichub Huala, thanks to the efforts of the savvy Kuna owner of the local hotel, who organizes regular local cleanups. About 400 Kuna live here, surviving on fishing from sleek *ulus* (dugout canoes).

To escape the throngs, hire a local boatman to take you to **Isla de los Perros.** Sometimes called Achutupu (not to be mistaken with another Achutupu farther east), this exquisite cay represents everything that an idyllic tropical island should be. Isla de los Perros

INSIDER TIP:

Gain an insider's view of the Kuna and tourism by reading the informative work of Cebaldo de León, a Kuna anthropologist.

—PROF. XERARDO PEREIRO
*National Geographic
field researcher*

is perfect for snorkeling, with coral reefs edging right up to the whiter-than-white beach that rings the isle; a small shipwreck lies off the south shore. Jet-skiing and water-skiing are not allowed. The silence is absolute except for the soft music of ripples washing ashore. A single family owns the coconut palms (though not the land) and is in attendance when visitors are present. There's a bench and table

---

Kuna Phrase Book

The Kuna language, Duleigaiya, has only recently been transcribed into a written form and there is no standard for spelling, so many words have variants. Likewise, grammatical rules are flexible. Duleigaiya is highly symbolic, and profound meaning is attached to expression, signified by suffixes and prefixes tacked on to specific words. Kuna consonants differ from their closest Spanish or English equivalents, and vowels are approximations.

Here are some key words and phrases to know:

Anugaden . . . , My name is . . .
Beikeni ginika? What's your name?
Eiyei, Yes
Nuwedi, Catchall phrase meaning "good" (good morning, thank you)
Nuweigambi, Nice to meet you
Paneimalo, Good night, see you later
Suli, No
Takeimalo, Goodbye!

---

under palms, and the Kuna caretakers will sometimes cook up a meal by request.

Cartí & Around

The island town of **Cartí Sugtupu,** one of the largest settlements in the Kuna comarca, lies a stone's throw from the mainland airstrip. A post office, public library, and other key services for the western isles are concentrated here, although the sole accommodation is a rustic dorm, and the trash littering the streets and shores is an eyesore. Favored as a port of call by cruise ships, Cartí can be congested with swarms of tourists. The highlight is the small **Kuna Museum of Culture,** honoring

El Porvenir
🗺 116 A2

Museo de la Nación Kuna
✉ El Porvenir
☎ 316-1232
💲 $
onmaked.nativeweb.org

Cartí Sugtupu
🗺 116 B2

Kuna Museum of Culture
✉ Cartí Sugtupu
☎ 299-9002 or 6085-9592
💲 $

local culture and mythology. Bilingual guides are on hand to explain the artifacts. Water taxis serve the mainland wharf, which can be accessed by a horrendously muddy road that connects to El Lano on the Interamerican Highway (see sidebar below).

A hop, skip, and jump across the waters, **Isla Aguja** offers a strikingly pristine contrast and is perfect for lazing all day on the beach beneath the shade of palms.

Cayos Los Grullos & Holandeses

The densely populated twin communities of **Río Sidra** (aka Ursadup) and neighboring **Nusatupo,** 9.5 miles (15 km) east of Cartí, are served by a mainland airstrip and are the main gateway to **Cayos Los Grullos,** a dozen or so tiny cays

grouped together some 6 miles (10 km) northeast of Nusatupo. Devoid of tourist facilities, the Los Grullos cays are prime snorkeling spots, with calm bays for yachters.

Competing for diamond-dust beaches and transparent blue waters, **Narasgandup Pipi** (sometimes called Naranjo Chico), 2 miles (3.5 km) northwest of Nusatupo, is another perfect spot in which to laze in a hammock beneath palm trees. It has crude accommodations.

Looking like it dropped from a picture postcard, **Kuanidup** is a diminutive, exquisite palm-shaded isle midway between El Porvenir and Río Sidra.

Recognized for its *mola*-making tradition, **Isla Máquina,** about 2 miles (3.2 km) from Río Sidra, is less polluted and more laid-back than the latter and makes for delightful strolling. On Río Sidra, local Kuna transvestite and master mola-maker Lisa Harris *(tel 6753-2085)* has a small museum of outstanding molas.

Sprinkled enticingly like pieces of eight over the edge of the continental shelf, the **Cayos Holandeses** compose a cluster of deserted isles about 19 miles (30 km) from shore. Surf crashes up against the jagged reef edge. **Wreck Reef** is named for the Spanish galleons and other ships that foundered there. Centuries later, sublime snorkeling awaits the adventurous traveler. English-speaking Kuna guide Elías Pérez *(tel 6708-5254)* can take you kayaking and snorkeling at Cayos Holandeses. ∎

Stick in the Mud

Cartí is great to visit, but the dirt road linking Cartí with the Interamerican Highway *(At El Llano, 11 miles/18 km E of Chepo)* **is not for the fainthearted. It's a brutal drive, especially in rainy season, when sinking deep into vacuum-like mud is likely. Even in dry season, the route is usually impassable to all but the biggest high-clearance, four-wheel-drive vehicles. Bring a chain for winching yourself out; you don't want to get stuck in the rain forest.**

Narganá & Central Isles

Hugging the coastline of the central *comarca,* with the Serranía de San Blas rising tight behind like a frozen sea of billowing waves, these widely dispersed isles are less traditional, for the most part, than islands to west and east. Nonetheless, you'll leave bearing a treasure of colorful memories.

Narganá is an administrative center joined by a long, arching footbridge to **Corazón de Jesús,** a small peninsula with an airstrip. These twin isles have little appeal, with mostly concrete houses, the community having been sucked into the vortex of Western modes. Still, Narganá has the only bank in Kuna Yala, plus a hospital. A bronze **statue of Carlos Inaediguine Robinson** (an educator and leader of the 1925 Kuna Revolt) marks the village square; his birthday is celebrated each August 20 with music, dance, and excessive drinking.

Río Azúcar, 3 miles (5 km) west of Narganá, is another crowded island with telephones, a medical center, and other services that draw yachters. It has been a focal point for missionary work in recent years, despite which it hosts a Carnaval bacchanal at Easter.

Culturally perhaps the most vibrant and intriguing of all the San Blas islands, **Isla Tigre,** some 4.5 miles (7 km) east of Narganá, is kept spic and span, its streets swept clean by conscientious Kuna. Uniquely, too, the local people go about their traditional lives with little regard for tourists. Visitors can roam freely without being badgered to buy, though you must still report upon arrival

Kuna children on Isla Playón Chico

to the local tourism commission. A dramatic reenactment of the Kuna Revolt of 1925 is held each February 25, and in mid-October the island hosts a weeklong festival of music and dance.

Small planes serve **Playón Chico,** another crowded modern community that serves as a jumping-off point for forays to neighboring isles such as tiny **Isla Yandup** (*yandupisland.com*), a coral-fringed cay good for snorkeling; it has a small hotel. Pinprick-size **Iskardup** boasts fine accommodations with the **Sapibenega Kuna Lodge** (see Travelwise p. 243). The English-speaking hotel owner leads jungle hikes into the mainland mountains, including to the **Ibe Igar** waterfall and a Kuna burial ground. ■

Narganá
🄼 116 B2

Kuna Culture

Fierce defenders of tribal tradition, the Kuna people cling tightly to an indigenous culture that is one of the most colorful and intact in the New World. Whether in Panama City, Penonomé, or the islands of their *comarca* (autonomous district), Kuna women are instantly recognizable in their colorful skirts and blouses adorned with *molas* in primary colors.

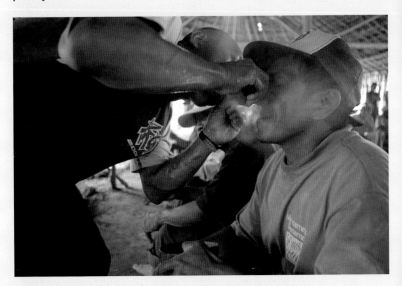

A Kuna blows smoke in an elder's nostril (above). Painted noses are marks of beauty (opposite).

According to their oral tradition, the Kuna (or Tule, as they sometimes refer to themselves) originally lived in the forests of Darién. Around the time of the Spanish arrival, warfare with the encroaching Emberá-Wounaan and, possibly, with the Spaniards forced the Kuna northward into the Serranía de Panamá and Caribbean plains and, later, to the islands offshore. About 70,000 Kuna survive today, of whom about 32,000 inhabit the islands and as many as 30,000 occupy the Panamanian diaspora.

A diminutive people averaging about 5 feet (1.5 m) in height—only the Pygmies of Africa are smaller—the Kuna have slender, sinewy limbs and disproportionately large heads, with aquiline noses esteemed as a sign of beauty.

They speak Duleigaiya, the Kuna language (see sidebar p. 119), and protect their tribal bloodlines assiduously: Anyone marrying outside the tribe is expelled. Insularity promotes interbreeding; perhaps as a result of this, rates of albinism here are the highest in the world. The ancient tradition of killing albinos at birth has given way to reverence. Today albinos are considered specially chosen and gifted "Moon children," born after a pregnant women is supposedly exposed to the full moon. Albino boys are trained in the ways of women and can often be seen stitching or selling *molas* in the cool shade.

Matriarchal Society

Kuna society is matriarchal. Women control the local real estate, mostly composing simple thatched huts walled with stiff reeds or cane and with bare earth for floors. The ground beneath their feet, however, is owned in common by the community and has prevented the division of Kuna society into "haves" and "have nots." A man moves into his lover's home to signal marriage and simply moves out again to enact a divorce. While the men don mask and flippers to dive for lobsters for sale to passing yachts and to tourists, the women fill the family coffers by stitching and selling their colorful molas to an international market.

A girl's passage into womanhood is celebrated by the entire community, when a surfeit of *chicha* is drunk. At puberty, women cut their hair short and henceforth cover their head with a bloodred *muswe* (shawl). Their daily attire is a *saburet* (skirt) worn over a *bicha* (petticoat) held by a *mudub* (belt). Although Western lipstick has made inroads, many women still paint their cheeks with *achiote,* a natural rouge obtained from the achiote seed, and paint a black line of tagua dye down the length of their nose. The ensemble is completed by large gold earrings and nose rings, plus necklaces of colored beads, used also to create beaded bracelets to decorate their forearms and ankles. By contrast, the men go unadorned in Western clothing.

Both women and men are skilled in their use of dugout *cayucos* or *ulus* (canoes), ferrying between islands propelled by paddle or urged along by a triangular sail. At daybreak, some men set sail to go lobstering and fishing, while others head to the mainland to fetch water, attend to subsistence lots, and collect coconuts for sale or barter to

EXPERIENCE: Appreciating the Indigenous Life

The Spanish occupation proved devastating to indigenous cultures throughout Central America, yet Panama today has several tribes that continue to thrive, despite various contemporary pressures. The Kuna, Emberá-Wounaan, and Ngöbe-Buglé live in scattered villages throughout their own semiautonomous *comarcas* (administrative units). Many Kuna villages now subsist almost exclusively on the tourist trade; some have become heavily westernized, while others cling tightly to their traditional customs.

Tourism is also now being promoted as a way of fostering a renewed pride in traditional beliefs, crafts, and customs among Emberá-Wounaan and Ngöbe-Buglé communities. Permits are not required to visit the reserves.

A visit to these indigenous communities will give you a sound appreciation of traditional lifestyles and the strength of indigenous pride:

The rustic **Bungalows Eco-Lodge La Chunga** (*tel 6655-0984, traveldarien panama.com*), at La Chunga, is set in the heart of an Emberá village. It is designed in traditional Wounaan manner, and guests dine with local villagers.

Kuna Yala offers dozens of islands where you can fully immerse yourself in colorful Kuna lifestyle. Base yourself at the **Sapibenega Kuna Lodge** (see Travelwise p. 243) on Iskardup.

Soposo Rainforest Adventures (*tel 6631-2222, soposo.com*), on the edge of Parque Internacional La Amistad upriver from Changuinola, is a Naso community with a rustic lodge.

Colombian schooners. As many as 30 million coconuts may be harvested in a year and sold at a price fixed (strictly enforced) by community elders. Although the beauty of Kuna women hides the economic plight of most Kuna families, they are not at all preoccupied with the fact that they are poor economically. In fact, the Kuna are rich in spirit and resourcefulness.

The Kuna comarca is divided into four districts, each presided over by an elected chief, or *sahila,* under a supreme sahila who chairs a six-monthly *congreso,* or *onmaket nega,* of village heads. Every village has its own daily congreso headed by its own sahila versed in Kuna traditions; all males over 18 must attend the Sunday sessions or face a fine. Custodians of sacred rites, the village *absoguedi* (chanter) and *nele* (shaman) employ spiritually alive wooden human figures called *nuchus* to divine and cure human sickness. Like scribes in a Dickensian novel, an army of secretaries maintains records and writes countless permits issued (for a fee) to individuals wishing, for example, to visit

INSIDER TIP:

Yandup Island Lodge *[tel 202-0854]* is the best intercultural experience in the area. There you can enjoy Kuna culture and nature in an intensive way.

—PROF. XERARDO PEREIRO
National Geographic field researcher

another village or travel outside the comarca.

The Kuna are deep believers in a spirit world, in which every natural thing is possessed of a positive guardian spirit. *Poni*—evil spirits—also roam the land; to guard against them, the Kuna use nuchus carved of balsa. The Kuna practice a kinship with the forests and land; to deforest the land, for example, will bring harm to the community. Nonetheless, the Kuna fish indiscriminately. The lobster population has suffered greatly, and marine turtles are now rarely seen in these waters.

A fisherman heads to work in a traditional Kuna watercraft as the sun rises over the Caribbean Sea near Achutupu in the San Blas Archipelago.

Eastern Isles

These dark green cays rising out of the water in a long line like a Spanish flotilla are beyond the reach of easy boat travel from points farther west. Airstrips serve the main islands. Boasting some of the most exquisite of all the San Blas islands, this part of the world offers visitors a chance to see Panama through the eyes of an explorer.

Lacking an offshore coral reef, these isles are subject to battering by high seas in stormy weather. Ocean passage can be tricky and even risky. Colombian drug-smuggling boats run these waters, while paramilitary and guerrilla groups occasionally infiltrate the coastal strip.

The main airstrip for the isles is in densely populated **Achutupu,** centered on a large community hall. A mere 200 yards (183 m) west of Achutupu, the more intimate **Isla Uaguitupo** (aka Uaguinega) is almost entirely taken up by the Dolphin Island Lodge (see Travelwise p. 242) one of the best hotels on the isle; tours are offered from here.

Ailigandí, 3 miles (5 km) west of Achutupu, crams 1,200 Kuna into its impossibly small compass. The isle is studded with statues and painted with political murals commemorating the 1925 Kuna revolt; the **Instituto Nacional de Cultura** teaches *mola* techniques. Nearby, less visited **Mamitupu** has a local cooperative making coconut oil products, such as soap. Worldly-wise local Kuna Pablo Núñez Perez acts as an informal tour guide and will paddle out to greet you in his dugout canoe if you arrive by yacht at Mamitupu.

Farther east, **Mulatupo,** with one of the largest populations in

A domesticated parrot takes in village life from its window perch in Ailigandi.

the San Blas chain, is a stepping-stone to the mainland coast. From here you can visit **Aclá,** founded in 1515 as the first Spanish settlement on the Spanish Main and, at **Punta Escosés,** New Edinburgh, founded in 1698 (see p. 30). ∎

Eastern Isles

⚠ 117 D2–F2

Shutter-Happy Etiquette

Kuna children with a photogenic smile and parrots on their shoulders will have you reaching for your camera posthaste. First, be sure you have plenty of dollar bills at hand. The rarely waived rule is $1 per photo. The rate usually doesn't apply to scenics or group shots, such as ceremonial dances, although pointing a camera at a group of Kuna women usually causes most of them to cover their faces. Never photograph without asking permission. Kuna village elders enforce the rules, and merely carrying a camcorder can result in being charged $10 to $50 or more. Some islands are more tolerant than others.

More Places to Visit in Kuna Yala

Área Silvestre Corregimiento de Narganá

The mountainous Narganá Wilderness Area—a 230-square-mile (596 sq km) swathe of virgin rain forest inhabited solely by wild animals—serves as a barrier intentionally isolating the *comarca* from the rest of the country. It is also a buffer zone against intrusion by non-Indians and by loggers with their eyes on deforestation. The park merges with Parque Nacional Chagres to the west and extends from the continental divide to the Caribbean coast. The birding is the equal of anywhere in Panama. More than 400 species have been seen here: keel-billed toucans, black-crowned antpittas, sulphur-rumped tanagers, blue-headed parrots, and more. Birding is best from December to June.

Molas

Layered in textured meaning, brightly colored *molas* are world-renowned symbols of Kuna culture. Originating as decorative blouse panels, these oblong works of art averaging about 18 inches (46 cm) wide are made of several layers of cotton cloth of contrasting colors. Patterns are cut into the separate layers, which are then hand-stitched together—a process called reverse appliqué. The basic designs usually represent parrots, butterflies, and other symbols of nature, although abstract patterns are also produced. The mutlilayering produces a 3-D effect.

On the islands, vendors display their molas in the open. Bargain, but expect no more than a 10 percent discount off the asking price, which begins at about $15. Larger, superior molas can cost $500 or more. Look for a well-balanced design, harmonious colors, evenly spaced lines, and almost invisible stitches.

Burbayar Lodge (see Travelwise p. 242) is a Kuna-run ecolodge on the edge of the reserve at a springlike 1,200-foot (375 m) elevation. Six trails (including the **Kuna Medicinal Forest Trail**) of varying difficulty lead into the lodge's own 122-acre (50 ha) rain forest reserve, good for spotting poison dart frogs, vine snakes, bats, iguanas, families of monkeys, pumas, jaguars, and tapirs. You can even hike to Cartí (6 to 10 hrs.). Access to Burbayar is easy by four-wheel-drive; beyond Burbayar, the road deteriorates rapidly.
🅐 116 A1–B2 ✉ Nusagandi, 12.5 miles (20 km) N of El Llano, on Interamerican Hwy. ☎ 236-6061

Bahía de Escribano

This serene bay, just outside the Kuna Yala comarca, about 10 miles (16 km) west of El Porvenir, is protected by an offshore barrier reef called Baja Escribano, 3 miles (4.8 km) out. Gin-clear waters wash onto beaches of pure white radiance. The pristine coral reefs offer breathtaking diving. Almost 70 species of hard corals and more than 60 species of sponges provide a pelagic playground for a star-studded cast: barracudas, giant groupers, manta rays, harmless nurse sharks, and moray eels peering out from their coral crevices at the dizzying array of damsels, tangs, wrasses and an extravaganza of other rainbow-hued fish. In 1501, Spanish explorer Rodrigo de Bastidas became the first European to land in Panama when he stepped ashore here. Later, pirates Henry Morgan and Sir Francis Drake used the bay as a staging ground to ambush Spanish galleons. For years the bay has drawn yachters to its white sands. In 2006, the first hotel opened. **Coral Lodge Resort** (see Travelwise p. 243), accessible solely by plane and boat, offers diving and kayaking.
🅐 116 A2 ✉ By yacht or by boat transfer from El Porvenir

The largest pristine wilderness habitat in Central America, a birder's and nature lover's dream

Darién

Many remote places are reached
by *cayuco*.

Darién

Named for an Indian chief, this vast eastern third of the country is renowned for rain forests so thick that the last leg of the Interamerican Highway still has not come through. A mother lode of biodiversity, sparsely populated Darién Province provides unexcelled birding and wildlife viewing—though relatively few places are accessible.

The Río Sambú snakes through the forests and clear-cut fields of Darién.

The Interamerican Highway, unfurling east as far as Yaviza, is the sole highway access to this region. Completed to this point in 1977, the road brought a rapid influx of mestizo settlers and massive deforestation. Today there are two Dariéns: the wounded western half speckled along the highway with recently established, albeit tiny, townships; and eastern Darién, still smothered in virginal rain forest enshrined within 2,236-square-mile (5,791 sq km) Parque Nacional Darién, a UNESCO World Heritage site.

Virtually uninhabited, this creepered Amazonian world is accessed by airstrips and by long narrow dugout *cayucos* (canoes). Up the black tannic rivers are remote Emberá and Wounaan Indian villages predominantly found in two semiautonomous districts, the Comarca Emberá Cémaco and Comarca Emberá Sambú. Although creeping Westernization is altering Emberá-Wounaan lifestyles, many ancient traditions endure, including hunting with *boroquera* (blowgun) and poison-tipped darts.

Framing the region to the northeast, the rugged Serranía del Darién coastal mountain range separates Darién from the Comarca de Kuna Yala. The long and lonesome western shoreline is also backed by the Serranía del Sapo and Sierra de Jungurudó, winding southward into the Colombian Andes. The mountains rise to heights exceeding 6,000 feet (1,800 m), and ethereal mists swirl through

NOT TO BE MISSED:

the treetops of classic montane cloud forest—one of Parque Nacional Darién's five distinct life zones. Countless rivers cascade onto broad plains to pour into the Golfo de San Miguel, where on September 25, 1513, Vasco Núñez de Balboa first sighted the Pacific Ocean.

The first Spanish colonial settlements in Panama were established in Darién, spawned by discovery of the Cana gold mines. The precious metal was ferried downriver in canoes and loaded on larger ships to be carried north to the Camino Real; Spanish forts built to guard the port at the mouth of the Río Tuira peer out from the luxuriant biomass. Today, Cana is a gold mine for hikers and birders. Punta Patiño Nature Reserve offers an alternative wildlife experience and is a short boat ride from

La Palma, the provincial capital, in the Golfo de San Miguel.

Many settlements are guarded by heavily armed police, a reminder that parts of the national park and the Comarca Emberá Cémaco are a hideout for a variety of outlaws spilling over the uncontrolled Colombian border. The best way to explore these zones is with an accredited guide or reputable tour company (see Travelwise p. 264). ■

Along the Interamerican Highway

Part of the Pan-American Highway stretching from the tip of Alaska to Tierra del Fuego, the 3,400-mile (5,470 km) Interamerican Highway links Central American nations from Nuevo Laredo, in Mexico, to Yaviza, 172 miles (276 km) east of Panama City. Forested mountains rise above the deforested landscape, a setting for welcoming Kuna and Emberá hamlets.

Villages along the Interamerican Highway such as Santa Fé provide glimpses into local life.

Interamerican Highway

🅰 129 A3, A4, B3, & C2

Visitor Information

☎ 500-0855 (ANAM) or 299-6530 (Metetí)

anam.gob.pa

Chepo to Ipetí

The gateway to Darién Province is **Chepo,** 33 miles (53 km) east of the heart of Panama City. While the town, which lies 2 miles (3.2 km) south of the highway, is within eastern Panamá Province, Panamanians consider this to be the Darién frontier, as it was here that the highway once ended. Onward travel was by canoe from **Puerto Coquira,** where *cayucos* still set out down the Río Chepo, roosting site for anhingas and the largest colony of cattle egrets in Panama.

East of Chepo, **Lago Bayano** spreads across the valley like a pool of mercury. Covering 86,000 acres (35,000 ha), the U-shaped lake was created in 1975 when the Ascanio Villalaz hydroelectric dam was built across the Río Bayano. You can rent a boat *($$$)* at **Bayano** for a 45-minute ride to **Cuevas Bayano,** bat-filled caves that lie along the Río Tigre. Feeling like Indiana Jones, you can explore the chambers—often up to your chest in cold water. **Panama Outdoors** *(tel 261-5043, panama outdoors.com/cuevas_bayano.html)* offers guided tours.

Most of the lake lies within the **Comarca de Kuna de Madugandí,** an 800-square-mile (2,073 sq km) semiautonomous region created in 1996 and adjoining the Comarca de Kuna Yala. About 5,000 Kuna inhabitants in 12 communities struggle to maintain their cultural identity since the opening of the Interamerican Highway. The community of **Ipetí Kuna,** tucked 1 mile (1.6 km) north of the highway, welcomes visitors with ceremonial dances. Local guide Igua Jiménez *(tel 6595-9500, redturs.org)* leads tours. The villagers of **Ipetí Emberá,** 0.6 mile (1 km) south of the highway, also perform traditional ceremonial dances, sell crafts, and offer trips by *piragua* along the Río Ipetí. The village has simple thatched lodging in a characteristic open-walled house raised on stilts.

Santa Fé to Yaviza

Santa Fé, 32 miles (51 km) east of Ipetí and 2 miles (3.2 km) west of the highway, is a river town on the east bank of the Río Sabanas. **ECODIC** *(tel 6739-0853)* is a community development project that makes soaps and colorful murals for sale; you can hike forest trails and learn about organic farming at its agricultural station, Finca Sonia *(tel 299-6951)*. At high tide, piraguas travel 5 miles (8 km) downriver to **Boca de Lara,** a Wounaan community also accessible from the Interamerican Highway by four-wheel-drive. Here you can sleep local fashion in a thatched open-walled lodge. **Canopy Camp Darien** *(Metetí, tel 264-5720, canopytower.com)* offers trips to Boca de Lara.

Giant cuipo trees tower over Canopy Camp Darien, adjoining a hydrological reserve east of Metetí. Surrounded by lowland tropical forest, this new safari-style ecolodge is a birder's dream: Tody flycatchers, barred puffbirds, and Golden-headed manakins are among the species easily seen from your tent's observation deck—a chance to also spy monkeys, kinkajous, tamanduas, and perhaps even snakes.

Metetí, the major settlement between Chepo and Yaviza, has spartan hotels. A paved road leads west 12 miles (20 km) to ramshackle Puerto Quimba, bustling

---

The Monster of Lago Bayano

The lake, one of Panama's few breeding sites for the Cocoi heron and neotropical cormorant, is named for a warrior leader of *cimarrones*—escaped African slaves—who led a fierce resistance to Spanish rule. According to local belief, a Loch Ness–like monster inhabits the lake.

---

with water traffic in the Golfo de San Miguel (see pp. 138–139).

Sordid accommodations fit the melancholy mood of **Yaviza,** at the end of the road 165 miles (266 km) from Panama City. Journeying solo beyond Yaviza is ill-advised. After registering your arrival at the police station, take time to scout the ruins of the **Fuerte San Jerónimo de Yaviza,** an 18th-century Spanish fortress overhanging the Río Chucunaque. ■

Driving the Interamerican Highway

This journey, an adventurous escape along perhaps the most famous highway in the world, delivers you quite literally to the end of the road. Beyond that, a 70-mile (106 km) swathe of dense rain forest spanning the country coast to coast comprises the infamous Darién Gap—the only unbridged section along the entire 16,000-mile (25,800 km) route of the highway between the tips of Alaska and Argentina.

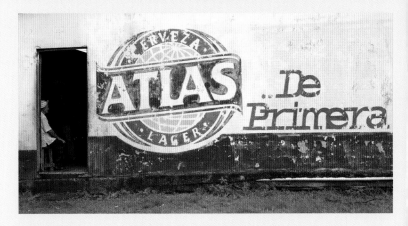

Simple roadside cantinas, such as this one in Cañita, provide gathering spots for locals.

Although the road is paved for the first three-quarters of the trip, conditions then deteriorate markedly and you will need a four-wheel-drive vehicle to proceed. Even so, reaching Yaviza, where the road peters out, may prove impossible in wet season.

The journey is mostly flat as the highway unfurls along a broad valley hemmed by the Serranía de San Blas and Serranía de Majé mountains. Cut into the virgin jungle in the 1970s, the highway's construction ushered in an era of deforestation. The few sites of interest are separated by long stretches of cattle pasture. Accommodations along the route are few and mostly dismal, and militarized police checkpoints are reminders that venturing beyond Yaviza is a foolhardy notion. Plan on a same-day, round-trip journey, setting out in early morning. *You will need your passport.*

NOT TO BE MISSED:

Lago Bayano • Ipetí Kuna • Ipetí Emberá • Zapallal

Begin in **Chepo ❶,** a quiet, colorful town discreetly hidden 2 miles (3.5 km) south of the Interamerican Highway, 33 miles (53 km) east of Panama City. A police checkpoint and a statue of St. Christopher with a child on his shoulder mark the junction, east of which the highway undulates along the southern lee of the Serranía de San Blás. After 24 miles (39 km), silvery **Lago Bayano ❷** (see pp. 130–131) comes into view. You'll need to present your passport at the police checkpoint in the community of **Bayano,** where Kuna women in traditional costumes add bright notes of color. Crossing over the lake on an iron bridge, you enter the Comarca de Kuna de Madugandí tribal territory. For the next 20 miles (32 km) the road is fringed by forest and is a veritable freeway for butterflies and parrots.

The forest fades beyond **Quebrada Calí**, opening the vistas southward toward the sawtoothed Serranía de Majé. Farther east, the tiny community of **Ipetí Kuna** ❸ (see p. 131) sells *molas*. After visiting this village and the nearby Emberá village of **Ipetí Emberá,** your route is now lined with pastures studded with freestanding mahoganies. The roadside community of **Tortí** is known for its *feria* featuring rodeos and bull taunting in late March, and for the manufacture of handcrafted saddles; the *talabarterías* (leather workshops) face each other across the street. Passing teak plantations, you

arrive at **Aguas Frías** ❹, with a police checkpoint and billboard that reads "Welcome to Darién." Some 13 miles (20 km) farther, take a break at **Emberá Arimae** (aka Los Monos), known for its artistic traditions; the community sells crafts and welcomes visitors.

The asphalt that begins in Alaska ends at the Afro-colonial community of **Zapallal** ❺. From here on, you'll kick up dust or mud as you slog south to **Metetí,** where police at the fortified checkpoint may discourage your onward passage. Metetí has a gas station and bank.

East of Metetí the highway becomes an embarrassment to road engineers; in wet season, you should call a halt here. Your speed is halved and then quartered as the going deteriorates with every mile until it fizzles out in **Yaviza** ❻, a dilapidated, vaguely menacing frontier town beyond which the fur-thick jungle takes over.

⬛ See also area map p. 129
➤ Chepo
🕐 5 hours one way
↔ 127 miles (204 km)
➤ Yaviza

Parque Nacional Darién

Larger than any other national park in Central America, Darién has earned a reputation for some of the region's best wildlife viewing. From tiny poison dart frogs to the world's largest eagle, this foreboding mini-Amazon is a crown jewel of rain forest and wetland biota whose enormous appeal is well worth the discomforts of sodden humidity and rains.

A hut with a view at Cana, deep in the heart of Parque Nacional Darién

Parque Nacional Darién

🏛 129 C1–C2

✉ El Real de Santa María

☎ 299-6965 or 299-6530

💲 $$ (permit compulsory)

anam.gob.pa

A vast oasis of biodiversity, the park was established in 1980 to protect 2,236 square miles (5,791 sq km) of lowland rain forest, as well as a range of other life zones extending from mangrove swamps to premontane rain forest atop 6,150-foot (1,875 m) **Cerro Tacarcuna.** Stretching virtually the length of the Panamanian-Colombian border, entire sections of the park are infiltrated by guerrillas, narco-traffickers, and bandits, and travel outside established secure zones is dangerous. Travel only with a knowledgeable guide and/or reputable tour company. The only facilities for overnighting are at Pirre and Cana.

The National Authority for the Environment (Autoridad Nacional del Ambiente, or ANAM) park headquarters is at the riverside town of El Real de Santa María (see p. 142), from which you can hike (4 hrs.; dry season only) or travel by canoe to ANAM's **Pirre Station,** on the banks of the Río Peresenico in the heart of the lowland rain forest. Pirre has a dormitory with meager facilities. Bring your own food and flashlight; there is no electricity.

Set deep in the heart of the park, **Cana,** at a 1,500-foot (457 m) elevation on the eastern slopes of **Cerro Pirre,** offers more comforts and is an exhilarating site for birding. It is accessible only by foot. This biological research station run by the Asociación para la Conservación de la Natureleza (ANCON) also serves as an ecolodge operated by Ancon Expeditions (see Travelwise p. 244).

Stupendous Wildlife

Declared a UNESCO World Heritage site in 1981 and a Biosphere Reserve in 1982, this biological Eden boasts wildlife in abundance. Darién hosts viable populations of 56 species endangered elsewhere. Harpy eagles are commonly sighted, as are tapirs. Chances of seeing any of the five big cat species are greater here than anywhere else in the nation. So, too, white-lipped peccaries, tamanduas, sloths, and a variety of monkeys.

Exotically painted poison dart frogs hop about on the dank forest floor; crocodiles and caimans splash about in the rivers. More than 450 bird species have been recorded here, including blue-and-yellow, great green, and red-and-green macaws.

Hiking

You need not venture far from Pirre or Cana to get close to the wildlife. Bring waterproof hiking shoes for the muddy trails, plus bug spray and water. Watch out for venomous snakes, not least for fer-de-lances, large, well-camouflaged pit vipers with brown-and-black backs whose bite can be fatal in minutes. *Do not hike without a guide.* If you get lost or are injured in the forest,

your odds of survival are slim.

From Pirre, a 1.5-mile-long (2 km) trail leads to a series of exquisite cascades; for safety, avoid the temptation to climb the falls. The steep **Sendero Cerro Pirre** offers a greater challenge going up Cerro Pirre but pays off with views over the river valley.

Four-Wheel Driving

If the Indiana Jones within is hankering to explore Panama, a four-wheel-drive (4WD) vehicle is a must (see Travelwise pp. 229–230). Access to much of the highlands (and Darién) is via badly potholed, rock-strewn, and/or corrugated unpaved roads.

Dusty in dry season, these roads turn to a bouillabaisse in the wet, when fording rivers can add to the challenge. Even paved roads can quickly wash out in rainy season. In some areas—notably Highway 4 over the Cordillera de Tabasará in Chiriquí—landslides are common.

Without doubt 4WD exploration can be fun, turning touring into a true adventure. However, even with 4WD vehicles you have to know when to quit. Most major agencies rent 4WDs.

Five trails originate at Cana. One, a short and easy hike along the **Sendero Máquina,** leads to rusted 19th-century locomotives. The 6-mile-long (9 km) **Sendero Cerro Pirre** ascends Cerro Pirre to a tent camp swaddled in high-elevation cloud forest; from here the **Sendero Bosque Nuboso** offers opportunities for spotting the golden-headed quetzal. Trails also lead from the ANAM ranger station at **Rancho Frío,** a three-hour walk from El Real; one leads to the summit of Pirre. ■

Poison Dart Frogs

Breathtaking in their beautiful coloration, poison dart frogs inhabit the warm moist forests of the neotropics of Central and South America. Most are no bigger than a thumbnail, though a few grow to 2 inches (5 cm) long. Notwithstanding their diminutive size, these tiny critters produce some of the deadliest toxins known to science.

Diminutive poison dart frogs can be deadly to predators.

The vividly colored frogs are members of the Dendrobatidae family. New species are still being discovered, such as *Dendrobates claudiae,* first identified on Panama's Isla Bastimentos in 2000. Of the 170 or so recognized species, only one-third are known to be toxic.

Poison dart frogs produce bitter-tasting alkaloid compounds that are stored in microscopic mucous glands beneath the frog's skin; they cause any hungry predator to instantly gag. The most potent toxin of all is batrachotoxin (from *batrachos,* the Greek word for "frog"), produced uniquely by the three extraordinarily lethal species of *Phyllobates* genus. Found only in Darién and Colombia's Andean lowlands, these are the true "poison dart" frogs after whom the entire family is named. Emberá-Wounaan

Indians have traditionally used *Phyllobates's* secretions to coat the tips of the blow darts they use to hunt monkeys and other game. The frogs typically secrete their deadly potions when they feel stressed or threatened. However, the silvery yellow, 2-inch-long (5 cm) *Phyllobates terribilis* even without being agitated is lethal to the touch for humans—the Emberá-Wounaan need do no more than wipe their darts along its back. This frog's rare neurotoxin, 250 times more potent than strychnine, is so deadly that a toxin-tipped dart can remain lethal for more than a year.

Toxicity

The frogs derive their specific toxicity from their diets. The *Phyllobates's* batrachotoxin, for example, is ingested from a little-known group of tiny beetles of the *Choresine* genus that contain high concentrations of the neurotoxin. When placed in captivity and removed from their natural diets, the amphibians gradually lose their toxicity.

Nature's neon touch-me-nots advertise their toxicity through brilliant coloration that serves as a warning to potential predators. While some are uniform in coloration, typically they have a predominant Day-Glo color on top (usually bright red, orange, green, or blue) and a secondary color (usually yellow, red, white, blue, or black) underneath, often appearing as spots or speckles. The frog species of Bocas del Toro Archipelago vary from island to island. For example, they are green on Isla Popa, green and black on Isla Taboga, dark blue on Cerro Brujo, yellow with

INSIDER TIP:

While surveying the forest floor, look for long lines of leaf-cutter ants marching along, each one hoisting a little green bit over its back.

—JENNIFER HOLLAND
National Geographic *magazine writer*

black dots on Isla Bocas, and ripe-strawberry red on Isla Bastimentos.

Most poison dart frogs are ground dwellers, looking like little enameled porcelain figures on the moist forest floor. Boldly diurnal, they hop around by day secure from predation. Males aggressively defend their territories against rivals and can often be seen wrestling chest to chest like miniature sumos. Uniquely immune to the frog's toxin, the fire-bellied snake *(Leimadophis epinephelus)* is the amphibians' only natural predator.

Poison dart frogs lay their eggs among the leaf litter and go to great lengths to safeguard their precious offspring, who lack toxins. Once

The Birds & the Bugs

The frogs' batrachotoxin is shared with New Guinea's insectivorous blue-capped ifrita and the *Pitohui* genus of birds, all of which have toxic feathers and skin. Both the birds and the *Phyllobates* frogs eat *Choresine* beetles, whose own batrachotoxin serves as defense against predation. The frogs and birds have evolved a resistance to the bug's toxin, guaranteeing them an exclusive food source.

the eggs hatch, one parent loads the tiny tadpoles on its back and carries them one at a time into the trees, where it deposits them in water-filled leafy funnels of bromeliads. While most other frog species typically abandon the young tadpoles, female poison dart frogs visit their babies every few days to feed them by depositing unfertilized eggs in the water.

Dendrobates azureus comes in various shades of blue, from powder to cobalt, although poison dart frogs can also be red, green, or yellow.

La Palma & Golfo de San Miguel

The Golfo de San Miguel forms the watery gateway to Darién. Humpback whales can often be seen frolicking in the ultrawarm waters into which Vasco Núñez de Balboa waded in 1513, sweating and laden with armor, after stepping from the jungle to claim the Pacific for Spain.

Ibises are among the many bird species easily seen along the shores of the Golfo de San Miguel.

La Palma

⬛ 129 B2

Visitor Information

✉ ATP, La Palma
c/o Mabel del
Carmen Viñuela

☎ 299-6337

darien@atp.gob.pa

La Palma, the region's ugly duckling provincial capital, occupies the tip of a crocodile-shaped peninsula at the mouth of the Río Tuira, with the Golfo de San Miguel spreading westward like a Spanish fan. Served by an airstrip and connected to the Interamerican Highway by boat via Puerto Quimba (water taxis leave every 30 mins. for a 20-min. journey), La Palma is primarily a base for exploring inland along the **Río Tuira** (see p. 140) and west

along the coast and up the Río Sambú into the **Comarca Emberá Sambú** (see pp. 140–141). Its small harbor is a hive of activity. During early Spanish colonial days the port served as a transshipment point for gold extracted upriver at the Cana gold mines. The ruins of 16th-century **Fuerte San Carlos** peer out from beneath a writhing sarcophagus of strangler vines on **Isla Boca Chica,** five minutes by boat from shore.

The local population is predominantly Afro-colonial. These *afrodarienitas*—descendants of African slaves imported to work the Espíritu Santo mines of Cana—are renowned for their musical traditions, considered to reach a zenith in the impoverished fishing village of **Punta Alegre,** 14 miles (22 km) southwest of La Palma. Linger awhile and people are sure to break out guitars, bongo drums, and maracas while dancers perform a sensual *bullerengue,* a dance whose roots can be traced to the Batá region of Africa's Spanish Guinea.

Beyond **Punta Patiño,** the huge sweep of **Ensenada de Garachiné** curls around to Punta Garachiné and the open Pacific. Boats to **Playa de Muerto** (see p. 141) can be hired in the Afro-colonial community of Garachiné, from which a road unfurls into the valley of the **Río Sambú** (see p. 141).

Reserva Natural Punta Patiño

Capybaras munch the marshy grasslands a short distance from the cozy nature lodge at Punta Patiño, a 117-square-mile (303 sq km) nature reserve owned by the Asociación para la Conservación de la Naturaleza (ANCON). These blunt-nosed rodents the size of small pigs are commonly seen as you hike the trails that lead through mangroves, coastal wetlands, and tropical dry and moist forests occupying a peninsula jutting out

into the Golfo de San Miguel. Much of the reserve is a former coconut plantation and cattle ranch that is being reforested. Amazingly diverse for such a small area, it claims 10 percent of the animal and bird species in Panama, including harpy eagles, great curassows, jaguars, ocelots, and pumas. The easy **Sendero Piedra de Candela** trail loops through coastal forest and is a good place to spot poison dart frogs.

Harpy Eagles

The endangered *Harpia harpyja*—Panama's national bird and the world's largest eagle—has a wingspan of 7 feet (2.1 m). With talons the size of grizzly bear claws, this powerful raptor lords it over the lowland rain forest, where it seizes tree-dwelling prey such as monkeys and sloths. Its range is now limited to pockets of Central and South America. Captive-bred harpy eagles are being released to the wild.

The reserve has a private airstrip and is a one-hour boat journey west from La Palma; a tractor pulls arriving boats ashore through the muddy flats as mosquitoes whine about your ears. Overnight visits must be reserved through Ancon Expeditions (see Travelwise p. 244), which offers package tours. ∎

Reserva Natural Punta Patiño

 129 B2

✉ 9 miles (14.5 km) SW of La Palma by boat

Emberá & Wounaan Comarcas

Spinning a magical mystery tour of homespun art and tribal traditions, river trips into Darién's interior provide an intriguing insight into the region's rich indigenous culture, while the fantastic journeys also guarantee astonishing wildlife viewing. The experience is one of the most rewarding to be had in the country.

Emberá youngsters beat the heat by leaping into the Río Mogue.

Comarca Emberá–Wounaan
🏔 129 B2, C2, & C3

Comarca Emberá–Cémaco
🏔 129 C2–C3

Comarca Emberá–Sambú
🏔 129 B2, C2, & C3

The Emberá-Wounaan peoples originated in Colombia and have lived in the forests of Darién for at least two centuries as hunter-gatherers. Only in recent decades have they begun to settle in villages. Their territorial rights were recognized in 1983 with formation of the Comarca Emberá-Wounaan, home to 10,000 people, mostly Emberá with a Wounaan minority. Covering a quarter of Darién Province, it comprises two *comarcas*.

The 1,112-square-mile (2,880 sq km) **Comarca Emberá Cémaco,** holding 28 native communities, occupies the Chucunaque-Tuira River Basin in the northeast. The wide **Río Tuira** twists in great loops, linking isolated communities of Emberá, Wounaan, and *afrodarienitas.* Travelers must register at every police checkpoint. Travel beyond (and sometimes to) **Boca de Cupe,** erstwhile headquarters for the Cana gold mines but today a virtual ghost town, is off-limits due to guerrilla infiltration.

The 502-square-mile (1,300 sq km) **Comarca Emberá Sambú,** in the southwest, is safer and easily accessed by river. The comarca's 12 major villages are all set up to receive tourists. Most villages offer basic accommodations and meals and are protected by heavily armed police brigades. **Mogue,** 3 miles (5 km) up the murky Río Mogue, midway between La Palma and Punta Patiño, is the most accessible community. It's a 20-minute walk from wharf to village. Trails lead into primary rain forest.

Río Sambú

The Río Sambú, a 90-minute boat ride from La Palma, is plied by *cayucos* and piraguas that follow the river as it snakes deep into the heart of Darién as far as Pavarandó, the easternmost Emberá village. Crocodiles slither down the muddy banks; swimming is best avoided.

La Chunga, on the Río Chunga tributary, is relatively touristy. The rustic **Bungalows Eco-Lodge La Chunga** (see sidebar p. 123) is operated by three Emberá brothers, is a perfect base for cultural and nature explorations. Farther upriver, **Sambú**—part Emberá, part Afro-Antillean—provides a study of diverse ethnic groups living in harmony. Guides lead forest hikes, including to a rock covered with pre-Columbian petroglyphs.

Travel farther upriver is a daylong affair. The journey can be arranged through **Ancon Expeditions** (see Travelwise p. 263). Bring along plenty of insect repellent.

Playa de Muerto

This unique coastal community is difficult to reach but well worth the effort. An early morning departure is best for the hired boat journey *(2 hrs.)* from Garachiné (register with the police before leaving), which lands you on a miles-long black-sand beach fronting the Emberá village. It's a staggering setting against darkly brooding mountains. The 225 inhabitants perform native dancing, sell exquisite artwork, and demonstrate medicinal plants. Guides lead hikes to **Playa Cocal,** where a trail leads through rain forest to a waterfall. Playa de Muerto has simple accommodations with the stentorian roar of howler monkeys for reveille. ■

Emissary of Darién

The Emberá-Wounaan can produce more income from a single tree in the rain forest than from 40 acres (16 ha) of cattle grazing, claims Jim Brunton, founder of the **Pajaro Jai Foundation** (PJF; *420 Post Rd., West #202, Westport, CT 06880, USA, tel 207/460-4184, sites.google.com/site/pajaro jaifoundation*). PJF works to promote the self-sufficiency and maintain the strength of Darién culture. Centered on the village of Mogue, the group fosters eco-sensitive projects such as native crafts for export, the opening of jungle lodges for ecotourism, and small-scale furniture factories producing dowels, frames, and furniture of bloodred *nazareno*, fiery gold *pino amarillo*, and coral-hued almond. PJF's primary educational tool is the *Pajaro Jai* (Enchanted Bird). The result of 15 years' labor by the Emberá, this 92-foot-long (28 m) oceangoing ketch was hand built and is crewed by Emberá-Wounaan in native dress.

More Places to Visit in Darién

Bahía Piña

Midway between Punta Garachiné and the Colombian border, this small bay pincered by narrow promontories boasts a setting of magnificent beauty. Waves crash against rocky cliffs backed by emerald forests spilling down the Sierra de Jungurudó. Humpback whales and bottlenose dolphins frequent the bay. An airstrip serves the hamlet of **Puerto Piña,** where Emberá often welcome visitors with traditional dances. The bay is the setting for **Tropic Star Lodge** (see Travelwise pp. 243–244), known for its hundreds of International Game Fish Association world-record catches culled from the churning waters of **Zane Grey Reef,** an underwater mountain 15 miles (25 km) from shore. A mountain trail leads to talcum white **Playa Blanca,** shelving into turquoise waters protected by a coral reef good for snorkeling.
129 B1

The lush rain forests of Darién are a treasure house of fabulous flora.

Jaqué

The southernmost settlement in Panama, 5 miles (8 km) south of Bahía Piña, is served by twice-weekly flights from Panama City. Many occupants are Colombian refugees.

Bridges across Borders (bridgesacrossborders .org) sponsors a women's cooperative that makes cards from recycled paper and natural fibers. And villagers gather and tend the eggs of leatherback turtles, which nest on the miles-long black-sand beaches. Simple accommodations are available. You can journey up the Río Jaqué to **Biroquera,** a Wounaan village, and to the Emberá villages of **Lucas, El Coco,** and **El Mamey**. However, venturing beyond Biroquera is foolhardy.
129 B1

El Real de Santa María

This ramshackle frontier town, with an airstrip ringed by jungle, is the main gateway to Parque Nacional Darién (see pp. 134–135). Solo travelers intent on visiting the park must register with ANAM (tel 299-6965). Situated on the Río Tuira, 40 miles (65 km) upriver from La Palma and 4 miles (6.4 km) downriver from Yaviza (see p. 131), the village dates back to the early 17th century, when it served as a stopover for gold from the Cana mines. The barely discernible ruins of a Spanish-built fort are overgrown by a fantasy of thick foliage. The town has accommodations available.
129 C2

Reserva Forestal de Canglón

On the north bank of the Río Tuira, midway between La Palma and El Real de Santa María, this 122-square-mile (316 sq km) wetland—also known as Humedal de Matusagaratí—protects a vital network of mangroves, riverine marshes, and tropical humid forest. Egrets, herons, and ibises pick among the sedge wetlands, where jacanas can be seen tiptoeing across lily pads, using the ultrawide span of their toes to disperse their weight. With luck you may spot capybaras, as well as crocodiles lurking in the river or sunning on the riverbank, motionless as logs.
anam.gob.pa 129 B2–C2 ☎ 299-6530

Magnificent hiking and a coast lined with beaches and
precious wetlands

Central Panama

Detail of a 1,200-year-old ceramic,
Museo de Veraguas, Santiago

Central Panama

This region is blessed with tourist attractions of every sort—fine beaches, magnificent mountain scenery, forests teeming with wildlife, even pre-Columbian sites and important colonial architecture. All are within a few hours' drive of Panama City. It's easy to understand why the provinces of Coclé and Veraguas have together become the premier vacation destination for residents of Panama City.

Mists shroud mountaintops in Parque Nacional Omar Torrijos.

Veraguas is the only Panamanian province that extends between the Caribbean and the Pacific. To the north, the region is bounded by the rugged mountains of the continental divide. Isolated Ngöbe-Buglé communities dot the mountains, and the coast is sparsely populated by Afro-colonial communities. No roads penetrate the Caribbean region that, with the Darién Gap, constitutes Panama's final frontier.

On the Pacific side, the rivers that tumble out of these steep mountains flow down to rolling flatlands and empty through swampy wetlands into the Bahía de Parita. East of the bay, 40 miles (64 km) of sun-kissed beaches with taupe sands stretch along the Pacific shore from Farallón to Punta Chame and the Bahía de Panamá (Bay of Panama). Though Panamanians flock to this coast, relatively few foreign tourists know of these beaches, which begin about one hour west of Panama City and are marked by signposts on the Interamerican Highway.

Most beach communities are loosely organized agglomerations of second homes and vacation rentals. Large all-inclusive resort hotels have recently opened (one has a golf course), appealing mainly to Panama's middle class. Other accommodations are limited; beach restaurants are even fewer.

The hilly interior invites cooler pleasures. The mountain settlement of El Valle de Antón, spread out in an ancient volcanic crater, basks in a springlike temperate climate year-round. You can delight in hiking and horseback rides, plus get a close look at the creatures you miss in the wild by visiting one of the country's two zoos. Wildlife is also the name of the game in rugged Parque Nacional y Reserva Biológica Altos de Campana—starkly beautiful high country from

NOT TO BE MISSED:

Viewing poison dart frogs in El Valle de Antón   147

A zipline ride at the Canopy Adventure   147

Kiteboarding at Punta Chame 148–149

Sunning at Playa Santa Clara   149

A walking tour of central Penonomé   150–151

Hiking in Parque Nacional Omar Torrijos   154–155

Snorkeling at Isla Granito de Oro   163

which all Panama seems to explode into view—and Parque Nacional Omar Torrijos. Together they offer some of the most spectacular mountain hiking in Panama, with lush forests bursting with epiphytes, orchids, and birdsong. Birders and orchid fans flock, too, to the end-of-the-road highland hamlet of Santa Fé.

The region is cut through by the Interamerican Highway, which grants easy access to every sight. The highway itself is a fast, rather unexciting drive, two lanes in each direction, well maintained (and heavily patrolled). The route is dotted with towns abuzz with modern vitality

yet containing time-warp Spanish-village centers. Penonomé is one such, living in another century entirely at its core. Natá is graced by the oldest Catholic church in the Western Hemisphere. Nearby Parque Arqueológico El Caño offers one of Panama's most important pre-Columbian sites. And Santiago boasts a fine museum brimming with archaeological relics.

West of Santiago, the Interamerican Highway narrows down to one lane in each direction and after about 25 miles (40 km) climbs over mountain ridges that separate Veraguas and Chiriquí Provinces. There are few settlements, nor even gas stations or hotels, along this long stretch of road, and it holds only a fistful of basic restaurants. Surfers and sportfishers typically divert south to the Golfo de Montijo for some of the best waves and angling thrills in the country. And Parque Nacional Isla Coiba is, not least, world renowned for its stupendous diving. ■

Altos de Campana

The wild, barren heights of Altos de Campana more closely resemble the whisky brown crags of the Scottish Highlands than the torrid tropics. The 12,170 acres (4,925 ha) of mountainous wilderness include severely deforested lower slopes, yet the breeze-swept heights are lush and lovely, with a large concentration of endemic species atop the highest peaks.

Parque Nacional y Reserva Biológica Altos de Campana

⚠ 145 D3

Visitor Information

✉ 2.8 miles (4.5 km) W of Interamerican Hwy., at Capira

☎ 254-2848

💲 $

anam.gob.pa

Established in 1966 as the country's first national park, **Parque Nacional y Reserva Biológica Altos de Campana** is shaped like a barbell. The dramatic mountain formations reflect the area's tormented volcanic origins. Lava fields and volcanic tors—sheer-sided, freestanding boulders—stipple the slopes, which range from about 1,300 feet (396 m) to 3,304 feet (1,007 m) atop **Cerro Chame.**

The main access road to the southerly Cerro Chame section begins 2 miles (3 km) west of Capira on the Interamerican Highway, from which a paved road with more curves than Miss Panama winds its way 3 miles

(5 km) up to the park entrance on the western side of the mountains. The road offers fantastic views over the coastal plains, best enjoyed from the mirador (lookout point) 200 yards (183 m) beyond the ranger station. Though much of the western and southern slopes is entirely denuded, forests await above. The well-maintained, 3-mile-long (5 km) **Sendero La Cruz** begins on the right about 3 miles (5 km) above the ranger station and ascends to the summit of **Cerro Campana,** topped by a cross. The more demanding **Sendero Cerro Campana** offers an alternate route.

The more lushly clad Atlantic slopes resound with chattering birds: bronze-tailed plumeleteers, scale-crested pygmy tyrants, and a variety of trogons are among the 267 species recorded. The area is known for its large numbers of reptiles and amphibians, including Panama's endangered golden frog, restricted to the northwest corner near El Valle de Antón.

Rugged 3,176-foot (968 m) **Cerro Trinidad** offers a steep and sometimes slippery three-hour hike to the summit, which rewards the visitor with 360-degree vistas as spectacular as any in Panama. From Capira, a four-wheel-drive track claws its way up the eastern slopes to the trailhead. Simple huts (refugios) are available for overnights. ∎

The Golden Frog

A national symbol of Panama, the golden frog (Atelopus zeteki) is found only in a small area of these mountains. It was revered by pre-Columbian Guaymí, who made gold frog talismans (huacas) representing fertility. According to legend, the frogs turn into huacas when they die; locals believe that seeing or possessing a live frog will bring good luck.

El Valle de Antón

Tucked in a valley at about 1,975 feet (602 m) with mountains all around, the breathtaking beauty of the town and region known as El Valle is equaled only by its sublime climate, while golden frogs, square trees, a market, exhilarating hikes, and a thrilling zipline ride through the forest canopy count among its attractions.

Flat as a billiard table and just as green, the valley floor after which El Valle is named was once a lakebed in an ancient volcanic crater. This jewel of a vale 16 miles (25 km) north of the Interamerican Highway at Las Uvas is a popular weekend retreat for Panama City's wealthy. The tranquil town is laid out on the east bank of the sparkling Río Antón.

Trails lead up the mountain known as **Cerro La India Dormida** (Sleeping Indian Woman). Look for exquisite orchids in shady niches. **Panama Explorer Tours** (see Travelwise p. 265) offers guided hikes and more.

Every Sunday, Ngöbe-Buglé Indians flock to the traditional **market** (*Ave. Central at Calle del Mercado*) to sell crafts, including figurines of *ranas doradas*—the endangered yellow-and-black poison dart frogs. To see the real thing, head to **El Níspero,** a botanic garden and zoo, displaying monkeys, agoutis, kinkajous, and ocelots—alas in tiny cages. Here, **El Valle Amphibian Conservation Center** (*fightforthefrogs.com/valle.html*), an exhibition center and laboratory, breeds *ranas doradas*. Nearby, the **Serpentario** (*Ave. Principal, tel 983-6680*) displays snakes. Thickly forested 3,888-foot (1,185 m) **Monumento Natural Cerro Gaital** is accessed by a trail

A colorful farmers market is held weekly in El Valle.

near Hotel Campestre (see Travelwise p. 248). Another trail behind the hotel leads to *árboles cuadrados* (square trees), although only the most vivid imagination would be able to discern the quadrangular form.

Canopy Adventure (*$$; see Travelwise p. 265*) lets you whiz thrillingly between the treetops on a zipline. The highlight is gliding over the **Chorro Macho,** a 150-foot (46 m) waterfall also accessed by good birding trails. Nearby, the **Piedra Pintada** boulder is carved with pre-Columbian symbols. Adjoining the tiny **Iglesia de San José** (*Ave. Central at Calle la Compaía*), the tinier **Museo El Valle** displays pre-Columbian petroglyphs, ceramics, and folkloric costumes. ■

El Valle de Antón

- 🅜 145 C3

Visitor Information

- ✉ Mercado Artesanal, Ave. Central
- ☎ 983-644

El Níspero

- ✉ Calle Carlos Arosemena, 0.75 mile (1.2 km) N of the police station, Ave. Central
- ☎ 983-6142
- 💲 $

Museo El Valle

- ✉ Ave. Central
- 🕐 Closed Mon.–Fri.
- 💲 $

The Beaches

Unraveling like a string bikini along the curvaceous coast of western Panamá Province and Coclé Province, silvery beaches run one into the other for 40 miles (64 km). Less than a two-hour drive from Panama City and thereby extremely popular with the city's middle class, the beaches can get packed on weekends and during fiestas. Ramshackle fishing hamlets speckle the shore, where marine turtles haul out to deposit their eggs above the high-water mark.

Local youth show off their soccer skills, and affiliations, on Playa Santa Clara.

The Beaches
◭ 145 C3–D3
Visitor Information
✉ ATP, Río Hato, Farallón main street
☎ 993-3241
🕒 Closed Sat.–Sun.

Most of the beaches are indicated by signposts on the Interamerican Highway, which runs inland of the shore. The sands—in colors from chocolate and taupe to black—are easily accessible by public bus from Panama City's Gran Terminal. Taxis ply the highway or await at the bus stops, ready to shuttle you to your beach.

Punta Chame & Around

Curling north like a fishhook around the eastern flank of **Bahía de Chame,** the needle-thin sandspit called Punta Chame divides two unique worlds. You'll thrill to gorgeous views as you follow the potholed, roller-coaster road to the tip of the point. The bay shore, lined with shrimp farms and mangroves, forms a vital nursery for caimans, turtles, and juvenile fish. Dolphins frolic in the blue-gray waters and kite-boarders scud across the bay. The nondescript community of Punta Chame is the capital of kiteboarding in Panama. To try your hand at the sport, contact MacheteKites (see Travelwise p. 265) or Nitro City Panama Action Sports Resort (see Travelwise pp. 246–247), which also has an MX motorcycle track, mountain bikes, and ATVs.

The bay's lush boomerang-shaped **Isla Taborcillo** is commonly known as Isla de John Wayne, who bought it after filming *Rio Bravo* in Panama in 1959. New owners have built a family-oriented hotel and entertainment complex in mock-Western fashion, staffed by live actors re-creating Wayne's swaggering cowboy aura. The isle is also an important nesting site for tricolored herons and yellow-crowned night-herons.

Punta Chame's waters are subject to undertow, and stingrays congregate here, burrowing down into the sandy shallows; wading is a hazard. Three species of marine turtles waddle ashore at full moon. Floating 9 miles (15 km) offshore, craggy **Islas Otoque, Boná,** and **Estivá** are important breeding sites for pelicans, frigate birds, and brown- and blue-footed boobies.

West of Punta Chame, **Playa Coronado** is speckled with the second homes of wealthy Panamanians and draws an upscale crowd. Many come to practice their swing at Coronado Golf & Beach Resort (see Travelwise p. 265) which has

an 18-hole golf course. Bring your ID to gain access.

Playa El Palmar to Farallón

Playa El Palmar, reached via San Carlos on the main highway, pulls in winds off the open sea. Its 10-foot (3 m) waves are nirvana for surfers; the **Palmar Point Surf Hotel** *(tel 240-8004)* doubles as a surf school. For a taste of laid-back fishing culture, head to **Playa San Carlos** or **Playa Río Mar.** Southward, **Playa Santa Clara** is one of the prettiest beaches and is well served by modest accommodations and seafood restaurants where you can dine beneath palms.

At **Playa Farallón,** the all-inclusive Royal Decameron Beach Resort & Casino is beloved of monied *panameños* on weekends; day passes can be bought. Beyond the resort, the sandy coastal track threads between rustic fishermen's shacks. Westward, on the snow-white sands of **Playa Blanca** fisherman's shacks now squat in the lee of ritzy resorts, including the luxurious Wyndam Grand Playa Blanca (see Travelwise p. 245). ∎

Playa El Palmar
🅼 145 D3

Playa Farallón
🅼 145 C3

Marine Turtles

Five of the world's seven species of marine turtle—from the diminutive olive Ridley to Cadillac-size leatherbacks—lay their eggs on Panama's beaches. Their populations are endangered throughout their range thanks to human depredations, though all the major nesting sites in Panama are now protected. Male turtles spend their lives at sea; only the female returns to land, normally to the beach where she was born, and usually at night during a full-moon high tide. Finding a spot above the high tide mark, she digs a pit in which she lays 100 or so spherical, golf ball–size eggs. After covering them up, she heads back to sea. The eggs hatch after incubating in the warm sand for about seven weeks. Hatchlings are usually the same gender in each nest according to the temperature of the sand (cooler for males).

Penonomé & Around

Striking for its charming colonial plaza, providing a whitewashed way station at the base of the Cordillera Central, otherwise hurly-burly Penonomé is a handy springboard for exploring the mountain parks that rise north and east.

Penonomé's graceful Iglesia San Juan Bautista dominates the town's central plaza.

Penonomé
🅰 145 C3
Visitor Information
☎ 997-7538
   (ANAM)

Museo de Penonomé
✉ Calle San Antonio
☎ 997-8490
💲 $

The provincial capital of Penonomé (pop. 21,000) was founded in 1581 as a *reducción de indios,* an area where Indians were resettled to form a pool for forced labor. After destruction of the original Panama City in 1671, Penonomé—the name derives from Indian chief Nomé, executed by the Spaniards here—served as the capital of the isthmus until today's Casco Antiguo (see pp. 60–67) was built.

This prosperous agricultural town is known for its *sombreros pintados* (straw hats; see sidebar p. 79), which can be bought at the **Mercado de Artesanías Coclé** *(19 miles/31 km NE of Penonomé via Vía Sonadora)*—itself built in the shape of a *sombrero*

montuño. Though the town whirls in a contemporary commercial vortex, it retains an exquisite colonial plaza: **Parque 8 de Diciembre,** shaded by blossoming flame trees and with a bandstand at its heart. The modest **Iglesia San Juan Bautista,** on the plaza's north side, boasts beautiful stained glass. Rising over the west side are the Gobernación (municipal government building) and a handsome police station in quasi-medieval style. A life-size bronze statue of Simón Bolívar gazes over the park, which extends south into an elongated *plazuela* studded by monuments and busts of former presidents.

The small **Museo de Penonomé,** in a row of four charming

blue-and-white 18th-century cottages, has pre-Columbian ceramics, colonial religious icons, and exhibits on local architecture and archaeology.

La Pintada

Fifteen miles (24 km) northwest of Penonomé, the agricultural town of La Pintada revolves around a pretty main square fringed by pines. Heady aromas emanate from **Cigarros Joyas de Panamá,** a simple hillside facility where 20 rollers use locally grown tobacco to produce 12 types of cigars. It's best to call in a day or two ahead to arrange a tour. The factory, 400 yards (366 m) southwest of the plaza, has signposts in town. In the center of town, the **Mercado de Artesanías de La Pintada** sells straw hats and *muñequitas* (dolls) dressed in folkloric clothes. Many of the hats originate in neighboring Pedregosa.

A rough road leads northwest from La Pintada to **El Copé,** gateway to rugged, remote **Parque Nacional Omar Torrijos** (see pp. 154–155). Continuing due north from La Pintada across the continental divide into Ngöbe-Buglé territory leads to **Molejón,** site of a huge gold-mining project opening veins once tapped by conquistadores.

Reserva Privada Távida

Part of a macadamia farm, reforestation project, and private college, this reserve with hilltop hotel—Villa Távida—welcomes visitors for birding and hiking. Its superlative setting in the **Serranía del Escaliche**—studded with soaring forest-tipped limestone peaks—is one of the finest birding sites in the country. Oropendolas . . . toucans . . . rufous-winged tanagers: Every blink of an eye brings something new.

The 800-yard-long (0.75 km) **Sendero Pozo Azul** winds through lush grounds to a lake and the *pozo azul* (blue well), where you can soak in mineral waters. A more demanding hike leads to the **Távida waterfall,** tumbling 92 feet (28 m) into a natural pool; en route, you'll pass a huge rock carved with pre-Columbian

Reserva Privada Távida

- 17 miles (27 km) NE of Penonomé via Carretera a Chiguirí Arriba
- 6485-0505
- $ $$–$$$$ (depending on activity)

posadalavieja.com

Shop Sustainably

Many craft and souvenir items for sale in Panama are made from endangered flora or fauna. Buying such items contributes to their demise. Trade in endangered products is illegal, and such items may be confiscated by Customs. Avoid jewelry made from turtle shell or coral; furs of ocelots or other animals; and items made from macaw or quetzal feathers. Only buy a tropical hardwood product if it was made from fallen trees. Shop with a conscience!

---

pictographs. If you're feeling especially adventurous, you can hike or ride a mule through the mountains to El Valle de Antón (see p. 147).

It's best to overnight here to fully appreciate the serenity broken only by birdsong. That strange metallic *bonk?* The call of a three-wattled bellbird. You awaken to views of **Cerro La Vieja** peeking out from beneath its own blanket of mist. ■

Penonomé to Reserva Privada Távida Drive

Break out your camera for this 32-mile-long (52 km) drive through the foothills of the Cordillera Central. It's a magnificent journey, with the scenery unfolding like a series of Hollywood stage sets.

The whitewashed church next to a park in La Pintada is typical of the *iglesias* that line this route.

Much of this journey is along a well-worn road that is badly potholed and even washed out in places. Though easily attempted by sedan, your backside will be glad for the more robust suspension provided by a four-wheel-drive vehicle.

Begin in the charming main plaza of **Penonomé ❶** (see pp. 150–151), departing via the road that begins on the square's north-west corner. Following the level valley of the Río Coclé, this wide, well-paved section gives a foretaste of the beauty that awaits as you pass through cattle country with sensuously rounded peaks in the distance to east, west, and ahead. After 9 miles (15 km) you arrive in **La Pintada ❷** (see p. 151), a small agricultural town lent beauty by the gleaming white **Iglesia de Candelaria.** A side road that begins beside the church leads east a short distance to **Charco Las Lavanderas,** natural pools

NOT TO BE MISSED:

Iglesia de Candelaria, La Pintada • Cigarros Joyas de Panamá • Capilla Católica de la Medalla Milagrosa • Reserva Privada Távida

whose waters are said to have healing powers.

Alternately, at the church plaza turn left and follow signs that lead you 400 yards (366 m) southwest along a winding road to **Cigarros Joyas de Panamá** (see p. 151), a cigar factory selling quality smokes for a pittance.

Retrace your route to the center of La Pintada. Turn right in the center of town toward **Las Minas ❸** and follow the partially paved road as it bores into ever more rugged terrain. As you ascend eastward you might stop to admire the view west toward **Cerro Ororari,** a flat-topped, sheer-walled mesa. The next few miles of the drive provide a stop-and-go selection of magnificent panoramas over forest-clad valleys and mountains—more than adequate compensation for the deteriorating state of the road.

Arriving in the community of **Toabré,** turn left at the crossroads for **Tambo ❹,** a twee village flanked on its west side by citrus plantations. Turn right beside the church in Tambo. Less than 2 miles (3.2 km) along, you'll pass a charming **cemetery** (on the left) against a backdrop of scalloped mountain ridges.

Dominating the scene is **Cerro Chiquiralí,** a free-standing nipple of volcanic rock rising majestically to the northeast. The peak lords it over the community of **Miraflores ❺,** with

its lovely church—the **Iglesia de San José—** enfolded by pines.

The road (unpaved in places) descends through conifer forest and cattle pasture to **Churuquita Grande ❻.** En route, the vistas open up through the trees, revealing lush valleys studded with spectacular limestone formations. Turn left at the junction with the paved road in Churuquita Grande. Coiling gradually upward, the road ascends a spur ridge to **Caimito,** graced by the charming little **Capilla Católica de la Medalla Milagrosa.** For the next few miles, the ridgetop route delivers an array of views that leave you breathless. The road narrows and grows steeper. After 32 miles (52 km), you arrive at your destination, **Reserva Privada Távida ❼,** where trails lead to waterfalls.

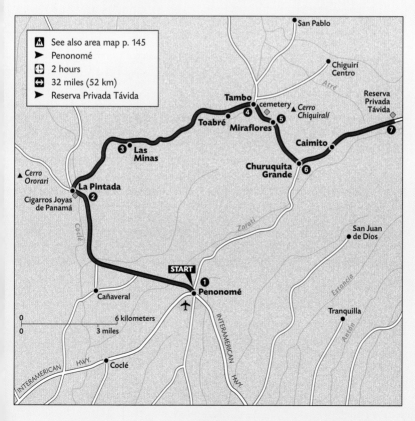

Parque Nacional Omar Torrijos

Swaddled in montane cloud forest on its upper slopes, this rugged park teems with wildlife and, though facilities are meager, hikers and birders are amply rewarded with the chance of rare species sightings. A spiderweb of trails is well maintained by the U.S. Peace Corps.

Torrential rainfall feeds magnificent cascades in Parque Nacional Omar Torrijos.

Known commonly as El Copé (for the *copé* tree) and officially as Parque Nacional General de División Omar Torrijos Herrera, the 62,454-acre (25,275 ha) national park straddles the continental divide. Created in 1986, it is named for Panama's populist military leader Maj. Gen. Omar Torrijos, who fell in love with the area, sponsored local community programs, and was killed when his plane crashed here in foul weather on July 31, 1981 (remnants of the wreck can still be seen, a somber curiosity for bush-whacking hikers; it's a five-hour hike from the ranger station).

The park protects the watersheds of Ríos Bermejo and Marta on the Pacific slopes and those of the Ríos Blanco, Guabal, and Lajas on the Caribbean, which are deluged in rains. Mists that rise from the Caribbean Sea swirl ethereally through the forests that envelop the cool highland slopes—a habitat for the endangered immaculate antbird, golden-olive woodpecker, red-fronted parrotlet, and bare-necked umbrellabird, boasting a coiffure that would do Elvis proud. Panama's endangered golden frog hops around the forest floor. El Copé is also one of the last refuges in central Panama for the jaguar, puma, and tapir.

Parque Nacional Omar Torrijos can be reached from the Interamerican Highway, 10 miles (16 km) west of Penonomé. The paved road rises 16 miles (26 km) northward to the village of El Copé, from which a rugged track leads uphill to the **ANAM ranger station.** A four-wheel drive is essential. A half-mile (0.7 km) hike beyond, the simple breeze-swept **Altos del Calvario Visitor Center** (with basic explanations on local ecology) is poised on a ridge with a vista toward the Caribbean through glass walls.

Trails & Lodging

An easily hiked **interpretative trail** begins at the visitor center and takes about one hour round-trip; another short trail leads to a mountaintop lookout with

Tapirs

Mate an elephant with a pig and the result might resemble Baird's tapir (*Tapirus bairdii*), a corpulent mammal with short legs and a nose like a miniature trunk. This plant-eating forest dweller—the largest terrestrial mammal in Central America—prefers to live near still water and can often be seen bathing in swamps. It has a keen sense of smell and good hearing. Adults have tough, bristly gray-brown skin; chestnut-brown calves are spotted and striped with white for camouflage. Their meat is considered a delicacy by hunters, who have brought the tapir to near extinction.

magnificent vistas. More rugged trails lead to the remote hamlet of **La Rica,** the **Chorros de Tife** cascades, and the summits of **Cerro Marta** and **Cerro Peña Blanca.** Seasoned hikers can even trek to the Caribbean (a guide and sufficient provisions are essential). A simple dorm with kitchen, lounge, and bunks is available in the park, and camping is permitted. Bring warm clothing for chilly nights. The local Asociación de Guías can provide guides (*$–$$ per person*).

Between El Copé and the park entrance, the community of **Barrigón** has established the Barrigón Grupo Boca (*tel 998-9130*), which offers guides and lodging. ∎

Parque Nacional Omar Torrijos

- 145 B3–C3
- 31 miles (50 km) NW of Penonomé; 5 miles (8 km) NW of El Copé
- 983-9089 or 997-7538 (Penonomé)
- $

anam.gob.pa

Aguadulce & Around

Long known as a center for salt and sugar production and for shrimp farming, Aguadulce occupies the flatlands of Coclé Province. Birders will thrill to migratory whimbrels and other waders in coastal wetlands, while the nearby Natá and El Caño hark back to the colonial and pre-Columbian past.

Harmonized in purples, a passerby blends into a mural depicting Aguadulce's colorful past.

Aguadulce

145 C2

Ingenio de Azúcar Santa Rosa

✉ 1 mile (1.6 km) N of El Roble, 15 miles (24 km) W of Aguadulce

☎ 987-8544

🕐 Closed Sun.; 24-hour notice required

azunal.com

An important industrial town in the midst of an otherwise semi-arid plain, Aguadulce, 115 miles (185 km) west of Panama City, is surrounded by lime green sugarcane fields dusted by delicate white blossoms in spring. During the December-to-April sugar harvest, smoke-smudged field hands in straw sombreros slash at the charred stalks with glinting machetes, and trucks trundle down the highway, dropping stalks of cut cane as they go.

Then, too, **Ingenio de Azúcar Santa Rosa,** the Santa Rosa Sugar Refinery, operates around the clock and black smoke rises from it in twirling tornadoes,

tainting the air with the stench of molasses. Visitors may take a tour, which includes the original mill-owner's home with period furniture.

Plaza 19 de Octubre

In town, the heart of affairs is Plaza 19 de Octubre, an unassuming square with the **Iglesia de San Juan Bautista** on its north side. The **Museo Regional Stella Sierra** (formerly the Museo de la Sal y el Azúcar), in a quaint two-story mansion dating from 1925, contains period furniture, stone axes, and other pre-Columbian artifacts, plus a tiny sugar press and other simple exhibits relating to the salt and sugar industries. The main drag has a median with a **monument of Rodolfo Chiari** (1869–1937), a local boy and president of Panama 1924–1928, at its north end.

East of town, salt pans (salinas) abandoned a decade ago recall the days when Aguadulce was a major salt producer. Adjoining shrimp ponds deliver juicy plump jumbo shrimp to restaurants throughout the country. The pans and ponds merge into brackish marshes and mangroves lining the shore of the **Bahía de Parita.** The **Aguadulce wetlands** are an important breeding ground for herons, wood storks, roseate spoonbills, and other stilt-legged waders jabbing with long beaks for exposed bugs. At high tide, locals love to splash around in four pools—**Las Piscinas**—built into rocks surrounded by the oozy mudflats.

Natá De Los Caballeros & Nearby

Exquisite in the quietude of its central colonial plaza, Natá, founded in 1517 and named for a local Indian chief of the time, lures visitors to its lovely church in the leafy main square. Begun in 1522, the **Basílica Menor de Santiago Apóstol** is said to be the oldest church on the Pacific coast of the Americas. Its simple, whitewashed facade ripples like notes in a fugue.

Within, the main altar is adorned with fruits and flowers crawling with feathered serpents, the work of Indian carvers. Note,

too, the simple beamed ceiling, the painting of the Holy Trinity, and the statue of the patron saint holding a Spanish flag in his hand.

Parque y Museo Arqueológico El Caño, 5 miles (8 km) northeast of Natá, is well worth a quick browse for the history-minded. Site of Panama's most abundant concentration of pre-Columbian discoveries, this ancient ceremonial center and burial ground, found in 1924, covers 20 acres (8 ha) and dates back 5,000 years. A row of Stonehenge-like stone stellae that rise from the meadow march enigmatically into the past.

Sugarcane

A source of both wealth and backbreaking labor in the Caribbean, sugarcane is a perennial grass. The giant plant is harvested throughout the year in the most productive locations, its roots left in the ground to regrow. In most of the world, harvesting is still accomplished by workers wielding long machetes in the tropical heat.

A burial site displays five skeletons in situ, curled in fetal positions and even stuffed into jars. Blocks of stone inscribed with anthropomorphic images, a reproduction of a cacique's hut, and a small colonial-era-style museum displaying ceramics, stone axes, and so forth, are among the attractions. ■

Museo Regional Stella Sierra

- ✉ Calle Fábrica Final, Aguadulce
- ☎ 997-4280
- 🕓 Closed Sat.–Sun.
- 💲 $

Parque y Museo Arqueológico El Caño

- ✉ 2 miles (3.2 km) N of Interamerican Hwy., 17 miles (27 km) W of Penonomé
- 🕓 Closed Mon.
- 💲 $

Santiago de Veraguas

A bustling commercial hub marking the midway point between Panama City and Costa Rica on the Interamerican Highway, Santiago delivers a trio of appealing sites.

Pilgrims flock to the Iglesia Atalaya in Atalaya during Lent to beseech miracles of a Christ figure.

Santiago de Veraguas

🅰 145 B2

Visitor Information

✉ ATP, Ave. Central

☎ 998-3929

visitpanama.com

Museo Regional de Veraguas

✉ Calle 2da at Ave. Juan Demóstenes Arosemena

☎ 998-4543

🕐 Closed Sat.–Sun.

💲 $

Santiago, 155 miles (249 km) west of Panama City, was founded in 1632. Today it is a thriving commercial and agricultural center. Broad Avenida Central unrolls past the **Mercado Artesanal de la Peña**—a good place to choose your *sombrero pintado*—to **Parque Juan Demóstenes Arosemena.** The plaza has a monument to the Santiago-born writer and politician (1879–1936) who died the year he was elected president.

Occupying a reproduction of the town's former jail, the **Museo Regional de Veraguas** has exhibits ranging from fossils of giant sloths to a re-creation of a pre-Columbian excavation site.

Santiago's crown jewel is the **Escuela Normal Superior Juan Demóstenes Arosemena** *(Calle 6ta, tel 998-4862),* a

teacher-training facility from the 1920s. This monument features masterful murals in the main hall by local artist Roberto Lewis.

Beyond Town

The quiet village of **San Francisco de la Montaña,** 10 miles (16 km) north of Santiago, was founded in 1671 and draws pilgrims nationwide to the **Iglesia San Francisco de la Montaña.** This simple stone church, erected in 1727 and recently restored, contains exquisite frescoes and statues. The baroque altar is carved with scenes from the Scriptures and Indian folklore. Another delightful church, the **Iglesia Atalaya** in Atalaya, 5 miles (8 km) southeast of Santiago, is remarkable for its painted windows and vaulted ceilings. ∎

Santa Fé & Around

A roller-coaster road ascends from Santiago into a dramatic mountain world of tumbling streams and rivers suitable for white-water rafting. Superlative birding and hiking originate from the delightful end-of-the-road hamlet of Santa Fé, known for orchids, fine coffee, and vibrant Ngöbe-Buglé peoples.

Tucked into a valley at a crisp 1,542 feet (470 m) of elevation in the shadow of **Cerro Tute,** only a few miles below the continental divide, Santa Fé has a springlike quality. This simple hamlet is laid out higgledy-piggledy, with a warren of narrow lanes snaking up and down the pine-studded hillsides. (Note that there's no gas station between Santiago and Santa Fé, a distance of 33 miles/53 km).

The settlement was founded in 1557 by conquistador Francisco Vásquez to be near the gold mines. The Spanish met fierce resistance from Indians led by warrior chieftain Urracá, commemorated today on Panama's 1 centavo coin. The indigenous presence is still strong. Ngöbe Indian women in their bright dresses can often be seen gathered around the grassy plaza or selling their *chácaras,* hand-stitched clothing and other handicrafts at the nearby **Mercado Agrícola y Artesanal Santa Fé**.

Orchids

The hamlet is known for its orchids, grown enthusiastically by local amateur gardeners. Berta Castrellón, former president of the Asociación de Orquideología de Panamá, opens her garden—**Orquideario y Cultivos Las Fragrancias de Santa Fé**—to visitors. You're welcome to push

Santa Fé
🅜 145 B3

Orquideario y Cultivos Las Fragrancias de Santa Fé
✉ 100 yards (91 m) N and 400 yards (366 m) E of the plaza
☎ 954-0910
$ By donation

EXPERIENCE: Learning About Coffee Culture

Although not as well known as Costa Rica as a coffee producer, Panama produces beans that rival the best in the world. The arabica coffee plant grows best in well-drained soils at elevations of 2,500 to 3,500 feet (760–1,070 m), with nearly constant temperatures between 59° and 82°F (15°–28°C) and a distinct wet and dry season.

The climate, slopes, and rich volcanic soils of the Chiriquí highlands are perfect for cultivation, combining to produce a distinctly flavored coffee—mellow and aromatic, with a hint of acidity.

The following venues will help you appreciate the intricacies of coffee production and the plant's place in the national psyche.

Café El Tute (Santa Fé, tel 954-0137, closed Sun.) roasts the beans grown by scores of the local cooperatives in the Santa Fé district. Tours are given during harvest.

Coffee Estate Inn (See p. 250; Boquete, tel 720-2211, coffeeestateinn.com) is a B&B inn on its own coffee estate. Guests get a tour and live-in experience.

Finca Lérida (Boquete, tel 720-2285, fincalerida.com), established in 1922, offers an in-depth interactive tour that includes the coffee fields and original processing plan, followed by a tasting.

**Parque Nacional
Santa Fé de
Veraguas**

145 B3

Visitor Information

998-0615 or
998-4387

anam.gob.pa

open the gate to her ridgetop home on the northeast side of town, in order to peruse the more than 260 species blooming on every branch.

August is the best time to visit; the flowers are in their most riotous bloom, and Santa Fé hosts an annual three-day orchid festival in autumn. The road past the orquideario leads down to the **Río Mulabá**, where inner tubes can be rented for float trips.

Aromas of fresh-roasted coffee draw you to **Café El Tute** (*980 feet/300 m N of plaza;* see sidebar p. 159), a tiny *beneficio* (roasting plant) where you can

indigenous families on land once owned by wealthy absentee landlords. (The Colombian priest who established the cooperative in the 1960s was murdered for overturning this feudal system.)

Look out for the cross in Santa Fé's **Plaza de Martires** that honors four Castro sympathizers killed trying to initiate a revolution in Panama.

Parque Nacional Santa Fé de Veraguas

Hikers and birders seek out trails through the montane wet forest and cloud forests of this 280-square-mile (725 sq km) national park, created in 2001 to protect a vital corridor for a wealth of wildlife: agoutis, anteaters, deer, and even jaguars and tapirs. The more than 400 bird species recorded here include olivaceous woodpeckers, spectacled antpittas, slaty-capped flycatchers, and others. The **Panama Audubon Society** (*tel 232-5977, audubonpanama .org*) runs bird-watching trips. Dedicated birder Berta Castrellón acts as a guide (*contact Audubon Society or tel 954-0910*).

A trail up **Alto de Piedra** is signed in town; the track (accessible to four-wheel-drive vehicles) is usually muddy, but the effort is rewarded as you ascend past *cafetales*—coffee farms—into forest full of birdsong. Another trail ascends to the summit of **Cerro Tute**, where mists play amid cloud forests. (This once made a cover for a band of guerrillas that aimed in 1959 to topple the Panamanian government.) ∎

EXPERIENCE: Hiking the Continental Divide

You can cross the Continental Divide (the watershed that divides eastward-flowing waters from westward-flowing waters) via the saddle between 4,633-foot (1,412 m) **Cerro Cabeza de Toro** and 4,980-foot (1,518 m) **Cerro Negro**. From there, you can drop down through the bejungled valley of the Río Calovébora to the Caribbean hamlet of Calovébora. However, this two-day hike is no cakewalk; a knowledgeable guide is essential. These trails can also be tackled on horseback by arrangement at the Hotel Santa Fé (*Carretera Santiago-Santa Fé, 600 Yards/550 m S of Santa Fé, tel 954-0941 or 954-0881; see Travelwise p. 247*), which also arranges guides.

---

watch organically grown coffee fresh from the fields being sun-dried, husked, and roasted. Run as a local *campesino* (peasant) cooperative, Esperanza de los Campesinos employs mostly

Golfo de Montijo

A marvelous repository of avian fauna at the mouth of Ríos San Pablo and San Pedro, the watery world of the Montijo Gulf supports not only large flocks of waterfowl but also crocodiles and mammals. Waves crashing onto beaches along the southern shores are nirvana to surfers. This region is as poor as any in Panama, and simple fishing villages eke out a living from the sea.

Wrapped in mangroves and marshy wetlands, the isle-studded gulf encompasses the **Humedal Golfo de Montijo** (Gulf of Montijo Wetlands), approximately 541 square miles (1,401 sq km) of coastal maritime ecosystems that include extensive tidal mudflats and gulf waters. The area—declared an Internationally Important Wetland under the Ramsar Convention—is a vital wintering area for migratory shorebirds. Such nationally threatened species as bare-throated tiger herons and muscovy ducks wade and waddle in large numbers. Crocodiles and caimans bask on the mud.

Access to the east-shore wetlands is by an all-weather road running south via **Mariato** to the fishing hamlet of **El Varadero,** gateway to Parque Nacional Cerro Hoya (see p. 183). Surf crashes into scalloped bays: **Playa Morrillo** has one of the most powerful beach breaks. Behind, copper-colored mountains loom over the dancing blue sea. The road climbs over headlands and offers magnificent views over the Pacific Ocean and **Isla Cébaco.** The gulf waters boil with bonito and billfish. **Cebaco Bay Sportfishing Club** (*tel 317-6890, cebacobay.com*), a floating hotel anchored off Isla Cébaco, caters to anglers.

Dawn breaks over fishing boats in Puerto Mutis, a launch point for vessels setting out for Isla Coiba.

On the west shore, a rolling road penetrates to **Playa Santa Catalina,** a funky favorite of the backpacking, surfing crowd. The former fishing village has morphed into Panama's top surf spot. Santa Catalina Boat Tours (see Travelwise p. 265) offers surfing and snorkeling tours, as does Santa Catalina Surf Shop (*tel 6963-0831, santacatalinasurfshop .com*); Panama Dive Center (*tel 6665-7879, panamadivecenter.com*) and Scuba Coiba (see Travelwise p. 265) offer diving and snorkeling trips to Isla Coiba. Buses run twice daily from Soná on the Interamerican Highway. Immediately east, **Playa El Estero** edges to the tip of the peninsula at **Punta Brava.** ■

Golfo de Montijo

△ 145 A1–B1

Parque Nacional Isla Coiba

Central America's largest marine park encircles rain forest–clad Isla Coiba and offers spectacular snorkeling, diving, and sportfishing in warm waters. Renowned until recently as a remote penal colony, the isle has a new focus on ecotourism.

Warmly inviting, the waters around Isla Granito de Oro are a snorkeling nirvana.

Coiba National Park encompasses 39 islands, including ox-jaw-shaped, 194-square-mile (502 sq km) Isla Coiba, the largest island in Panama. (The island is reachable only by boat from Puerto Mutis, by cruise ship, or by charter plane.) Virgin rain forest smothers 85 percent of the isle—a Noah's ark where crocodiles slosh about in the estuarine muds and howler and white-faced monkeys cavort in the trees. This howler monkey is a subspecies endemic to Coiba, as are 21 of its 147 bird species, including the brown-and-white Coiba spinetail. Coiba is a last refuge for the endangered crested eagle. And Panama's largest nesting colony of scarlet macaws congregates at **Barco Quebrado**. You're sure to see them flying at night in pairs, squawking to their mates.

In 1918 the Panamanian government converted Isla Coiba into a Panamanian version of Devil's Island. The unfenced prison has been phased out, although a few dozen prisoners now work as park rangers. Hiking is currently limited to the vicinity of the **ANAM ranger station** and **biological research station**, tucked into a sandy cove in the island's northeast; a small natural history exhibit features pickled snakes and even the skeleton

INSIDER TIP:

Stay the night on Parque Nacional Isla Coiba. You'll need to hire a boat to get there, and don't forget to bring your own food, gas, and bedding.

—CORY BROWN VEIZAGA
*National Geographic
contributor*

of a humpback whale. A resident crocodile is often present in the shallows near the ranger station. Duplex cabins can be rented by reservation. **Sendero del Observatorio**—a 20-minute amble—leads to an elevated lookout, with views toward Isla Coibita. **Sendero de los Monos** (Monkey Trail), accessed by a 20-minute boat ride from the ranger station, is good for monkey sightings and provides an exhilarating one-hour loop as howlers and capuchin monkeys charge along branches overhead.

On the **Isla Granito de Oro**, you can wade in off a golden beach beneath rocky headlands to snorkel with green and hawksbill turtles and harmless nurse sharks. Tour operators in the Golfo de Montijo (see p. 161) offer visits.

On the east side of the main island, the reefs of **Bahía Damas** spread across 334 acres (135 ha), the largest reef system in Central America. A kaleidoscope of dotted, dappled, and zebra-striped fish dart in and out of spectacular coral reefs encircling jagged

undersea pinnacles. Humpback whales, Cuvier's beaked whales, pilot whales, sperm whales, and even orcas slice through these waters. Giant manta rays and sharks—hammerhead, tiger, white-tip, and harmless whale sharks—are also common, as are marlin, sailfish, and tuna. Sportfishing is permitted, and the **Hannibal Bank,** between Isla Coiba and Isla Montuosa, is especially favored.

Howlers

Visitors to Panama's forests may not always see the country's treetop dwelling howler monkeys, but they will almost certainly hear them. Said to be the loudest animals in the New World, these big primates possess an enlarged hyoid bone in their necks that amplifies their calls like a drum, projecting the sound up to 5 miles (3 km). As they travel in slow-moving groups, the males mark and defend their territories with these gruff barklike cries. Frequent vocalizations indicate that several groups are in the area.

Mantled howlers, distinguished by long guard hairs along their sides, are common in Panama. The Coiba Island howler (*Alouatta coibensis*), however, is a threatened subspecies. If you happen to walk beneath a group, beware! Sticks, fruit, and less pleasant missiles may be accurately dropped on your head.

The small, uninhabited **Islas Contreras,** northwest of Isla Coiba, are beloved of yachters in search of untamed places. Coconut palms shade sheltered coves with blazing white sands backed by dense forest. A submerged rock called **Sombrero de Pelo** is rated world class for dives. ■

**Parque Nacional
Isla Coiba**

⚠ 145 A1

✉ By private charter flight or boat from Puerto Mutis (3 hrs.)

☎ 998-4271 or 998-0615

$ $$

anam.gob.pa

Playground for Whales

Panama's offshore waters have enough whale excitement to outdo Marine World. The warm tropical oceans and shallows draw dozens of species of dolphins and larger cetaceans. Some are seasonal visitors that can dependably be seen at predictable times of the year. Others are year-round dwellers.

Birthed in Panama's warm waters, a juvenile humpback accompanies its mother.

Although humpback whales and, occasionally, other whale species can be seen off the Caribbean seaboard, the prime Panamanian habitats for cetaceans are the waters surrounding Isla Coiba and Las Perlas Archipelago. The sweeping action of nearby Pacific equatorial currents scoops up oceanic nutrients from the deep, resulting in a rich supply of planktonic soup and shoaling fish. The warm, clear waters off Panama, Colombia, and Costa Rica are also perfect for breeding and calving.

Humpbacks from the southeast Pacific summer in the cold oceans off the south coast of Chile, where they gorge themselves on Antarctic krill. As winter approaches, they migrate north to their tropical breeding and birthing grounds in the Gulfs of Panama and Chiriquí. The first animals begin arriving in June, their slow progress betrayed by explosive exhalations of breath. By October, they begin heading back to southern Pacific waters. Humpback whales—identifiable by their elongated jaws, white underbellies, and long pectoral fins—are felicitous lovers. Promiscuous, too. Males push and shove each other to mate with a female in heat, while the females commonly mate with several males in succession. Nonetheless, during copulation, much tender touching takes place. The subsequent year, pregnant females return to the same waters to give birth to their 2,500-pound (1,150 kg) offspring and about one month later are in estrus again.

Bryde's whales, fin whales, pilot whales, four species of beaked whale, and even blue whales—at up to 150 tons (136 metric tons), the largest creatures on Earth—are also seen in Panamanian waters. While they prefer deeper oceanic surroundings, North Atlantic blue whales have been reported off Cristóbal, near the northern terminus of the Panama Canal.

Pods of orcas can be seen at certain times of year around Isla Coiba and the Gulf of Panama. Like humpbacks, orcas (the largest members of the dolphin family) visit during annual feeding and breeding migrations. Almost always traveling in groups related by birth, these "wolves of the sea" come into Panamanian waters to hunt prey, such as smaller dolphins. They are easily distinguished by their tall, sharply pointed dorsal fins and black bodies streamlined for speedy attacks, with a distinctive white saddle and eye patch.

Close encounters of the first kind are

INSIDER TIP:

You can see whales, rays, guitar fish, dolphins, and sea turtles around Isla Coiba [see pp. 162–163], which is only accessible by private charter boat or plane.

—BEN HIRSCH
National Geographic field researcher

virtually guaranteed on whale-watching trips, especially during summer months, when male humpbacks' songs haunt the oceans and resonate through the hull of your boat. A special thrill is the sight of a massive whale surging out of the water. Most whale species make Herculean leaps, even pirouetting midair like ballet dancers before crashing down with an explosive splash that echoes across the water like the boom of distant artillery. Panama's environmental authorities recently declared Las Perlas Archipelago a marine corridor and have joined forces with the Smithsonian Tropical Research Institute (STRI) to protect the whales and draft appropriate whale-watching guidelines.

EXPERIENCE: Try Eyeball-to-Eyeball Encounters

The Pacific waters off Panama offer some of the world's premier whale-watching. During autumn and winter, the warm ocean waters of the Golfo de Chiriquí and Golfo de Panamá are a kind of cetacean Grand Central Terminal. Though not as well-developed as they are in neighboring Colombia, excursions are catching on fast.

The main centers for trips are Boca Chica, Santa Catalina, and Isla Contadora. Strict regulations are in effect, including a ban on swimming with whales.

The following companies offer whale-watching excursions:

Gone Fishing Panama *(tel 6480-5296,* *gonefishingpanama.com)* has trips from Boca Chica, August through October.

National Geographic Expeditions *(tel 888/966-9687, nationalgeographic expeditions.com)* features whale-watching opportunities on its weeklong "Costa Rica & the Panama Canal" trips.

Panama Tours *(tel 6980-4710,* *panamatours.info)* offers private whale-watching trips from Panama City on a high-speed 30-foot (9 m) Scarab.

Whale Watching Panama *(tel 6758-7600, whalewatchingpanama.com)* has two- to five-day trips in the Las Perlas Archipelago; plus one-day trips around Isla Taboga, departing Panama City.

More Places to Visit in Central Panama

Golfo de los Mosquitos

One of Panama's last frontiers, the Caribbean coast of Veraguas borders the well-named Golfo de los Mosquitos. Isolated by thick jungle, the region is reachable only by boat or rugged jungle trails over the continental divide. Scant habitations are populated by Afro-colonial *playeros* (beach people)—descendants of Africans sent to work 16th-century gold mines. It is possible to hike the coast from **Coclé del Norte** (site for **Las Bahías,** a nascent ecological tourism project) to **Belén** (with a statue of rebel Indian chief Quibián), and from there to **Calovébora**—but only for well-provisioned Indiana Jones types with a guide armed with a machete. Trails that begin in Santa Fé (see p. 159), Parque Nacional Omar Torrijos (see pp. 154–155), and Molejón penetrate the jungled valleys to these remote coast settlements, from which irregular supply boats connect to Colón. Tourist services are few. Las Bahías, at the remote hamlet of Coclé del Norte, offers simple accommodations

and makes a good base for exploring. Boats connect Coclé del Norte to Gobea, in Colón Province. Alternately, take a bus from Penonomé (see p. 150) to Coclesito, then rent a *cayuco* for the five-hour journey downriver. January through March is best.
🅰 145 A4–B4

Las Palmas

The sleepy village of Las Palmas in the hills of southwest Veraguas Province once lay along the old Pan-American Highway. Now a little-trafficked back road, the badly deteriorated route is a rolling ride offering magnificent scenery as it sidles south to **Soná** (a four-wheel-drive vehicle is recommended). One minute you're looking down over verdant meadows; the next you're scrambling up a forested mountainside. A dirt road leads from Las Palmas cemetery to a gorge where **El Salto,** a waterfall (accessed by an improved road), kicks up a spray. The cascade is the node of a 6,172-acre (2,498 ha) **Área Natural Recreativa,** although there are no facilities.
🅰 145 A2 ✉ 35 miles (56 km) W of Santiago via Interamerican Hwy., then 7 miles (11 km) S

Reserva Forestal la Laguna de la Yeguada

Drawing Panamanians on weekends and holidays, this pine-studded upland forest reserve covers 17,000 acres (70 sq km) surrounding a man-made lake that shimmers within an extinct volcanic crater. The crisp mountain air and rugged terrain bear an unlikely resemblance to England's Lake District. You can hike trails to a 100-foot (30 m) waterfall. Accessible by paved road, the reserve is a popular camping spot, but has no facilities.
🅰 145 B3 ✉ 40 miles (65 km) NE of Santiago, via Pedrogoso ☎ 998-0615

Gold Fever

When Columbus visited the Veraguas region in 1502, he met Indians who wore breastplates of gold. The gold fever that drew Columbus is still alive and well. Gold-bearing veins and fluvial gravels are common on the Caribbean slopes of Coclé Province, and the mines established by Spanish conquistadores opened and closed as the price of gold rose and fell. Small-time *oreros* still sift alluvial gravel at *lavaderos* in the soupy rivers, seeking their pot of gold at the end of the rainbow, while the mammoth Molejón Gold Project will tap a recently discovered vein containing an estimated 893,000 ounces (25,316 kg) of gold.

Home to cowboy towns, folkloric traditions, and offshore isles that are prime nesting sites for marine turtles

Azuero Peninsula

A *diablito* (devil) mask, Los Santos

Azuero Peninsula

Azuero, comprising Los Santos and Herrera Provinces, has a beguilingly enigmatic appeal wholly unique in the nation. Remarkably overlooked by tourists, this 2,941-square-mile (7,616 sq km) trapezoid of land extending into the Pacific Ocean is considered the soul of the nation. Nowhere else in the country seems so antique as Azuero, with its creaky museums, whitewashed churches, and exquisite colonial homes in calming pastels.

Christian traditions remain strong in churches such as Santo Domingo in Los Santos.

This is Panama's dry quarter, with the sun beating down hard as a hammer in the summer. Once a lush paradise, Azuero was deforested during the course of two centuries to make way for cattle. The barren wasteland of Parque Nacional Sarigua, in the extreme northeast, shows the ravaging long-term effect on the land. Mountainous western Azuero is much greener, but slash-and-burn agriculture still gnaws away at the forests. The peninsula is cowboy country par excellence. Men on *paso fino* horses, lassos at their sides, add an intriguing appeal to the savanna landscape.

Azuero is proud of its heritage. Almost every male above rap-appreciation age dons a *sombrero montuño* (see sidebar p. 79), the traditional straw hat that is an integral part of the national costume. Hat weaving is a local tradition, with Ocú the main center. Pottery is fired in old-fashioned adobe ovens in towns such as La Arena. And entire communities, such as Guararé and San José, keep *pollera* lacemaking traditions alive.

The region is famed for its festive spirit: Azuero hosts more than 500 festivals yearly, when the streets are full of young women exquisitely dressed in polleras. Pre-Lenten Carnaval celebrations draw thousands of visitors from around the country. And every community devotes a day to its patron saint.

The oldest archaeological sites in the nation are found along the eastern seaboard, notably the Sitio Arqueológico Cerro Juan Díaz, an important burial site dating back more than 2,000 years. Here, too, precious mangrove habitats gird mudflats that support profuse birdlife, protected by a string of wildlife refuges. Farther east, Refugio de Vida Silvestre Isla de Cañas is one of the hemisphere's prime marine turtle nesting sites. And snorkelers and scuba divers are rapturous about Refugio de Vida Silvestre Isla Iguana's coral reefs.

Two roads penetrate the peninsula from the Interamerican Highway. The easterly Carretera Nacional begins at Divisa and unfurls along a flat coastal plain. The more westerly route runs through the heart of Azuero, linking Ocú to Tonosí. Dipping and rising along the eastern flank of rugged mountains, this route passes through hamlets of simple rustic *bohíos* (huts). No roads span the mountains, and the narrow coastal plain on the western side lies a world away in Veraguas Province.

There are relatively few tourist facilities or hotels and even fewer restaurants outside the towns. Reserve accommodations well in

advance during festivals. Hotel investment has started near the beaches, and former president Mireya Moscoso's private airstrip near Pedasí has been opened as a public airport. ∎

NOT TO BE MISSED:

Los Santos' Museo de la
    Nacionalidad   171

Parque Nacional Sariqua   173

Birding at Refugio de Vida Silvestre
    Peñón de la Honda   174

Watching *sombreros ocueños* being
    made in Ocú   175

The Festival de la Pollera in
    Las Tablas   178

Snorkeling the coral reefs of
    Isla Iguana   179

Surfing at Playa Venado   182

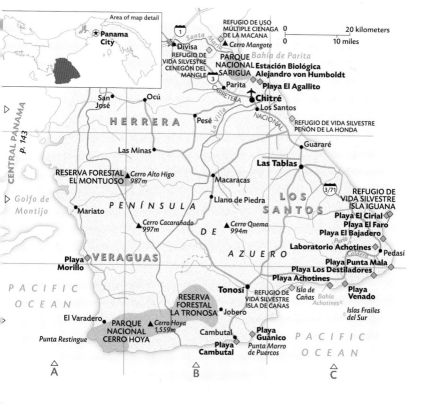

Chitré & Around

Cast in a quintessential colonial time warp, the towns of northeast Azuero boast whitewashed churches and a miscellany of modest attractions. While the beaches—popular with locals—have limited appeal, the shoreline wetlands teem with migratory and nesting birds.

There's always time for news from afar in Chitré.

Chitré

⬛ 169 B3

Visitor Information

✉ ATP,
   Circumvalacion
   La Arena, Chitré

☎ 974-4532

Museo de Herrera

✉ Calle Manuel
   Maria Correa
   & Ave. Julio
   Arjona, Chitré

☎ 996-0077

🕐 Closed
   Sun.–Mon.

💲 $

Chitré

The largest urban center, Chitré is a whirlwind of modern commercialism surrounding a colonial core. The town, founded in 1848 and named for an Indian *cacique,* is graced by row houses with red tile roofs, fronted by iron-studded doors and twirled wood window grills.

The leafy **Parque Unión** is highlighted by a *glorieta* (bandstand) and busts of local heroes. Casting cool shadows over the square, the **Catedral de San Juan Bautista** (built 1896–1910) has a fabulous gilt-and-mahogany altar, plus lovely stained-glass windows adorning an otherwise simple interior. The building shows few hints of being a post-colonial creation.

Housed in a merchant's mansion that later served as the town post office, the small **Museo de Herrera** traces the history of Azuero back to the antediluvian dawn. A mammoth fossil, pre-Columbian pottery and *huacas* (gold ornaments), and even a skeleton of a cacique buried with gold are among the museum's highlights. The upstairs room displays *polleras* and devil costumes. Sala Herrera is dedicated to the history of Chitré.

Playa El Agallito, 4 miles (7 km) north of Chitré, is one of Panama's prime birding sites. Vast mudflats extending more than a mile out to sea are exposed at low tide, when spoonbills, terns, egrets, phalaropes, stilts, and other shorebird species flock in their thousands, long bills stabbing the silt for tasty morsels while humans poke in the mud for *concha negra* clams. Many of the birds migrate from as far afield as Alaska and Argentina. At high tide, the birds hop over to the adjacent pond-pocked salt marshes. Guides can be hired at the Estación Biológica Alejandro von Humboldt.

The Río La Villa marks the divide between Chitré and Los Santos Provinces and between their twin namesake towns.

Villa de los Santos

Founded in 1557, Villa de los Santos—the "town of the saints"—is dear to Panamanians' hearts. The *grito de la Villa* ("scream of Los Santos") emanated from here on November 10, 1821, launching the revolution that culminated 18 days later in independence from Spanish rule. Panama's president flies in for the annual celebration that marks the occasion.

The old town's compact main square, **Plaza Simón Bolívar,** features busts of the South American hero, as well as of José Vallarino (1792–1865), a local lad who rose to become general of the royal vault. The plaza is dominated by the **Iglesia de San Atanasio,** dating from 1782. Its simple wooden interior, painted white, features a baroque gilt altar and walls embedded with a plaque of former priests interred within, plus rococo altar screens and a retable that pre-date the church. The life-size wooden figure of Christ in the glass sepulcher is paraded by candlelight on Good Friday.

The jewel in the local crown is the **Museo de la Nacionalidad,** in an 18th-century building where the nation's Declaration of Independence was signed in 1821. Painted in a delightful yellow, white, and turquoise combo, it is original in every regard, with walls of reed and adobe and well-worn terra-cotta floors. The charming gabled home opens to a beautiful courtyard with mortar and pestle, the remains of an old cart, and a reproduction of a traditional colonial country kitchen with clay *horno*

INSIDER TIP:

Take in the parade and other festivities every November 10 in Villa de los Santos, as Panamanians celebrate independence.

—PATRICIA DANIELS
National Geographic Books editor

(oven). Despite its diminutive size, this exquisite museum focusing on the quest for independence from Spain and the eventual creation of a nation is the region's most appealing. Exhibits include a collection of pistols, sabers, and muskets. The Instituto Nacional de Cultura's **Centro de Estudios Superiores**

Museo de la Nacionalidad

✉ Calle Jose Vallarino, Villa de los Santos

☎ 966-8192

🕐 Closed Mon.

💲 $

anam.gob.pa

Parita

169 B3

de Folklore Dora Pérez de Zárate (*Calle Vallarino, Plaza Simón Bolívar, tel 6819-7365*)—a school for students of folklore—can be visited by appointment.

The town is renowned for its festival of Corpus Christi (*May/ June; see sidebar opposite*), lasting two weeks and featuring more than one hundred performers in various costume. Master maskmaker **Carlos Ivan de León** (*Calle Tomas Herrera , tel 966-9194*) welcomes visitors to his studio to admire his fearsome devil masks.

Important archaeological finds are still being unearthed at **Sitio Arqueológico Cerro Juan Díaz** on a hill 3 miles (5 km) from Los Santos. The most important pre-Columbian burial site yet found in

Panama, it dates back more than 2,000 years. Be forewarned: The site has no facilities.

Parita

This quintessential charming 18th-century colonial town, 6 miles (10 km) northwest of Chitré, takes you back in time. The streets are lined with adobe dwellings, each painted in two-tone pastels. In the heat of mid-afternoon the village is surreally quiet.

At its heart is a small park where mock bullfights are held during the town's patron saint festival in early August. On its east side, the **Iglesia de Santo Domingo de Guzmán** dates from 1656; its steeple sparkles

Participants in the Corpus Christi festival, taking place in May and June, break for lunch.

with mother-of-pearl. Its interior has an elaborately carved pulpit plus a baroque altar supported by serpents. Silver candelabras and other religious icons gleam in the tiny **Museo de Arte Religioso Colonial** (closed Sat.–Sun.) in the adjoining chapel.

Parque Nacional Sarigua

With lunar landscapes evocative of the Sahara, this park encompasses a dramatically sculpted arid environment that makes a stark contrast to the distant backdrop of lush green mountains. Tracts of rare dry forest pock the fragile ecosystem, a devastating legacy of slash-and-burn agriculture during the past hundred years. Stripped of vegetation for cattle farms, the thin tropical soils were soon blown and washed away, leaving an infertile wasteland of rocks, wind-tossed sands, and deeply eroded gullies.

Though terrestrial wildlife is scarce, more than 160 bird species (mostly migratory) flock to salty lagoons and mangroves that fringe the shore. Pre-Columbian settlements dating back 11,000 years (older than anywhere else on the isthmus) have been found, though there is no excavation site to explore. A lookout at the **ANAM ranger station** provides sweeping views. Time your visit for the cool morning hours; afternoons can be insufferably hot.

Fully 50 percent of the 20,000-acre (8,000 ha) national park comprises marine environment extending 6 miles (9.5 km) from shore. Commercial shrimp farms can be visited.

Devil Dancers

The *danza de los diablos* (dance of the devils) is performed during Los Santos's Corpus Christi festival and is highlighted by the fight between *diablos sucios* (dirty devils), representing evil, and the *diablo blanco* (white devil, alias Archangel Michael), representing good. The diablos sucios don red-and-black-striped jumpsuits, red capes, and papier-mâché masks adorned with macaw feathers, usually representing demons or animals. Recalling pagan festivities, the dance can be traced back to Spain.

Birds of a Feather

Take your pick from a fistful of nature reserves protecting vitally important bird habitats in the Bahía de Parita—second only to the Bahía de Panamá for the quantity and variety of migratory shorebirds. At 5,000 acres (2,000 ha), **Refugio de Uso Múltiple Ciénaga de la Macana** is the largest freshwater wetland in Azuero and the only known breeding site in Panama for fulvous whistling-ducks and killdeer. Extending along the floodplain of the Río Santa María, its marshes surround a small lake covered with floating water hyacinths. Limpkins strut about, scavenging for snails,

Parque Nacional Sarigua

⛰ 169 B3

✉ 6 miles (10 km) NE of Parita

☎ 996-8216

$ $

anam.gob.pa

Refugio de Uso Múltiple Ciénaga de la Macana

⛰ 169 B3

✉ 1.2 miles (2 km) of El Rincón, 12 miles (20 km) N of Parita

Refugio de Vida Silvestre Cenegón del Mangle

🅰 169 B3

✉ 4 miles (6 km) E of Paris, 6 miles (10 km) N of Parita

Refugio de Vida Silvestre Peñón de la Honda

🅰 169 C3

✉ 1.5 miles (2.5 km) E of Playa Rompio

while snail kites watch from treetop perches. Birders in search of the glossy ibis should head to **Ciénaga del Rey,** a small marsh immediately west of La Macana and the bird's only known breeding site in Panama.

Refugio de Vida Silvestre Cenegón del Mangle protects 2,063 acres (835 ha) of mangroves, brackish wetlands, and dry scrub at the mouth of the Río Santa María. Boardwalks permit easy viewing of birdlife; anhingas, black-crowned night-herons,

The turnoff is marked by signs at the junction for Paris, 10 miles (16 km) south from the Interamerican Highway; a four-wheel-drive vehicle is useful.

Farther south, **Refugio de Vida Silvestre Peñón de la Honda** spreads over 58 square miles (150 sq km). It centers on tiny, rocky Isla Peñón de la Honda (2.5 miles/4 km offshore), a nesting site for blue-footed boobies, black-crowned night herons, magnificent frigate birds, and white ibises. Also included is a narrow

Parque Nacional Sarigua shows the devastating effect of slash-and-burn agriculture.

and boat-billed herons are its star draws. Snakes, caimans, and iguanas are commonly seen, and crocodiles are sometimes spotted.

The mudflats bubble with pools—*los pozos*—of cool waters that locals believe have curative powers. **Cerro Mangote,** a shell midden, dates back at least 7,000 years. The enthusiastic and knowledgeable ranger offers visitors the option of several guided walks.

strip of beach, tidal mudflats, and coastal wetlands and mangroves at the mouth of the Ríos Monjas and Bayano. Sandpipers, short-billed dowitchers, willets, and whimbrels abound. More than three-quarters of the refuge protects inshore waters where marine turtles breed and females gather, waiting for the full moon before coming ashore to lay their eggs. ■

Central Azuero

Forsaken by tourists yet superbly scenic, the Azuero interior is dominated by a broad mountain chain that runs clear down the peninsula. Twistier than a snake, the narrow highway through central Azuero steals away the hours as you coil along mountain ridges and curl through valleys whose traditional villages resound to the clip-clop of hooves.

Sleepy **Ocú** is known for its *sombreros ocueños*—the village's trademark straw hats trimmed in black and woven solely by women, such as Elena Montilla *(tel 974-1365)*. Local seamstresses also make *polleras* with a unique *punto de cruz* (point of the cross) embroidered stitch. **San José,** 4 miles (7 km) west of Ocú, is another epicenter of local ocueño traditions.

Occupying a fertile plain, quaint **Pesé,** 15 miles (24 km) east of Ocú, is surrounded by fields of sugarcane. Facing the village church is the **Destilería Don José** *(tel 974-9491, closed Sun.),* founded in 1936 and producing Seco Herrerano cane spirit. The distillery, open to visitors, evolved from the first sugar mill in the country, established in 1908. The crushing mill is open during the January-to-March harvest; tours are granted with one week's notice.

Mountain Roads

South of Ocú, the deteriorated road takes you up to **Las Minas,** a charming pine-studded mountain village, before dropping down to **Macaracas,** featuring a *talabartería* (saddlery) on the main street. **Llano de Piedra,** 6 miles (9 km) south of Macaracas, is a trip back in time, its

colonial houses fronted by well-trimmed lawns.

Southward, the road rises over the saddle between 3,271-foot (997 m) **Cerro Cacarañado** and 3,261-foot (994 m) **Cerro Quema**—a stupendously scenic switchback route. On the western flanks, **Reserva Forestal el Montuoso** covers 40 square miles (104 sq km) of tropical and premontane forest. A nature trail leads to the summit of 3,239-foot (987 m) **Cerro Alto Higo.** A bus from Las Minas serves Chepo, the reserve's gateway.

Tanager Tourism *(tel 6676-0220, tanagertourism.com)* offers ecotours into these scenic mountains and welcomes volunteer workers to participate in its reforestation projects. ∎

INSIDER TIP:

Guararé and Ocú are among the best places in Panama to buy *polleras.* Just don't expect them to come cheap—authentic polleras can cost $1,000 or more.

—PATRICIA DANIELS
National Geographic Books editor

Central Azuero
🗺 169 A2–B3

Reserva Forestal El Montuoso
🗺 169 A2
✉ 7.5 miles (12 km) W of Las Minas
☎ 500-0855
anam.gob.pa

Polleras

Panamanian women are never more graceful than when *empollerada*—dressed in their *polleras*—for festive occasions. Evolving from humble origins, Panama's beautiful national costume is today worn with pride by the daughters of the peasantry and the aristocracy alike.

Women display their *polleras* in Las Tablas's Festival Nacional de la Pollera.

The exquisite *pollera de gala* consists of a short-sleeved ruffled blouse, two-tiered full-length skirt, and petticoat; it derives from a Gypsy dress worn in Spain at the time of the 16th-century conquistadores. The simple white skirt, embroidered with floral designs, was perfectly suited to hot tropical climes. Spanish society ladies, sweltering in their heavy brocades and satins, enviously eyed the lightweight garment worn by their maids and servants and then appropriated it, further elaborating on the embroidery and decoration.

In Panama, the large, lavish hairpins of Spain's Valencia and Salamanca were enhanced by *tembleques* (tremblers) of gold and tortoise shell embellished with pearls, while chains of gold coins and precious jewels were also added to the outfit.

Accepted as the national dress by the time

of independence from Spain, the pollera and templeques have continued to evolve since that time, with several regional variations. However, the provinces of Herrera and Los Santos have jealously guarded their own pollera tradition, and their elaborate polleras de gala have been adopted throughout the nation. The finest polleras can cost tens of thousands of dollars and may take a year to complete.

A girl's *pollera* is completed by ribbons, chains, and *templeques*.

Ingredients of a Pollera

A pollera may be made either with cambric or fine linen, although the ground cloth must always be white. About 13 yards (12 m) of material is required. The blouse consists of two lace-edged ruffles and is worn off the shoulder, its neckline bordered with lace. The skirt is gathered on a waistband studded with gold buttons and consists of two or three ruffles that are raised to the sides, like a peacock's tail or mantilla fan.

The ruffles of blouse and skirt are adorned with motifs of birds, flowers, or native designs finely executed in *talco en sombra* (hand-sewn appliqué) of a chosen color. Brightly colored wool is woven in and out of the neckline border, a large matching *mota* (pom-pom) is centered at both chest and back, and four matching *gallardetes* (graceful streamers) or ribbons hang from the waist at front and back.

Five *cabestrillos*—chains of gold coins—hang from the *empollerada's* neck to her waist. A gold cross or medallion on a black velvet ribbon is worn as a choker. And a *monedero* (silk purse) suspended from the waistline is fastened with gold brooches. To complete the outfit, the woman slips on satin slippers.

The hair, typically tied in a bun behind the ears, is held in place by three large gold combs exquisitely filigreed, adorned with

pearls, and worn like a crown. More fanciful still are the templeques, elaborate "quivering pins" patterned after flowers or butterflies. Strung with pearls and sometimes with fish scales, the decorations tremble with the empollerada's every move.

Finally come the *zarcillos* (earrings) of intricately orna-mented gold or coral, and sometimes *dolores*—small gold discs tied to the hair at the temples.

Local Variations

The simpler *pollera montuna,* considered a daily dress, typically features a blouse with only one flounce, a skirt of solid color lacking embroidery, and a single gold chain and pendant earrings and perhaps an arrangement of natural flowers in the hair.

In the *pollera montuna ocueña,* from Ocú, the hair adornments disappear altogether, replaced by a traditional straw hat. And the *pollera basquiña,* once daily attire among country women, replaces the shoulderless blouse with a fitted white jacket-style blouse with buttoned collar, shoulder pleats, and flared hem.

Southeast Azuero

Heartland of Panama's folkloric tradition, this arid quarter is known for its festivals and party spirit. The best embroidered lace skirts in the country are produced in colonial towns ablaze with bougainvillea, while lonesome beaches accessed by dirt roads and until now known only to surfers are on the cusp of development as hoteliers are rushing in.

A surfer searches for the sweet spot on Playa Venado.

Southeast Azuero

169 B1–C2

Visitor Information

✉ ATP, Via Playa El Arenal, Pedasí

☎ 995-2339

✉ ANAM, Los Santos

☎ 966-9352

🕐 Closed Sat.–Sun.

visitpanama.com

Las Tablas & the *Polleras* Communities

The provincial capital of Las Tablas is an important center for *polleras* and each July 22 hosts the Festival de la Pollera (as well as the nation's wildest Carnaval). Its most interesting sites are found around **Parque Porras,** dominated by **Iglesia de Santa Librada.** The church was completed in 1789, although most of what you see is a reproduction following a devastating fire in 1950. The red-and-gold retables decorated with angels' heads are originals; so, too, the cruciform Virgin. **Museo Belisario Porras** honors the three-time (between 1912 and 1924) president of Panama; it occupies the home where Porras (1856–1942) was born. Porras bought a simple country house, built in 1889, which he used for cabinet meetings; today it contains exhibits relating to his life.

Northwest of Las Tablas, somnolent **Guararé** is a center for pollera production and for the distinctive five-string guitars known as *mejorana*s (note the giant mejorana at the northern entrance to town). The single-room **Casa Museo Manuel F. Zárate** (*Calle 21 Enero, tel 994-5644, closed Mon., $*) displays polleras from different regions alongside musical instruments and devil masks. Pollera-maker **Dilsa Vergara de Saavedra** (*Vía El Puerto Eloy Espino, tel 994-5221 or 6529-0445*) is renowned nationwide and welcomes visits. Despite its small size and quietude, Guararé comes alive each September during the Festival Nacional de la Mejorana, the country's most important folkloric festival. Then, ox-drawn wagons creaking with age parade through the streets bearing girls dressed in polleras.

Refugio de Vida Silvestre Isla Iguana

Created in 1981, Iguana Island Wildlife Refuge protects 131 acres (53 ha) of terrestrial and ocean realm. The islet, 3 miles (4.3 km) offshore from Playa El Bajadero (*2 miles/3 km NE of Pedasí*), is home to the largest nesting colony of magnificent frigate birds in Panama. During the midwinter mating season, males—they're the ones with inflatable red throat sacs—sit atop their nests, wings extended, puffing up their credentials as mates and ululating loudly. Brown pelicans also nest in certain years. Oystercatchers scurry along the beach, and five species of marine turtles arrive to nest between April and September.

Forty acres (16 ha) of coral reefs surround the isle. Twelve species of corals and more than 200 species of fish guarantee superb snorkeling with equally rewarding scuba diving farther out. Dolphins and harmless nurse sharks are commonly seen. Marine turtles flap by with leisurely sovereignty. And humpback whales migrate from colder waters to breed and give birth in the warm shallows between June and November.

Carnaval!

Las Tablas's streets vibrate with festive color, and never more so than during Carnaval, when the otherwise somnolent town explodes in party fever. For four days preceding Ash Wednesday, the town divides into Calle Arriba and Calle Abajo (High Road and Low Road). Each chooses a queen and competes to produce the best costume and music, while jesters toss tinted water at passersby. Each night after sundown, flamboyant floats with local beauties in their sequined, befeathered bikinis lead Brazilian-style parades, fireworks explode too close for comfort, and partying spectators (many of them drunk) crowd into the plaza for the slightly salacious fun. Each night is themed, culminating on Tuesday with women dressed in *polleras*.

Boats for Iguana leave from **Playa El Arenal** and **Playa El Bajadero.** However, service is fickle, and you need to clamber aboard through the surf. Trips can also be arranged through Buzos de Azuero (*tel 995-2405*).

The 20-minute boat ride puts you ashore on gorgeous **Playa El Cirial,** where you are greeted by swarms of tiny hermit crabs. The beach has a ranger station and tiny (continued on p. 182)

Museo Belisario Porras

✉ Ave. Belisario Porras, Parque Central, Las Tablas

☎ 994-6326

🕐 Closed Mon.; guides available Tues.–Sat.

💲 $

Refugio de Vida Silvestre Isla Iguana

🅼 169 C2

Visitor Information

✉ 3 miles (4.3 km) offshore of Playa El Bajadero; boats leave from Playa El Arenal & Playa El Bajadero

☎ 500-0921 or 994-6676 (ANAM, Las Tablas)

💲 $

A Drive Through Southeast Azuero

The ambitiously named Carretera Nacional (National Highway) runs inland of the eastern seaboard, skipping between a string of colonial towns and villages. The journey is a form of time travel, taking you back metaphorically one year with every mile.

Villa Camilla, near Pedasí, is one of Panama's most inviting hotels.

Begin by turning south at **Divisa** ❶ on the Interamerican Highway. Follow the Carretera Nacional for 14 miles (23 km) and divert north to visit **Parque Nacional Sarigua** ❷ (see p. 173) before continuing south to **Parita** ❸ (see pp. 172–173) to stroll quaint colonial streets bolstered by a historic church of note. Opposite the Shell gas station as you enter town, stop at the home and maskmaking studio of Dario López *(Carretera Nacional, 300 feet/100 m north of the gas station; see Travelwise p. 259),* a world-famous maker of papier-mâché devil masks. A gracious host, Dario displays his works, plus *diablitos* in red-and-black striped costumes.

More shopping awaits in **La Arena**, a tidy colonial village famous for ceramic workshops. The road is lined with artisans' stores; stop by **Cerámica Calderón** (see Travelwise p. 259), where patriarch Angel Calderón takes pride in showing his traditional spinning wheel and ovens.

NOT TO BE MISSED:

Parque Nacional Sarigua • Casa de Dario López • Museo de Herrera

Four miles (6.5 km) farther along the highway, the *carretera* delivers you to **Chitré** ❹ (see pp. 170–171), where you should peruse the **Museo de Herrera** and **Catedral de San Juan Bautista** on Parque Unión. From the southeast corner, follow Calle Aminta Burgos de Amado east, turn right onto Calle Carmelo Spadafora Abate (Carretera Nacional), and on to **Villa de los Santos** (see pp. 171–172). After viewing the main sites, call in at the **home of maskmaker Carlos Ivan de León** (see Travelwise p. 259).

Look for the roadside **La Casa de Pipa**

5.5 miles (9 km) south of Los Santos; stop here for fresh coconut water from a husked *pipa* (unripe coconut). After 14 miles (22 km), you enter **Guararé** ❺ (see pp. 178–179). Visit the **Casa Museo Manuel F. Zárate,** then follow the dirt road north to La Enea. Midway, stop at the **Casa de Dilsa Vergara de Saavedra** (see Travelwise p. 259), renowned nationwide for her *polleras.* Sra. Saavedra will explain and demonstrate her craft and happily pose with her medals won for the best skirts at the Concurso Nacional de Pollera. She can make a pollera to order.

Continue to **Las Tablas** ❻ (see p. 178), stopping to view the church and museum. For the final 26 miles (42 km) to the sleepy town of **Pedasí** ❼ (see p. 182), you pass through an increasingly impoverished and somnolent landscape where the opposing vehicle is likely to be a creaky ox-drawn cart.

End your day with an overnight at **Villa Marina** (see Travelwise p. 249) or **Hacienda Doña Carmen** (*tel 6672-7108, haciendadona-carmen.com*) with a second day given to visiting the **Isla Iguana** and **Isla Cañas wildlife reserves** (see pp. 179, 182, 184).

To turn this drive into a loop, continue west from Pedasí and follow the southern shore to **El Cacao,** then turn north to return to Las Tablas. This latter section via **Flores** and **El Muñoz** winds upward through exquisite mountain scenery, giving you magnificent views east over the coastal plains and Pacific Ocean.

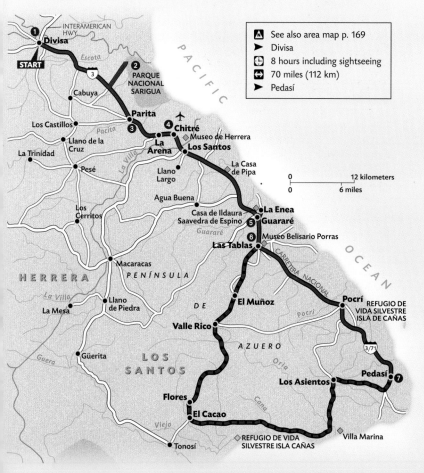

Mejorana guitars are made in Guararé.

Refugio de Vida Silvestre Pablo Arturo Barrios

✉ ANAM, Los Santos, 1.2 miles (2 km) E of Pedasí

☎ 966-9352

anam.gob.pa

visitor center. A nature trail connects El Cirial (on the west side) with **Playa El Faro** (on the ocean side), framed by rugged black rocks. High waves sometimes crash on El Faro; swimmers should use caution.

Camping is permitted beneath a shelter at the ranger station, which also has a dorm. There is no electricity, and self-sufficiency is a must. Don't go wandering off the trails, due to the presence of unexploded ordnance from World War II.

Pedasí & Around

A once sleepy fishing village at the southeastern tip of the Azuero Peninsula, Pedasí is

ground zero for a wave of tourism development in the region and provides a base for exploring beaches farther afield. **Pedasi Sports Club** (see Travelwise p. 265) offers scuba diving, fishing, and ecotours, and **Marco Díaz** (*tel 678-7272, islaiguana.com*) specializes in trips to Isla Iguana. Tuna fishermen set out from **Playa Punta Mala** to catch yellowfin and marlin; nearby, **Playa Los Destiladores** tempts with its gorgeous palm-fringed brown sands washed by surf.

Beyond Destiladores, **Playa Venado** (aka Playa Venao) is also beloved of surfers. This vast, scalloped 2-mile-long (3.5 km) stretch of gray sand is the setting for international surfing competitions. Large-scale resorts are rising behind the beach, and the bay is the site of a Smithsonian Tropical Research Institute reforestation project. Next door, the white sands of **Playa Achotines** gleam next to a cove; the headland is the setting for Laboratorio Achotines, a hatchery and laboratory (see p. 184). On the horizon, the twin **Islas Frailes del Sur** are the only nesting site in Panama for sooty and bridled terns.

Neotropic cormorants and black-crowned night-herons roost at **Refugio de Vida Silvestre Pablo Arturo Barrios,** extending along 12.5 miles (20 km) of shoreline between Ríos Purio and Caldera. It protects 37 square miles (96 sq km) of coastal wetlands and offshore waters. ∎

Parque Nacional Cerro Hoya

Secluded in the extreme southwest of the Azuero Peninsula, Cerro Hoya—an island of dense primary vegetation amid a sea of deforested land—receives only a handful of visitors. Yet ranging from offshore coral reefs to cool mountain heights, the park teems with precious wildlife.

Occupying 80,450 acres (32,557 ha), and with elevations ranging from sea level to 5,115 feet (1,559 m) atop Cerro Hoya, the park's climate varies considerably. Giant cedar, mahogany, and ceiba trees tower over tropical forests (moist, premontane, and montane). At lower elevations,

INSIDER TIP:

You have to have a really good eye to spot a sloth, but you might catch one on the (very slow) move.

—JENNIFER HOLLAND
National Geographic
magazine writer

much of the park is regenerating after decades of deforestation.

The forests resound with the calls of scarlet macaws and painted parakeets, two among 95 bird species recorded here. Sightings of tamanduas, sloths, agoutis, and squirrel monkeys reward adventure seekers.

Extending south into the Pacific Ocean, the park protects coral reefs and mangrove swamps as well as tiny offshore islands. By night, marine turtles arrive to nest on virginal beaches. The park has two ranger stations, plus administrative centers at **Restingue** (in Veraguas Province)

and outside the park at **Tonosí** (in Los Santos Province). The easiest access is from the west via the road from Santiago to El Varadero, beyond which with four-wheel-drive you can reach Restingue, a short hike from the park. From the east, you can enter the park on horseback or foot from **Jobero,** 16 miles (22 km) west of Tonosí, at the gateway to **Reserva Forestal La Tronosa,** a forest reserve adjoining the park. Alternately, you can hire a boat at **Playa Cambutal** (see p. 184) to the park boundary at **Tembladera;** you can even hike the shore at low tide—an overnight journey involving river crossings (a tide chart is essential), or drive partway with a four-wheel-drive vehicle depending on conditions. Basic accommodations and a *merendero* (snack shack) exist midway. Otherwise, you will need a tent and supplies. ∎

Parque Nacional Cerro Hoya
🅰 169 A1–B1

Reserva Forestal La Tronosa
🅰 169 B1
✉ ANAM, Los Santos, 1.2 miles (2 km) W of Jobero
☎ 500-0839
💲 $
anam.gob.pa

Arribadas

The olive Ridley turtle has hit on a clever idea to ensure its survival: an occurrence known locally as an arribada. When the moon is full, thousands of turtles congregate offshore, then surge ashore in an astonishing example of synchronized reproduction. Each arribada can occupy an entire week. So many eggs are laid (and destroyed by turtles digging up existing nests) that residents are granted rights to collect a limited number in a designated harvest zone.

More Places to Visit in Azuero Peninsula

Laboratorio Achotines

This hatchery and laboratory where scientists study tuna ecology borders beautiful Bahía de Achotines, whose welling marine currents provide a year-round spawning ground for tuna. Operated by the Inter-American Tropical Tuna Commission (IATTC, *tel 858/546-7100, iattc.org*), the facility is part of IATTC's Tuna-Billfish Program, which researches the early stages of tuna life. It has incubation pools and tanks where juvenile tuna fatten. The site also includes 173 acres (70 ha) of tropical dry forest inhabited by howler monkeys, iguanas, and toucans. Guided tours are offered by appointment, Monday through Thursday.

iattc.org 169 C2 Bahía de Achotines, 19 miles (31 km) SW of Pedasí 995-8166 $ (tours)

A male frigate bird inflates its chest in a show of proving itself a viable mate.

Playas Cambutal & Guánico

Playa Cambutal is a dark gray beach in three parts, hemmed in to the ocean by rugged mountains. Punta Morro de Puercos separates it from neighboring Playa Guánico, farther east. Until recently drawing only surfers, these lonesome lovelies have finally been discovered. Upscale residential resorts have been built, and the beach is now the setting for the Reef Classic Cambutal-Panama. Cambutal is a launch site via rented fishing boat for visits to nearby Parque Nacional Cerro Hoya (see p. 183), which can also be accessed by a rugged coastal hike. ANAM has an office in the fishing village of **Cambutal,** about 0.6 mile (1 km) inland.

169 B1 15.5 miles (25 km) SW of Tonosí 995-8180 (ANAM)

Refugio de Vida Silvestre Isla de Cañas

Cañas Island Wildlife Refuge was created in 1947 to protect Panama's most important marine turtle nesting site. Hawksbills, leatherbacks, loggerheads, olive Ridleys, and Pacific greens struggle ashore to lay their eggs on the gray-brown sands of this 9-mile-long (14 km) island, with August through November the peak nesting season.

The 98-square-mile (254 sq km) refuge—four-fifths of which extends out to sea—also includes mangroves that provide roosts for nesting colonies of cattle egrets, scissor-tail frigate birds, and white ibises. At night, the lagoon waters literally glow, thanks to microscopic dinoflagellates that emit a spectral bioluminescence when disturbed. Swimming is discouraged due to crocodiles . . . with luck you might see one moving stealthily, enveloped by a greenish glow.

To get to the refuge, turn off the Pedasí–Tonosí road at the hamlet of Agua Buena; the junction is poorly marked, and four-wheel drive is required in wet season for the 3-mile (5 km) dirt road. Boatmen will run you across the channel: Summon one with a metal clanger. The cooperative also offers compulsory guide service, basic accommodation, and a snack bar. **Isla Cañas Marina** *(tel 507/6980-0110, islacañasmarina.com),* inland of the island, offers paddleboard, kayak, and nighttime turtle-viewing tours.

anam.gob.pa 169 A1, B1 ANAM, Los Santos 994-7313 $$

Remote surf-washed beaches, mist-shrouded volcanic heights, and cool coffee-clad mountain vales

Chiriquí & the Cordillera

Ginger plant, Sitio Barriles, near Volcán

Chiriquí & the Cordillera

The most varied of Panama's provinces, ranging from beaches like fresh-fallen snow to misty cloud forest, this region requires at least a full week. Plunging gorges and razorback ridges, marine wetlands and offshore isles teeming with game fish, and cool highland valleys sheltering flower gardens and coffee farms compose a vastly diverse array of appealing options.

A busy commercial node and Panama's third largest city, David is the gateway to this region, divided between a long coastal plain narrowing eastward and a parallel mountain chain that is rugged in the extreme. Banana plantations and sugarcane smother much of the *llanura* (plain) west of town. Closer to shore, rivers meander through some of Central America's largest swamp systems:

important nesting sites for wading and shore-birds. The coastline is strung with gray-sand beaches popular equally with marine turtles and surfers. A necklace of isles redolent with forest is protected within Parque Nacional Marino Golfo de Chiriquí. The surrounding waters are world famous for sportfishing.

The lowlands can be suffocatingly hot and dry around David and oppressively humid by the shore. In contrast, the crisp highlands are marked by dozens of mild microclimates. The rivers cascade downhill

PARQUE INTERNACIONAL LA AMISTAD
Las Nubes
Cerro Punta
Nueva Suiza
Bambito
Guadalupe
PARQUE NACIONAL VOLCÁN BARÚ
Volcán ▲ 3,475m Barú
La Unión 42
Río Sereno
Volcán
Volcancito
Jungla de Panamá Wildlife Center

BOCAS DEL TORO p. 207

Cerro Horqueta 2,232m
Alto Lino
Boquete
Alto Boquete
Cerro La Estrella
Lago Fortuna
Panamá
RESERVA FORESTAL FORTUNA
Finca La Suiza
Central Hidroeléctrica Fortuna
4
Gualaca

NGÖBE-BUGLÉ

COSTA RICA

Macho de Monte
David
Chiriquí

41
43
Chiriquí
Charcha

CHIRIQUÍ

INTERAMERICAN HWY. de
Paso Canoa
El Tejar
Carta Vieja Rum Factory
1
David
Chiriquí
Alanje
Pedregal
Horconcitos
Chico
Manglares de David
Las Olas Beach Resort
Playa Barqueta
REFUGIO DE VIDA SILVESTRE PLAYA DE LA BARQUETA AGRÍCOLA
Bahía de Charco Azúl
Boca de San Pedro
Bahía de Muertos
Boca Chica
Playa Gallinaza
Playa Grande
Playa Hermosa
Isla Boca Brava
Puerto Armuelles
Isla Palenque
Isla San José
ARCHIPIÉLAGO DE Isla Gámez
Isla Parida LAS ISLAS PARIDAS
Isla Bolaños
PARQUE NACIONAL MARINO GOLFO DE CHIRIQUÍ

Golfo de Chiriquí

Islas Sec

0   20 kilometers
0   10 miles
Bella Vista
Punta Burica
A   B   C

1
2
3
4

A Ngöbe-Buglé family pictured on their _comarca_ (territory)

in leaps and bounds, perfect for challenging Class III and IV white-water runs.

The country's highest peak offers exhilarating hikes through the cloud forests of Parque Nacional Volcán Barú and Parque Internacional La Amistad, a million-acre (400,000 ha) reserve shared with Costa Rica. The parks are literally steps from the mountain resort towns of Boquete—Panama's "Little Switzerland"—and Cerro Punta. Tourists flock to the delightful hotels, gourmet restaurants, and cafés serving fresh-roasted coffees. Sitio Barriles preserves mementos of a pre-Columbian culture wiped out by a volcanic explosion.

Chiriquí is an ancient Guaymi word meaning "Valley of the Moon." The Guaymi, known today as Ngöbe-Buglé, live in remote mountain villages, many within a _comarca_ (autonomous reserve) established in 1998.

Direct flights serve David from Panama City. Alternately, the drive takes about five hours along the Interamerican Highway. The eastern section linking Veraguas Province is badly deteriorated; with one lane in each direction, it requires caution and should be avoided at night. The Interamerican runs to the Costa Rican border at Paso Canoa, about 290 miles (470 km) west of Panama City. _Careful!_ It is easy to drive straight through the border post. ∎

Area of map detail

★ **Panama City**

INTERAMERICAN HWY. •Tolé ①

CENTRAL PANAMA p. 143

◆ **Playa Las Lajas**

Isla Silva de Afuera

△ D △ E _Isla Ensenada_

NOT TO BE MISSED:

Along the Coastline

David, Panama's second largest city (pop. 90,000) sits on a coastal plain and, though short on sightseeing attractions, is centrally placed for hub-and-spoke exploration of Chiriquí Province. Along the humid coastline you will find mangroves, beaches washed by high surf, stupendous diving and fishing, and myriad emerald isles strewn like jewels in a sapphire sea.

Bananas are sorted in Puerto Armuelles.

David

⚑ 186 C2

Visitor Information

✉ ATP, Edificio
Don José, Ave.
Domingo Díaz,
bet. Calles
5ta & 6ta

☎ 775-2839

🕐 Closed Sat.–Sun.

ipat.gob.pa

**Museo de
História y Arte
José de Obaldía**

✉ Ave. 8a Este, bet.
Calle A Norte &
Calle Central

David & Around

Congested David (dav-EED) is known most for its weeklong mid-March fiesta honoring the city's patron saint, but despite its overriding modernity also boasts a handful of modest historic draws.

A major agricultural center, David is surrounded by cattle country (rodeos are frequently held on Sundays). Although founded in 1602, there is comparatively little sense of the past (in 1732 the town was razed by indigenous peoples). The crowded town center bustles with business. The whirligig of commercialism revolves around **Parque Cervantes,** overlooked by a ho-hum

church, the 19th-century **Iglesia de la Sagrada Familia.**

Barrio Bolívar, the historic core, lies south of the main square and clings to a slower pace. David's few sites of interest are here. The **Museo de História y Arte José de Obaldía** occupies the former two-story home of the namesake founder (1806–1889) of Chiriquí Province. Built in 1880, its timbers creak with age. At press time it was in the final stages of a five-year restoration and when reopened will display period furniture, pre-Columbian relics, colonial-era pieces, and religious items.

The restoration also includes the adjacent and equally charming colonial structure; it is intended to once again house the **Fundación Gallegos y Culturama,** a research library with a miscellany of intriguing exhibits that include a 19th-century printing press plus pre-Columbian ceramics. Nearby stands **La Hermita San José de David** *(Ave. 10 Este at Calle A Norte),* with a recently restored (albeit weathered) stone bell tower now made complete by the addition of a church.

Boats can be rented at the port of **Pedregal,** 3 miles (5 km) south of David, for trips through the Manglares de David and to **Parque Nacional Marino Golfo de Chiriquí** (see p. 191). David is

INSIDER TIP:

Panamanian *montuño* hats are distinguished from "Panama" hats (made in Ecuador) by their flat brims and multicolored designs.

—JUSTIN KAVANAGH
National Geographic Travel Books editor

also linked by air to Panama City, Bocas del Toro, and San José, Costa Rica.

Golfo de Chiriquí Shoreline

South of David, the **Manglares de David**—the largest mangrove system in Panama—spans 28 miles (45 km) of estuaries in the delta of Ríos Chiriquí, Chico, and David, which merge into Boca de San Pedro. The waterways form a con-voluted lacework through dense mangroves and mudflats teeming with migratory shorebirds. Part of the system comprises **Refugio de Vida Silvestre Playa de la**

Barqueta Agrícola, extending west from Boca San Pedro. Three-quarters of this 14,665-acre (5,935 ha) reserve protects off-shore waters where marine turtles mate before nesting on **Playa Barqueta.** Driftwood adds to the dramatic beauty of this desolate, lonesome beach unspooling for 10 miles (16 km) like a ribbon of silver lamé. (Bring insect repellent to ward off the *chitras,* no-see-ums that are particularly active around dawn and dusk.) Savage waves may tempt you to bodysurf, but caution is required due to fierce riptides (see sidebar below). Other than the bargain-priced all-inclusive Las Olas Beach Resort (which sells passes for day or night visits; see Travelwise p. 253), the only facilities are two simple restaurants.

The eastern shoreline of Chiriquí is heaven for surfers seek-ing a less crowded wave. A top draw is **Playa Las Lajas,** a 7-mile (11 km) slingshot of dun sands where tourism is beginning to stir. Offshore **Isla Silva de Afuera** is a small island with Big Kahuna rides.

Golfo de Chiriquí Shoreline

⛰ 186–187 B2–D2, E1–E2

Visitor Information

✉ ATP, Edificio Don José, Ave. Domingo Díaz, bet. Calles 5ta & 6ta
☎ 775-2839
🕐 Closed Sat.–Sun.

Refugio de Vida Silvestre Playa de la Barqueta Agrícola

⛰ 186 B2
☎ 774-6671 or 6716-8301
🕐 Closed Sat.–Sun.

Don't Drown! What to Know About Riptides

By far the greatest danger facing visitors to Panama off the roads is that of being caught in a riptide. These ferocious ocean currents claim more lives every year than snakebites, sunstroke, and natural disas-ters combined.

Riptides are associated with beaches subject to heavy surf. When waves form a dam preventing the water's retreat, any weak point can allow a fast-moving out-bound channel. Swimmers caught in the current will be dragged out to sea.

The natural instinct is to strike for shore—a big mistake. Even the strongest swimmer can quickly tire and drown. Since the channel is usually relatively narrow, the key to escaping is to swim parallel to shore (i.e., perpendicular to the current).

Riptides are not static, but migrate along the beach, and can form and dis-sipate quickly. Their presence is often betrayed by a still, glassy surface in the midst of waves.

Boca Chica

⚊ 186 C2

Isla Boca Brava

⚊ 186 C2

Boca Chica

The mainland fishing village of Boca Chica lies 18 miles (25 km) south of the Interamerican Highway via the community of **Horconcitos** (a roadside hamlet known for its saddlemakers). The road, which once resembled a tank-training course, has been paved. Several ritzy hotels have recently opened. Residential resorts have broken ground at **Playa Hermosa** and **Playa Gallinaza.** The new

---

Crude Oil

Charco Azul (Blue Ditch), 6 miles (10 km) west of Puerto Armuelles, is the Pacific terminus of an oil pipeline that crosses the continental divide, linking Charco Azul to Chiriquí Grande in Bocas del Toro Province. The 81-mile-long (131 km) pipeline, operated by Petroterminal de Panamá, was completed in 1982. Supertankers carrying oil from Alaska and Ecuador are too big for the canal. Hence, they discharge their cargo here for shipment to refineries in Houston and the Gulf states.

Cala Mia Boutique Hotel (see Travelwise p. 249) resort is a good base and offers visitors a host of facilities including a spa. It also offers outings including horseback riding, mangrove tours, scuba diving, and several other activities.

Isla Boca Brava

Isla Boca Brava floats in the Bahía de Muertos, about one-half mile (0.8 km) from Boca Chica; water taxis link the two. Howler monkeys holler as you hike trails through thick forest teeming with wildlife.

Activities include seasonal whale-watching. Gone Fishing Panama Resort Hotel (see Travelwise p. 265) and Panama Big Game Fishing Club (see Travelwise p. 265) offer sportfishing in the Hannibal Bank, and Panama Surf Tours (see Travelwise p. 264) can take you surfing.

Punta Burica

A needle-thin peninsula pierces the Pacific, marking Panama's extreme western tip. The gateway to this lonesome promontory is **Puerto Armuelles,** a rambling, relatively prosperous town surrounded by banana groves. Once farmed by the United Fruit Company (now Chiquita Brands), the fields are now tended by a worker's cooperative. The company legacy still stands south of town in a *barrio* (district) of colorful, albeit tumbledown, clapboard houses. Beyond, a gray-sand beach, palm-lined, curls gently south toward the Petroterminal de Panamá oil terminal.

The end of the road comes at Petroterminal, beyond which—at outgoing tide only!—you take to the beach as a roadway (after signing in at the terminal guardhouse). Mountains wrapped in dark folds of forest rise up behind. Panama Surf Tours (see Travelwise p. 264) offers eight-day surfing tours. Truck-buses run inland of the beach along a tortuous mud track to the hamlet of **Bella Vista,** from which it's an hour-long hike to the tip of Punta Burica.

Sugar-fine sands dissolve into azure waters on Isla San José.

Parque Nacional Marino Golfo de Chiriquí

Anchored in the middle of the Golfo de Chiriquí, this stellar marine park known for its glorious beaches and pristine coral reefs embodies many of the attributes that visitors to Panama might hope to see. Overflowing with wildlife, the hard-to-access park offers stupendous birding opportunities and great white-sand beaches.

The Gulf of Chiriquí Marine Park was established in 1994 to protect some 57 square miles (148 sq km) of marine ecosystems and the two dozen or so islands of the **Archipiélago de las Islas Paridas** that speckle these Pacific waters.

The real Goliath among these isles is Isla Parida. Its rolling hills are swathed in moist tropical forest and fringed by dense mangroves—perfect roosts for magnificent frigate birds, which wheel and slide overhead like kites on invisible strings. The forests vibrate with the squawks of parakeets and the stentorian roar of howler monkeys.

ANAM has a ranger station located here.

Jade-colored and bathtub warm, the waters around **Isla San José** are a snorkeler's dream. So, too, are those surrounding **Isla Bolaños,** where at night hawksbill and leatherback turtles come ashore to lay their eggs. By day, turtles graze among coral reefs nibbled upon by parrot fish in their Joseph's coats of many colors. Anglers rave about the explosive strike of cubera snapper, roosterfish, and other game fish.

Boaters are drawn to **Isla Gámez,** half a mile (0.8 km) northeast of Parida. Unfortunately, its beaches are often strewn with trash. Access to the park is by boat from Boca Chica (see p. 190).

Fundación MarViva (*marviva.net*) has sponsored the formation of Aventuras Rurales del Golfo (ARUG, *arugpanama .com*), a cooperative of fishermen and coastal dwellers that offers a range of adventure activities including snorkeling, turtle-viewing trips, and various other eco-friendly excursions in the gulf. ■

Parque Nacional Marino Golfo de Chiriquí

🗺 186 C1

Visitor Information

✉ ANAM, Vía Red Grey, David

☎ 775-3163

🕐 Closed Sat.–Sun.

anam.gob.pa

Parrots & Macaws

Panama boasts 18 of the world's 330-plus species of parrots, including 6 of the 16 macaws. The quintessential avians of the neotropics, these gregarious birds (flocks of several hundred are common) are characterized by their uncanny intelligence and gift of the gab.

Uniquely, parrots possess four toes on each foot, with two facing forward and two rearward, providing the dexterity to grasp fruits and nuts just as if the birds had opposable thumbs. Their hooked and immensely strong beaks have evolved to slice through nuts and

Scarlet macaws are among the most beautifully plumed of parrots.

seeds like metal cutters, while rasp-like ridges inside the upper bill can grind even the hardest pits to dust.

Most parrots are lime green, with varying colored markings that separate the species and subspecies. The most common genus includes the more than 50 species of so-called Amazon parrots—medium-size, stocky birds with heavy bills and slightly rounded, truncated tails. Savvy beyond their size, they have the intelligence and temperament of a two-year-old child. The country's very own Panama Amazon or yellow-fronted Amazon (*Amazona ochrocepala panamenis*) is the smallest and least colorful of the Amazons, its sole distinguishing marks being gray eye-rings, orange epaulets, and a small patch of yellow on the forehead. Found only along the Pacific coast, the Panama Amazon prefers savannas and woodlands. An inquisitive and talkative fellow, the Panama adapts well to captivity and is an expert mimic renowned for its linguistic abilities. Most birds waterproof their feathers using a special gland in the middle of their lower back with secretions that act as both an antibacterial and antifungal agent. The Amazons lack this gland and instead uses a powder from their down feathers.

Macaws

The gaily colored macaws—the giants of the parrot kingdom—are as haughty and elaborately plumed as emperors, with authoritative voices to match. Five of the six species of Panama's macaws are endangered due to deforestation and to poaching both for the pet market and for their long trailing tail feathers, plucked for use in folkloric ceremonies.

Although not yet considered endangered, the rust-red green-winged macaw (*Ara*

Blame the Devil Dancers

The devil dancers of Azuero (see sidebar p. 173) are partly to blame for the demise of macaws. Many top their costumes with headdresses of quivering red macaw feathers to create an illusion of flaming hair, representing the blazing fire of the devil.

Demand fueled illegal hunting. However, recent conservation efforts have trimmed the trade. An education program aims to educate the *diablos sucios* about the effect their passion has on macaw populations. Meanwhile, the dancers can now rent from a "bank" of macaw feathers donated by zoos, etc.

Others are learning to use feathers from geese and pheasants, which can be colored red and orange.

The conservation effort, initiated by Francisco Delgado, a professor from the University of Panama in Santiago de Veraguas, has had great success, not least because the dancers can buy artificial macaw feathers for a fraction of the price of the real thing. As a result, the value of real macaw feathers has been depressed, deterring illegal hunting while rescuing macaws from a sad fate and preserving a cultural tradition.

chloroptera) has nonetheless disappeared from part of its former range in Panama. The scarlet macaw (*Ara macao*), called *guacamayo* locally, is today found only in Cerro Hoya and Isla Coiba National Parks; named for its bloodred plumage, the scarlet macaw has wings of bold royal blue and yellow. The Caribbean-dwelling great green, or Buffon's macaw, has all but vanished in the wild and like most of Panama's macaw species is found only in Darién Province;

INSIDER TIP:

Parrots, particularly Amazons, can be found almost everywhere in Panama, but you'll need to seek out the much rarer macaws in remote locations.

—PATRICIA DANIELS
National Geographic Books editor

The blue-and-gold macaw in flight

too, occupies the lowlands of eastern Panama, albeit in diminishing numbers. Measuring more than 3 feet (1 m) to the tip of its tail feathers, it's also the largest of the six macaws.

Parrots and macaws make their nests in hollowed-out tree trunks. Males feed their partners by regurgitating food while females incubate the eggs and feed the young. Monogamous for life, parrots are often seen flying in pairs, the male and female squawking love notes as they sail overhead like double rainbows with their wings almost touching.

uniquely, these bright green birds blush when excited, their white featherless cheeks turning rose-petal pink. The amiable blue-and-gold macaw (*Ara ararauna*) is recognizable by its dazzling coat of teal blue and chest of yellow. It,

The Highlands

Known as the city of eternal spring, the popular highland destination of Boquete enjoys an enviably scenic location on the eastern flank of Volcán Barú. Roads lined with angel trumpet-vine herald a world of exquisite beauty. Coffee estates, white-water rafting, and trails that offer superb hiking and birding are among the key draws of the highlands.

A native Kuna picks ripe coffee cherries during coffee harvest season, between November and March.

Boquete
🅜 186 B4
Visitor Information
✉ CEFATI, Alto Boquete
☎ 720-4060

Boquete

The road from David ascends as smoothly as a line in a logarithmic equation—a 25-mile (40 km) straight shot that delivers you to the **Centro de Información Turística** (CEFATI) atop a bluff known as **Mirador de la Virgen de la Gruta** in Alto Boquete (Upper Boquete). CEFATI offers fabulous views over the town center, known as Bajo Boquete (Lower Boquete), laid out below in the tight valley of the Río Caldera at an elevation of 3,950 feet (1,300 m). Boquete is cupped by lush mountains, with the brooding mass of Volcán

Barú to the west and Cerro Azul and Cerro La Estrella to the east.

Founded in 1911, Boquete was settled early last century by immigrants from central Europe. The Swiss, Germans, and even Slavs left their mark in building styles.

The past decade has witnessed an explosion in tourism along with an influx of foreign residents and an associated real estate boom. The area is also home to one of the largest concentrations of Ngöbe-Buglé Indians in the country, their simple dresses in primary colors adding to the charm of Boquete.

Gently sloping Bajo Boquete makes for delightful ambling.

The heart of affairs is **Parque Domingo Médica,** where locals gather to gossip beneath redolent pines. On weekends, Ngöbe-Buglé set up stalls to sell their exquisite crafts. An **antique railroad car** marooned on a slice of track on the plaza's east side is a reminder of the railway, built in 1912, that once linked Boquete to the coast. Diagonally across the plaza, **Parque de las Madres** features a statue of mother and child. A five-minute uphill walk to the lovely **Panamonte Inn & Spa** (see Travelwise p. 250), dating from 1914, is well rewarded for its charming gardens and ambience.

Orientation tours by jeep are offered by Boquete Mountain Safari (tel 6627-8829, boquete safari.com), which also offers ATV tours and rafting.

Bloomin' Lovely: Plants and shrubs love Boquete's climate. Flower cultivation is a local industry. Many *viveros* grow lilies, carnations, and even roses, while locals coddle their plants with an almost English obsession.

Mi Jardín es Su Jardín (Ave. Central, 0.5 mile/0.8 km NW of Boquete) is a riot of color and scents. Spread over 12 acres (5 ha), the private garden of the González family draws visitors to admire ferns, azaleas, impatiens, hibiscus, and roses laid out in semi-formal fashion. Psychedelic cows and cut-out human figurines are among the eclectic oddities (the owner's house is off-limits).

Each January, the Fería Internacional de las Flores y el Café (Ave. Buenos Aires, tel 720-1466, feriadeboquete.com), the Flower and Coffee Fair, displays the local gardeners' arts and crafts. The showground on the east bank of the Río Caldera boasts 10,000 varieties of flowers. It is open year-round, but is best seen during the Feria de las Orquídeas each April.

Jungla de Panama Wildlife Refuge is Panama's only licensed

Jungla de Panama Wildlife Refuge

- ✉ Palmira Centro, 1 mile (1.6 km) W of Boquete
- ☎ 6981-3755 or 6968-6010
- 💲 $$

jungladepanama.org

EXPERIENCE: Try White-water Rafting

Rafting the rivers under the care and control of professional guides provides the ultimate combination of natural beauty and thrills. Intoxicating rides will have you laughing with delight as you paddle through tricky cascades, while tranquil stretches allow quiet contemplation of the scenery and fleeting wildlife. The rivers are at their best May to December, but can be rafted year-round.

Close to Panama City, the **Río Chagres** is surrounded by rain forest and offers Class II and III runs, with the chance to pull ashore at Emberá villages. To the west, Ríos **Chiriquí, Chiriquí**

Viejo, and **Majagua** pour off the slopes of Volcán Barú and cascade down to the Pacific plains.

Aventuras Panamá (tel 260-0044 or 6679-4404, aventuraspanama.com) has one-day trips on the Chagres, which reaches its peak in November.

Boquete Outdoor Adventures (tel 720-2284, boqueteoutdooradventures.com) leads raft and kayak trips on the Chiriquí and Majagua.

Chiriqui River Rafting (tel 6879-4382, panama-rafting.com) offers trips of the Chiriquí and Chiriquí Viejo aboard self-bailing rafts.

Finca Lérida

✉ Alto Quiel, 6
miles (9.6 km)
NW of Boquete

☎ 720-2285 or
720-1111

$ $

fincalerida.com

**Beneficio
Cafetalero
Café Ruíz**

✉ Hwy. 43, Alto
Boquete

☎ 720-1000 or
6672-3786

🕐 1- and 3-hr.
tours by appt.

$ $$$

caferuiz.com

animal sanctuary—a chance to see
ocelots, margays, coatis, monkeys,
and other creatures that were
orphaned or rescued. You can
even stay overnight: Accommoda-
tions range from a hostel to an
upscale casita.

Coffee Tours: Panama's fin-
est coffee is grown in Boquete,
whose slopes are patterned in
rows of green corduroy. Several
producers and roasters welcome
visitors to their *beneficios* (coffee
mills). During harvest season,
Ngöbe-Buglé Indians compose
the workforce and flock to
pick ripe beans from the dark
green bushes.

The loveliest *cafetal* (coffee
plantation) is **Finca Lérida**, com-
bining a 110-acre (44.5 ha) coffee
estate with 640 acres (259 ha)
of primary forest and another
140 acres (57 ha) given to crops
such as lettuce and carrots.
Visitors can savor a fresh-roasted
brew in the coffeehouse overlook-
ing the original beneficio, now a
museum with exhibits relating to

coffee production. Five miles
(8 km) of manicured trails lead
into the adjacent cloud-forest
reserve where the two-tone
whistles of quetzals promise
potential sightings. Guided and
self-guided tours are offered. Finca
Lérida operates a lovely bed-and-
breakfast (see Travelwise p. 251).

**Beneficio Cafetalero Café
Ruíz** also offers tours that include
the coffee fields in Palmira and
beneficio in Boquete, ending with
a delicious tasting in the coffee
shop. You can sign up for a tour

Boquete Coffee

The arabica coffee plant grows best in
well-drained soils at elevations of 2,500
to 3,500 feet (760–1,070 m), with nearly
constant temperatures between 59°F and
82°F (15°–28°C) and a distinct wet and dry
season. The climate, slopes, and rich soils
of the Chiriquí highlands are perfect for
coffee cultivation and produce a distinctly
flavored coffee—mellow and aromatic,
with a hint of acidity—that connoisseurs
say is among the best in the world.

The glossy green bushes begin fruiting
by their fourth year, announced at the

onset of rainy season by the appearance
of tiny white blossoms that scent the air
with a jasminelike fragrance. The beans
are surrounded by lush green berries that
turn bloodred by October, the time of the
seasonal harvest.

The hand-picked berries are shipped to
beneficios, where the fleshy outer layers are
removed to expose the beans, which are
blow-dried or spread out in the sun in the
traditional manner. The leathery skins are
then stripped away, the beans are roasted
and . . . java!

A climber seeks a route up a rock face of hexagonal basalt near Boquete.

at Café Ruiz at CEFATI in Boquete.

Estate Palo Alto, northeast of Boquete, offers daily group tours that include the **Kotowa Coffee Tour,** where visitors are shown the processing plant and a coffee mill—the oldest in Panama—that doubles as a cupping room for tastings. There are no signs to Estate Palo Alto, as drop-ins without reservations are discouraged. Kotowa hosts the **Boquete Tree Trek** (see Travelwise p. 265), a three-hour zipline ride along steel cables strung between treetop platforms.

Mountains Highs: To visit Boquete and not hike is akin to visiting France without tasting the wine. There are trails for every ability. Local hotels can recommend reputable guides.

Three short loops lead from Bajo Boquete to the trailheads. The most southerly loop departs the center of town and ascends through lush coffee fields to **Volcancito,** from which the hale and hearty can hike to the summit of **Volcán Barú** (see pp. 198–199). A second loop leads northeast to **Alto Lino,** where a less challenging trail leads up 7,323-foot (2,232 m) **Cerro Horqueta.** Another trail from Alto Lino transcends the continental divide and descends through **Parque Internacional La Amistad** (see pp. 222–223) to the Caribbean lowlands—an arduous four-day adventure.

The most dramatic drive is the 13-mile (20 km) **Bajo Mono** loop, switchbacking sharply upward through a canyon framed by a wall of hexagonal basalt columns formed by magma from an eons-old volcanic eruption. You can drive to the end of the road at **Alto Chiquero,** step from your car, and start walking the aptly named Sendero Los Quetzales

Kotowa Coffee Tour

✉ Estate Palo Alto, 3 miles (5 km) NE of Boquete

☎ 720-3852 or 6634-4698

🕐 Tours Mon.– Sat. 2 p.m.; Sun. & private tours by appt. through Coffee Adventures, tel 720-3852, *coffeadventures.net*

💲 $$$$

kotowacoffee.com

The Sendero Los Quetzales offers fine views over Cerro Punta.

Parque Nacional Volcán Barú

▲ 186 B4

Visitor Information

✉ ANAM, Vía Aeropuerto

☎ 774-6671 or 775-2055

(see opposite), which wends around the northern slopes of Volcán Barú. If you've ever wanted to see a quetzal, then this is as good as it gets.

You can even drive all the way to the summit on a "Volcano Jeep Tour" with Boquete Mountain Safari *(tel 6627-8829, boquetesafari .com)*, using customized Jeeps. The journey begins before dawn, and you ascend through five climate zones in time to view both the Caribbean and the Pacific Ocean.

Parque Nacional Volcán Barú

Protecting the brawny, thickly forested flanks of Panama's sole volcano, this park is easily accessed, providing fantastic, albeit challenging hikes and prime quetzal viewing. On clear days you can see both the Caribbean Sea and Pacific Ocean from the mountain's summit—the highest point in the country.

The 55-square-mile (142 sq km)

park abutting Parque Internacional La Amistad is centered on the eponymous 11,398-foot (3,475 m) volcano, which has slumbered peacefully for the last 500 years. Seven craters pock the summit (topped by communication towers). They are attainable from the east by the 8.5-mile-long (13.5 km) trail that begins at the ANAM ranger station above **Volcancito,** 5 miles (8 km) west of Boquete. Driving the steep rocky track to the station requires a high-ground-clearance, four-wheel-drive vehicle with off-road tires; otherwise, it's a 45-minute hike from the end of the paved road at Volcancito. The summit trail is a challenging five-hour hike from the ranger station (the boulder-strewn track can also be driven—a brutal ordeal guaranteed to shake your teeth loose).

From the west side, a track that begins roadside about 2.5 miles (4 km) north of **Volcán** leads 4 miles (7 km) east to the summit trailhead. This is a steeper route than the Boquete trail; allow a good ten hours minimum to summit and return.

Hiking with a seasoned guide enhances the possibilities of spotting quetzals, whose melodious two-note whistles lure you on like the mysterious calls of Rima the bird girl from *Green Mansions*. Black-bellied and brown violet ear hummingbirds flit past, the metallic clang of the endangered three-wattled bellbird rings through the forest, and hikers thrill to sightings of such endemics as yellow-thighed finches and black-chested warblers. Set out before dawn to beat the clouds that often blanket the upper heights by mid-morning, and bring warm clothing and rain gear.

The **Sendero Los Quetzales** trail threads the lush green blankets of the north slope and links the ANAM ranger stations at **Alto Chiquero,** which has a dorm with cold shower, and **El Respingo** at Bajo Grande, near Cerro Punta (see pp. 201–203). Six hours should be sufficient for this 12-mile (19 km) mostly uphill trail, which is well named. More than 300 breeding pairs of quetzals inhabit the park, and they are often seen tending their nests or in sweeping dip-and-rise flight. A government attempt to turn Sendero Los Quetzales into a paved highway was canceled due to outraged public reaction following a campaign led by Fundación para el Desarrollo Integral de Cerro Punta (FUNDICCEP; *tel 771-2171, e-mail: fundiccep@cwpanama.net*), a group that sponsors local sustainability projects.

The park's thriving mammal population includes all five species of cats. Pumas are particularly common, although infrequently seen. Wildlife viewing is enhanced by participating in guided hikes, offered from Boquete by Coffee Adventures *(tel 720-3852, coffeeadventures.net)* and Los Quetzales *(tel 771-2291, losquetzales.com).*

Around Volcán

The town of Volcán enjoys a gloriously scenic setting on the western flank of Volcán Barú. Though its own appeal is limited, it draws adventure-minded

Quetzals

The resplendent quetzal, a member of the trogon family, is an exotic and elusive species that draws many birders to Panama (see p. 47). Its iridescent emerald plumage is so luxuriant that the Maya worshiped it as a sacred bird.

The endangered pigeon-size bird is common at elevations of 3,500 feet (1,070 m), where cloud forests are found. The male boasts a chest of brilliant crimson and trailing tail feathers sinuous as feather boas, which it puts to good use in its mating displays. The quetzal prefers the avocado-like fruit of the aguacatillo, which it plucks from below in mid-flight.

visitors keen on kayaking, hiking, or birding, while coffee estates line a spectacular ridgetop drive that extends west to the Costa Rica border.

All services locally are centered on the town of **Hato de Volcán** (more commonly known as Volcán), on a bare, high plateau on the southwestern slopes of Volcán

Barú. The area was first settled by Swiss immigrants a century ago, and their architectural legacy is evident. The nondescript town serves as a gateway to sites farther afield. Plans to build a new road to link Cuesta de Piedra, 7 miles (10 km) south of town, with Boquete promise to increase tourist traffic.

Worth a quick visit, **Janson's Coffee Farm** (tel 6569-7494, lagunasadventures.com, closed Sun.) is a hilltop coffee roaster and café above the company beneficio on the south side of town. Free tours of the company's **La Torcaza Estate** coffee farm and beneficio

A pre-Columbian ceramic urn at Sitio Barriles

are given by request. After sampling the coffees, birders should head to nearby **Lagunas de Volcán.** These three small lagoons enveloped by wetlands covering 352 acres (143 ha) are an important stop for migratory waterfowl. The muddy access road begins on the north side of the airstrip and is suitable for four-wheel-drive vehicles only. Don't swim here, as it's easy to get caught in the weeds.

The Río Macho de Monte rises on the west flank of Volcán Barú and drops through the sheer-walled **Cañón Macho de Monte,** with waterfalls tumbling dramatically into cool pools. Access off the highway is via the track to a hydroelectricity plant that begins 7 miles (12 km) south of Volcán. Thrilling raft trips are offered by Chiriquí River Rafting (see Travelwise p. 265), and inner tubes can be rented from Casa Grande Bambito Resort (see Travelwise p. 251) for floats upriver.

West of Volcán

The proverbially long and winding road that leads to Río Sereno west of Volcán is to be enjoyed for its own sake as it snakes through mountains draped in cloud forest and coffee fields.

The small roadside coffee farm of José Luis and Edna Landau doubles as an archaeological site—**Sitio Barriles**—where the remains of a culture dating from 300 to 600 B.C. include a tomb, a large rock carved with an ancient map, plus remnants of what may have been an ancient temple. Pottery fragments and other

Living in Panama

International Living recently rated Panama the best retirement destination in the world. It has a stable democratic government, an educated workforce, inexpensive yet quality medical care, and a relatively high standard of living. It's also relatively cheap and offers excellent financial incentives to lure foreign investors. Panama does not tax foreign income, for example, and newcomers who buy or build a new house pay no property taxes for 20 years.

Foreigners have five options for residency. The first four allow you to own a business; the fifth let you work for wages:

Turisto Pensionado (pensioner) requires you to prove at least $1,000 a month in pension income.

Rentista requires a deposit sufficient to generate at least $750 per month of income. It grants the right of a Panamanian travel passport (but not citizenship).

Solvencia Económica Propia is for individuals who don't intend to work. It requires a Certificate of Deposit of at least $200,000 and grants the right to citizenship after five years.

Inversionista de Pequeña Empresa grants one-year residency to small business investors who invest at least $40,000 and hire three Panamanian employees.

Países Amistosos de Residencia Permanente requires a $5,000 deposit, plus proof of investment or offer of work.

---

pre-Columbian figurines are displayed higgledy-piggledy. In 1947, 18 life-size human figures hewn from basalt were discovered here (they are now in the Museo Antropológico Reina Torres de Araúz in Panama City; see p. 88). The culture was probably destroyed by an eruption.

Owned and operated by a keen conservationist, the **Finca Hartmann** coffee farm has its own forest reserve. The farm has two units. **Ojo de Agua** has a small museum with displays on coffee production, a large insect collection (from exquisite butterflies to rhinoceros beetles), and pre-Columbian artifacts, as well as accommodations in a lovely wooden lodge. At **Palo Verde** (the main coffee farm), 3 miles (5 km) of self-guided trails lead into 12 acres (5 ha) of primary forest. Toucans, tinamous, and motmots are among the nearly 300 bird species commonly seen; armadillos, deer, ocelots, and monkeys abound.

Tucked in the forest nearby are **Los Pozos Termales Tisingal,** hot-water pools reached by four-wheel drive via a convoluted dirt road. The road begins at a turnoff 6 miles (10 km) west of Volcán; signs to the springs are found along the way.

Río Sereno, 22 miles (35 km) west of Volcán, is a pleasant border town centered on a grassy plaza with a marble obelisk. A dirt road leads northwest from town through coffee fields to **La Unión,** where the (easily missed) Costa Rican border is marked by an obelisk on the southwest side of town.

Around Cerro Punta

Quintessentially alpine Cerro Punta is a most unlikely tropical setting, conjuring images of *The Sound of Music* without the snow.

Volcán
🅰 186 B3

Sitio Barriles
✉ 4 miles (6.4 km) W of Volcán
☎ 6575-1828
💲 Donation

Finca Hartmann
✉ Hwy. 42, 17 miles (27 km) W of Volcán
☎ 6450-1853
🕐 24 hrs. notice required
💲 $$$
fincahartmann.com

You'll be glad for blankets at night in this flower-filled high-mountain valley at the gateway to Parque Internacional La Amistad. Orchid, strawberry, and horse-breeding farms and a large Ngöbe-Buglé population should

A *Dracula vampira* orchid displays its spectacular petals at Finca Drácula orchid farm.

Cerro Punta
🏔 186 B4

Finca Drácula
✉ 0.75 mile (1.2 km) NE of Guadalupe
☎ 771-2070
💲 $$

fincadracula.com

keep visitors enthralled when not hiking and birding in the area's cloud forests.

North of Volcán, the road ascends through **El Llano**—The Plain—created by an ancient lava flow; it is studded with massive boulders and striated with old riverbeds. Set amid pines between Volcán and Cerro Punta, the twin communities of **Bambito** and **Nueva Suiza** (New Switzerland) cause you to do a double take with their Tyrolean-style houses and lodges (many with sod roofs)

graced by gingerbread trim and hanging baskets full of pink, red, and white impatiens (locally called *novia*). **Truchas de Bambito** (*on main road in Bambito, tel 771-4265*) breeds trout and rents rods—it's like catching fish in a barrel.

About 2,200 feet (670 m) higher than Boquete, **Cerro Punta,** at 6,463 feet (1,970 m) elevation, occupies the crater of an extinct volcano, with mountains all around. The mild alpine climate and fertile soils are perfect for cultivation of arable crops, flowers, and strawberries. Cerro Punta is also a center for the raising of Thoroughbred horses, a tradition of animal husbandry dating back a century. **Haras Cerro Punta** (*on main road, 0.3 mile/0.5 km N of Cerro Punta, tel 771-2057, haras cerropunta.com*) stud farm offers tours of its impressive facilities, where championship racehorses and French Percheron drays munch contentedly in lime green pastures. Foaling season (*Jan.–May*) is especially rewarding.

Above Cerro Punta, exquisite **Guadalupe,** the highest village in Panama, is the flower-festooned setting for **Ecolodge & Spa Los Quetzales** (see Travelwise p. 251), an excellent base for riverside spa treatments and for hiking and birding in the hotel's 865-acre (350 ha) private reserve. Nearby, **Finca Drácula** orchid sanctuary displays more than 2,200 orchid species—supposedly the largest collection in the Americas—including several from the genus *Dracula vampira* for which the *orquideario* is named. Guided tours of the greenhouses and laboratories (which produce 250,000 plants a year) provide orchid lovers with plenty to sink their teeth into.

At Guadalupe, the road loops and returns to Cerro Punta, a beautiful 4-mile-long (6.5 km) circular drive past flower and strawberry farms: **Panaflores** *(tel 771-2105)* welcomes visits to its spectacular flower farm.

Cloud Forest Hikes

Only 158 acres (62 ha) of the 799-square-mile (2,069 sq km) **Parque Internacional La Amistad** (see pp. 222–223) is located in Chiriquí Province, yet the principal entrance and most accessible trails are here. Hiking La Amistad's lush cloud forests is reason enough to visit this region. The main entry and ANAM ranger station is 4 miles (7 km) northwest of Cerro Punta at Las Nubes. Three trails begin at the ranger station. The mile-long (1.6 km) **Sendero La Cascada** offers lookout points en route to a spectacular waterfall; slightly longer **Sendero El Retoño** ascends into the cloud forest, as does the more challenging **Sendero La Montaña.** The **Asociación Agroecoturística La Amistad** (ASAELA; *tel 771-2620*), a local cooperative, runs a fine open-air restaurant at the entrance, plus accommodations nearby. The ranger station, a five-minute hike uphill, has a tiny exhibition center, plus a simple dorm and kitchen (bring your own food).

You can also set out along Sendero Los Quetzales (see p. 199), which begins at Bajo

INSIDER TIP:

Visit Finca Drácula and take a guided tour through the greenhouses and orchid-filled grounds.

—CHRISTIAN ZIEGLER
*Smithsonian Tropical Research
Institute photographer*

Grande *(3 miles/5 km E of Cerro Punta–Guadalupe road)* and crosses the northern shoulder of **Parque Internacional Volcán Barú** before depositing you in Boquete (see pp. 194–196). The shorter and easier **Sendero Las Tres Rocas** leads to a rock formation and lookout with spectacular views. Ecolodge & Spa Los Quetzales's private reserve (see opposite) lies within the park and has trails that extend into Parque Internacional La Amistad. ■

Orchids

Orchids, generally held to be delicate, hothouse plants, are in fact adaptable survivors. Their tiny seeds are easily dispersed by the wind, taking orchids into every corner of the world, from deserts to tropics to land above the Arctic Circle. More than 20,000 species are known, with flowers ranging in size from a pinpoint 0.1 inch (2 mm) to an expansive 15 inches (38 cm).

Panama's misty mountainsides are a prime habitat for the genus. More than one thousand species grow naturally here, making it one of the richest orchid habitats in the world. Thousands more are cultivated in orchid farms. They can be seen year-round, but prime viewing is in the spring months of March and April.

Driving Across the Continental Divide

Surmounting Panama's serrated spine, this mountain drive begins almost at sea level and reaches cloud-draped heights before spiraling down to the Caribbean coastal plain. Stupendously scenic, the journey features numerous way stations of interest. While unpaved in part, the route described here is suitable for most sedans, although occasional landslides, fogs, and steep switchbacks require caution.

Storm clouds gather over Lago Fortuna on the Caribbean side of the continental divide.

NOT TO BE MISSED:

Optical illusion • Reserva Forestal Fortuna • Centro de Visitantes, Lago Fortuna • Malí

Highway 4 begins at **Chiriquí ❶**, a nondescript town at the junction with the Interamerican Highway. From here the well-paved road sweeps north through cattle country clad with green meadows. Drawing you forward are the rounded peaks of the Cordillera de Tabasará floating on the horizon. Turn left at the Y-fork at the entrance to **Gualaca ❷**, then left at the gas station half a mile (0.8 km) farther along. Soon the road begins to climb foothills strewn with volcanic boulders.

After 18 miles (29 km), a sheer-walled canyon parallels the road, which appears to slope downhill. You'll be shocked to note water running in the opposite direction—the apparent slope is an **optical illusion.** A short distance farther you cross **Presa Chiriquí,** a dam tapping the Río Chiriquí for electricity.

Four miles (6.4 km) farther, turn right at the T-junction. Beyond the tiny community of

Caldera **❸** you'll pass a short trail to **Piedra Pintada,** a giant riverside boulder carved with pre-Columbian petroglyphs, and a 1.5-mile-long (2.5 km) trail to the **Pozos de Aguas Termales** thermal springs (102°–108°F/39°–42°C), known locally as Las Calderas. Soaking in these tepid pools, ringed by stone walls and shaded by fruit trees, provides a pleasant break. Continuing, dramatic views open up as the road begins a roller-coaster ascent into the mountains.

Some 36 miles (58 km) after starting out, turn right onto the dirt road at the junction marked Casa de Control (the left fork ends at the control center for the Central Hidroeléctrica Fortuna; see p. 206).

After 6.5 miles (10.5 km) you meet Highway 4; turn left. Immediately you enter **Reserva Forestal Fortuna ❹,** where trails lead up through 75 square miles (194 sq km) of protected forests swaddled in clouds. Beyond the **Centro Para la Investigación y Conservación de la Biodiversidad Tropical,** where the Smithsonian Tropical Research Institute has a research facility *(closed to the public),* the road coils sharply downhill into the Valle de Las Sierpes and **Presa Edwin Fábrega,** a 100-foot-high (30 m) dam containing the

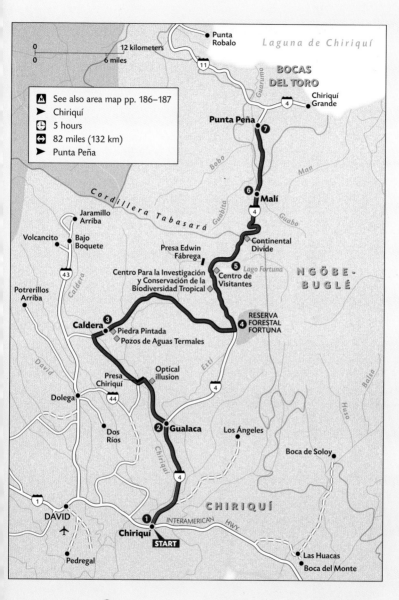

waters of **Lago Fortuna** ⑤. Stop to peruse the nature exhibitions (in Spanish only) in the **Centro de Visitantes.**

Hereon, the mountain vistas inspire awe as you cross the continental divide. Drive with care as you descend the forest-clad eastern slopes with the road falling sharply, sinuous as a snake,

to the Ngöbe-Buglé Indian village of **Malí** ⑥— a drop of some 5,000 feet (1,524 m). The road then follows the Río Guarumo through a lush valley framed by dramatic mountain scenes. The drive ends in **Punta Peña** ⑦, whose inhabitants are employed in the pineapple plantations north of town.

More Places to Visit in Chiriquí & the Cordillera

Carta Vieja Rum Factory

The plains west of David are covered in cane fields, and the yeasty smell of molasses hovers over them, luring you toward one of the oldest *centrales* (sugarcane processing factories) in Panama. The Central Industrial Chiricana rum factory, in the village of El Tejar, about 12 miles (20 km) west of David, was founded in 1915. It is known for making Panama's esteemed Carta Vieja—a dark, full-flavored rum aged for four years in white birch casks, which lend their own color and flavor. The distillery offers weekday tours. Two original stills are displayed outside. *cartaviejapanama.com* ⚊ 186 B2 ✉ El Tejar, 2 miles (3.2 km) NW of Alanje (10 miles/ 16 km W of David) ☎ 772-7073 🕐 Closed Sat.–Sun. 💲 Free

Central Hidroeléctrica Fortuna

The Fortuna Hydroelectricity Station, opened in 1984, generates 39 percent of Panama's electricity needs. Its three 100 MW turbines are fed by the waters of Lago Fortuna (see pp. 204–205) 20 miles (32 km) away. The waters speed 4 miles (6 km) downhill through a pressure tunnel, dropping some 2,392 feet (765 m) to the turbine station. The Casa de Máquinas—the turbine facility—occupies a vast cavern 1,419 feet deep (430 m) and is accessed via a mile-long (1.6 km) tunnel. Guided tours are offered with one week's advance notice. Long pants and covered shoes must be worn. ⚊ 186 C3 ✉ 3 miles (5 km) NW of Gualacá (19 miles/31 km NE of David) ☎ 206-1800 (Panama City) 🕐 Closed Sat.–Sun.

Finca La Suiza

Set on 500 acres (200 ha) of premontane forest on the southeastern slopes of Volcán Barú, this Swiss-run lodge offers hiking along four well-marked and manicured forest trails—some steep, all-day adventures— that ascend into cloud forest full of chattering birdsong. Day access is offered to nonguests for a fee. The postprandial strawberry sundae is reason enough to overnight at the lodge. *fincalasuizapanama.com* ⚊ 186 C3 ✉ 2.5 miles (4 km) N of Los Planes & 11 miles (18 km) N of Gualacá ☎ 6615-3774 🕐 Closed Oct. 💲 $$

Islas Secas

The Islas Secas Archipelago, southeast of Parque Nacional Marino Golfo de Chiriquí, is a privately owned archipelago of 16 small islands with one hotel served by its own charter plane. Limned by talcum-soft beaches, these isles answer the longing for a luxury take on the Robinson Crusoe experience. Each isle is distinct as a thumbprint, though most are craggy, densely forested, and ringed by coral reefs. Some have trails good for birding. White-tipped sharks are common, patrolling reefs that guarantee fantastic snorkeling and diving. Hawksbill, leatherback, and olive Ridley turtles flap leisurely by and, by night, haul out to nest in hidden coves. *islassecas.com* ⚊ 186 D1 ✉ 22 miles (35 km) SE of Boca Chica by charter boat or private charter flight ☎ 800/377-8877

Tolé

Tolé is the most accessible of the Ngöbe-Buglé communities and sprawls across the foothills separating Veraguas and Chiriquí Provinces. During the coffee harvest, entire families commute to work around Boquete. You can watch *chácaras* (handbags; see sidebar p. 52), woven baskets, and dresses being made. If you're in a hiking mood, a trail that begins at **El Nancito**, 5 miles (8 km) west of Tolé, leads to boulders etched with pre-Columbian petroglyphs. ⚊ 187 E2 ✉ 51 miles (82 km) E of David via Interamerican Hwy., then 1.5 miles (2 km) N

The charm of Caribbean island culture mixed with the thrill of premier snorkeling and surfing

Bocas del Toro

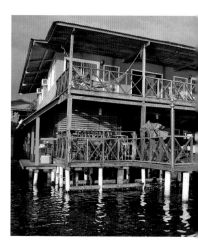

Waterfront living, Bocas Town

Bocas del Toro

The most popular tourist destination beyond Panama City, Bocas del Toro Province is known for its funky, laid-back island lifestyle. There are really two Bocas del Toro, however: island and mainland. A huge chunk of the mainland province lies within Parque Internacional La Amistad and the Bosque Protector Palo Seco buffer zone. This wild and rugged region—a realm of peccaries, jaguars, and pumas—is virtually unexplored.

The sunlit waterfront of Bocas Town, an increasingly popular tourist destination

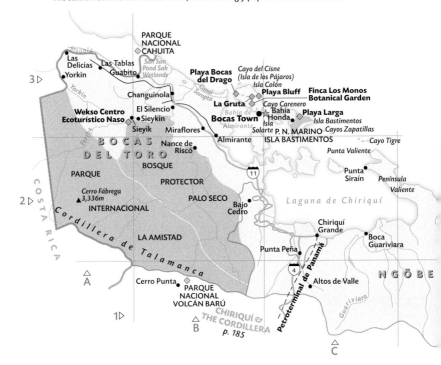

The offshore isles synonymous with the name Bocas del Toro—referred to simply as "Bocas" by locals—are another world altogether. This archipelago of about six major islands and several score atolls and cays is a watery world where water taxis are the only means of travel. Catching a wave, chilling in a hammock, or sipping cold beers in raffish tumbledown bars—such are the ways of the laid-back Bocas lifestyle (exemplified by the local use of *tranquilo* as a response when asked how things are). Foreign investors have recently discovered Bocas's appeal, however. Big resorts and residential projects are bursting forth like mushrooms on a wet log, threatening to change the casual mood.

The vast majority of visitors to the region limit their visit to these islands, which rise up from year-round warm water where coral reefs support 74 of the Caribbean's 79 coral species. Snorkeling and diving are superb, although visibility is often an issue (especially after heavy rains) due to silt from the banana plantations. Patches of rain forest tower over the waters. Several species of poison dart frogs are endemic to the islands, as is a small sloth that resides among the mangrove leaves. Bring insect repellent against mosquitoes and *chitras*, tiny annoying sand flies that will eat you alive.

A key attraction in the area are the Ngöbe-Buglé communities, many still clinging to their

---

NOT TO BE MISSED:

Lounging in Bocas Town   210–211

Surfing at Playa Bluff   212

Looking for poison dart frogs on Sendero de la Rana Roja   215

A boat tour between the islands   216–217

Snorkeling at Cayo Zapatilla Oeste   217

Hiking the rain forests of Parque Internacional La Amistad 222–223

Spotting manatees in San San Pond Sak   224

Ngabere language and culture in the face of hardship. Located throughout the archipelago and mainland (where many communities line the coast highway between Punta Peña and Almirante), they are accessible to every traveler. Increasingly, indigenous peoples throughout the region are turning to ecotourism. Though facilities are simple and often remote, visits to ecolodges such as Wekso provide a chance to experience the diversity of Panama while contributing to the well-being and eco-consciousness of indigenous people. (From necessity, many still hunt wildlife, including turtles, illegally; visitors should refrain from eating turtle meat and even lobster, which is being overfished.)

While the mainland population is mostly mestizo and Ngöbe Indian, a majority of islanders are black—descendants of slaves and of 19th-century Jamaican laborers. Most speak both Spanish and English, though the region's lingua franca is a lilting English patois laced with indigenous and Spanish terms called Guari-Guari.

Come prepared for rain. February through March and the month of June offer you a better-than-average chance of enjoying sunny weather. ∎

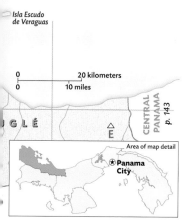

Isla Escudo de Veraguas

0   20 kilometers
0   10 miles

CENTRAL PANAMA p. 143

GLÉ

E

Area of map detail

⊛ Panama City

CENTRAL PANAMA p. 143

Isla Colón

This 24-square-mile (61 sq km) island is the largest and by far the most populated of Bocas's isles, with the majority of hotels, restaurants, and services. Though its prime appeal is the mellow charm of the Bocas Town lifestyle, the island has patches of primary forest to explore, plus spectacular beaches seemingly tailored for surfing and for turtle viewing by night.

At offbeat, vibrant restaurants and pubs throughout Isla Colón—such as here at Bocas Town's El Pecador del Sabor restaurant—locals and visitors mingle in laid-back ease.

Bocas Town, the archipelago's commercial hub, was founded in 1826 and was a base for British loggers and for harvesting sea turtles. In 1889, the United Fruit Company established its local headquarters here; the building, erected in 1905, is now the **Gran Hotel Bahía** (tel 757-9626, ghbahia.com). Jamaican laborers

followed. The early 20th-century boom died along with banana plants when the company moved to the mainland. Meanwhile, a series of fires destroyed much of the town—a charming ensemble of clapboard houses, gingerbread trim, and facades painted in tropical ice cream flavors. After "Big Fruit" pulled out, the isle slumbered in limbo until two decades or so ago, when backpackers put Bocas on the map.

Though the past few years have seen an explosion in tourism, this close-knit community still appeals mostly to independent-minded travelers whose idea of a good time is lazing in a hammock until sundown, then chilling over reggae riffs and a cool beer in funky waterfront bars. Most hotels nestle over the waters, and many have their own wharves and restaurants resting on stilts, good for watching fiery vermilion sunsets.

Around Town

The town is laid out in a simple grid with every place of import strung along the two main waterfront streets: Calle 1 and Calle 3. Between the two, and the heart of affairs, is **Parque Simón Bolívar,** shaded by fig trees full of birdsong. A bronze **bust of Simón Bolívar** is the town's sole monument. The **Biblioteca Pública de Bocas** (Calle 3, closed Sat.–Sun.), or library, has an exhibition on marine turtle ecology; and the **ATP office** has exhibits on history and ecology.

Cayo Carenero floats atop the waters just a three-minute boat-ride to the north. A crumbling cement path winds through its village—a smaller, sleepier version of Bocas Town—and leads to a killer reef break that lures surfers.

Bocas Town's beach, **Playa el Istmito,** a ten-minute walk north from the park along Avenida G, is the setting for the annual four-day Fería del Mar in September, when the entire community grooves to reggae. The beach has a volleyball court and a party atmosphere, although there are more scenic beaches farther out. The Smithsonian Tropical Research Institute operates a **scientific research station** (tel 212-8574, stri.org, open Thurs.–Fri. 3–5 p.m.) at the west end of

INSIDER TIP:

February through April offer the best conditions for snorkeling and scuba diving in Bocas del Toro.

—NEIL SHEA
National Geographic
magazine writer

Playa el Istmito. It has marine exhibits. Nearby, English expats David and Lin Gillingham have created a superb hilltop tropical garden, **Finca Los Monos Botanical Garden,** spanning 20 acres (9 ha). Birds are drawn in by the score; birding tours are offered twice weekly. And lepidoptera flit about the tiny **Bocas Butterfly Farm** (tel 757-9008, $$), set amid mangroves a two-minute boat ride across Bahía de Almirante.

Windward Shore

Two dirt roads lead north from Bocas Town. One follows the eastern shore past the community of Big Creek to **Playa Paunch,** which tempts surfers

---

Isla Colón

⚑ 208 B3

Visitor Information

✉ ATP, Calle 1, Bocas Town

☎ 757-9642

🕓 Closed Sat.–Sun.

Finca Los Monos Botanical Garden

☎ 757-9461

🕓 Guided tours Mon. 1 p.m. & Fri. 8:30 a.m.; other times by appointment

bocasdeltorobotanic algarden.com

GETTING TO BOCAS TOWN

By air: Bocas Town is served by air from Panama City, David, & Costa Rica.

By water taxi: Contact Boteros Bocatoreños Unidos, tel 757-9760, e-mail: boterosbocas@ yahoo.com

Expreso Taxi 25: Operates to & from Almirante & neighboring isles, tel 758-3498.

By car ferry: A car ferry operates between Chiriquí Grande, Almirante, and Bocas Town.

with its reef break, and **Playa Bluff,** where nonsurfers can kick back and watch experienced surf dudes practicing on Hawaiian-size killer tubes. Riptides and high surf preclude swimming. Stretching for 2 miles (3.5 km), this brown-sand beach is an important nesting site for marine turtles, June to September. The **Asociación Natural Bocas Carey** (tel 6843-7244 or 6671-5794, anaboca.org) offers guided tours at night. By day, you can follow a trail beyond Playa Bluff to **La Piscina,** a lagoon with safe swimming. Inland, the forests teem with parakeets, monkeys, and sloths.

Birders will be enthralled by rare sightings at **Cayo Cisne** (Swan Cay), sometimes called Isla de los Pájaros (Bird Island). Rising 131 feet (40 m), this small rugged islet 1 mile (1.6 km) off the north coast of Isla Colón is the only known nesting site in the southwest Caribbean for red-billed tropic birds (see sidebar).

Leeward Shore

A second, unpaved road cuts north through the heart of the island to **La Colonia Santeña,** a small community surrounded by cattle pastures. (You'll be glad for four-wheel drive in the wet season.) Half a mile (0.8 km) east of town, a cavern known as the **Santuario Natural Nuestra Señora de la Gruta,** or more commonly as La Gruta (the grotto), contains a statuette of the Virgin Mary. Push aside the ferns and vines that curtain the entrance to discover a surreal world full of dripstone formations. Fruit bats roost in ceiling crevices, and the pungent smell of ammonia seeps up from their excrement, soft underfoot (wear a bandanna mask to guard against inhaling toxic spores).

INSIDER TIP:

The road from Bocas Town takes you to a wonderful destination at Bocas del Drago. The food at Yarisnori restaurant [see Travelwise p. 255] is divine.

—MAUREEN DONNELLY
*National Geographic
field researcher*

Red-Billed Tropic Bird

The red-billed tropic bird (*Phaethon aethereus*) is a Holy Grail for birders. About the size of a pigeon, yet with a yard-long wingspan, these slender snow-white birds have sooty black eyebands and bright red, scissorlike beaks. Their wings are tipped in inky black, and their back is barred with gray. They are most remarkable, however, for their two very long center tail feathers (in both male and female), sinuous as feather boas.

The seabirds roam the tropical oceans, although they are occasionally seen in temperate climes as far north as Canada and Great Britain. Individuals have recorded some of the longest migrations in the avian kingdom. They typically feed on fish and other sea life by plunge diving or by picking their food off the ocean surface while in flight. Females nest on the ground or on cliff ledges and lay a single egg.

The waterfront hotels of Bocas del Toro invite relaxation on decks with a view.

The site draws pilgrims, especially each July 16 for the Festival de la Virgen del Carmen.

The dirt road, a fun cycling experience in the dry season, ends at **Bocas del Drago,** a sheltered bay with a gorgeous white-sand beach at the isle's northwest tip. It's a great place to relax, and the beachfront restaurant rents pedal boats and snorkeling gear. Boat taxis will run you here; it's wise to arrange a return pickup. ■

Boca del Drago

 11 miles (18 km) NE of Bocas Town

Islas Bastimentos & Solarte

These twin cays paralleling each other east of Isla Colón boast rain forest with rewarding hikes, world-class snorkeling spots, and interesting Ngöbe-Buglé villages. Surfers rave about Hawaiian-size waves on Bastimentos, which is also known for its strawberry poison dart frogs; one-third of the isle is protected as a national park that extends into the marine environment.

Islas Bastimentos & Solarte

🅼 208 C3 & 217

Visitor Information

✉ ANAM, Calle 1, Bocas Town

☎ 758-6822

🕐 Closed Sat.–Sun.

anam.gob.pa

Isla Bastimentos

Appealing mainly to nature lovers, this lush, 20-square-mile (52 sq km) island also pulses to the heartbeat of Afro-Antillean culture, centered on the small, down-at-heels settlement of **Old Bank** (also called Bastimentos Town). A ten-minute boat ride from Bocas Town, this funky, colorful community snuggles in a sheltered cove

Isla Solarte's waters provide great snorkeling.

on the isle's southwest side. Dogs snoozing in the dust and old-timers playing dominoes in pools of shade sum up the pace of life. The predominantly Afro-Antillean population (most of whom speak the local Guari-Guari dialect) lives by fishing, by guiding tourists, or by selling Afro-Antillean cuisine, such as johnnycakes and *rondon,* a spicy Caribbean seafood stew. Reggae riffs mingle with the surf, and locals pick up the beat on Monday night calypso sessions by the Bastimentos Beach Boys.

A track begins near the football field and cuts east across the island, providing a rain forest experience and stringing together a necklace of spectacular beaches (however, muggings have been reported; do not hike alone). First up is **Playa Primera** (also called Wizard's Beach). Like most north-shore beaches, it is pummeled by high surf and unsafe for swimming. Farther east, frosty white **Playa Rana Roja** (Red Frog Beach) is the setting for the region's only deluxe resort (see Travelwise p. 253) and for the **Bastimentos Sky Zipline Canopy Tour,** letting you whiz through the rain forest canopy. Beyond surf crashes ashore onto **Playa Larga,** whose miles-long sugary sands draw nesting sea turtles. The beach

EXPERIENCE: Learn Yoga in Panama

Seeking to balance your mind, body, and spirit in an environment of natural beauty and tranquility? Panama has lately been fast evolving as a leading tropical destination for yoga vacations. You can choose from a fistful of dedicated yoga facilities, or from several wilderness lodges and deluxe beachfront hotels with yoga dojos. Here are a few key venues.

Bocas Yoga & Massage Center (Isla Colón, Bocas del Toro, tel 6658-1355, bocasyoga.com), run by Arizona transplant Laura Kay and Panamanian Anabel del Carmen, offers classes six days a week, including private sessions.

Panama Yoga Retreat (El Valle de Ancón, retreatspanama.com) offers seven-day yoga retreats that include sightseeing between Panama City and the lovely Los Mandarinos Spa hotel. A trio—Anna Karina Gutiérrez, María José Fasano, and Lileana Ledezma—together offer yoga, hypnosis, Reiki, and massage. And gourmet meals are served at the acclaimed La Casas de Lourdes.

Prashanta Yoga at **Bluff Beach Retreat** (Bluff Beach, Isla Colón, Bocas del Toro, tel 6677/8867, bluffbeachretreat.com) uses the sands of Bluff Beach and a lovely hotel setting adjoining its own organic farm for regular yoga retreats.

---

lies within **Parque Nacional Marino Isla Bastimentos** (see p. 218), whose inland forests can be accessed from here by trails. Nearby, **The Silverback** is so named because its waves can snap your board like a twig; this is the Big Kahuna of Bocas surfing with waves that on occasion reach 25 feet (7.5 m).

Connecting Playa Rana Roja to the southern, inward shore, the jungle-shaded **Sendero de la Rana Roja**—named for the many enameled strawberry-red frogs hopping among the leaf litter—leads via pools full of caimans to the tiny Ngöbe-Buglé community of **Bahía Honda**. Here, guides will take you out in *cayucos* to spot crocodiles and caimans and the region's endemic species of mangrove-munching sloth. **Nivida Cave,** tucked up a small creek off Bahía Honda, can be reached by sea kayak. Exploring involves wading chest deep through grottoes.

Isla Solarte

Slung beneath the underbelly of Isla Bastimentos and 1.5 miles (2 km) east of Bocas Town, the 3-mile-long (5 km) by half-mile-wide (0.8 km) isle that locals call Cayo Nancy hosts the delightful clifftop hotel, Garden of Eden (see Travelwise p. 255).

For now the island has few houses and no roads. Bicycles and golf carts follow narrow trails. A short trail ascends through the forest from the humble community of **Solarte,** where the mostly Ngöbe-Buglé inhabitants live simply by fishing and lobstering.

There's great snorkeling and diving to be enjoyed in the little bay off the western tip of **Punta Hospital,** although it can sometimes get overcrowded with tour boats. Starfleet Scuba (see Travelwise p. 265) offers dive trips. ■

Bastimentos Sky Zipline Canopy Tour

☎ 6987-8661

🕐 Tours 10 a.m., 1 p.m., 3:30 p.m.

💲 $$$$$

redfrogbeach.com

A Boat Tour Around the Archipelago

Sprinkled across almost 60 miles (100 km) of teal waters, the Bocas del Toro archipelago offers isles within isles. All the islands have things in common, but each has its own character and even distinct culture and natural wonders. This full-day boat tour combines cultural highlights, wildlife encounters, and opportunities for snorkeling in bathtub-warm waters the color of melted peridots.

Ngöbe-Buglé Indians paddle a hand-hewn log canoe past Cayo Agua.

Several boat operators in **Bocas Town** ❶ offer tours or hire out a boat and guide for a personal tour. They can be found at the waterfront docks on Calle 1; Bocatoreños Unidos *(tel 757-9760)* is a local cooperative. The price can top $100 for a day's boat ride and is best shared with a group. Be sure that the boat is seaworthy and has life jackets—which you should wear—and a 75-hp motor. You'll be at sea all day, so a sun hat and sunscreen are de rigueur. Take snorkel gear, which can be rented in Bocas Town.

Begin by heading south for **Isla San Cristóbal** ❷—note the lighthouse on the northwestern point marking the channel through which large cargo ships pass en route to load bananas at Almirante. Cruising along the mangrove-lined shoreline, your destination is **Laguna Bocatorito,** a calm lagoon teeming with fish. Bottlenose dolphins are almost always around and seem to delight in leaping alongside

NOT TO BE MISSED:

Laguna Bocatorito • Cayo Zapatilla Oeste • Cayo Crawl

speeding boats. The Ngöbe-Buglé community of **Bocatorito** overlooks the lagoon. Step ashore briefly to learn about the Comité Local de Conservación y Pesca, a local fish conservation group that has established tanks of tilapia to feed the impoverished village.

Next head to **Isla Popa** ❸, passing **Popa II,** a Ngöbe-Buglé community that lives on fishing. An ecotourism project sponsored by ANAM has laid trails; the **Sendero de Sandubidi** provides a magnificent rain forest experience should you choose to stop and hike (be aware of your surroundings at all times, as fearsome fer-de-lance snakes abound here). If hungry, you can eat at the restaurant here, or continue east along the shore of Isla Popa to **Punta Cayo Tigre** and the rocky isle that rises from the channel to its east; here, **Restaurante El Morro** offers lunch from a perch with a view, and you can snorkel close to shore.

It's a five-minute ride to the next island, **Cayo Agua ➍**, drawing few visitors but fascinating for its colorful homesteads overhanging the waters. Passing **Playa Punta Limón** at the isle's northwest point, note the exposed coral embedded in cliffs more than three million years old. Next, turn north across open water toward the enchanting **Cayo Zapatilla Oeste ➎**, whose white sands beckon you for snorkeling in the glassy shallows, with coral only 9 feet (3 m) down. Stay close in to shore due to strong currents farther out.

Satisfied? Head back west toward **Isla Bastimentos** and the landlocked community of

Quebrada Sal ➏ (Salt Creek), where a mix of Ngöbe-Buglé and *afrocaribeños* live surrounded by mangroves; look for sloths as you motor up the channel. The community still practices traditional healing, and guides will lead you along a mile-long (1.6 km) forest trail to a mirador with lovely views back to Cayo Zapatilla. Then, continue south around the tip of Isla Bastimentos, passing **Cayo Crawl ➐**, a tiny cay off the southeast tip of Bastimentos. Stop to snorkel the reefs in crystal-clear shallows.

Return to Bocas Town via the channel between Isla Bastimentos and Isla Solarte.

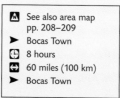

- 🅰 See also area map pp. 208–209
- ► Bocas Town
- 🕗 8 hours
- ↔ 60 miles (100 km)
- ► Bocas Town

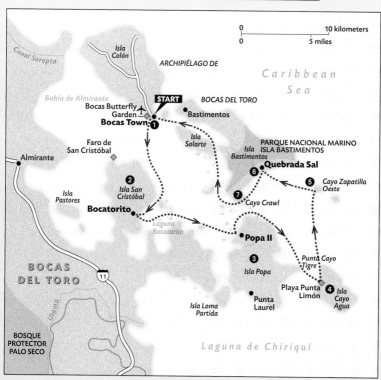

Parque Nacional Marino Isla Bastimentos

Covering 51 square miles (132 sq km) of lush Isla Bastimentos and surrounding tropical waters and cays, this marine park was established in 1988 to protect the most extensive coral reefs and Caribbean mangrove swamps in the country. Superlative snorkeling and spectacular wildlife viewing are key appeals.

Hawksbill turtle at Parque Nacional Marino Isla Bastimentos

Parque Nacional Marino Isla Bastimentos

⯅ 208 C2–C3

Visitor Information

✉ ANAM, Calle 1, Bocas Town

☎ 758-6822

🕐 Closed Sat.–Sun.

💲 $$ (purchase permit in Bocas Town)

anam.gob.pa

Girding the wide waist of Isla Bastimentos, the park covers one-third of the island. Along the shores, channels braid through vast expanses of mangroves. Inland, dense moist tropical forest makes a fecund habitat for capuchin and night monkeys, sloths, agoutis, and 28 other species of mammal, including bulldog bats that swoop over **Laguna de Bastimentos** after dusk to seize fish on the fly. The freshwater lagoon is a hangout for turtles, caimans, and crocodiles: Swim at your own risk! You may spy the strawberry poison dart frog, one of 28 reptile and amphibian species in the park. Trails into the forest are basic. Hire a local guide.

You can follow a trail from Old Bank to access the park at **Playa Larga.** Four marine turtle species nest along this 8-mile-long (13 km) beach.

Two-thirds of the park spans the waters to both west and east of the island. Stealing the show are the **Cayos Zapatillas,** named for the *zapatilla* fruit that grows here. Sitting atop a coral plateau,

INSIDER TIP:

Spend a couple of nights in La Loma Jungle Lodge [see Travelwise p. 254], an eco-friendly place with wonderful hosts and a chocolate farm.

—CHRISTIAN ZIEGLER
Smithsonian Tropical Research Institute photographer

these twin isles are ringed by palm-shaded talcum-fine beaches. Nurse sharks cruise among the coral heads. Ashore, the **Bosque Detrás del Arrecife** interpretive trail begins at the ANAM ranger station on Cayo Zapatilla Este, where camping is permitted for a small fee. ■

Bosque Protector Palo Seco

Forming a buffer between Parque Internacional La Amistad and the coast, this 413,650-acre (167,400 ha) protected zone acts as a biological corridor for wildlife connecting the park with Reserva Forestal Fortuna.

The fragile ecological region incorporates six different forest types extending from about 600 feet (182 m) to more than 6,500 feet (1,981 m) above sea level. Most of the terrain is rugged, mountainous, and jungle clad. The vistas looking up from the lowlands are dramatic. Nonetheless, the lowland terrain bordering the zone is under pressure. Slash-and-burn agriculture and illicit logging have followed the recent opening of the Punta Peña–Almirante highway. Nonetheless, the forests are rich with wildlife. The big cats are here, along with arboreal mammals such as the olingo.

Two projects—Corredor Biológico Mesoamericano del Atlántico Panameño and the Modelo de Comunidad Ecológica los Valles—work with small Ngöbe-Buglé communities throughout the lowlands to establish sustainable ecological models. Several are focusing their efforts on ecotourism, including the community of **Bajo Cedro,** which has a women's crafts cooperative using natural fibers and dyes, 3 miles (5 km) west of the highway, about 22 miles (35 km) south of Almirante. The community of **Nance de Riscó,** about 3 miles (5 km) inland of Almirante, lies within the Bosque Protector and is a center for the production of woven handbags and other indigenous crafts. And nearby **Miraflores,** on the highway 4 miles (6.5 km) north of Almirante, has a *zoocriadero* (breeding farm) for iguanas. All these communities are active in reforestation and offer guide services into the nearby forest along community trails.

ANAM has a ranger station at Km 68.5 on the Fortuna highway, near Altos de Valle, 18 miles (29 km) south of Chiriquí Grande. Here, the **Sendero Los Tucanes** leads through montane forest. ∎

Bosque Protector Palo Seco
🅰 208 B2
Visitor Information
✉ ANAM, Changuinola, Bocas Town
☎ 758-6822
anam.gob.pa

Iguanas

The iguana is found in forested lowlands from Mexico to Brazil. Primarily herbivorous, it spends most of its time in the treetops or basking in the sun in forest clearings. It can grow up to 6 feet (1.8 m), half of which comprises a flickable tail ribbed with spines. This hardy, solitary creature is capable of withstanding a 50-foot (15 m) fall from a tree; it's a good swimmer, and its rough, scaly skin is water-resistant. Nonetheless, the iguana faces threats from hunting, loss of habitat, and capture for the pet trade. Impoverished *campesinos* consider its meat and eggs to be delicacies, and indigenous communities also kill iguanas for medicinal purposes. The Smithsonian Tropical Research Institute *(stri.org)* heads a successful breeding program in Panama.

Wild Cats

Of the ten species of neotropical wild cats, six are present in Panama and are found from the shoreline to the highest mountain slopes. Supremely camouflaged and armed with keen vision, these elusive hunters stealthily prowl their habitats, silent as a cloud.

Like most big cats, the ocelot has been hunted to near extinction for its exquisite fur.

Four species of these cats—the jaguar, margay, ocelot, and oncilla—have spotted coats; all are listed as facing extinction due to poaching and deforestation. The puma and jaguarundi, with their single-colored coats, fare slightly better.

Worshiped by pre-Columbian Indians, the muscular jaguar *(Panthera onca)* can weigh up to 330 pounds (150 kg) and measure almost 9 feet (2.7 m) in length, nose to tail. It has short, stocky legs and a large head with power-ful jaws built for piercing its prey's skull with one bite *(yaguara* is a South American Indian word meaning "a beast that kills its prey with one bound"). An adept swimmer, this forest dweller lives close to water and is skilled at scooping up fish. Despite its size, it can even scale trees to hunt monkeys. Melanistic or black jaguars are frequently born into litters

alongside normally colored siblings; their rosette markings can faintly be seen, slate against jet-black sheen. The jaguar is one of the first animals to disappear in habitat suffering deforestation.

Found throughout Panama in a wide range of environments, the sleek and furtive ocelot *(Leopardus pardalis),* known locally as the *mani-gordo,* is the phantom of the night. About twice as long as a house cat, this agile climber spends most of its time slinking along branches like a catwalk diva. Ocelots often pair up to stalk prey. The cat's exquisite fur can vary from a rich yellow cream in arid areas to a deeper rust brown in darker forests. Its white-tipped ears are well rounded and dotted with a white spot on the back; white markings surround the eyes and mouth and twin black lines run up over its shoulders. Rows of beige blotches ringed in black run along its body, while its short tail is ringed in black bands like a raccoon.

The ocelot's smaller cousin, the margay (*Leopardus wiedii*), known to Panamanians as the *tigrillo,* also prefers a life in the trees and has evolved specially adapted claws and a unique ankle joint—which it can rotate 180 degrees for pirouetting like a ballerina—for an arboreal lifestyle. It can even run headfirst down trees! The margay has a longer tail and legs than the ocelot, and its rosettes are less distinct, sometimes appearing as solid blotches. The population has dwindled dramatically, and the margay is now found only in isolated pockets of Panama. The similarly colored, house cat–size oncilla (*Leopardus tigrinus*), or tiger cat, is found in higher elevation forests in Panama's cordilleras. Far less adept at arboreal living than its larger cousins, it hunts on the ground, feeding primarily on rodents, reptiles, and insects. It has a shorter tail than the margay and a narrower body.

Known to North Americans as the mountain lion, the puma (*Puma concolor*) is common throughout the isthmus and South America. Colored from tawny to taupe or chocolate, the 6-foot-long (1.8 m) cat has a small, broad head with small rounded ears, a long slender body, and an equally long black-tipped tail.

INSIDER TIP:

To spot jaguars and other wild cats in Panama, a planned excursion with an expert is necessary. Even then, you won't always come across these secretive creatures.

—PETER GWIN
National Geographic *magazine writer*

A full-grown adult can tackle domestic cattle with trademark running jumps ending with a huge lunge of its powerful hind legs.

The long-tailed jaguarundi (*Herpailurus yagouaroundi*) has an elongated slender body, short front legs, slightly longer hind legs, and a small head with tiny weasel-like ears and narrow yellowish eyes. This lowland dweller is expert at scooping up fish with its probing front paws. A full-grown male can measure up to 30 inches (76 cm) and, though spotted at birth, its lustrous adult coat is solid, ranging from coffee-colored to chocolate or even charcoal. Known to Panamanians as the *león breñero* (scrub lion), the jaguarundi is the most adaptable of the neotropical cat species to environmental changes wrought by humans.

Paseo Pantera

Jaguars range from Mexico to Paraguay and require vast territories for hunting. They've even been observed swimming across the Panama Canal. Many local communities fear jaguars and continue to hunt them, as do ranchers. Hunting and habitat loss have eradicated jaguars from 40 percent of their former range. Today they are listed as Near Threatened by the International Union for the Conservation of Nature.

Two decades ago, governments throughout the Americas agreed to cooperate in creating a system of interconnected parks and reserves to form the Paseo Pantera (Path of the Jaguar)—today known as the **Mesoamerican Biological Corridor**—linking North America to South America. The associated Jaguar Corridor Initiative, established by Panthera (*panthera.org*), aims to preserve habitat connectivity, guard against genetic isolation, and educate local communities. Panthera has been working with the Panamanian government on a national strategy for jaguar preservation and mitigation of conflicts with ranchers.

Parque Internacional La Amistad

Beyond the edge of human incursion, the vast Talamanca massif is a last frontier for tourism. Panama's wildest mountain terrain has been enshrined for posterity in a mammoth park that the country shares with its northern neighbor, Costa Rica. Panama's portion lies almost wholly within Bocas del Toro Province, though the tiny fraction that spills westward into Chiriquí offers by far the easiest access.

Parque Internacional La Amistad

⚠ 208 A2–B2

Visitor Information

✉ ANAM, Changuinola; & Vía Aeropuerto, David

☎ 775-3163 (Changuinola), 758-8967 (Teribe), or 720-3057 (Boquete)

anam.gob.pa

Spanning 1,550 square miles (4,000 sq km) of Panama and Costa Rica, the International Friendship Park girdles the rugged Cordillera Talamanca mountains, a great tectonic massif thrust from the ocean over several million years and twisted into a number of ranges. Rising with a heart-aching loveliness from 150 feet (46 m) above sea level on the Caribbean lowlands to a cool 10,945 feet (3,336 m) atop the dizzying heights of **Cerro Fábrega,** these mountains span a width of 50 miles (80 km). The steep knife-edged peaks are rain-sodden year-round.

Panama's 799-square-mile (2,069 sq km) portion spans seven of the country's 12 life zones. Vegetation varies from rain-drenched lowland tropical rain forest to a prodigious expanse of cloud forest—home to the largest concentration of quetzals in Central America. Named a UNESCO World Heritage site in 1990, this pristine wilderness is a last refuge for many endangered species. The wildlife viewing is superlative, offering creatures from tapirs to tayras. Poison dart frogs are abundant underfoot, and

INSIDER TIP:

La Amistad has some of the best bird-watching anywhere. You can find trailheads on the Volcán side of Volcán Barú.

—CORY BROWN VEIZAGA
National Geographic contributor

well-camouflaged fer-de-lances lie coiled in deathly anticipation of passing prey.

Birders are no less rewarded: More than 225 species have been recorded within the park. Harpy eagles, locally extinct in much of Central America, still soar over the southern Talamancas. In all, the park holds at least 60 percent of the nation's species of flora and fauna.

Three indigenous tribes—the Bribrí, the Ngöbe-Buglé, and the Naso-Teribe—also cling to vestiges of their traditional lifestyles in the park's remote lowland valleys. The vast majority of this wild and choking terrain, however, is uncharted, uninhabited, and immensely difficult to explore.

Festooned with epiphytes and mosses, the rain forests of Parque Internacional La Amistad are a mecca for birders.

Hiking is a true adventure and should be undertaken only with adequate preparation and never alone. Access on the Caribbean side requires a 40-minute boat trip up the Río Teribe from **El Silencio,** 6 miles (10 km) south of Changuinola. Kingfishers, parrots, and river otters are frequently seen. The ANAM ranger station is at Teribe, near the hamlet of **Wekso,** where a short trail leads into the park. Other barely discernible trails penetrate the mountainous heart of La Amistad along remote, often overgrown, muddy tracks. A guide is essential, as are food and camping gear for overnights. It's best to hike in the dry season (Dec.–April).

Even more appealing are the subalpine highlands. The best base for exploring these areas is **Cerro Punta** (see pp. 201–203) in the Chiriquí highlands, where you do not have to be Indiana Jones to make your way to the park. ■

Around Changuinola

This zone, in the far northwest corner of the country, is engulfed in a sea of bananas. The unlovely regional center of Changuinola offers no inherent attractions and is a place to pass through en route to valuable wetlands and to indigenous communities that are evolving an ecotouristic aesthetic.

The black waters of San San Pond Sak open out to the sea.

Changuinola
🗺 208 B3

San San Pond Sak Wetlands
🗺 208 B3
✉ AAMVECONA, 3 miles (5 km) N of Changuinola
☎ 6678-7238
💲 $

aamvecona.com

The famous fruit company now known as Chiquita Brands established Changuinola and built most of the town infrastructure, including a canal (see p. 226) stretching 9 miles (15 km) to Bahía de Almirante. Bocas Marine & Tours (*tel 758-9033*) operates a scheduled water taxi service from Changuinola to Bocas Town.

San San Pond Sak Wetlands

These coastal wetlands cover 39,845 acres (16,125 ha) extending 14 miles (22 km) from Río Sixaola—along the Costa Rica border—to Bahía de Almirante. They include seasonally flooded forest dominated by oreys (a swamp-loving tree), mangroves, and peat marshes. Rain forest rises up from ink black waters. Iguanas,

sloths, and dozens of waterbird species can also be seen.

San San Pond Sak was designated an Internationally Important Wetland under the Ramsar Convention in 1994 and is a habitat for endangered species, including manatees, river otters, and the tucuxi dolphin. The ecosystem, a spawning ground for tarpon, is threatened by agricultural chemicals washing out from the banana plantations and by hunting from the hard-pressed community of **San San Pond Sak**.

The **Asociación de Amigos y Vecinos de la Costa y la Naturaleza** (AAMVECONA) manages the humedal and sponsors ecotourism. A boardwalk leads from the visitor center at the entrance to a nesting beach for green, hawksbill, and leatherback turtles. Guides offer tours to view nesting turtles and can also take you by boat to a manatee viewing platform.

Comarca Naso

The Naso-Teribe indigenous people live in 27 communities—**Sieykin** and **Sieyik** are the largest—in the Río Teribe valley, on the border with Parque Internacional La Amistad (see pp. 222–223). They retain their own language and are attempting to revitalize centuries-old practices of shamanism and medicinal plant use. A hydroelectric project planned for the Teribe Valley has split the community, which awaits the government's legalization of a Naso-Teribe autonomous district. The **Proyecto ODESEN—Organization for the Sustainable Development of Naso Ecotourism** *(tel 758-9137)*—was established in 1995 to orient these people toward sustainable practices, including reforestation and crafts. A visit to its two ecotourist projects proves a rich cultural experience.

Soposo Rainforest Adventures, on the banks of the Teribe, is a Naso-run ecolodge a 30-minute boat journey from El Silencio, 2 miles (3 km) west of Changuinola. Community members lead trips to Sieyik and the adjoining Parque Internacional La Amistad. Packages are sold in Bocas del Toro. **Wekso Centro Ecotúristico Naso,** farther upriver, occupies the site of a former military jungle survival school. Trails include the relatively easy 2-mile (3.5 km) **Sendero Los Heliconias** loop trail; sloths, monkeys, and red-eyed tree frogs are easily seen. Guided hikes are offered to Sieyik, returning via an exciting rafting trip.

Valle de Talamanca

This lush valley extends west from the border town of **Guabito** and follows the Río Sixaola. A railway track runs to **Las Tablas,** 11 miles (18 km) west of Guabito. Jeep taxis in Las Tablas negotiate the rugged track to the Bribrí Indian community of **Las Delicias.** Locals now focus on ecotourism and the establishment of a nascent nature reserve. Two short trails that begin at the ecolodge lead to a lookout with fine views. You can ride on horseback or hike to the **Catarata Colorado** waterfall, plus take river trips up the Río Yorkín to the Bribrí community of Yorkín. Las Delicias has basic thatched accommodations. ∎

Soposo Rainforest Adventures

✉ 5 miles (8 km) W of Changuinola

☎ 6875-8125 or 6631-2222

soposo.com

Wekso Centro Ecotúristico Naso

✉ About 10 miles (16 km) SW of Changuinola via dirt road to El Silencio, then 1-hour, 5-mile (8 km) boat ride

☎ 6574-9874 or 6569-2844

odesen.bocasdeltoro.org

Las Delicias

✉ 20 miles (32 km) W of Guabito

☎ 6600-4042

EXPERIENCE: Join Voluntourism Projects

Nothing is as soul satisfying as knowing that you have contributed to ecological and cultural welfare at a grassroots level. One way to do this is by giving your time, skills, and energy to specific projects that seek international volunteers. Here are some of the key organizations:

Build a Bridge Foundation (tel 6070-1342, www.buildabridgefoundation.org) helps indigenous communities protect their traditions and create sustainable prosperity through intercultural activities. Participants provide volunteer assistance and leadership in community projects, interspersed with adventures and excursions as a tourist.

New Zealand-based **Global Volunteer Network** (tel 800/963-1198 in U.S. or 800/032-5035 in U.K., globalvolunteernetwork.org) offers programs in literacy, community outreach, and growth and development programs for children.

The **Peace Corps** (tel 1855-855-1961, peacecorps.gov) has programs assisting community development, English tuition, plus environment, health, and agriculture.

Tanager Tourism (Palmilla [aka Malena], Golfo de Montijo, tel 6676-0220, tanagertourism.com) is a Dutch-run ecotourism project that aids with reforestation and with protecting the nesting sites of marine turtles.

More Places to Visit in Bocas del Toro

Almirante

Fascinating for its Caribbean vernacular wooden houses (many in ramshackle condition) built over estuaries, this sprawling, hardscrabble banana-loading port and fishing village is the gateway to Bocas del Toro via water taxis that leave from unmarked *muelles* (wharves). Anyone arriving by car will be hit upon by locals eager to guide you to the wharves, which are otherwise a devil to find. The Ngöbe indigenous community of Río Oeste hosts ecotours to view chocolate being made in traditional manner at **Orebä Chocolate Nativo** *(tel 6649-1457, facebook .com/Orebachocolate),* a simple cacao plantation reached by a steep muddy trail.
🅰 208 B3 ✉ 18 miles (29 km) SE of Changuinola

Manatees

The West Indian manatee inhabits warm coastal tropical and subtropical waters from Florida through Panama to northern Brazil. This gray marine mammal resembles a tuskless walrus and propels itself using its spatulate tail. Males grow to 10 feet (3 m) in length and can weigh 1,200 pounds (540 kg). Manatees live in shallow, slow-moving river estuaries and calm saltwater bays, eating aquatic plants. They can live for 60 years, but reproductive rates are low: Females calve on average every two years. Although protected as an endangered species, they are threatened by loss of habitat, pesticides, and accidents with boats.

Canal Soropta

Commonly called the Changuinola Canal, this artificial waterway runs parallel to the Caribbean shore and extends from the Río Changuinola to the western edge of Bahía de Almirante. Completed in 1903 to permit shipment of bananas by barge, it was abandoned following construction of a railroad. The canal is still a liquid highway of commerce used by public water taxis—usually fast-paced launches—and slower dugout *cayucos* ferrying bananas and other agricultural produce. Cut through tropical rain forest and wetland, the 100-foot-wide (30 m) channel has been severely deforested in recent years. Still, it's a thrilling journey as your boatman runs your craft with the throttle wide open; ask him to slow down to maximize wildlife viewing. Freshwater turtles and small caimans sunning themselves on logs will plop into the water as you putter past. Egrets and other stilt-legged waders stalk the grassy banks. Jacanas strut across water hyacinths munched on by manatees. Early morning and late afternoon are best.
🅰 208 B3 ✉ 7 miles (11 km) E of Changuinola 🚢 Water taxi from Finca 63 or Bocas Town

Laguna de Chiriquí & Península Valiente

The Bocas del Toro Archipelago shelters Chiriquí Lagoon, held in the grip of the claw-like Península Valiente, and lined with mangroves and freshwater swamps. Most of the land lies within the Comarca Ngöbe-Buglé. The indigenous village of **Boca Guariviara,** at the mouth of the Río Guariviara, can be reached by four-wheel-drive vehicle from Chiriquí Grande and has a women's artisan cooperative; the village of **Punta Siraín,** at the tip of Península Valiente, can be accessed only by boat. Game fish put up a fight to remember in the sheltered waters off **Punta Valiente.** Offshore, **Cayo Tigre** (Tiger Cay) is one of only two known nesting sites for Audubon's shearwater in the southwest Caribbean. Brown boobies nest on **Isla Escudo de Veraguas,** 11 miles (18 km) offshore.
🅰 208 C2–D2

Travelwise

Bocas del Toro nightlife

TRAVELWISE

PLANNING YOUR TRIP
When to Go

Time your visit to Panama according to the area you wish to visit, as the country's climate varies by region. In general, December through April is "dry season," which in most parts of the country means less rainy; "wet season" is May through November. The *arco seco*, a dry belt centered on the Azuero Peninsula, sizzles during the dry season when temperatures soar. Elsewhere, be prepared for stifling humidity in the lowlands. The Caribbean coast can be cooler in summer, when the trade winds pick up. In Darién Province, torrential rains can occur at any time of year.

Temperatures vary with elevation, rather than with latitude. The highlands of central Panama and Chiriquí enjoy a year-round springlike climate.

Most tourists visit in the dry season, when Panamanians also vacation en masse—mostly at beach resorts, which can be sold out at this time. November is also busy, especially in Azuero, as towns nationwide host their patron saint festivals. Lenten week is the biggest holiday in Panama, and much of the country shuts down; hotels in cities hosting Carnavales are usually fully booked. The end of the wet season is a perfect time to visit, when everything is lush.

What to Take

Panama has a hot, tropical climate, so dress accordingly. Lightweight, loose-fitting cotton and synthetic clothes are best. You'll want some elegant wear for nighttime. A sweater and/or lightweight jacket are useful for the heavily air-conditioned restaurants and stores and essential for visits to highland areas. A poncho works well against downpours.

Hiking shoes will prove useful on mountain trails or in wilderness areas, where you should expect to get muddy. Avoid bright colors (which can frighten away wildlife) if you plan on birding or nature hikes.

You'll need insect repellent, particularly for coastal areas and during the wet season, even in cities.

Sunglasses are a necessity, as the tropical light is intense, and a hat is mandatory outdoors.

Medicines are widely available. However, you should bring a basic first-aid kit that includes aspirin, Lomotil, antiseptic lotions, Band-Aids, and essential medications. Make a note of the generic name of any prescription medications you take before you leave home; they may be sold by a different trade name in Panama.

Insurance

Travel insurance is a wise investment. Companies that provide coverage for Panama include:
Travelers, tel 888/695-4625, travelers.com
TravelGuard International, tel 800/826-4919, travelguard.com
Assistcard, tel 877/369-2774, assist-card.com. Based in Florida, it has a regional assistance center in Panama.

Entry Formalities

Citizens of the United States, Canada, and most European nations require a valid passport and a return ticket to enter Panama. No visas are necessary for these citizens. A tourist visa is no longer required for stays up to 90 days. For longer stays, contact the **Dirección Nacional de Migración,** Ave. Cuba & Calle 28, Panama City, tel 507-1800. There are also immigration offices in David, Chitré, Changuinola, and Santiago.

Further Reading

The Birds of Panama: A Field Guide (2010) by George R. Angehr & Robert Dean. A beautifully illustrated field guide to local birds and key birding sites.

Emperors in the Jungle: The Hidden History of the U.S in Panama (2003) by John Lindsay-Poland. A sweeping account of U.S. involvement in shaping Panama.

Getting to Know the General (1984) by Graham Greene. Britain's beloved novelist writes of his real-life friendship with Panamanian strongman Gen. Omar Torrijos.

The Path Between the Seas: The Creation of the Panama Canal (1977) by David McCullough. Mesmerizing text tells the history of construction of the Panama Canal.

The Tailor of Panama (1996) by John Le Carré. A tale of espionage, blackmail, and deceit.

HOW TO GET TO PANAMA
By Air

Most flights arrive at Tocumen International Airport, tel 238-2700, 15 miles (25 km) east of Panama City. A small number of international flights land at David's Aeropuerto Enrique Malek, tel 721-1072, in the northwest of the country. Bocas Town, in Bocas del Toro, is served in Panama by daily flights on Aeroperlas and Air Panama.

The national carrier, **Copa Airlines,** tel 800/359-2672, or 217-2672 in Panama, copaair.com, serves more than 30 destinations throughout the Americas, including several in North America.

The following U.S. airlines offer regular flights to Panama:

American Airlines, tel 800/433-7300, aa.com

Delta Airlines, tel 800/221-1212, delta.com.

United Airlines, tel 800/864-8331, united.com

By Sea

More than a dozen major cruise lines include Panama on their itineraries. Many feature a transit of the Panama Canal. For information, contact the **Cruise Lines International Association,** tel 212/921-0066, cruising.org.

National Geographic Expeditions, tel 888/966-8687, nationalgeographicexpeditions.com, and **Windstar Cruises,** tel 866/898-6418, windstarcruises.com, offer in-depth educational cruises of Panama and Costa Rica.

Group Tours

Most packaged tours cater to anglers, scuba divers, and surfers. A few others focus on nature (especially birding) and cultural encounters. Contact the **Autoridad de Turismo de Panama** (ATP; see p. 232) for a list of recommended tour companies.

GETTING AROUND
In Panama City
By Bus & Subway

The *diablos rojos* (red devils) buses that operate throughout Panama City have been phased out in favor of a new Metro Bus system (mibus.com.pa) with modern buses and a prepaid card system, including a single-track subway and overland train route through the city center. The main terminal is Albrook Terminal, on Corredor Norte. No public buses serve the airport.

By Taxi

Taxis are the staple form of transportation in town. They are safe, cheap, and numerous. Point-to-point fares in Panama City are based on a zone system. For touring and multiple points, rates are negotiable. Tourists are usually charged more than locals. Stick with local taxis; taxis with "SET" on their license plates are Servicio Especial Turista, which charge considerably more. The official rate for a tourist taxi between Tocumen International Airport and downtown is $25 for one person, $14 per person for two people, and $10 per person for up to four people, tel 238-4305. Local taxis are not allowed there, but penny-pinchers can catch them outside the airport.

Around Panama
By Air

Flights departing Aeropuerto Marcos A. Gelabert, tel 501-9292, in Albrook, connect Panama City with key tourist destinations throughout the country. Smaller charter planes serve the country's 150 or so airstrips. Be prepared for white-knuckle rides.

Air Panama, tel 316-9000, flyairpanama.com. Flies to 22 destinations throughout Panama, using aircraft from four-passenger Cessnas to Boeing 737s.

By Boat

Travel between islands within the San Blas and Bocas del Toro Archipelagos, and along the coast and rivers of Darién, is primarily by motorized water taxis *(lanchas)*, motorized dugout canoes *(piraguas)*, or paddled dugouts *(cayucos)*. Except for Bocas del Toro, where regular services operate, prices are often negotiable; be sure that any agreed-upon price includes fuel. Usually only lanchas operate with life jackets.

Calypso Queen Ferries, tel 314-1730, depart every day from Amador Causeway to Isla Taboga. The round-trip ticket is $11 for adults and $7 for children.

Sea Las Perlas, tel 6780-8000, sealasperlas.com, operates ferries daily between Panama City and the Las Perlas Archipelago.

By Bus

Buses to destinations throughout Panama depart **Gran Terminal de Transporte,** tel 303-3030, in the Albrook district of Panama City. There is no national network. Several private companies compete and offer fast *(directo)* and slower *(regular)* service. Long-distance service is typically by large, modern, air-conditioned bus. However, regional buses can mean anything from a former school bus to minivans *(chivas)*.

Buses are usually crowded; avoid travel on weekends if possible, and guard against pickpockets and luggage theft. Most companies sell advance tickets; on others you pay when boarding.

By Car

To rent a car you should be over 25 (some agencies permit younger drivers with credit cards) and hold a passport and a valid driver's license (a U.S. license is fine). You will also need a credit card and will have to leave a hefty deposit (about $500). Beware additional charges that might appear on your bill when you return the car or get your credit card statement. Loss damage waiver *(renuncia a daños o pérdida)* and liability insurance are mandatory; some companies refuse to honor insurance issued abroad. For off-road driving, a rugged four-wheel-drive vehicle *(carro con doble)* is essential. Rental cars cannot be taken into Costa Rica.

Most major international car rental companies are represented:

Alamo, tel 238-4142, alamo.com

Avis, tel 238-4037, avis.com

Budget, tel 263-8777, budgetpanama.com

Dollar, tel 270-0355, dollarpanama.com

Hertz, tel 315-6044

National, tel 265-2222, nationalpanama.com.

Main roads throughout the country are in excellent condition. However, portions of the Interamerican Highway (notably in Chiriquí Province) are in poor repair and should be avoided at night. A four-wheel-drive vehicle is recommended for remote areas, including Darién east of Metetí, and for access to many national parks. Many Panamanian drivers are reckless—drive slowly, and be on your guard. Talking on a cell phone while driving is illegal, and wearing a seatbelt is mandatory. See page 233 for what to do in a car accident.

By Train

The country's sole railroad connects Panama City with Colón and runs alongside the Panama Canal. Trains leave Panama City's Corozal train station at 7:15 a.m. and return at 5:15 p.m. Contact the **Panama Canal Railway Company,** tel 317-6070, panarail.com.

Group Tours

Panama has several dozen reputable tour agencies, including:

Ancon Expeditions, tel 269-9415, anconexpeditions.com. Renowned for its ecotours and top-ranked bilingual nature guides. Operates nature lodges in Darién.

Panama Travel Experts, tel 6671-7923, panamatravelexperts.com. Specializes in half-day and daylong excursions.

PRACTICAL ADVICE
Communications
E-mail & Internet

Most towns and villages have Internet cafés (usually charging $1–$2 per hour), and most tourist hotels are wired for Internet use or have business centers, though fees can be high. Many cafés, restaurants, and retailers have free Wi-Fi "hot spots."

Post Offices

It costs $0.35 to mail a letter or postcard to North America, and $0.75 to Europe. Never mail anything of value; theft is common. Most towns have a post office, usually open 7 a.m. to 5:45 p.m. Allow a week for mail to the U.S. or Canada, and at least ten days for mail to Europe.

There is no home delivery in Panama. Mail is delivered to postal boxes (*apartados postales,* abbreviated *Apdo.*). However, service is unreliable, and many people use private mail and courier services.

Telephones

Public pay phones are yellow or blue and usually accept both coins and prepaid phone cards (some accept only phone cards), which can be bought at supermarkets and Claro (*claro.com .pa),* Móvil (Cable & Wireless; *cwpanama.com*), and Movistar (*www.movistar.com.pa*) outlets nationwide. Insert the card into the phone, and the cost of your call is deducted. "Telechip Total" cards can be used in any phone booth; "Telechip International" cards work only in specific phones. In remote areas, the public phone may serve the entire community.

Making Calls

Local calls cost $0.10 per minute. Some Internet cafés double as call centers and have cheaper rates than most hotels.

For direct-dial international calls from Panama, dial 00, the country code (U.S.: 1; U.K.: 44) and area code, then the number. For operator-assisted calls inside Panama, dial 101. For operator-assisted calls to countries outside, dial 106. For directory inquiries, call 102.

Calling to Panama from the U.S., dial 011 plus Panama's country code 507 and the number. From the U.K., dial 00 plus Panama's country code 507 and the number.

Cellular numbers within Panama have eight digits starting with 6.

Electricity

Panama operates on 110-volt AC (60 cycles) nationwide, although a few more-remote places use 220 volts. Most outlets use U.S. flat, two-, or three-pin plugs. Many remote parts of the country do not have electricity; here restaurants and hotels rely on generators or solar power, and often service is limited to certain hours of the day.

Etiquette & Local Customs

Panamanian society is diverse. Life in Panama City is cosmopolitan and relatively liberal, while smaller towns and rural villages are far more conservative. Society remains extremely class conscious. Panamanians respect professional titles and use them when addressing titleholders, such as engineers (e.g., Ingeniero Arosemena) and architects (Arquitecto García).

Adults are addressed as Señor (Mr.), Señora (Mrs.), or Señorita (Miss). The terms Don (for men) and Doña (for women) are used for high-ranking or respected individuals and senior citizens.

Panamanians are courteous and normally use the formal *usted* form of "you," while the informal *tu* form is reserved for intimates. Hugs and kisses are generally used only among close friends and family.

Panamanians are proud of their country and sensitive to criticism by foreigners, particularly U.S. citizens. The Kuna Indians of the San Blas Islands are extremely sensitive to intrusions or insults to their culture: Dress modestly away from the beach, and photograph individuals only if you are prepared to pay the expected $1 per photo.

Outside the main tourist areas and business centers, you may not be understood in English, so it is advisable to learn a few Spanish phrases. Most restaurants in cities have menus in English.

Holidays

In addition to Christmas, New Year's, and Easter, Panama observes the following national holidays:

January 9, Martyrs' Day
May 1, Labor Day
August 15, Foundation of
    Old Panama
November 3, Independence From
    Colombia Day
November 4, Flag Day
November 10, First Call for
    Independence (Primer Grito
    de Independencia)
November 28, Independence From
    Spain Day
December 8, Mother's Day.

The biggest holiday of the year is Carnaval, the four days leading up to Ash Wednesday. Most tourist sites and services stay open for these holidays, but banks and government offices close.

Liquor Laws

Drinking alcoholic beverages is legal at 18 in Panama, though the law is rarely enforced.

Driving while under the influence is illegal; a conviction of drunk driving will nullify any insurance coverage you are carrying on a rented car.

Media

Newspapers & Magazines

Panama has three major national newspapers. The excellent daily *La Prensa* is the most conservative and complete, and covers everything from politics to fashion; *El Panama América* and *La Estrella de Panama* are also good.

The weekly *Panama News,* thepanamanews.com, and *Newsroom Panama*, newsroompanama .com, publish news online in English.

Television & Radio

Television reaches everywhere in Panama, which has five TV stations. Panama also has dozens of radio stations. All but a few broadcast local news and Latin music. The BBC World Service and Voice of America offer English-language news.

Money Matters

Currency

Panama's official currency is the balboa, which is pegged to the U.S. dollar (1 balboa = 1 dollar). There are 100 centesimos to a balboa. Circulating paper money is dollars, and U.S. coins are accepted as well as Panamanian ones.

Some international banks in larger towns have foreign-exchange counters to serve travelers arriving without U.S. dollars, but you shouldn't count on this; most banks have no such service. The state-owned Banco Nacional tends to be less efficient than other, private, banks. There are few private exchange bureaus.

Take all the cash you think you'll need for a stay in the San Blas Islands; there are only two banks in the entire *comarca,* and banks in Darién are also few and far between. In these out-of-the-way spots, it is best to carry plenty of small-denomination bills, as $50 and $100 bills often cannot be changed.

Visitors may experience trouble cashing traveler's checks anywhere but banks, due to widespread fraud and holds imposed by banks. Many shops will refuse to accept them.

Automated Teller Machines

Most banks have 24-hour automated teller machines (ATMs). There is usually a small charge. Avoid using ATMs in poor neighborhoods and in dark locations, where crime may be a problem.

Credit Cards

Credit cards *(tarjetas de crédito)* are widely accepted. Visa is the most commonly accepted, followed by MasterCard and American Express. In the San Blas Islands and Darién, you will need to operate on a cash-only basis.

Opening Times

Most stores are open Monday to Saturday 9 a.m. to 6 p.m., but malls, supermarkets, and many souvenir stores have longer hours and also open on Sundays.

Banks are typically open Monday through Friday 8 a.m. to 3 p.m. (some until 6 p.m.) and Saturdays 9 a.m. to noon. Businesses are typically open Monday through Friday 9:30 a.m. to 7 p.m.; travel agencies and tourist-related businesses are also open on Saturdays 8 a.m. to noon and do not close for lunch. Most government offices are open weekdays 7:30 a.m. to 3:30 p.m.

Places of Worship/ Religion

Most communities have at least one Roman Catholic church and often a Protestant church. Panama City also has mosques. Local tourist information offices and leading hotels can usually supply a list of places of worship.

Restrooms

There are very few public restroom facilities (baños). Most restaurants and bus stations have restrooms, although standards of cleanliness vary.

In the San Blas Islands, most accommodations have only shared bathrooms (many are over-the-water affairs that dump waste directly into the sea), as do some budget hotels in Bocas del Toro and Darién. Toilet paper is rarely available in these places; bring your own.

Smoking

Smoking is officially forbidden in public areas, including offices, restaurants, bars, nightclubs, and other venues that can be considered workplaces. Violators face steep fines.

Time Differences

Panama time is the same as U.S. Eastern Standard Time (EST), five hours behind Greenwich Mean Time (GMT). Panama does not observe daylight savings time.

Tipping

Tipping is not a fact of life in Panama except in tourist areas. However, a tip is an acknowledgment of good service: If the service is not satisfactory, do not tip.

A 10 percent service charge is often added onto restaurant bills, where a tip should be given for good service. Many cafés and budget eateries do not expect to receive tips. Hotel porters should be given 50 cents per bag (airport porters expect $1), and room service staff $1 per day. Taxi drivers do not expect a tip.

In the countryside, park rangers, boat guides, etc., often provide services for which a tip is in order, albeit not expected.

Travelers With Disabilities

Although paying lip service to the theme, Panama does not display great sensitivity to the needs of visitors with disabilities. Few buildings have wheelchair access or provide special toilets. Buses are not adapted for wheelchairs, and few curbs are dropped at corners. Some modern, upscale hotels and a few restaurants in Panama City have wheelchair access, and a few hotels provide special suites.

The following agencies provide information for visitors with disabilities:

Gimp on the Go, gimponthego.com. An Internet-based newsletter and forum for disabled travelers.

Instituto Panameño de Habilitación Especial (Panamanian Institute for Special Rehabilitation), tel 501-0510, iphe.gob.pa. A government organization to assist disabled people.

Society for Accessible Travel & Hospitality, 347 5th Ave. Ste. 610, New York, NY 10016, tel 212/447-7284, sath.org.

Visitor Information

Panama's environmental agency, **Autoridad Nacional del Ambiente** (ANAM; anam.gob.pa), administers national parks and other protected areas throughout Panama. Though the main office in Panama City provides little help to visitors, the regional offices are generally more helpful; they're also essential stops before visiting parks where permits are needed or if you want to spend the night in a refuge.

Panama's government also runs the **Autoridad de Turismo de Panama** (ATP; Edif. BICSA, Ave. Balboa & Aquilino de la Guardia, tel 526-7000 or 800/231-0568 in the U.S., visitpanama.com). ATP is headquartered at Tocumen International Airport and has regional bureaus throughout the country.

Focus Panama is a tourist-oriented publication published twice yearly in English and Spanish and widely available in hotels. The Panama Visitor newspaper is published twice-monthly in Spanish and English.

EMERGENCIES
Crime & Police

Panama is a relatively safe destination and crime is no more prevalent than in most North American towns and cities; overall, violent crime against tourists is extremely rare. However, caution should be exercised at all times, particularly in impoverished parts of Panama City (including the El Chorrillo area bordering Casco Viejo and Curundú, northeast of Ancón) and in Colón, where the threat of muggings is severe. In towns, there is a danger of pickpockets and snatch-and-grab theft, so be especially wary in crowded areas, such as buses and markets. Scams are common, especially in private street transactions; never take your eyes off any items you purchase. And keep your possessions in a locked suitcase in hotels, as theft by cleaning staff is common

Never hike alone, particularly in national parks close to Panama City and the Canal Zone, where robberies have been known. And never leave items unguarded on beaches. Avoid leaving luggage or valuables in cars; do not carry large quantities of cash or wear expensive-looking jewelry, and keep passports and credit cards out of sight. If anything is stolen, report it immediately to the police and/or to your hotel.

The eastern half of Darién Province close to the Colombia border is considered unsafe for travel due to infiltration by guerrillas, armed insurgents, drug traffickers, and lawless bandits. A heavily armed branch of the police maintains fortified bases throughout the region, but cannot guarantee travelers' safety.

Tourism police patrol Casco Viejo and a few other heavily touristed areas, including Colón. Traffic police (tránsitos) patrol the highways. A new professionalism to Panama's police force belies their reputation for corruption. However, dishonest officials still exist. The **Policía Técnica Judicial** (PTJ; tel 512-2222, policia .gob.pa), handles criminal investigations, including reports of police corruption.

Embassies & Consulates

U.S. Embassy, Ave. Demetrio Basilio Lakas, Clayton, Panama City, tel 317-5000, panama .usembassy.gov, e-mail: Panama web@state.gov

British Embassy, Calle 53, Marbella, Panama City, tel 297-6550, gov.uk/government/world /organisations/british-embassy -panama-city

Canadian Embassy, Torres de las Américas, Tower A, Punta Pacifica, Panama City, tel 294-2500, canadainternational.gc.ca

Emergency Telephone Numbers

Most, but not all, communities are served by the following emergency numbers:

Fire (bomberos), tel 103
Police (policia), tel 104
Tourism police, tel 511-9260 or 527-9873 (Casco Viejo)
Tourism hotline, tel 178

Ambulance service is provided by the **Red Cross,** tel 315-1388, and private companies such as **SEMM,** tel 366-0122.

Emergency care is free in public hospitals, in Panama City's **Hospital Santo Tomás,** in the Central Provinces, **Hospital Cecilio Castillero** (Los Santos) and **Aquilino Tejeira** (Penonomé), but all other medical services cost.

Health

Most towns have private physicians and clinics. In Panama City and David, medical service is up to North American standards. In Panama City, three of the best facilities are the **Hospital Nacional,** Ave. Cuba & Calles 38 and 39, tel 207-8100; **Centro Médico Paitilla,** Ave. Balboa & Calle 53, tel 265-8800; and **Clinica Hospital San Fernando,** Vía España, Las Sabanas, tel 303-6300. Government-run centros de salud (health centers) serve virtually every town and offer treatment for nominal fees. However, the service is of low standard, and visitors are advised to seek treatment at private facilities.

Full travel insurance should cover all medical costs. A medical evacuation clause is also important in case you need to return home.

Most hotels keep a list of doctors and medical centers. Keep receipts or paperwork for insurance claims.

Panama's main health hazards—other than traffic accidents—relate to its tropical climate, where bacteria and germs breed profusely. Wash all cuts and scrapes with warm water and rubbing alcohol. The tap water is safe in most of the country. However, avoid drinking water from faucets in Bocas del Toro and other destinations along the Caribbean shore, and in all other impoverished communities, where you should drink (and brush your teeth with) bottled water. Boil water when camping to eliminate giardia, a parasite that thrives in warm water. Avoid uncooked seafood (except ceviche, which is normally safe) and vegetables, unwashed salads, and unpeeled fruits.

Be liberal with sunscreen and build up your tan slowly, as the tropical sun is intense. Drink plenty of water to guard against dehydration.

Biting insects abound, particularly in the humid lowlands. Malaria is present in lowland areas and is a problem mainly on the Caribbean coast and Darién. Consult your doctor for a suitable malaria prophylaxis. Dengue fever is also spread by mosquitos, and occasional outbreaks are reported in the Caribbean and Pacific lowlands. There is no preventative medication, so it is wise to try to avoid being bitten. Use insect repellents liberally, and wear earth-colored clothing with long sleeves and full-length pants when hiking.

Venomous snakes are common in wilderness areas. Wear closed-toed shoes that cover the ankle to reduce the chance of snakebites, and don't put your hand in places you can't see. Give snakes a wide berth. If you are bitten, get immediate medical help. Avoid wading in the shallows along the central Pacific shore, where stingrays abound.

Riptides (see sidebar p. 189) are an extreme danger along much of the coast, particularly where high surf comes ashore.

What to Do in a Car Accident

In the event of an accident, do not move the vehicle or permit the other vehicle to be moved. Take down the license plate numbers and cédula (legal identification) of any witnesses. Call the transit police and await their arrival; they will fill out a report that you will need for insurance.

If someone is seriously injured or killed, contact your embassy.

Hotels & Restaurants

Accommodations in Panama are varied and reasonably priced, although standards vary widely. There are great differences between the facilities available, and it will help you to understand these differences when deciding where to stay. Remember that large areas of the country are remote, and the availability of accommodations is limited; more desirable accommodations can fill quickly during busy months and especially during festivals such as Carnaval. In much of Darién and the San Blas Islands, the only available accommodation may be extremely basic. Eating out can be a great pleasure in Panama City, which offers a wide variety of possibilities, including many world-class options. Elsewhere, menus are typically restricted to traditional fare and seafood, with more cosmopolitan options in tourist destinations and upscale hotels. In the San Blas Islands, meals are often bland and your options are extremely limited.

ACCOMMODATIONS

There are several types of accommodations. Panama City is blessed with top-of-the-class hotels to international standards. These range from small, family-run boutique hotels that combine intimacy and charm to high-rise international chain hotels, usually with business and or convention facilities. Several have casinos. Some of these hotel chains have toll-free numbers:

Country Inn & Suites
tel 800/830-5222,
countryinns.com
Intercontinental Hotels Group
tel 888/424-6835,
intercontinental.com
Marriott Hotels & Resorts
tel 888/236-2427,
marriott.com
Radisson, tel 800/967-9033,
radisson.com

Many new hotels have opened in the past few years in response to the tourism boom. The El Valle and Boquete regions have some of the best accommodations in the country, including intimate bed-and-breakfast country inns, and Bocas del Toro also offers wide options. Large-scale beach resorts are relatively few in number; the few that exist are generally all-inclusive and cater mainly to a local clientele. Mid-range hotels are widely available, offering a modicum of services; standards vary. However, certain areas of the country, such as Azuero, have relatively few hotels; the options that exist sell out fast during Carnaval, when accommodations can be impossible to find.

Panama has relatively few wilderness lodges. Exceptions are in Darién as well as the Chiriquí highlands, where facilities range from tent camps to cozy, no-frills wooden lodges and a couple of more sophisticated options with spas and saunas. Specialized lodges also serve anglers and surfers, although most of the latter are fairly simple. Camping is available along beaches and in most of the national parks.

In the San Blas Archipelago, hotels are few and invariably basic, even spartan: Expect homespun cabanas made of palm trunks and bamboo reeds, with thatch or tin for a roof. Few have electricity (lighting is usually kerosene lanterns), and fewer still have flushing toilets—over-the-water outhouses are the norm.

Vacation rental and long-term properties—everything from beachfront bungalows to Spanish colonial haciendas—can be rented through **Viviun International Property Listings,** viviun.com.

In budget hotels, sink plugs may be missing, showers are often cold, and mattresses are thin and usually past their prime. Warm (tepid) water may be provided by an electric element above the shower. Ensure windows and doors are secure.

Avoid "motels," which are usually rented by the hour for sexual trysts.

Unless otherwise stated, all hotels listed here have dining rooms and private bathrooms and are open year-round.

Hotel rates generally are about 15 percent higher in high season, December through April. In mid-range and budget hotels, ask to see several rooms, as the same price often applies to rooms of vastly different size and standard.

A 10 percent sales tax is added to most hotel bills.

RESTAURANTS

Seafood is the staple along the coasts, while chicken and pork form the heart of typical Panamanian fare. Restaurants usually open 11 a.m. to 2 p.m. and 6 p.m. to 11 p.m. Many close on Mondays. Make reservations for the more expensive restaurants, particularly on weekends. In Panama City, service is usually fast, but elsewhere it is often slow.

Local fare can be enjoyed for less than $5. Look for *comida corriente,* set lunch plates (usually a choice of meat, rice, beans, and vegetables, or salad) at bargain prices.

In the San Blas Islands, restaurants can be counted on one hand; most are extremely basic. Here,

PRICES

HOTELS

An indication of the cost of a double room in the high season is given by $ signs.

$$$$$	Over $200
$$$$	$100–$200
$$$	$50–$100
$$	$25–$50
$	Under $25

RESTAURANTS

An indication of the cost of a three-course meal without drinks is given by $ signs.

$$$$$	Over $35
$$$$	$20–$35
$$$	$10–$20
$$	$5–$10
$	Under $5

expect to eat rather blandly in your hotel; avoid lobster (if possible) due to overexploitation, and squid, which are often fished by dumping bleach in the water.

A selection of the best quality restaurants for each area is given below.

Making Reservations

Although we have tried to give comprehensive information, please check details before booking. This applies particularly to facilities for disabled guests or nonsmoking rooms, acceptance of credit cards, and rates. Do not rely on booking by mail; fax or e-mail your hotel reservation, and take your written confirmation with you.

If a Panamanian tour operator informs you that the hotel of your choice is full, check directly with the hotel; even the most reputable tour operators have been known to intentionally steer clients toward hotels that pay preferential commissions.

For disabled access, it is recommended that you check with the establishment to verify the extent of their facilities.

Organization

The hotels and restaurants listed here have been grouped first according to their region (by chapter), then listed alphabetically by price category.
L = lunch   D = dinner

Credit Cards

Giving a card number is often the only way to reserve rooms in upscale hotels. Some hotels add a fee of up to 3 percent for credit card payments. Most quality restaurants accept payment by credit card.

Abbreviations used are:
AE (American Express),
DC (Diners Club),
MC (MasterCard),
V (Visa).

▓ PANAMA CITY

HOTELS

SOMETHING SPECIAL

🏨 HOTEL BRISTOL
🍴 $$$$$

CALLE AQUILINO DE LA
GUARDIA, CALLES 51 & 52
TEL 264-0000
thebristol.com
This splendid boutique option—a member of the Leading Hotels of the World—sparkles with mahogany and marble while exuding London-style Old World class and charm. Tastefully deluxe furnishings include locally themed highlights, such as colorful *mola* pillows. The restaurant Salsipuedes (see p. 237) is among the city's finest.

🛈 119 🅿 🚻 🅢 🍸
🅢 AE, MC, V

🏨 TANTALO HOTEL
🍴 $$$$$

CALLES B & 8,
CASCO VIEJO
TEL 262-4030
tantalohotel.com
This newcomer has turned a colonial edifice into Panama City's hippest hotel. Its über-sophisticated suites are individually styled with designer furniture and chic art. It has a superb tapas restaurant, **Tantalo Kitchen** (see p. 238), and the rooftop lounge club throbs. Complimentary breakfast, plus free Wi-Fi and bicycle rental.

🛈 13 🅢 🅢 🅢 AE, MC, V

SOMETHING SPECIAL

🏨 TRUMP OCEAN CLUB INTERNATIONAL HOTEL
$$$$$

CALLE PUNTA COLÓN,
PUNTA PACIFICA
TEL 215-8800
trumphotelcollection.com
Rising magnificently some 70 stories over Punta Pacifica, this avant-garde landmark hotel is shaped like a wind-filled sail. Defining luxury with its divine gasp-inducing styling and decor, its soothing guest rooms feature en suite bathtubs. A pool deck features five infinity pools and private cabanas, and a catamaran offers complimentary service to a private beach club.

🛈 396 🅿 🚻 🅢 🅢 🏊 🍸
🅢 All major cards

🏨 WALDORF ASTORIA PANAMERA
$$$$$

CALLES 47 & URUGUAY,
BELLA VISTA
TEL 294-8000
waldorfastoria3.hilton.com
Furnished throughout in whites, creams, and taupes, this sumptuous and suavely contemporary hotel opened in 2013. Many rooms boast

🅢 Nonsmoking 🅢 Air-conditioning 🖼 Indoor Pool 🖼 Outdoor Pool 🍸 Health Club 🅢 Credit Cards

balcony spa-tubs. Choose from four stylish restaurants. Service is exemplary.

🛏 130 (118 apartments) 🅿 🔄 Ⓢ Ⓒ ⛱ 🍴 🍽 ◈ All major cards

SOMETHING SPECIAL

🏨 CANAL HOUSE
$$$$
CALLE 1RA & AVE. A,
CASCO VIEJO
TEL 228-1907
canalhousepanama.com

There's a reason Daniel Craig slept here while filming *Quantum of Solace.* Exuding sophistication, this intimate boutique hotel in the midst of Casco Viejo combines colonial ambience with state-of-the-art accoutrements, including plasma TVs, Wi-Fi, and iPod docking stations. Its three suites have king beds with 600 thread-count linens. A library and lounge/dining room add further notes of stylish elegance. Rent the entire house!

🛏 3 🅿 Ⓢ Ⓒ ◈ AE, MC, V

SOMETHING SPECIAL

🏨 LAS CLEMENTINAS
$$$$
CALLE 11 & AVE. B, CASCO VIEJO
TEL 228-7613
lasclementinas.com

A sibling to the Canal House, this gorgeous property in a retored four-story 1930s corner building displays exemplary taste. No detail has been overlooked in creating a soothing, sophisticated boutique hotel. Furnishings play up yesteryear, yet offer 21st-century accoutrements in the large, sumptous suites, enlivened with contemporary art. The lobby bar and café are justifiably popular with local expats for the chic mood and Chef Javier Lamarca's Panamanian-inspired fusion dishes, which can be enjoyed in a palm-shaded garden.

🛏 6 Ⓢ Ⓒ ◈ All major cards

🏨 CROWNE PLAZA
$$$$
AVE. MANUEL ESPINOSA
BAUTISTA
TEL 206-5500
cppanama.com

This full-service upscale hotel in the heart of the commercial zone has tastefully appointed rooms with all modern conveniences. Rooftop pool and sports bar are highlights. Breakfast is included.

🛏 149 🅿 🔄 Ⓢ Ⓒ ⛱ 🍽 ◈ All major cards

🏨 HOTEL DEVILLE
🍴 **$$$$**
AVE. BEATRIZ CABAL,
N OF CALLE 50
TEL 206-3100
devillehotel.com.pa

Furnished with an eclectic assemblage of globe-spanning pieces, this all-suite luxury boutique hotel combines the best of both worlds: tasteful, old world decor and comprehensive, modern accoutrements. Themed rooms and cavernous bathrooms sparkle with marble floors topped with oriental throw rugs. Guaranteeing angelic slumber are orthopedic mattresses, Egyptian cotton linens, and pillows as soft as a sigh. The hip **Alkimia** restaurant (see p. 237) is a treat, too.

🛏 33 🅿 🔄 Ⓢ Ⓒ ◈ AE, MC, V

🏨 INTERCONTINENTAL
🍴 **MIRAMAR PANAMA**
$$$$
MIRAMAR PLAZA, AVE. BALBOA
TEL 206-8888
miramarpanama.com

Soaring 25 stories over Panama Bay, this handsome, contemporary high-rise combines luxe and convenience, including a full-service business center and banqueting facilities, plus Turkish baths. Spacious rooms are beautifully appointed and are wired for Internet. Spectacular views through wall-of-glass windows are a high point. The fifth-floor **Miramar Restaurant** is noted for its gourmet seafood.

🛏 186 🅿 🔄 Ⓢ Ⓒ ⛱ 🍽 ◈ AE, MC, V

🏨 RADISSON DECAPOLIS
🍴 **$$$$**
AVE. BALBOA, BEHIND
MULTICENTRO PLAZA
TEL 215-5000
radisson.com

This slick avant-garde high-rise thrusting some 29 stories over Marbella boasts minimalist contemporary furnishings, fabulous views, a range of hip dining options at the **Sushi Bar, Luxor,** or **Fusion Restaurant,** plus the fashionable **Martini Bar.** Business travelers are well served, and all rooms have

---

🏨 Hotel 🍴 Restaurant 🛏 No. of Guest Rooms 🔄 No. of Seats 🅿 Parking 🕐 Closed 🔃 Elevator

broadband Internet. A casino and shopping mall adjoin. Breakfast included.

🚪 240 P ⬆ 🚫 🌀 🌊 🏋
🅰 AE, MC, V

🏨 ALBROOK INN
$$$
CALLE LAS MAGNOLIAS NO. 4, ANCÓN
TEL 315-1789
albrookinn.com
In the far west of the city and close to the airport, perfect for exploring Ancón and Balboa. Graciously furnished with white fabrics, dark contemporary hardwoods, and cream walls. Suites have large kitchenettes. Small free-form pool in pleasant garden.

🚪 30 P 🚫 🌀 🌊 🏋
🅰 AE, MC, V

🏨 THE BALBOA INN
$$$
2311 CALLE CRUCES, BALBOA
TEL 314-1520 OR 6618-4088
thebalboainn.com
Lovingly tended by Dutch live-in owners, Saskia Swartz and Thorwald Westmaas, this inn is perfect for exploring Balboa. Rooms are cozy rather than luxurious and have Wi-Fi, safes, and ceiling fans.

🚪 9 P 🚫 🌀 🅰 MC, V

🏨 PLAZA PAITILLA INN
$$$
VÍA ITALIA, PUNTA PAITILLA
TEL 208-0600
plazapaitillainn.com
Modern, circular high-rise with fabulous city views through walls of glass. Pleasant decor and understated elegance in guest rooms. Special rates offer bargains.

🚪 255 P ⬆ 🚫 🌀 🌊
🅰 AE, MC, V

🏨 ARCOS DE BELLA VISTA B&B
$$
CALLE 49 & AVE. FEDERICO BOYD, BELLA VISTA

TEL 6713-7165
pattyscasitas.com
Live-in owners Patty Polte and Rudy Ariana welcome guests into their 1940s art deco mansion, with a two-bedroom suite. Simply furnished.

🚪 2 🚫 🌀 🅰 No credit cards

🏨 LUNA'S CASTLE HOSTEL
$
CALLE 9NA ESTE 3–28, CASCO VIEJO
TEL 262-1540
lunascastlehostel.com
Beloved of backpackers, this hostel in a dusty old mansion enlivened with colorful art is a choice pick for budget hounds. Free coffee, Internet, and Wi-Fi.

🚪 255 P ⬆ 🚫 🌀 🌊
🅰 AE, MC, V

RESTAURANTS

🍴 ORÍGENES
$$$$
CALLE 58, BELLA VISTA
TEL 393-2416
origenespanama.com
Sharp, sophisticated, and youthful Spanish fusion restaurant lit by multihued neon. A perfect meal might combine garlic and mushroom soup, seafood zarzuela or pan-seared duck with caramelized apple and merlot sauce, and chocolate lava cake. Excellent service.

🪑 72 🚫 🌀 🅰 MC, V

🍴 SALSIPUEDES
$$$$
HOTEL BRISTOL, CALLE AQUILINO DE LA GUARDIA, CALLES 51 & 52
TEL 264-0000
salsipuedespanama.com
Mahogany panels and classical European elegance at an upscale restaurant in the Hotel Bristol (see p. 235). Exemplary service. Chef Cuquita Arias de Calvo—famed, not least for her TV cooking show—oversees

a menu of divine Latin fusion dishes such as tamal soup, crocodile with wasabi and ginger, and lobster tortellini with mint and onion broth.

🪑 80 P 🚫 🌀
🅰 AE,MC, V

🍴 ALKIMIA
$$$
CALLE 50 & BEATRIZ CABAL, INSIDE HOTEL DEVILLE, EL CANGREJO
TEL 213-8250
devillehotel.com.pa
The hip new restaurant in Hotel Deville (see p. 236) is a sophisticated eye-pleaser. Trendy contemporary decor, plus progressive music in the lounge bar. The Mediterranean mood–blue lighting against white walls–is reflected in the menu featuring Spanish cheeses and a Serrano ham appetizer, plus paella and langosta (large prawns) with basil.

🪑 50 P 🚫 🌀 🅰 AE, MC, V

🍴 THE FISH MARKET
$$$
CALLE FELIPE, CASCO VIEJO
TEL 6721-6445
facebook.com/fish.market.panama
As much an "experience" as a dining treat, this casual Caribbean-style open-air venue occupies a former colonial ruin (complete with Romanesque columns). Owner Mike Thompson guarantees superfresh Thai ceviche, fish tacos, tuna *poke*, and daily specials using ingredients straight from the real *mercado de mariscos* nearby. Maybe opt for a delicious lobster ceviche washed down by ice-cold Balboa beer, or try the traditional English fish 'n' chips with a hearty real ale.

🪑 60 🕐 Closed Mon. & Tues.
P 🚫 🌀 🅰 No credit cards

🚫 Nonsmoking 🌀 Air-conditioning Indoor Pool 🌊 Outdoor Pool 🏋 Health Club 🅰 Credit Cards

HABIBI'S
$$$

CALLE RICARDO ARIAS

TEL 264-3647

habibispanama.com

Popular Levantine-themed restaurant in a converted colonial mansion with a contemporary motif and mellow vibe. The menu features staples such as hummus, shish kebab, and shashlik, but also Western favorites. Belly dancers perform on weekends. Hookahs are passed around upstairs in the tented lounge.

🔢 60 🅿 🔲 🔲 🔲 MC, V

LAS TINAJAS
$$$

CALLE 51, BELLA VISTA

TEL 263-7890

tinajaspanama.com

A touristy restaurant renowned for its traditional folkloric shows (*Tues. & Thurs.–Sat. at 9 p.m., $5 cover*) featuring women dressed in *polleras*. The menu plays on a local theme, with dishes such as *sopa borracha*, tamales, and *frituras*. Rustic colonial-themed decor. Reservations essential for dinner shows.

🔢 80 🅿 🔲 🔲 🔲 MC, V

SOMETHING SPECIAL

MANOLO CARACOL
$$$

CALLE 3RA & AVE. CENTRAL, CASCO VIEJO

TEL 228-4640

manolocaracol.net

This fashionable conversion of a colonial structure has lively, eclectic decor and an open kitchen. It features superbly executed fusion dishes and tapas using fresh ingredients. The Spanish-inspired menu includes such delights as gazpacho Andaluz with cucumber and sorbet, but runs to sashimi tuna. Prix-fixe daily menu. Doubles as an art gallery, with regularly

changing exhibitions.

🔢 100 🕐 Closed Sun. & L Sat. 🔲 🔲 🔲 MC, V

SUKHI
$$$

EDIFICIO AMÉRICA, AVE. RICARDO ARIAS

TEL 395-6081

sukhionline.com

This agreeably clean, contemporary restaurant serves dishes from throughout Southeast Asia. The pad thai with langostinos, jungle prawn curry, and tempura tilapia are recommended. Curry buffet on Wednesday afternoons. The staff are friendly and speak good English.

🔢 40 🕐 Closed Sun. 🅿 🔲 🔲 🔲 MC, V

SUSHI ITTO
$$$

REAR OF EDIFICIO PLAZA OBARRIO, BET. CALLES SAMUEL LEWIS & 55

TEL 265-1222

sushi-itto.com

Milan meets Tokyo in this contemporary Japanese restaurant. Sophisticated without being pretentious, it has walls of glass and bright lighting. The varied menu includes such non-Japanese oddities as pastas, alongside sushi, tempura, and other Japanese staples of average quality. Patio dining is an attractive option.

🔢 80 🅿 🔲 🔲 🔲 MC, V

TANTALO KITCHEN
$$$

AVE. B & CALLE 8, CASCO VIEJO

TEL 262-4030

tantalohotel.com

Chic fun-fueled newcomer draws the *farandula* (youthful in-crowd) to dine beneath a spiderweb of halogens. The vast menu spans pizzas, grilled octopus, pad thai, and risotto with porcini mushroom. After dinner, step up to the rooftop

lounge deck to party around the neon-lit bar.

🔢 80 🔲 🔲 🔲 AE, MC, V

TAURO
$$$

MULTICENTRO, AVE. BALBOA

TEL 380-1111

hrhpanamamegapolis.com

In the Hard Rock Hotel, this exciting interpretation of a classic steak house also serves market fresh seafood dishes, from smoked salmon, fajitas, and chicken finger appetizers to a 14-ounce ribeye. Avant-garde black and red decor. The service can be slow.

🔢 48 🅿 ♿ 🔲 🔲 🔲 AE, MC, V

CASA SUCRE COFFEEHOUSE
$$

CALLE 8 & AVE. B, CASCO VIEJO

TEL 393-6130

casasucrecoffeehouse.com

A bohemian hangout with a

PRICES

HOTELS

An indication of the cost of a double room in the high season is given by **$** signs.

$$$$$	Over $200
$$$$	$100–$200
$$$	$50–$100
$$	$25–$50
$	Under $25

RESTAURANTS

An indication of the cost of a three-course meal without drinks is given by **$** signs.

$$$$$	Over $35
$$$$	$20–$35
$$$	$10–$20
$$	$5–$10
$	Under $5

🏨 Hotel   🍴 Restaurant   🛏 No. of Guest Rooms   🔢 No. of Seats   🅿 Parking   🕐 Closed   🛗 Elevator

Parisian vibe and comfy chairs in the heart of the old city, Casa Sucre is perfect for lingering over espresso, cappuccino, or iced latte. Budget-priced bagel, egg, bacon, cream cheese breakfast. Free Wi-Fi.

🛏 30 🚭 ❄ 🅾 MC, V

🍴 EGO Y NARSICO
$$
CALLE ANTONIO SUCRE, PLAZA BOLÍVAR, CASCO VIEJO
TEL 262-2045
Bohemians gather at this Spanish tapas restaurant where tables spill onto the cobbled plaza. Wash down your spicy ceviche or shrimp brochette with hearty sangria.

🛏 20 🕐 Closed Sun.
🚭 ❄ 🅾 All major cards

🍴 EL TRAPICHE
$$
VÍA ARGENTINA, EL CANGREJO
TEL 269-4353
Hearty traditional Panamanian fare from the central provinces. Start with chicken-stuffed fritters or ceviche followed by the "Panamanian Fiesta" combo. Decor includes a *trapiche*: a traditional sugar press, which is worth a look, as service can be slow.

🛏 44 🅿 🚭 ❄ 🅾 MC, V

🍴 CASA VEGETARIANA
$
CALLE RICARDO ARIAS & AVE. 3 SUR
TEL 269-1876
A heaven-sent option for vegans and vegetarians, this Taiwanese-run hole-in-the-wall offers fill-your-plate, four-item buffets for a mere $2. Free miso soup with a fifth item. Homemade natural juices.

🛏 10 🚭 🅾 No credit cards

🍴 GRANCLÉMENT
$
AVE. CENTRAL & CALLE 3RA, CASCO VIEJO
TEL 208-0737
granclement.com
Gourmet ice creams and sorbets made from all-natural ingredients. Flavors range from pineapple and mango to cinnamon and Earl Grey tea. Cool colonial surroundings.

🛏 6 🚭 ❄ 🅾 No credit cards

🍴 NIKO'S CAFÉ
$
ANTIGUA BOLERA, BALBOA
TEL 228-8888
nikoscafe.com
Excellent value at this large, popular, buffet-style café-restaurant. An excellent range of tasty local fare, including desserts. Panoramic black-and-white historic photos of the Canal Zone.

🛏 120 🅿 🚭 ❄
🅾 No credit cards

■ CENTRAL CARIBBEAN & THE CANAL

ARCHIPIÉLAGO DE LAS PERLAS

SOMETHING SPECIAL

🏨 HACIENDA DEL MAR
🍴 **$$$$$**
ISLA SAN JOSÉ
TEL 832-5439
haciendadelmar.net
Billed as an "eco-resort by the sea," this gorgeous hotel is an escape from the modern world in every way imaginable. No TVs. No phones. No stress. Just rest and relaxation. A 20-minute flight from the mainland. Poised on a promontory with balconies suspended over azure waters, the bungalows here are cozy and include junior suites and two-room VIP cabanas. The hacienda includes a slate-lined swimming pool. Superb (albeit expensive) seafood in the dramatic open-air restaurant. Sportfishing, all-terrain-vehicle tours, and more are available at extra charge.

🛏 14 🚭 ❄ 🏊 🏋
🅾 AE, MC, V

SOMETHING SPECIAL

🏨 PERLA REAL INN
$$$$
ISLA CONTADORA
TEL 6513-9064
perlareal.com
Spanish-colonial-themed inn with courtyard fountain, minutes from gorgeous white beaches. Classically elegant rooms boast wrought-iron pieces, gaily colored walls with stencil designs, pure white linens, and hand-painted blue-and-white tilework and sinks in spacious bathrooms. Offers tours and activities. Breakfast included. A solid bargain.

🛏 6 🚭 ❄ 🏊 🅾 MC, V

🏨 THE POINT
$$$
ISLA CONTADORA
TEL 836-5434
hotelthepoint.com
Set amid landscaped, palm-shaded grounds with a raised beachfront boardwalk, this gracious property has gone upscale under a new Italian owner, who has turned it into a heavenly island retreat. The Point offers an exquisite free-form pool and open-air beachfront restaurant serving pastas and seafood.

🛏 48 🅿 🚭 ❄ 🏊 🅾 MC, V

🏨 VILLA ROMÁNTICA
$$$
ISLA CONTADORA
TEL 202-7426
visitcontadoraisland.com
A slightly dated yet quirkily romantic French-owned inn with charming, even kitschy rooms with ceiling fans. Lovely open-air oceanfront restaurant. Wi-Fi.

🛏 17 🚭 ❄ 🅾 MC, V

CERRO AZÚL

SOMETHING SPECIAL

 **HOSTAL CASA DE CAMPO COUNTRY INN & SPA**
$$$
28 MILES (45 KM) E OF
PANAMA CITY
TEL 226-0274
panamacasadecampo.com
Delightful modern family-run hilltop inn decorated in Old World style. Rooms in cabins set on lush grounds boast rich color schemes and fabrics. Home-cooked meals are served, and the spa has wide-ranging treatments. Minutes from Parque Nacional Chagres. Birding tours are offered.
[]11 P S ▨ MC, V

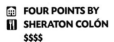 **SIERRA LLORONA**
$$$
SABANITAS, SANTA RITA ARRIBA, 12 MILES (19 KM) SE OF COLÓN
TEL 202-3166
sierrallorona.com
A handsome contemporary-style two-story nature lodge set amid rain forest and popular for birding. Airy, spacious bedrooms featuring tile floors, wicker and Spanish colonial furniture, and ceiling fans open to verandas with hammocks. Dining is family style, and there's a cozy lounge with bar. Guided birding, hiking, and mountain biking are offered.
[]7 P S S DC, MC, V

COLÓN

FOUR POINTS BY SHERATON COLÓN
$$$$
MILLENNIUM PLAZA, AVE. AHMAD WAKED
TEL 447-1000
starwoodhotels.com
Bringing a touch of class to Colón, this superchic high-rise

cruise-port hotel is designed to resemble a ship's prow. Inside, stylish decor combines with 21st-century accoutrements, including Wi-Fi in the café and high-speed modems (extra charge) in guest rooms done up in trendy combinations of chocolate, olive, and orange. **Café Portobelo** has the finest dining in town.
[]243 ▨ S S ▨
All major cards

RADISSON COLÓN 2,000 HOTEL & CASINO
$$$$
PASEO GORGAS & CALLE 13
TEL 446-2000
radisson.com
A neighbor and rival to the Four Points, it wins no points for good looks but comfy guest rooms offer Edwardian elegance and all modern conveniences.
[]102 ▨ S S ▨ ▨
All major cards

NEW WASHINGTON HOTEL
$$$
CALLE 1, AVE. BOLÍVAR
TEL 441-7133
newhotelwashington.net
This venerable grande dame of a hotel received a much needed facelift in recent years. Chandeliers and marble staircases gleam, although rooms remain dull. A casino adjoins, and the restaurant offers a broad seafood menu.
[]124 P S ▨ AE, MC, V

LAS CUMBRES

HOTEL AVALON GRAND PANAMA
$$$$
5 MILES (8 KM) N OF
PANAMA CITY
TEL 268-4499 OR 800/261-5014
FAX: 268-8654
hotelavalongrandpanama.com
Hilltop rain forest setting adjoining Parque Nacional

Camino de Cruces, accessed by trails. Elegantly appointed guest rooms and villas. Children's water park.
[]37 P S ▨ ▨
AE, MC, V

GAMBOA

GAMBOA RAINFOREST RESORT
$$$$
AVE. GAILLARD, 15.5 MILES (25 KM) NW OF PANAMA CITY
TEL 314-5000
FAX 314-9020
gamboaresort.com
Large, modern facility enjoying a supremely beautiful position overlooking the Río Chagres. The resort offers forest trails and a wide range of nature-oriented activities. Spacious rooms are tastefully furnished and have balconies overlooking the grounds, Río Chagres, and the rain forest. Also available are 48 apartments in renovated 1930s Panama Canal Administration homes decorated with charming tropical furniture. Choice of eateries includes the elegant **Chagres River View** restaurant and the lakeside **Los Lagartos** for Sunday brunch.
[]107 P S S ▨ ▨
DC, MC, V

ISLA GRANDE

SISTER MOON ECOLODGE
$$$
14 MILES (22.5 KM) E
OF PORTOBELO
TEL 6948-1990
hotelsistermoon.com
Shaded by palms on the slopes of a rocky cove. Thatched stilt-legged cabins, including bunks for budget travelers. Billiard table and darts in the sundeck bar. Water sports and fishing. Breakfast included.
[]11 P S ▨ MC, V

ISLA TABOGA

CERRITO TROPICAL
$$$
ISLA TABOGA
TEL 390-8999 OR 6489-0074
cerritotropicalpanama.com
Reached by a steep path, this quaint hillside B&B has simple rooms and larger yet cozy apartments, all with ceiling fans and adorned with lively tropical colors. At **Garden Ranchito** restaurant, guests are always invited to dine with owners, who serve up hearty breakfasts on the veranda.

3 (2 apts.) MC, V

VEREDA TROPICAL HOTEL
$$$
ISLA TABOGA
TEL 250-2154
This colorful hotel has a cliff-top perch with lovely beach views. Tastefully furnished rooms around a central court-yard are themed to span the globe; colorful tilework is a highlight. Guests can enjoy the ocean-view restaurant.

14 (some rooms) MC, V

LAGO GATÚN

MELIÁ PANAMA CANAL
$$$$
LAGO GATÚN, 4 MILES (6.4 KM) W OF COLÓN
TEL 470-1100 OR 888-956-3592
meliapanamacanal.com
Stylish conversion of former U.S. military headquarters on the shores of Lake Gatún. Spacious rooms offer elegant Edwardian-style furnishings; "Royal Service" suites have butler service. Convention center, choice of restaurants, plentiful sports options, plus a treetop zipline.

285 All major cards

JUNGLE LAND PANAMA
$$
LAGO GATÚN
TEL 213-1172
junglelandpanama.com
Imagine a floating hotel anchored in a cove in the midst of Gatún Lake. This one-of-a-kind two-story wooden houseboat is an excellent venue for fishing and viewing wildlife. Family-style dining on a shaded deck slung with hammocks is offered. Organized tours including kayaking and even jungle survival are also available.

8 MC, V

MARIA CHIQUITA

BALA BALA BEACH RESORT
$$$$
MARIA CHIQUITA, 10 MILES (16 KM) E OF COLÓN
TEL 202-0282
balabeach.com
A stunning contemporary-style, high-rise, all-inclusive condo-hotel, opened in 2013, with city-slicker sophistica-tion. Choose fom studios to penthouse lofts, all with full kitchens, walk-out balconies, and Wi-Fi. Wide array of water sports and activities.

117 MC, V

MIRAFLORES

TOP DECK
$$$
MIRAFLORES LOCKS VISITOR CENTER, 5 MILES (8 KM) W OF BALBOA
TEL 276-8325
An excellent all-you-can-eat buffet restaurant with shaded terrace for a bird's-eye view over the Miraflores Locks. Ground-floor snack bar with sandwiches, salads, and coffees. You will need to pay an entrance fee to the visitor center for the

upper-level restaurant.

60 MC, V

PARQUE NACIONAL SOBERANÍA

SOMETHING SPECIAL

CANOPY TOWER ECOLODGE & NATURE OBSERVATORY
$$$$
PARQUE NACIONAL SOBERANÍA
TEL 264-5720
canopytower.com
An ascetic conversion of a former radar facility, this unusual entity appeals mostly to birders. First impressions upon entering are of being inside a grain silo, with its bare metal walls and "industrial" beams. Expensive first-story rooms are small, basic, and share bathroom facilities. Upper-story rooms, shaped like pie slices, are more spacious and romantically furnished. Avoid rooms with views into the parking lot. A cozy library doubles as a dining room. A rooftop observatory looks down over the forest. Meals and birding tour included.

12 DC, MC, V

PLAYA BONITA

WESTIN PLAYA BONITA
$$$$$
KM 6 CAMINO A VERACRUZ, PLAYA BONITA
TEL 304-6600
starwoodhotels.com
This stunning modern, high-rise, all-inclusive beach resort opened in 2012. Six types of rooms all boast chic minimalist decor and furnishings and ocean views through walls of glass. The hotel is loaded with facilities, including a kids club and vast oceanfront swimming pool.

611 All major cards

 Nonsmoking  Air-conditioning Indoor Pool Outdoor Pool Health Club Credit Cards

PORTOBELO

COCO PLUM
$$$

3 MILES (5 KM) W OF
PORTOBELO
TEL 448-2102
cocoplum-panama.com
Lovely beachfront hotel with
water sports and beach games.
Colorful decor in spacious
rooms with cool tiles underfoot. Upkeep here is an issue.
The airy **Restaurante Las
Anclas** specializes in seafood
and Colombian-style *patacones*
(fried plantain slices).

🛈 12 🅿 🔧 🚫 AE, MC, V

🍴 RESTAURANTE LOS CAÑONES
$$

0.5 MILE (0.8 KM) W OF
PORTOBELO
TEL 448-2980
This thatched restaurant overlooking a cove specializes in
seafood. The house specialty is
pulpo en leche de coco: octopus
in tomato sauce on coconut
rice. A word of warning:
Chitras strike at dusk—bring
a can of insect repellent.

🪑 34 🅿 🚫 No credit cards

▪ KUNA YALA

ACHUTUPU

🏨 DOLPHIN ISLAND
🍴 LODGE
$$$

ISLA UAGUITUPO, 400 YARDS
(366 M) E OF ACHUTUPU
TEL 838-9885
dolphinlodgesanblas.com
On its own private island.
Two types of thatched,
beachfront cabins, served
with satellite Internet.
Delightful, albeit rustic,
bamboo-sided junior suites
with hardwood floors are
preferred to the simpler
concrete-and-wood standards.
Private bathrooms have flush

toilets and cold showers.
Facilities include hammocks
and volleyball court, plus
waterfront bar and the seafood **Bohío Restaurant** with
ocean views (rates include
meals). Solar electricity
during set hours.

🛈 11 🚫 MC, V

AILIGANDÍ

🏨 DAD IBE ISLAND
🍴 LODGE
$$$$

10-MIN. BOAT RIDE FROM
DOMESTIC AIRPORT
TEL 6112-5448
dadibelodge.net
Lovely, comfy, and colorfully
furnished thatch-and-bamboo
huts overhang waters sur-
rounding this tiny island, with
safe waters for swimming
thanks to flush toilets and
septic tank. Simple restaurant.
Rates include meals. Bilingual
guides available.

🛈 3 🚫 No credit cards

AKWADUP

🏨 AKWADUP LODGE
$$$$

AKWADUP
TEL 832-5144 OR 6078-7397
akwaduplodge.com
This family-run ecolodge
has thatched cottages with
24-hour electricity, tile
floors, modern bathrooms
with showers, plus balconies
overhanging the ocean. Rates
include all meals, and tour
are offered.

🛈 7 🅿 🔧 🏊 🚫 MC, V

ÁREA SILVESTRE PROTEGIDA NARGANÁ

SOMETHING SPECIAL

🏨 BURBAYAR LODGE
🍴 $$$

NUSUGANDI, 9 MILES
(14.5 KM) N OF EL LLANO
(ON INTERAMERICAN HWY.)

TEL 236-6061 OR 6949-5700
burbayar.net
Sitting astride the summit
of the Serranía San Blas, this
rustic family-run ecolodge
immerses guests in unspoiled
nature. Run to strict ecological principles, the simple
wood-and-thatch lodge has
rustic bamboo-and-hardwood
cabanas with basic furnishings,
shared bathrooms, and solar-
powered lamps. Some rooms
have bunks. Delicious meals
served family style at candlelit
rough-hewn tables with
lovely views over landscaped
grounds and forest (meals
are included in rates).
Guided hikes. Gates are
locked in the evening;
advance reservations
are essential.

🛈 7 🅿 🚫 No credit cards

BAHÍA EL ESCRIBANO

SOMETHING SPECIAL

 CORAL LODGE
RESORT
$$$$$
COSTA ARRIBA, COLÓN,
SAN BLAS
TEL 838-9988
corallodge.com
This intimate, Polynesian-inspired, U.S.-owned and -operated resort, on the western boundary of the Kuna Yala *comarca,* features thatched, octagonal "water villas" on piers overhanging the turquoise waters. Sitting rooms feature glass floors for close-up viewing of reef life, while king-size beds with wraparound net drapes, hammocks slung on sundecks, rattan furnishings, and whirlpool tubs with ocean views add to the romantic ambience. Casual elegance is the watchword. Scuba diving and kayaking are specialties. Two restaurants. Wi-Fi.

7 MC, V

ISKARDUP

**SAPIBENEGA KUNA
LODGE**
$$$$$
3 MILES (4.8 KM) W OF
PLAYÓN CHICO
TEL 215-1406
sapibenega.com
Squeezed onto a tiny islet, this pleasant lodge operates under the motto "Nature is our life." Bamboo-walled duplex cabins on stilts over the water have private flush toilets and tiled showers. Fresh seafood is served in an open-air waterfront restaurant lit by tiki lights at night. Guided nature hikes and cultural tours. Meals included in rates. Solar power and generator supply electricity 24 hours.

13 MC, V

ISLA YANDUP

CABAÑAS YANDUP
$$$
0.75 MILE (1.2 KM) NE OF
PLAYÓN CHICO
TEL 202-0854
yandupisland.com
Pleasant, albeit simple, thatched bamboo-walled cabins with orthopedic mattresses, stylish fabrics, ocean-front patios, and shared toilets. Forest hikes, snorkeling, and meals (served in an open-air dining room) included in rates. Bring insect repellent.

14 No credit cards

KUANIDUP

CABAÑAS KUANIDUP
$$$
KUANIDUP, 4.5 MILES (7.2 KM)
N OF RÍO SIDRA
TEL 6635-6737 OR 6742-7656
kuanidup.com
Simple thatched, woven-bamboo cabins enjoy a splendid, unpolluted beach-side location. Rough-hewn beds with foam mattresses, sandy floors, and outside shared toilets. Rates include all meals, snorkeling, plus transfers from Río Sidra airstrip.

7 MC, V

NARGANÁ

**RESTAURANTE NALI'S
CAFÉ**
$
NARGANÁ
TEL 299-9009 (PUBLIC PHONE)
One of the few restaurants in the archipelago. Seafood is tasty and usually trustworthy. Lobster, fresh crab, rice, and beans are the staples. Traditional American breakfasts are served.

20 No credit cards

EL PORVENIR

 **UKUPTUPU HOTEL**
$$$
UKUPTUPU, 0.2 MILE (0.3 KM)
W OF EL PORVENIR
TEL 6746-5088
ukuptupu.com
This former Smithsonian Institution research facility takes up most of the tiny isle and offers delightful vistas. Spacious yet basic accommodations have tin roofs, bamboo walls, foam mattresses, and linoleum floors. Shared bathrooms have flush toilets. Hammocks are slung on shaded balconies. Rates include meals.

15 No credit cards

KUNA NISKUA LODGE
$$
ISLA WAILIDUP, 0.5 MILE (0.8 KM)
SW OF EL PORVENIR
TEL 259-3471
No frills at this simple, clean, thatch-and-bamboo lodge where corner rooms are preferable. Three rooms have shared bathrooms and solar electricity. Seafood served at a simple thatched restaurant. Meals and snorkeling included.

9

DARIÉN

BAHÍA PIÑA

TROPIC STAR LODGE
$$$$$
BAHIA PIÑA
TEL 407/423-9931 OR
800/682-3424 (U.S.)
tropicstar.com
This upscale U.S.-owned sportfishing lodge enjoys a tranquil setting on the mountain-rimmed east shore of Pineapple Bay. Accommodations are a mix of cabins and rooms, some with king beds, furnished in Old World colonial

style. El Palacio, the original owner's three-bedroom ridge-top home, can be rented and is reached by funicular or a flight of 122 steps. Dining is family style and features top-notch meals, predominantly seafood, enjoyed while fishing videos are screened. Fishing is aboard a fleet of 31-foot (9.5 m) Bertrams. One-week minimum stay during high season.

🛏 18 🌊 🏊 ⛷ AE, MC, V

METETÍ

SOMETHING SPECIAL

🏨 **FILO DEL TALLO LODGE**
$$$$
2 MILES (3 KM) W OF METETÍ
TEL 6673-5381
panamaexoticadventures.com
Offering both an immersion in indigenous culture and endearing comfort, this hilltop retreat in a Wounaan village combines traditional palm-and-bamboo architecture with simple yet sophisticated decor. The wall-less lounge and dining area in a circular *palenque* has grandstand views, enjoyed while lounging in poured-concrete sofas with plump pillows. Guided birding, hikes, and horseback rides are offered.

🛏 3 🌐 ⛷ No credit cards

PARQUE NACIONAL DARIÉN

🏨 **CANA FIELD STATION**
$$$$
CANA, PARQUE NACIONAL DARIÉN
TEL 269-9415
anconexpeditions.com
At 1,600 feet (488 m) of elevation in the heart of Parque Nacional Darién, this simple nature lodge is administered by Ancon Expeditions, which has sole use of the facility. Surrounded by rain forest offering spectacular birding.

Communal bathrooms. The dining room looks out to the forest. Accommodation is usually provided only as a multiday package. Ancillary accommodation is offered at a cloud-forest tent camp at 4,200 feet (1,280 m), a 6-mile (9.6 km) hike.

🛏 8 ⛷ MC, V

PUNTA PATIÑO

🏨 **PUNTA PATIÑO LODGE**
$$$$
RESERVA NATURAL PUNTA PATIÑO
TEL 269-9415
anconexpeditions.com
A blufftop nature lodge within Punta Patiño Nature Reserve, with magnificent views. Individual cabins in tropical pastels set amid lawns have loft bedrooms and private bathrooms with cold showers; six cabins are air-conditioned. A balcony wrapping around the dining room has hammocks for lounging with lovely views. Nature hikes are a specialty. Bugs abound. Bring some insect repellent.

🛏 10 🅿 🌐 ⛷ MC, V

RÍO SAMBÚ

🏨 **SAMBÚ HAUSE BED & BREAKFAST**
$$$
SAMBÚ
TEL 268-6905 OR 6766-5102
sambuhausedarien panama.com
This spacious wooden lodge with a BBQ deck and mosquito screens offers a true jungle experience with many modern comforts in the heart of a small Emberá indigenous community. Two of the rooms share a bathroom; a third is air-conditioned and has its own bathroom. A jungle treehouse is to be added. The owners offer guided birding and cultural trips. Meals

are included.

🛏 4 🌊 ⛷ No credit cards

▥ CENTRAL PANAMA

MARIATO

🏨 **HELICONIA B&B ECOLODGE**
$$$
MARIATO, 38 MILES (60 KM) S OF SANTIAGO
TEL 6676-0220
hotelheliconiapanama.com
Upscale camping within a self-sustainable ecological project run by Dutch biologists Loes Roos and Kees Groenendijk. Spacious safari-style tents atop stilt platforms with thatch roofs, twin camp beds with mattresses, and hammocks on decks. Artsy stone-floored open-air bathrooms and showers. Volunteer for reforestation projects. Guided birding, hiking, and kayaking. A four-room hotel and self-catering cottages are to be added.

🛏 8 🌐 ⛷ No credit cards

PARQUE NACIONAL ALTOS DE CAMPANA

🏨 **HOSTAL HACIENDA DOÑA VICTORIA**
$$
CAMPANA, 2 MILES (3.2 KM) W OF CAPIRA
TEL 393-7379
hostalvictoriapanama.com
Set within a beautiful garden, this intimate, yet simply furnished, old Spanish hacienda is fronted by a stone courtyard with fountain, wrought-iron grills, and hammocks on terra-cotta patios. It has a lovely swimming pool with waterfall. Horseback riding and a carriage tour are offered. Meals included.

🛏 9 🅿 🌊 ⛷ MC, V

PARQUE NACIONAL COIBA

🏨 PESCA PANAMA
$$$$$
ISLA COIBA
TEL 800/946-3474
pescapanama.com
A floating lodge catering primarily to sportfishers. Cozy wood-paneled bar/lounge with bamboo furnishings, plus outdoor dining. Sleeps 12, including bunks. Scuba diving and kayaking are offered. Fishing is available aboard 27-foot (8 m) center-console boats. Weeklong packages only.
🛏 3 🚭 ❄ 🃏 MC, V

PENONOMÉ

SOMETHING SPECIAL

🏨 LA IGUANA
🍴 ECO-RESORT
$$$
CHURUQUITA GRANDE, 9 MILES (14 KM) NE OF PENONOMÉ
TEL 6981-1517 OR 6798-8650
laiguanaresort.com
Approached by a long glade, this thatched nature lodge in the foothills is perfect for birders, although it is slightly run-down. Simply appointed rooms decorated with pre-Columbian motifs; some have loft bedrooms. Cold showers only. Meals served indoors and on a lovely patio. Trails lead to a waterfall and into a forest teeming with wildlife.
🛏 8 🅿 🚭 🌊 No credit cards

PLAYA BLANCA

SOMETHING SPECIAL

🏨 WYNDHAM GRAND
🍴 PLAYA BLANCA
$$$$$
PLAYA BLANCA
TEL 908-3800

wyndham.com
This all-inclusive beach resort induces gasps of delight for its eye-pleasing design and über-chic decor. Guest rooms in six-story towers are arrayed around a huge infinity pool complex and feature lush linens, 32-inch flat-screen TVs, iPod docking stations, and a host of other high-tech amenities. Its five restaurants include Mediterranean and Japanese options. Kids get an arcade room. Free Wi-Fi throughout.
🛏 211 🅿 ❄ 🚭 🌊 ☔ 💪
🃏 All major cards

🏨 PLAYA BLANCA BEACH RESORT & SPA
$$$$
6 MILES (9.6 KM) SW OF RÍO HATO
TEL 264-6444 OR 908-3500
playablancaresort.com
An all-inclusive beach resort catering to Panama's middle-class and international package groups. Guest rooms occupy a series of three-story units arranged haphazardly around two large free-form pools. Lively contemporary decor. Complete dining, entertainment, and activities such as water sports included in the fee. Boisterous on weekends and holidays.
🛏 340 🅿 ❄ 🚭 🌊 ☔ 💪
🃏 MC, V

🍴 PIPA'S BEACH RESTAURANTE
$$
FARALLÓN, 1 MILE (1.6 KM) W OF DECAMERON
TEL 6252-8430
pipasbeach.com
Ramshackle and colorful beach bar and restaurant serving delicious seafood. Listen to reggae tunes, play beach volleyball, and dine with the sand between your toes. Usually open until the last guest leaves.
🍴 20 🅿 🃏 No credit cards

PLAYA CORONADO

🏨 🍴 CORONADO GOLF & BEACH RESORT
$$$$$
PLAYA CORONADO
TEL 264-3164 (PANAMA CITY) OR 240-4444
coronadoresort.com
Based around a championship 18-hole golf course, this low-rise upscale resort can be boisterous on weekends when the Panama City crowd flocks in. The resort's wide-ranging facilities include eight restaurants, a spa, plus tennis, a stable, water sports, and convention facilities.
🛏 78 🅿 ❄ 🚭 🌊 ☔ 💪
🃏 All major cards

PLAYA FARALLÓN

SOMETHING SPECIAL

🏨 JW MARRIOTT
🍴 **$$$$$**
PLAYA FARALLÓN
TEL 264-0000
marriott.com
Opened in 2009 in the heart of the sprawling Buenaventura residential resort, the JW Marriott is built around a Nicklaus Design par-72 championship golf course. The suites are spacious and sumptuously appointed and have four-poster king beds plus state-of-the-art amenities. Justifiably a member of the Leading Hotels of the World. Guests will also relish the gourmet dining on offer in the hotel restaurant and at the hotel beach club. Also available on the property are 18 four-bedroom villas. A panoply of water sports and fun activities includes ziplining.
🛏 114 🅿 ❄ 🚭 🌊 ☔ 💪
🃏 All major cards

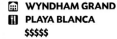

PLAYA KOBBE

🏨 **INTERCONTINENTAL**
🍴 **PLAYA BONITA RESORT**
& SPA
$$$$
4 MILES (6.4 KM) W OF
PANAMA CITY
TEL 211-8600 OR 206-8880
ihg.com

A sprawling Mediterranean-inspired hotel set amid 20 acres (8 ha) of lush rain forest along a mile-long (1.6 km) stretch of brown sand. Guest rooms are a classy indulgence, with rich hardwood furnishings, divinely comfortable king beds, and wireless Internet access. The resort includes four swimming pools, three restaurants, and a huge spa. Open-air oceanfront dining under thatch.

🚪303 🅿 ⬆ Ⓢ 🈂 ⛱ 🍸
🈂 All major cards

PLAYA SANTA CATALINA

🏨 **HOTEL SANTA**
CATALINA
$$$
50 YARDS (50 M) INLAND
OF PLAYA SANTA CATALINA
TEL 6571-4387
hotelsantacatalina
panama.com

The best option for miles. U.S.-run oceanfront boutique hotel designed as an old hacienda with aged timbers and terra-cotta roofs with ceiling fans and luxe line; some have bunks.

🚪5 🅿 Ⓢ 🈂 🈂 MC, V

🍴 **PIZZERÍA JAMMIN'**
$
BET. PLAYA SANTA
CATALINA & PUNTA BRAVA
A favorite of surfers, who flock here for the thin-crust pizzas served beneath thatch. Has hammocks and bench tables for a laid-back feel.

🪑24 🅿 🕐 Closed Mon.
🈂 No credit cards

PLAYA SANTA CLARA

SOMETHING SPECIAL

🏨 **ART LODGE LAND ART**
$$
ISLA GOBERNADORA, 6 MILES
(10 KM) SE OF SANTA CATALINA
TEL 6636-5180
artlodgepanama.com

A budget travel maven's dream, this island lodge is the creation of two French artists, Valérie and Yves. Back-to-nature types will love the open-air king-size platform beds with mosquito nets, beneath thatched roofs. Artsy touches include mosaics in the rain forest (open-air) bathrooms.

🚪3 🈂 No credit cards

🏨 **HIBISCUS GARDEN**
🍴 **& RESTAURANT**
$$
PLAYA LAGARTERO,
SANTA CATALINA
TEL 6615-6097
hibiscusgarden.com

Two California-raised surfers, Mike and Ollie, have turned a formerly ho-hum lodge into a classy budget option. Minimal yet tasteful furnishings. Shared kitchen. Surf lessons. The open-air oceanfront restaurant slung with hammocks serves goat cheese salads, burgers, and turkey sandwiches.

🚪4 Ⓢ 🈂 No credit cards

🏨 **XS MEMORIES**
$$
INTERAMERICAN HWY.,
PLAYA SANTA CLARA
TEL 993-3069
xsmemories.com

U.S. expats Dennis and Sheila Parsick run this RV park, offering hookups and facilities for 22 motor homes. It also has camping facilities, plus three cabins with ceiling

---

PRICES

HOTELS
An indication of the cost of a double room in the high season is given by $ signs.

$$$$$	Over $200
$$$$	$100–$200
$$$	$50–$100
$$	$25–$50
$	Under $25

RESTAURANTS
An indication of the cost of a three-course meal without drinks is given by $ signs.

$$$$$	Over $35
$$$$	$20–$35
$$$	$10–$20
$$	$5–$10
$	Under $5

---

fans. Sports bar. Kayak Panama is based here.

🚪3 🅿 Ⓢ 🈂 🈂 MC, V

PUNTA CHAME

SOMETHING SPECIAL

🏨 **NITRO CITY PANAMA**
🍴 **ACTION SPORTS**
RESORT
$$$$
CARRETERA BEJUCO,
PUNTA CHAME
TEL 202-6875 OR 223-1747
nitrocitypanama.com

Designed for young sports-minded travelers, the theme is play hard by day, party hearty by night. Deluxe rooms with chic decor include suites, all with heaps of light pouring in through sliding glass walls. The **Pit-Stop Restaurant** offers simple fare, from seafood soup to burgers, while the chill **Refuel Bar** has a pool table, fusbol, and serious partying. Paint ball, MotoX, and water

sports are some of the fun-filled activities.

🚹 36 🅿 🚭 ❄ 🏊 💚
💳 MC, V

SANTA FÉ

🏨 HOSTAL LA QHIA GUEST HOUSE
$$
SANTA FÉ
TEL 954-0903 OR 6592-5589
panamamountainhouse.com
A Swiss-style summer home of a wealthy Panamanian businessman is now a lovely alpine retreat in a gorgeous garden. Rooms, which include a dorm, are almost ascetic with their minimal (almost spartan) furnishings. Run by a Belgian/Argentine couple.

🚹 4 💳 No credit cards

🏨 HOTEL SANTA FÉ
$$
CARRETERA SANTIAGO–SANTA FÉ, 600 YARDS (550 M) S OF SANTA FÉ
TEL 954-0941
hotelsantafepanama.com
A favorite of birders, this hotel on the edge of the village has lovely valley views. Simply yet cozily furnished rooms with cold showers; some are air-conditioned. Guided hiking and birding tours are offered, plus horse rental.

🚹 16 🅿 🚭 Some rooms
💳 No credit cards

SANTIAGO

🏨 HOTEL VISTA LAGO ECORESORT
$$$
INTERAMERICAN HWY. KM 258, SANTIAGO DE VERAGUA
TEL 954-9916 OR 6206-6065
hotelvistalagopanama.com
Almost incongruous given its lovely lakeside setting, this minimalist contemporary hotel has urbane furnishings in the lounge. Guest rooms are

simpler, almost disappointing. Gourmet restaurant with lake views serves fusion dishes.

🚹 24 🅿 🚭 🏊 💚 💳 MC, V

🏨 HOTEL LA HACIENDA
🍴 **$$**
INTERAMERICAN HWY., 1.5 MILES (2.4 KM) W OF TOWN CENTER
TEL 958-8580
hotel-lahacienda.net
A hotel with a sunny disposi-tion, this colorful Mexican-themed stopover beside the Interamerican Highway is a popular way station for busi-ness travelers and is the nicest hotel in town. Ceramic sun and moon faces smile at every turn. Rooms are furnished in simple hacienda style. Firm mattresses are a bonus. Italian fare in the colorful restaurant.

🚹 42 🅿 🚭 ❄ 🏊 💳 MC, V

🍴 RESTAURANTE LOS TUCANES
$$$
CENTRO COMERCIAL VERAGUENSE, INTERAMERICAN HWY.
TEL 998-3197
A favorite stop for buses, this popular roadside restaurant is a good place for sandwiches, salads, and Panamanian staples, from fried chicken to spicy shrimp *criolla* (in tomato sauce).

🚹 60 🅿 🚭 💳 MC, V

SORÁ

🏨 TANGLEWOOD WELLNESS CENTER
$$$$
9 MILES (14.5 KM) NW OF BEJUCO
TEL 6671-9965 OR 202/652-4694 (U.S.)
tanglewoodwellness center.com
A health and fasting retreat enjoying a superb mountain setting at a 1,500-foot (460 m) elevation. Guest lounge with wicker furnishings and library. Cozy cottages. Organic meals

are served. Best suited to trav-elers seeking a wellness pack-age. One week minimum.

🚹 10 🅿 🚭 💚
💳 All major cards

EL VALLE DE ANTÓN

SOMETHING SPECIAL

🏨 LOS MANDARINOS BOUTIQUE SPA HOTEL/ LA TASCA DE TRIANA
🍴 **$$$$$**
200 YARDS (185 M) W OF ESCUELA DE PRIMER CICLO, OFF CALLE EL CICLO
TEL 983-6645 (EL VALLE) OR 6608-2743
Recalling a Tuscan villa, this gem tucked into a quiet corner of El Valle is one of Panama's finest boutique hotels. Exquisite gardens. Tile floors and elegant furnishings, including four-poster beds in spacious rooms and villas. Doubles as the weekend home of Chef Lourdes Fábrega de Ward, owner of Panama City's acclaimed Golosina restaurant. The hotel has two restaurants, one an **Irish Pub** serving shepherd's pie and fish 'n' chips. Spanish-themed **La Tasca de Triana** serves deli-cious tapas such as garlic clams and gallega octopus, plus paella and even pork chops. A spa offers a complete range of treatments.

🚹 52 🅿 🚭 🏊 💚
💳 AE, MC, V

🏨 CANOPY LODGE
$$$$
CALLE CERRO MACHO
TEL 264-5720
canopylodge.com
Lovely contemporary river-side hotel in a private nature reserve next to the protected area of Cerro Gaital Natural Monument. Birding is a spe-cialty. Light and spacious guest rooms with Japanese-inspired aesthetic open to terraces

🚭 Nonsmoking ❄ Air-conditioning 🏊 Indoor Pool 🏊 Outdoor Pool 💚 Health Club 💳 Credit Cards

overlooking the forest, as do the airy public spaces.

🛈 12 🅿 ⏹ 🌀 AE, MC, V

🏨 CRATER VALLEY RESORT & ADVENTURE SPA
$$$$
CALLE CATIRITA &
RANITA DE ORO
TEL 215-2328
FAX 215-2329
crater-valley.com

Gorgeous landscaped grounds provide a perfect setting within this large estate hotel and spa. Spacious but modestly furnished rooms have beamed wooden ceilings and ceramic floors, warm earth tones, and heaps of light. The spa offers a panoply of treatments. Continental breakfast included.

🛈 8 🅿 ⏹ 🌀 ⛱ 🍸 🌀 MC, V

SOMETHING SPECIAL

🏨 PARK EDEN BED & BREAKFAST
$$$$
CALLE ESPAVE NO. 7
TEL 983-6167 OR 6695-6190
parkeden.com

An exquisite garden sets off this European-style timber-and-stone lodge. Intimate decor in individually styled rooms, which vary in size; all have ceiling fans. The live-in Panamanian-Ecuadorian owners lavish pride on their fine home-hotel, which also includes a two-bedroom house for rent. Full-course breakfasts are a treat, and English tea is served mid-afternoon.

🛈 6 🅿 ⏹ 🌀 (some rooms) 🌀 AE, MC, V

🏨 HOTEL CAMPESTRE
$$$
CALLE EL HATO
TEL 983-6146
hotelcampestre.com

This charmingly rustic alpine lodge at the base of mountains has heaps of ambience, although furnishings remain dowdy despite a reconstruction that has replaced much of the old structure.

🛈 40 🅿 ⏹ 🌀 🌀 MC, V

🏨🍴 RINCÓN VALLERO HOTEL
$$$
100 YARDS (90 M) S OF CALLE DE LOS MILIONARIOS
TEL 983-6175
hotelrinconvallero.com

Hacienda-style hotel with flagstone floors set on lovely grounds with artificial lake and waterfall. Offers tastefully appointed, individually themed rooms and bungalows, including a honeymoon suite with sunken stone whirlpool. Lovely **El Pez de Oro** restaurant and bar are romantically inviting. Try the fried ceviche.

🛈 14 🅿 ⏹ 🌀 🌀 MC, V

🍴 ARTASH FRESH CHOICE
$$
1 CALLE LA PLANTA
TEL 6980-2734

A garden restaurant serving health-conscious diners. Owner-chef Arturo Wong dishes up artfully presented veggie stir-fries and wraps, washed down by smoothies and cappuccinos.

🪑 20 🕐 Closed Tues.
🅿 ⏹ 🌀 🌀 No credit cards

AZUERO PENINSULA

CHITRÉ

🏨🍴 HOTEL LOS GUAYACANES
$$$
VÍA CIRCUNVALACIÓN
TEL 996-9758
losguayacanes.com

A quality albeit soulless hotel

in quasi-Teutonic style around an artificial lake with waterfall. Hand-carved hardwood furnishings in guest rooms. Facilities include tennis courts, disco, and convention space. The open-air **Restaurante Las Brisas**—graced by glistening hardwoods—has an interesting and eclectic menu. Try the grilled chicken breast in lemon mushroom sauce.

🛏 64 🅿 ⏹ 🌀 ⛱ 🌀 AE, MC, V

🏨 HOTEL VERSALLES
$$
EL PASEO ENRIQUE GEENZIER
TEL 996-3133
hotelversalles.com

This clean, no-frills modern hotel on the main road on the outskirts of town offers simple comforts. Spacious family rooms are a better value than smaller standards. High-speed Internet is a bonus, but the swimming pool is tiny.

🛈 60 🅿 ⏹ 🌀 ⛱ 🌀 MC, V

🍴 RESTAURANTE EL MESÓN
$$
HOTEL REX,
CALLE MELITÓN MARTÍN
TEL 996-2408

You get value for money at this pleasant restaurant with patio overlooking the main square. Everything from sandwiches to lasagna, seafood, and excellent Mexican fare. Paella is served on Sundays. The roast pork *(loma al horno)* is recommended any day.

🪑 66 🌀 🌀 AE, MC, V

PEDASÍ

🏨 CASA DE CAMPO
$$$
400 YARDS (430 M) S OF THE GAS STATION, PEDASÍ
TEL 6780-5280 OR 995-2733
casacampopedasi.com

Surrounded by tree-shaded

grounds in the heart of downtown Pedasí. Beamed ceilings and poured concrete floors blend colonial and modern touches, but stylish fixtures in cozy bedrooms are state-of-the-art. Billiard table and rockers under thatch. Massages also offered.

🛏5 ⓢ 🏊 ⓢ MC, V

🏨 CASITA MARGARITA
🍴 BOUTIQUE INN
$$$

CALLE PRINCIPAL, PEDASÍ
TEL 995-2898
pedasihotel.com

Another heart-of-Pedasí newbie, this modest option has a surfeit of shiny hardwood features, including furniture in tasteful guest rooms with Wi-Fi and satellite TV. Ceiling fans. Hammocks on balconies. Meals are served in a stone-lined dining room.

🛏5 P ⓢ ⓢ MC, V

SOMETHING SPECIAL

🏨 LA ROSA DE
🍴 LOS VIENTOS
$$$

1 MILE (1.6 KM) E OF PEDASÍ
TEL 6778-0627 OR 6530-4939
bedandbreakfastpedasi.com

Set on lush grounds, this intimate hacienda-style hotel oozes traditional charm. Simply furnished rooms have glazed cement floors and Guatemalan tapestries. Hospitable live-in owners offer free bicycle use, and horseback riding is offered.

🛏3 P ⓢ ⓢ MC, V

🍴 RISTORANTE PASTE
E VINO
$$

E SIDE OF PEDASÍ ON ROAD
TO PLAYA TORO
TEL 6695-2689

Simple yet charming bargain-priced restaurant in a private home. Owners Daniel and

Elena serve authentic Italian dishes, such as cannelloni and pizza spaghetti bolognese, served alfresco in a flower-filled garden. Excellent veggie platter.

🛏24 P ⓢ
ⓢ No credit cards

PLAYA DESTILADEROS

🏨 BEACH SUITES BY
🍴 VILLA CAMILLA
$$$$

50 YARDS (50 M) INLAND OF
PLAYA DESTILADEROSÍ
TEL 994-3100
villacamillapanama.com

Spacious, attractively furnished oceanfront condo-style villas and studios with kitchens amid oceanfront lawns. Villa 14 has a private lap pool. Restaurant serves fresh salads and seafood.

🛏6 P ⓢ ⓢ ⓢ MC, V

🏨 POSADA LOS
🍴 DESTILADEROS
$$$$

7 MILES (11.3 KM) SW OF PEDASÍ
TEL 995-2771
panamabambu.net

French-run ecolodge made entirely of hardwoods and thatch. Cross-ventilated Amazonian-themed rooms exude a one-with-nature feel. Exquisite touches include hand-carved wooden wash-basins. Ocean views from wooden deck with Adirondack chairs. Gourmet cuisine by a French professional chef. Free Wi-Fi.

ⓘ18 P 🏊 ⓢ MC, V

PLAYA VENADO

SOMETHING SPECIAL

🏨 VILLA MARINA
🍴 $$$$

PLAYA VENADO
TEL 397-1058
villamarinapanama.com

Set on 220 acres (90 ha) of grounds, this gorgeous historic

Spanish hacienda–style beach property revolves around a terra-cotta courtyard with fountain. Red-tile roofs and traditional blue-and-white painted walls and posts add to the gracious yesteryear ambience, as do antiques in guest rooms, which have tasteful fabrics plus French doors opening onto ocean-view balconies with hammocks beneath shady eaves. Some rooms share bathrooms. The main house has graceful lounges. Lush lawns sweep down to the 1.2-mile-wide (2 km) beach. Quality meals are served in the atmospheric dining room. Horseback rides are a specialty and a 23-foot (7 m) Boston Whaler is available for sportfishing.

ⓘ9 P ⓢ ⓢ AE, MC, V

CHIRIQUÍ & THE CORDILLERA

BOCA CHICA

SOMETHING SPECIAL

🏨 CALA MIA
🍴 BOUTIQUE HOTEL
$$$$$

TEL 851-0059 OR 6747-0111
boutiquehotelcalamia.com

Solar-powered, this luxury hotel bills itself as an ecolodge. Perched over the ocean, it has an enviable setting on the otherwise virtually uninhabited Isla Boca Brava. Accommodation is in thatched *ranchos* with handcrafted, rustic-themed hardwood furniture; some have king beds. The horizon pool and wooden deck are highlights. Mediterranean-inspired gourmet cuisine with indoor and outdoor seating.

🛏11 ⓢ 🏊 ⓢ MC, V

🏨 BOCAS DEL MAR
🍽 $$$$
1 MILE (1.6 KM) E OF
BOCA CHICA
TEL 6395-8757
bocasdelmar.com
This is a gorgeous Belgian-run ultra-mod hillside hotel overlooking the gulf. Bright, airy bungalows with deluxe contemporary furnishings and terraces; some with whirlpool tubs. One unit is a two-story suite. Alfresco and indooor dining on seafood.
ℹ 16 🅿 �''''' 🌊 MC, V

🏨 SEAGULL COVE LODGE
$$$$
BOCA CHICA
TEL 851-0036
seagullcovelodge.com
This upscale hillside hotel is styled in Spanish neocolonial fashion. Gracious furnishings include colorful Guatemalan bedspreads and 400-thread-count linens, plus ceiling fans and terra-cotta tile floors. Bungalows are set amid effusively landscaped grounds. The lodge has its own dock. Family run.
🛏 6 🅿 🌊 MC, V

BOQUETE

🏨 LOS ESTABLOS
$$$$$
JARAMILLO ARRIBA, 1.5 MILES (2.4 KM) NE OF BOQUETE
TEL 720-2685
losestablos.net
A lovely boutique inn with fantastic views. Converted from horse stables, this luxury hotel is surrounded by lawns and coffee fields. Lovely furnishings include antiques; guest quarters have patios and marble bathrooms. Internet access is available and breakfast is included.
ℹ 7 🅿 🌊 MC, V

SOMETHING SPECIAL

🏨 PANAMONTE INN &
🍽 SPA
$$$$$
BOQUETE
TEL 720-1324 OR 720-1327
panamonte.com
This family-run gem dates back to 1914. It exudes warmth and individuality, multiplied by the presence of gracious hostess Inga Collins. A log fire burns in the cocktail lounge that opens onto lush gardens. Individually styled nonsmoking guest rooms are cozy in the manner of a classic English country inn; all have ceiling fans, Internet service, and telephones. The restaurant offers top-notch traditional staples, including fresh trout and succulent Black Angus beef dishes, served with fresh local vegetables and conjured into a sublime treat by Chef Charlie Collins. Who can resist his grilled pork chop served with onion ragout and potatoes, with a veal stock reduction wine sauce? The signature dessert is the inn's famous lemon pie. A spa offers all manner of treatments.
ℹ 19 🅿 🌊 AE, MC, V

SOMETHING SPECIAL

🏨 COFFEE ESTATE INN
$$$$
JARAMILLO ARRIBA, 1 MILE (1.6 KM) NE OF BOQUETE
TEL/FAX 720-2211
coffeeestateinn.com
Chiriquí's preeminent family-run inn exudes a home-away-from-home appeal. Surrounded by lush forest at 4,200 feet (1,280 m) of elevation, this coffee and citrus estate proves that a fine jewel is made complete by its setting. The inn offers stupendous volcano views from the cozy, delightfully furnished bungalows, each with

bedroom, bathroom, kitchen, and terrace; comfy beds feature down-filled duvets and pillows. Run lovingly by an erudite Canadian couple who pay meticulous attention to guests' well-being and comfort. Candlelit gourmet dinners are served alfresco on your balcony, and the owners will prepare boxed lunches. Free Internet is a bonus, and the charming and conscientious owners are a trove of useful tour information. Trails offer fabulous birding.
ℹ 3 🅿 🌊 MC, V

🏨 BOQUETE GARDEN INN
$$$
PALO ALTO, 1.75 MILES (2.8 KM) N OF BOQUETE
TEL 720-2376
boquetegardeninn.com
On the banks of the Río Palo Alto, amid effusive gardens, this charming hotel is steeped in nature. Guest rooms are

🏨 Hotel 🍽 Restaurant ℹ No. of Guest Rooms 🛏 No. of Seats 🅿 Parking 🕐 Closed 🛗 Elevator sumptuously furnished, with rich earth tones, crisp linens, and warm duvets. The Canadian/American owners run their inn with caring concern for detail.

🛈 10 🅿 🚭 🕸 MC, V

🏨 FINCA LÉRIDA BED & BREAKFAST
$$$
ALTO QUIEL, 6 MILES (9.6 KM) NW OF BOQUETE
TEL 720-2285 OR 720-1111
fincalerida.com
In the heart of a coffee estate, this delightful romantic inn appeals to nature lovers and oozes ambience and good taste. Choose one of the rooms in the vintage family home (or adjoining cottages) built in 1922 and wood-paneled throughout in cedar. The cozy lounge-library has a stone fireplace. Furnishings are original period pieces; bathrooms are Swiss-clean. Some rooms have private porches with Adirondack chairs. Newer rooms in a modern block overlook the manicured lawns and coffee fields; one room is equipped for handicapped visitors. Trails lead into the forest, and tours are offered on the estate.

🛈 21 🅿 🚭 🕸 MC, V

🍽 DELICIAS DEL PERÚ
$$$
AVE. LOS FUNDADORES & CALLE 2DA
TEL 720-1966
Terrific seafood restaurant with a cozy ambience and superlative ceviche and other regional dishes. Outdoor dining patio with view.

🍴 80 🚭 🕸 AE, MC, V

🍽 MACHU PICCHU
$$$
AVE. BELISARIO PORRAS
TEL 720-1502
Attentive Peruvian chef Jaime Breña Aristoteles conjures

outstanding Peruvian seafood and meat dishes. Rich decor of royal blue and white, with blond wood furniture.

🍴 65 🚭 🕸 AE, MC, V

🍽 IL PIANISTA
$$$
PALO ALTO, BOQUETE
TEL 720-2728
Worth the hilly drive, this creekside Italian restaurant serves genuine Sicilian fare plus local trout specialties. Rustic decor includes riverstone walls. Leisurely service. Waterfall views from patio.

🍴 20 🅿 🕒 Closed Mon. 🚭 🕸 AE, MC, V

🍽 BISTRO BOQUETE
$$
AVE. CENTRAL & CALLE 1RA SUR
TEL 730-9599
A delightful main-street bistro with eclectic menu: salads, sandwiches, quesadillas, trout dishes, filet mignon, even curried chicken. Cheesecakes to die for.

🍴 40 🕒 Closed Mon. 🚭 🕸 MC, V

🍽 CAFÉ KOTOWA
$
CEFATI, ALTO BOQUETE
TEL 720-4060
Adjoining IPAT's information office, this coffee shop boasts fabulous views over Boquete—perfect for enjoying cappuccino and a chocolate brownie or other scrumptious desserts.

🛈 20 🚭 🕸 MC, V

CERRO PUNTA

🏨 CASA GRANDE
🍽 BAMBITO RESORT
$$$$
BAMBITO, 3 MILES (4.8 KM) S OF CERRO PUNTA
TEL 201-5555
casagrandebambito.com
Facing manicured grounds on one side and lush forest

on the other, the former El Manantial Spa & Resort has been redesigned as a luxury boutique hotel. And what a stunner! Massage and other treatments in a spa with stone-walled hot tubs. **La Carreta** restaurant has walls of glass with forest views and a patio for dining on sunny days. River tubing and other activities.

🛈 20 🅿 🚭 🕎 🕸 AE, MC, V

🏨 ECOLODGE & SPA
🍽 LOS QUETZALES
$$$$
GUADALUPE, 2 MILES (3.2 KM) NE OF CERRO PUNTA
TEL 771-2291 OR 774-5555 (DAVID)
losquetzales.com
Nature-themed Swiss-style alpine lodge with rooms, chalets, and suites. Cozy library-lounge and charming restaurant serving excellent and filling fare. Five spacious, rustic cabins within Parque Internacional La Amistad (quetzals are often seen from the balconies) have butane-powered lamps and stoves; meals can be delivered from the lodge. Guided birding and hikes.

🛈 24 🅿 🕸 AE, MC, V

🏨 CIELITO SUR BED & BREAKFAST
$$$
NUEVA SUIZA, 2 MILES (3.2 KM) S OF CERRO PUNTA
TEL 771-2038
cielitosur.com
This peaceful bed-and-breakfast enjoys a magnificent setting overlooking the trout-filled Río Caldera. Spacious, quaintly furnished alpine cottages, plus open-air dining on a shaded porch with fireplace good for birding. A thatched *bohio* has hammocks, and a bathhouse has a hot tub.

🛈 4 🅿 🕒 Closed Oct. 🚭 🕸 MC, V

🚭 Nonsmoking   🌀 Air-conditioning   🏊 Indoor Pool   🏊 Outdoor Pool   🕎 Health Club   🕸 Credit Cards

🏨 HOTEL BAMBITO
🍴 RESORT
$$$
BAMBITO, 3 MILES (4.8 KM)
S OF CERRO PUNTA
TEL 771-4265 OR 771-4251
hotelbambito.com
This beautifully appointed, contemporary-themed hotel with strong alpine hints has a lovely garden setting with duck pond and cascade, plus modestly furnished accommodations. Glass-enclosed heated indoor pool, plus activities such as guided horseback rides and hiking. Weekend all-inclusive package rates are a bargain. **Restaurante Las Truchas** specializes in trout; a prix-fixe Sunday brunch offers an all-you-can-eat treat.
🛈 47 🅿 🔄 🚫 🐾 🎦
🌐 AE, MC, V

DAVID

🏨 GRAN HOTEL
NACIONAL
$$$
CALLE CENTRAL & AVE. 1 ESTE
TEL 775-2222
hotelnacionalpanama.com
Favored by the local business crowd, this modern option is the best of an uninspiring choice of hotels. Modest-size rooms have comfortable mattresses but cramped bathrooms. Irregular Wi-Fi. A casino adjoins.
🛈 75 🅿 🚫 🔄 🔄
🌐 AE, MC, V

🍴 CUATRO
$$$
AVE. OBALDIA
& CALLE ESTUDIANTE
TEL 730-5638
e-mail: info@restaurante
cuatro.com
Unpretentious honey setting for gourmet Panamanian and fusion dishes such as shrimp spring rolls, grilled octopus, and chicken roulade. Divine desserts include chocolate

fondant and *cuatro de leches* cake. Fair prices and very attentive service.
🍴 30 🕐 Closed L & Sun.
🅿 🚫 No credit cards

🍴 RESTAURANTE
EL FOGÓN
$$$
AVE. 1 ESTE BET. CALLES A & B
TEL 775-7091
A pleasant open-air ambience pervades this modern restaurant serving a large menu of meat and seafood dishes. Latin music usually adds to the atmosphere.
🍴 90 🅿 🕐 Closed L Sun.
🚫 🔄 🌐 MC, V

ISLA BOCA BRAVA

SOMETHING SPECIAL

🏨 THE RESORT AT ISLA
🍴 PALENQUE
$$$$$
SE OF ISLA BOCA BRAVA
TEL 777-9260
amble.com
This striking boutique beach resort occupies a small private island and guarantees laid-back luxury in its tent suites and deluxe "Estate Rooms" perched over beaches to each side of the isle. The architecturally stunning, suavely furnished suites are hemmed by forest and have cantilevered ceilings and private infinity lap pools Two restaurants serve gourmet fare, and torchlit beach dinners are offered. Kayaking, island tours, and sportfishing. Free Wi-Fi.
🍴 6 (4 tent suites) 🅿
🌐 MC, V

🏨 HOTEL BOCA BRAVA
$–$$$
ISLA BOCA BRAVA
TEL 851-0017
hotelbocabrava.com
Atop a breeze-swept bluff, choose from backpackers'

hammocks to charming cabins at this lonesome island escape, with hammocks slung on tiled balconies. Ceiling fans and Wi-Fi. Simple meals. Kayaks.
🛈 16 🅿 🚫 🌐 MC, V

ISLAS SECAS

SOMETHING SPECIAL

🏨 ISLAS SECAS RESORT
$$$$$
ISLA CAVADA
TEL 805/729-2737 (U.S.)
islassecas.com
Unpretentious luxury at this eco-conscious resort spread over 10 acres (4 ha) of palm-studded coastline. Spacious cabins—totally upgraded in 2014—overlooking an ocean-front cove come with queen bed, wraparound screened open windows, and sensuous decor. Absent are TV, phone, or radio—you come here for a Robinson Crusoe escape. Gourmet fare on the deck beneath spreading mango trees might start with plantain-crusted crab cakes, followed by Manchego cheese and roasted garlic aioli as an entrée. Rates include meals, alcoholic beverages, and water sports such as scuba diving. Arrival is by charter plane. Four-night minimum.
🛈 6 🚫 🔄 🌐 AE, MC, V

LOS PLANES

🏨 LOST AND FOUND
LODGE
$$
HWY. 4, 26 MILES (42 KM)
N OF CHIRIQUÍ
TEL 6920-3036
lostandfoundlodge.com
This budget hostel at the edge of cloud forest appeals primarily to backpackers. It has private rooms, plus dorms, all artfully decorated. Communal kitchen, and meals prepared by request. Stunning views.

It's an uphill hike to reach the lodge from the road.

🛈 5 🚫 No credit cards

PLAYA BARQUETA

🏨 LAS OLAS BEACH RESORT
$$$$

PLAYA BARQUETA, 16 MILES
(26 KM) SW OF DAVID
TEL 772-3000 OR 6212-9236
lasolasresort.com
Modern, all-inclusive hotel adjoining the wildlife refuge. Pink rooms all have ocean-front terraces; standards are small, and junior suites offer a better bargain. Activities from beach volleyball to horseback rides, plus spa.

🛈 39 🅿 🚫 ❄ 🏋
🚫 AE, MC, V

PUNTA BURICA

🏨 MONO FELIZ
$$

BELLA VISTA, 28 MILES (45 KM)
S OF BOQUETE
TEL 6595-0388 OR 6459-0707
E-MAIL: mono_feliz@hotmail
.com
End-of-the-road, North American–run nature lodge at the tip of Punta Burica. Fabulous wildlife viewing. Simple cabins have mosquito nets and cold showers, and camping is permitted; guests have use of a kitchen, but meals are also served for an extra fee. Getting here requires hiking.

🛈 5 ❄ 🚫 No credit cards

VOLCÁN

🏨 HOTEL DOS RÍOS
$$$

1.5 MILES (2.4 KM) W OF
VOLCÁN
TEL 771-5555
dosrios.com.pa
Colorful, modestly equipped rooms at this friendly, service-oriented, all-wood riverside

hotel set in lovely gardens. Outdoor-indoor restaurant with a quaint country feel (but quality meals), plus a pizza restaurant. Breakfast included.

🛈 18 🅿 🚫 🚫 MC, V

SOMETHING SPECIAL

🍽 CERRO BRUJO GOURMET
$$$$

CALLE PRINCIPAL, VOLCÁN
TEL 6669-9196
Artist Patricia Miranda Allen doubles as gourmet chef at this gorgeous cottage restaurant, where you dine surrounded by a carefully tended garden in the lee of Volcán Barú. A porch is a perfect perch for enjoying such creative and artfully presented dishes as herbed rabbit or chicken with green curry. Organic salads fresh from the garden, or soups such as creamy yellow split pea, accompany all entrées.

🍴 10 🅿 🚫
🚫 No credit cards

▮ BOCAS DEL TORO

CHANGUINOLA

🏨 SOPOSO
🍽 $$

RÍO TERIBE, 5 MILES (8 KM)
W OF CHANGUINOLA
TEL 6631-2222 OR 6875-8125
soposo.com
This rustic lodge provides an immersion in Naso indigenous culture. The two thatched huts on stilts are rustic, but have mosquito nets, solar lanterns, porches with hammocks, and shared outside showers and latrines. Hearty meals.

🛈 5 🚫 No credit cards

🏨 WEKSO CENTRO ECOTURÍSTICO NASO
$$

APPROX. 12 MILES (19 KM)
W OF CHANGUINOLA
TEL 620-0192
E-MAIL: turismonaso
_odesen@hotmail.com
odesen.bocasdeltoro.org
Isolated, rustic riverside ecolodge run by the Naso Indian community on the edge of Parque Internacional La Amistad. Guests stay in simple thatched accommodations in stilt-legged cabins surrounded by jungle; cold showers. Hearty meals, but bring bottled water. Transportation is by boat from El Silencio.

🛈 6 🚫 No credit cards

ISLA BASTIMENTOS

🏨 RED FROG BEACH
🍽 ISLAND RESORT & SPA
$$$$$

RED FROG BEACH
TEL 836-5501
redfrogbeach.com
Opened in 2013, this deluxe resort features a Balinese-style lodge and one-to-five-bedroom villas, each with plunge pool and BBQ grill. Separate beach grill and rain forest restaurants, plus private in-villa chef service. Full service marina offers sportfishing and sunset cruises. Activity center with zipline.

🛈 41 🚫 🚫 ❄
🚫 All major credit cards

🏨 TRANQUILO BAY ECO-ADVENTURE LODGE
$$$$$

CAYO CRAWL
TEL 838-0021 OR 713/589-6952
tranquilobay.com
Amid mangroves, modest tin-roofed cabins on stilts have simple handmade furniture, granite countertops, and raised oceanfront porches with

🚫 Nonsmoking 🚫 Air-conditioning 🚫 Indoor Pool ❄ Outdoor Pool 🏋 Health Club 🚫 Credit Cards hammocks and Adirondack chairs. Main lodge has a bar, TV lounge, and canopy observation tower. Meals included in all-inclusive package rate.

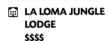 6 ⊗ ⊗ ⊗ AE, MC, V

SOMETHING SPECIAL

🏨 LA LOMA JUNGLE LODGE
$$$$

BAHÍA HONDA, 6.5 MILES (10.5 KM) E OF OLD BANK
TEL 6592-5162
thejunglelodge.com
Accessible solely by boat, this ecolodge borders the national park. The location of the lodge offers incredible snorkeling and wildlife viewing. The accommodation is welcoming with romantic decor. Open-walled bamboo-and-thatch ranchos with glistening hardwood floors and simple, locally crafted furniture; beds have hardwood planks spanning tree trunks. Private bathrooms have hot water. Two cabins require a steep climb. Meals for the health-conscious are included. Wooden *cayucos* available.

🛈 4 ⊗ ⊗ No credit cards

ISLA CARENERO

🏨 BUCCANEER RESORT
$$$

SE SHORE
TEL/FAX 757-9042
bocasbuccaneerresort.com
Upscale jungle-themed lodge with thatched, wood-paneled bungalows (including two-story suites) and cabins shaded by palms. There is also a cheerful, thatched open-air bar-restaurant that hangs over the waters. Catches the thumping beat from nearby disco bars.

🛈 9 ⊗ ⊗ ⊗ MC, V

ISLA COLÓN

SOMETHING SPECIAL

🏨 PUNTA CARACOL
🍴 ACQUA-LODGE
$$$$$

PUNTA CARACOL
TEL 6612-1088 OR 757-9410
puntacaracol.com
Romantic, eco-sensitive, Polynesian-style lodge. A boardwalk leads to thatched wooden cabanas on stilts above jade waters. Quality handcrafted hardwood furnishings include king-size four-poster beds with netting. Soothing Caribbean pastel schemes grace the choice of one- or two-story suites. Solar-powered electricity, biodigesters for waste water, and state-of-the-art aerobic sewage treatment earn thumbs-up. The open-air restaurant focuses on seafood with local flavors, such as snapper in virgin olive oil and rock salt with rice, and *guandú* in coconut milk.

🛈 9 ⊗ ⊗ ⊗ AE, MC, V

🏨 PLAYA TORTUGA HOTEL
🍴 & BEACH RESORT
$$$$

2 MILES (3 KM) W OF BOCAS TOWN
TEL 300-1893
hotelplayatortuga.com
The first true full-scale beach resort in Bocas, this three-story hotel has ocean-view rooms strung along palm-fringed sands. The contemporary aesthetic is sophisticated yet understated. Gorgeous bi-level swimming pool has built-in lounge chairs. Wi-Fi throughout. Two restaurants. Unfortunately, a smell of sewage is pervasive.

🛈 117 P ⊗ ⛱ ▽ ⊗ AE, MC, V

🏨 TROPICAL SUITES
$$$$

CALLE 1RA NEXT TO POLICÍA NACIONAL AND IPAT, BOCAS TOWN
TEL 757-9880 OR 678/400-0535
bocastropical.com
For travelers preferring a self-catering option with excellent service. Functional but uninspired suites with a maid service have orthopedic mattresses and tile floors. Watercraft are available and the property has its own dock, lending the whole property a *Miami Vice* vibe.

🛈 16 P ⊟ ⊗ ⊗ ⊗ MC, V

🏨 BOCAS INN
$$$

CALLE 3 & AVE. G, BOCAS TOWN
TEL 757-9600 OR 269-9415
anconexpeditions.com
This well-respected establishment run by Ancon Expeditions hangs over the waters on the northeast side of town. Spacious, modestly furnished,

wood-paneled rooms open onto broad verandas with hammocks. Filling breakfasts are served, and there's a tiny bar.

🚹 6 ❄️ ⛱️ AE, MC, V

🏨 EL LIMBO ON THE SEA
$$$

CALLE 2DA, BOCAS TOWN

TEL 757-9062 OR 757 9227

ellimbo.com

Lovely little three-story hotel on the water with large windows opening to balconies. Waterfront bar, plus sea kayaks and snorkeling gear for rent.

🚹 18 🅿️ ❄️ ⛱️ AE, MC, V

🏨 HOTEL SWAN'S CAY
🍴 **$$$**

CALLE 3, BET. AVES. E & F, BOCAS TOWN

TEL 757-9090

swanscayhotel.com

Striking exterior with lush hardwoods bespeaks a natty rehab for this aged building. Rooms around an atrium courtyard have colorful, albeit dowdy, furnishings. Italian-themed restaurant, plus oceanfront pool in a nearby annex. Wi-Fi available.

🚹 46 🅿️ ❄️ 🏊 ⛱️ MC, V

🍴 LEMONGRASS
$$$$

CALLE 2, BOCAS TOWN

TEL 6847-9306

This seafood restaurant is upstairs in a creaky wooden building poised over the Caribbean. Founding owner Mike Thompson has moved on, but new Dutch owners still serve delicious world-spanning fare, from Caribbean curry to samosas and pad thai. It gets packed for its live music and special parties.

🍽️ 30 🅿️ ⛱️ No credit cards

🍴 LILI'S CAFE
$$

CALLE 1, BOCAS DEL TORO

TEL 6560-8777

Local cook Lili's permanent smile welcomes patrons to her hole-in-the-wall waterfront deck restaurant—perfect for omelet or banana pancake breakfasts, grilled sandwiches, or local seafood dinner spiced up with Lili's homemade, not-for-the-faint-of-heart Killin' Me Man pepper sauce.

🍽️ 12 🕐 Closed D Sun. ⛱️ No credit cards

🍴 OM CAFE
$$

AVE. H, BET. CALLES 3 & 4, BOCAS TOWN

TEL 6624-0898

facebook.com/ OmCafePanama

Iconoclastic restaurant in a creaky old home serving superb East Indian fare on an upstairs balcony to a hip world-music beat. Bargain rates, including for vegetarian dishes and tropical fruit *lassis*. Also filling breakfasts (such as spicy eggs vindaloo).

🚹 20 🅿️ 🕐 Closed Wed. ⛱️ No credit cards

🍴 RAW
$$

CALLE 3 & AVE. E, BOCAS TOWN

TEL 6938-8473

Hole-in-the-wall Asian fusion and sushi restaurant. Superb rolls and fresh *nigiri*. Candlelit at night. Popular for its sake martinis and daily happy hour.

🍽️ 30 🕐 Closed Mon. 🅿️ 🚭 ⛱️ No credit cards

🍴 YARISNORI
$$

BOCAS DEL DRAGO, 9 MILES (14.5 KM) NW OF BOCAS TOWN

TEL 6615-5580 OR 6498-5606

yarisnori.com

This pleasant beachfront bar and restaurant with sand

underfoot and shady open-air dining, includes medieval-style tents. Lobster, shrimp, and other artfully presented gourmet seafood such as red snapper with coconut rice are on the menu. Hammocks, snorkeling, and a kiddie playground are all available.

🚹 60 🅿️ 🕐 Closed Tues. ⛱️ No credit cards

ISLA POPA

🏨 POPA PARADISE
🍴 BEACH RESORT
$$$$

ISLA POPA, BOCAS DEL TORO

TEL 6550-2505

popaparadisebeachresort.com

Wrapped in forest by the edge of the sea, this upscale newcomer on one of the more remote islands combines the best of both worlds. Choose from simple yet endearingly appointed budget cottages to free-standing casitas with suites, and even a two-bedroom penthouse with kitchen. Jungle trail, snorkeling, and kayak safaris. Landscaped pool. Coral reef offshore.

🚹 17 ❄️ 🏊 ⛱️ MC, V

ISLA SOLARTE

🏨 GARDEN OF EDEN
$$$$

ISLA SOLARTE

TEL 6967-0187

gardenofedenbocas.com

Perched atop the cliffs, this private gem was formerly Panama's only clothing-optional hotel; not so under a more conservative new owner. Rooms boast beautiful decor. A local chef produces all the meals.

🚹 3 ❄️ 🚭 🏊 ⛱️ No credit cards

🚭 Nonsmoking ❄️ Air-conditioning 🏊 Indoor Pool ⛱️ Outdoor Pool 💪 Health Club ⛱️ Credit Cards

Shopping in Panama

As a major crossroads of the world, Panama is a shopping mecca, not least for such high-end goods as jewelry and designer clothing. The Colón Free Zone (one of the world's largest free-trade zones) supplies many retailers in Panama City, which pass on the benefits from low freight costs. Large malls in Marbella and the Tumba Muerto district of Panama City offer a complete selection of world-renowned names from Bulgari to Yves Saint-Laurent.

Panama's other strong suit is indigenous crafts. Most upscale hotels have gift stores selling high-quality crafts. However, artisans' markets have by far the widest choice, and you might have more fun bargaining with the artisans themselves. Almost every town has an artisans' market selling intricate woven baskets, colorful bead necklaces (chaquiras), intricately knitted Ngöbe-Buglé bags called chácaras, small animal figurines carved from the tagua palm nut, and colorful stitched-appliqué molas. Many crafts use hardwoods, such as lignum vitae, purpleheart, and rosewood, often carved into the form of jungle animals and birds or cayucos. Other mementos include devil masks from the Azuero region, sombrero montuño straw hats, and dolls dressed up in polleras.

Bargaining is expected for crafts and, unlike most Central American nations, even for items such as electronics and jewelry.

The country's renowned coffee is available nationwide. And Panamanian cigars make a popular souvenir. (Cuban cigars are also sold; it is illegal for U.S. citizens to purchase them here.)

Opening Times

See p. 231.

■ PANAMA CITY

Panama City's main shopping street is Vía España. The shopping district centered in Marbella and El Cangrejo districts is chock-full of designer stores and malls, including Multiplaza Pacific Mall (multicentropanama.com.pa), at Punta Pacífica and Multicentro. The Albrook Mall (near Aeropuerto Marcos A. Gelabert) sprawls over almost 5 million square feet (460,000 sq m). Kuna Indian women sell their crafts streetside in Casco Viejo and in dedicated artisans' markets where crafts from every indigenous group in the country are represented. Pedestrian-only Avenida Central is lined with street vendors and shops—beware of pickpockets.

Arts & Antiques

Allegro Galería Calle 73 #16, San Francisco, Panama City, tel 226-6967, allegrogallery.com. Avant-garde works from almost two dozen leading local artists.

Dgriss Art Gallery Torre de las Américas, Punta Pacífica, tel 201-5550, dgriss.com. Avant-garde contemporary Panamanian art.

Galería Mateo Sariel Calle 79E #14, Panama City, tel 270-2404, mateosariel.com. This gallery displays and sells works by two dozen of the nation's top artists.

Legacy Fine Art Condominio Los Delfines, Ave Balboa

Marbella, tel 265-8151, legacy fineartpanama.com. Represents many of the best contemporary Panamanian artists.

Books & Maps

Exedra Books Vía España & Vía Brasil, tel 264-4252, exedrabooks.com. Modest range of texts in both Spanish and English, plus magazines.

Instituto Geográfico Nacional Tommy Guardia Calle 57 Oeste & Ave. 6a Norte (off Vía Simón Bolívar), tel 238-1844, ignpanama.gob.pa. Detailed maps of all kinds, especially useful for hikers; does not sell tourist maps.

Librería Argosy Vía Argentina & Vía España, tel 223-5344. Small, cluttered bookstore is a treasure trove of antiquarian and new books, with a strong emphasis on Panama.

Clothes & Accessories

Boutique Breebaart Calle Abel Bravo #5, Obarrio, tel 264-5937, breebaartpanama.com. Contemporary womenswear by fashion designer Hélène Breebaart, featuring Kuna molas.

La Fortuna Vía España, 50 yards (45 m) E of Vía Argentina, tel 236-6434, lafortunapanama .com. Suits and shirts from the real tailor of Panama. Anyone who is anyone dresses here (see pp. 78–79).

Victor's Panama Hats Calle 3 between Ave Central & A, Casco Viejo, no tel. The name says it all! Local *montuños* and genuine Panama hats from Ecuador.

Crafts & Jewelry

El Farol Calle 1 Este, Casto Viejo, tel 2280-8597. Quality indigenous crafts and clothing.

Galería de Artes Indígenas Plaza de Francia, Casco Viejo, tel 228-9557. In Las Bóvedas. Large selection of indigenous crafts and souvenirs, plus fine art.

Museo de la Esmeralda Calle Pedro Sosa & Calle 6, Casco Viejo, tel 220-3373. Fine Colombian emeralds, loose and set.

Reprosa Ave. Samuel Lewis & Santuario Nacional St., Obarrio, tel 271-0033, reprosa.com. Pre-Columbian gold reproductions *(huacas)* plus contemporary jewelry. Shopping includes a factory tour.

La Ronda Calle Primera, Casco Viejo, tel 211-1001. *The* place for quality indigenous crafts, such as Emberá-Wounaan baskets, Ngöbe jewelry, and *sombreros montuños.*

Gifts & Miscellaneous

Panafoto Calle 50 & Calle 49a Este, tel 263-0102, panafoto .com. Electronics store with a modest selection of cameras and photographic equipment, plus binoculars.

Papiro y Yo Calle 4 bet. Aves. Central & B, Casco Viejo, tel 391-3800. Unique paper-based gifts such as booklets and special stationary.

Malls

Albrook Mall Corredor Norte, tel 303-6255, albrookmall.com. A huge mall with more than one hundred stores.

Multicentro Mall Ave. Balboa, Marbella, tel 208-2500, multicentropanama.com.pa. Multi-story complex incorporating a casino and hotel.

Multiplaza Pacific Vía Israel, Punta Pacífica, tel 302-5380, mallmultiplazapacific.com. Multi-story complex with 7 department stores and 52 stores.

Markets

Mercado de Buhonerías y Artesanias Ave. 4 Sur & Calle 23 Este, Calidonia. Outdoor market where artisans from around the country sell *molas* and other indigenous crafts, plus *sombreros montuños,* hammocks, and more.

Mercado Nacional de Artesanias Vía Cincuentario, Panamá Viejo. Dozens of stalls attended by Kuna Indians and other indigenous people selling everything from straw hats to hammocks.

Mi Pueblito Ave. de los Mártires, Ancón. This re-creation of typical Spanish colonial, Caribbean, Kuna, and Emberá villages has stores selling crafts representative of each region.

■ CENTRAL CARIBBEAN & THE CANAL

Colón is the main entrepôt for goods entering and leaving Panama via the Zona Libre de Colón (Colón Free Zone). This vast complex serves wholesalers and retailers. Strict customs regulations apply to retail sale to tourists, who cannot leave the zone with any items. Purchased items must be sent to the airport or cruise port, where they are delivered to departing passengers. Colón's cruise ports have arts-and-crafts markets, and you can journey to Emberá Indian villages to buy exquisite baskets, necklaces, and other items at the source.

Crafts & Jewelry

Emberá Parará Púru, Emberá Drua, and **Emberá Púru** Parque Nacional Chagres. Indigenous villages selling native bead jewelry, wood and tagua-nut carvings, carved gourds, beautiful woven baskets and plates, plus traditional masks. Bring small-denomination bills for payment.

Gifts & Miscellaneous

Colón 2000 Paseo Gorgas, tel 447-3197, colon2000.com. This small but modern cruise-ship port has half a dozen duty-free and souvenir stores, plus folkloric performances when ships are in port.

Miraflores Visitor Center Miraflores Locks, tel 276-8325. Splendid gift shop with everything you could wish to relating to the canal, from trinkets such as mugs and key-chain rings to books and fine-art prints.

MUCEC Calle 2 & Ave. Amador Guerrero, Colón, tel 447-0828, mucec.org. This nonprofit charity supports distressed omen in Colón and has a development workshop producing pillowcases, children's clothing, pottery, and other goods sold in the on-site store.

Malls

Zona Libre de Colón Ave. Roosevelt & Calle 13, tel 475-9500, zonalibredecolon.com.pa. This city-size entity sprawls over 1,000 acres (400 ha) and has scores of warehouses and showrooms stocked with every imaginable item sold duty-free. Permits, obtainable at the main gate, are required to enter. Most items sold here that are of interest to tourists can be bought as cheaply at airport duty-free stores.

Markets

Mercado de Artesanía 50 yards (45 m) SW of Iglesia de San Felipe de Portobelo, Portobelo. This tiny market on the west side of the plaza hosts Kuna Indians selling *molas*, hammocks, and jewelry.

▨ KUNA YALA

Ground zero for the production of gorgeous, brightly colored *molas*, the San Blas Islands are a magical mystery tour of indigenous Kuna crafts, which include beaded bracelets, coral and shell jewelry, Pan-style wooden flutes, and embroidered blouses and shirts with appliqué panels. Certain islands excel. There are no fixed-roof stores: Vendors display their wares along village pathways, while others paddle out in their watercraft to pitch to cruise ships and yachts. Vendors can be quite aggressive in their sales pitch. Although a limited degree of bargaining is acceptable, the Kuna are tough negotiators and most prices are fair to begin with. Expect to pay at least $15 for *molas*, with the largest and highest quality examples costing several hundred dollars. When buying *molas*, look for the following: a well-balanced design with harmonic contrasts of color; evenly spaced lines with smooth edges; small, almost invisible stitches. Also look for *nuchunaga* wooden figures representing spirit gods.

Avoid the islands of Wichub-Huala and Cartí Suituipo when the cruise ships are in. Credit cards are not accepted. You will need lots of small-denomination bills. Narganá has a bank if you run out of cash.

▨ DARIÉN

The Emberá-Wounaan people are gifted at crafts. While their exquisite products can be bought in Panama City, bargaining with the artist directly in an Emberá or Wounaan village is far more fun. The local communities are trying to adjust to environmental threats, such as deforestation, by turning to ecotourism and a more productive use of their natural habitat than slash-and-burn. Sales of crafts to tourists now form a significant source of income.

Look for highly colored *chaquiras* of colorful shells and/or beads; bowls, animal figurines, and miniature canoes carved from iron-hard *cocobolo* hardwood; and smaller figurines—anteaters, marine turtles, macaws, and sloths—hewn from the ivorylike, hen-egg-size nut of the tagua palm. Most impressive are the decorative baskets made of *naguala* and *chunga* palm fibers. The cream-colored baskets and platters are woven by Emberá women using a coil technique, and inlaid with black and red geometric shapes or representations of animals and birds. The finest examples can take two months or longer to make. Expect to pay at least $10 for a platter, and no less than $50 for a basket.

Most communities set up stalls selling their crafts upon arrival of visitors. Afro-colonial people also inhabit the region; some sell drums and other musical instruments.

Crafts & Jewelry

The following villages are good sources:

Boca Lara 4 miles (6.4 km) S of Santa Fé and 5 miles (8 km) SW of the Interamerican Hwy. Wounaan community prized for the quality of its crafts.

Emberá Arimae Interamerican Hwy., 18 miles (29 km) W of Metetí. Emberá community known for its crafts.

Ipetí Emberá 1 mile (1.6 km) S of Interamerican Hwy., 54 miles (87 km) E of Chepo. Emberá community selling crafts.

Ipetí Kuna 1 mile (1.6 km) N of Interamerican Hwy., 53 miles (85 km) E of Chepo. Small Kuna community selling *molas* and other typical Kuna craft items.

Vista Alegre Río Tuira, 2.5 miles (4 km) E of El Real de Santa María. The entire community makes handwoven plates and baskets.

Wererá Perú 2 miles (3.2 km) W of Sambú. Emberá and Afro-colonial community with an artisan's workshop selling crafts.

Gifts & Miscellaneous

ECODIC Santa Fé, 2 miles (3.2 km) W of the Interamerican Hwy. and 92 miles (148 km) E of Chepo, tel 6739-0853. Indigenous community workshop producing and selling medicinal plants, paintings (including murals by local youths), and scented soaps.

Pajaro Jai Furniture Factory Mogue, 3 miles (4.8 km) up the Río Mogue, 15 miles (24 km) SW of La Palma, sites.google.com/site/kaimokarainc. A small-scale furniture factory run by the Emberá community that makes world-class hardwood benches and other furniture for export.

Talabartería Echao Palante
Tortí, Interamerican Hwy. Pedro Guerra owns this saddlery where you can have a handcrafted saddle custom-made in a single day.

CENTRAL PANAMA

The road that winds up to El Valle de Antón is lined with stalls selling wicker crafts and ceramics, while *viveros* (nurseries) sell orchids. This is one of the best areas in the country to buy a *sombrero montuño* (cream-colored with narrow trims of black or brown), made locally around the community of La Pintada and sold here for about half the price of one in Panama City. Lesser quality hats can be bought for as little as $15, although the best hats sell for $100 and up. Look for a barely discernible weave. Other good bargains include embroidered *montuno* men's shirts (similar to the Cuban *guayabera*) and dolls dressed in *polleras*.

Crafts & Jewelry
David's Shop Ave. Central, El Valle de Antón, tel 983-6536. This crafts store and workshop represents a wide range of crafts, many made on-site in the workshop to the rear. Folk art from throughout the Americas is represented.

Gifts & Miscellaneous
Artesanías Típicas Panameñas Interamerican Hwy., Villa del Carmén, Km 50 near Capira, tel 248-5313. This roadside store sells devil masks and ceramics from Azuero, as well as a wide choice of hammocks, plus rustic rocking chairs of leather and lathe-turned wood.

Café El Tute Santa Fé, tel 954-0801 or 954-0737. This Ngöbe-Buglé worker's cooperative sells organic coffees fresh from the roaster.

Cigarros Joyas de Panama La Pintada. A small cigar factory where you can buy any of 12 types of high-quality hand-rolled smokes for a pittance. A box of Churchills costs $45, and individual cigars cost $1–$2.

Markets
Cooperativa Santa Fé Santa Fé. Good for Ngöbe-Buglé *chácaras* and jewelry.

Mercado Artesanal Veraguas La Peña Interamerican Hwy., 3 miles (4.8 km) W of Santiago. This small artisan's market is worth the stop for its reproduction pre-Columbian figurines, plus contemporary indigenous crafts.

Mercado de Artesanías Ave. Central, El Valle de Antón. This small, pulsating market is one of Panama's best, especially on Sunday when a wide variety of Ngöbe-Buglé jewelry, soapstone carvings, and other crafts, plus *sombreros pintados*, hammocks, and Kuna *molas*, are sold. Specialties include orchids, hardwood serving trays *(bateas)*, and painted figurines.

Mercado de Artesanías Coclé Interamerican Hwy., Penonomé. Good selection of traditional craft items, from hammocks to men's embroidered *montuno* shirts.

AZUERO PENINSULA

Azuero is renowned for the production of *polleras* and *diablitos* (devil masks), while La Arena, on the outskirts of Chitré, is the nation's leading ceramics center. Feel free to enter *talleres* (workshops) to see ceramics being fired in clay wood-burning ovens.

Guararé and Ocú are centers for *polleras*, which can take six months or longer to make and cost $1,000 or more.

Clothes & Accessories
Casa de Dilsa Vergara de Saavedra Via El Puerto Eloy Espino, La Enea, tel 994-5221 or 6529-0445. Sra. Vergara de Saavedra is renowned for the quality of her hand-sewn *polleras*.

Talabartería 5 Hermanos de Arnulfo Calle Moisés Espino, Las Tablas, tel 994-6743. Saddlery and leather shop, with fine belts.

Crafts & Jewelry
Artesanía Ocueña San José, 3 miles (4.8 km) W of Ocútel, tel 974-1047. Makes *sombreros montuños* and *montuno* shirts for men and *polleras* for women. Also lace tablecloths.

Casa de Carlos Ivan de León Calle Tomás Herrera, Los Santos, tel 966-9149. A foremost maskmaker; his masks are collectibles.

Casa de Dario López Carretera Nacional, opposite the Shell gas station, La Parita. Fearsome papier-mâché devil masks from one of the most acclaimed maskmakers in Panama.

Cerámica Calderón Carretera Nacional, La Arena, tel 947-4946. This *taller* produces some of the nicest ceramic pieces in town, including dinner sets and pre-Columbian reproductions made to order.

Markets
Mercado de Artesanías de Herrera Carretera Nacional, La Arena. This two-story building represents works by several ceramic *talleres*.

Mercado de Artesanías de Las Tablas Carretera Nacional, Las Tablas. Comparatively small market good for devil and other masks.

CHIRIQUÍ & THE CORDILLERA

Ngöbe-Buglé people produce exquisite bead jewelry and woven bags. The Interamerican Highway is lined with indigenous crafts stalls. Boquete has several quality gift stores, as well as superb coffee, which can be bought fresh roasted on the estates. David has malls and the main street is a major commercial thoroughfare. Paso Canoa is lined with duty-free shops selling CDs, cheap clothes, and the like.

Books & Maps
Bookmark Dolega, 10 miles (16 km) N of Interamerican Hwy., tel 776-1688, booksr4reading .wordpress.com. U.S.-owned secondhand bookshop full to the rafters; many rare travel books.

Crafts & Jewelry
Artesanías Cruz Volcán Carretera 41, Volcán, tel 6622-1502. The studio-store of local artist José de la Cruz sells his stained-glass and wood creations.

Casa Artesanal Ngöbe-Buglé Cruce San Felix, Interamerican Hwy., 2 miles (3.2 km) N of Las Lajas. Large Ngöbe-Buglé cooperative with the widest range of indigenous crafts in the region.

Tolé Interamerican Hwy. Ngöbe-Buglé center of crafts, sold roadside.

Gifts & Miscellaneous
Conservas de Antaño 400 yards (366 m) SE of Parque Domingo Médica, Boquete, tel 720-1539.

Homemade tropical fruit jams.

Finca Drácula Guadalupe, tel 223-8633, fincadracula.com. Rare orchids sold in vials ready for export.

Galería de Arte Ave. Belisario Porras, tel 6769-6090. Good source of indigenous crafts and clothing, plus ceramics, jewelry, and quality artwork.

Hacienda Carta Vieja El Tejar, 2 miles (3.2 km) NW of Alanje, tel 772-7073. Quality rum can be purchased after a factory tour.

Souvenir El Cacique SW corner of Parque Domingo Médica, Boquete, tel 720-2217. Quality Ngöbe-Buglé crafts, plus books, maps, and more.

Markets
Avenida 3 de Noviembre David. Stores and stalls selling CDs, hammocks, clothes, and other goods.

Mercado Municipal NE corner of Parque Domingo Médica, Boquete. Market crammed with fresh produce stalls.

BOCAS DEL TORO

Bocas Town has lots of shops selling hammocks, *molas,* and other indigenous crafts, which can also be bought at the source in Ngöbe-Buglé and Bribrí villages in the Bosque Protector Palo Seco and isles of the Bocas del Toro Archipelago. Many places sell chocolate bars made from locally grown organic cocoa.

Clothes & Accessories
Tropix Surf Shop Calle 3A, Isla Colón, Bocas Town, tel 757-9801, tropixsurf.tripod.com. Custom surfboards and surf duds.

Crafts & Jewelry
Artesanías Bri-brí Emanuel Calle 3, Bocas Town, tel 757-9652. Large selection of native crafts and souvenirs.

Pachamama Calle 3, Bocas Town. Hammocks and other indigenous crafts.

Up in the Hill Old Town, Isla Bastimentos, tel 6607-8962, upinthehill.com. Organic soaps, oils, and balms, plus mosaic and wood craft items.

Markets
Super Gourmet Calle 3 & Ave. Central, next to Gran Hotel Bahía, Bocas Town, tel 757-9357. Specialty food store, including gourmet coffees and locally produced artisanal chocolates.

Entertainment

Panama City has something for everyone, from theater and movies to casinos, sports bars, and nightclubs, many concentrated in the Bella Vista and El Cangrejo districts. Nightclubs and bars in Panama City begin to get in the groove on Wednesday, peak on Friday, and wind down on Saturday. Folkloric festivals are a staple of Azuero Province, which also hosts the nation's wildest Carnaval. Festivals and events are listed in *La Prensa*.

■ PANAMA CITY

The Arts

Asociación Nacional de Conciertos tel 214-7236, conciertospanama.org. Promotes the performing arts.

Atlapa Convention Center tel 526-7200, atlapa.gob.pa. The city's main venue for classical performances and shows.

Ballet Nacional de Panama tel 501-4150, inac.gob.pa. Acclaimed ballet company performs at the Teatro Nacional.

Orquestra Sinfónica Nacional tel 501-4111

Teatro Balboa tel 501-4109. Art deco theater hosting classical performances and plays.

Teatro Nacional tel 501-4107. The city's leading theater.

Casinos

Crown Continental Casino Vía España, tel 395-8000

Royal Casino Hotel Marriott, Calle 52 & Ave. Ricardo Arias, tel 205-7777

Trump Ocean Club Casino Calle Punta Colón, trump oceanclub.com

Veneto Hotel & Casino Vía Veneto bet. Vía España & El Cangrejo, tel 340-8888, venetopanama.com

Festivals

Panama City Jazz Festival (Jan.), panamajazzfestival.com. Four days of music with international performers.

Festival Internacional del Cine (Apr.), tel 202-0867, iffpanama.org. Local and international films.

Festival Nacional de Ballet (Oct.), tel 501-4959. International ballet festival.

Nightlife

Most dance clubs don't get going until well past midnight.

HabanaPanama Calle Eloy Alfaro & Calle 12 Este, Casco Viejo, tel 212-0152, habanapanama.com. Hot salsa dance club.

Hard Rock Hotel Ave. José de la Cruz Herrera, Marbella, tel 294-4000, hrhpanamamegapolis.com. Four club bars including rooftop; live bands rock.

Isabella Multiplaza Pacífica, Vía Israel, tel 391-6008. Upscale nightclub and lounge bar for dancing the night away.

Relic Bar Calle 9na, Casco Viejo, tel 262-1640, relicbar.com. Popular stone-walled cellar bar.

Tantalo Roof Bar Ave B & Calle 8, tel 262-4030, tantalohotel.com. Youthfully hip lounge bar.

Zona Viva Amador Causeway. This area has about a dozen bars and nightclubs.

■ CENTRAL CARIBBEAN & THE CANAL

Casinos

Crown Casino Radisson Colón 2000 Hotel & Casino, Paseo Gorgas, tel 446-2000

Festivals

Festival de Diablos y Congos (New Year's Eve & March 3), Portobelo. Satirical festival recalling slave days.

Los Congos (Jan.–Feb.), Escobal, 15 miles (24 km) SW of Colón. Celebration of Afro-colonial heritage. Draws large crowds.

Carnaval (4 days preceding Ash Wednesday), Isla Grande. Costumed revelry calypso style.

Patronales de la Virgen del Carmen (July 16), Isla Grande. Religious procession by sea and land.

Día de la Raza (Oct. 12), Viento Frío, Colón. Celebration of Columbus's landing.

Black Christ Festival (Oct. 21), Portobelo. Pilgrimage with religious parade, as well as music, dance, and feasting.

Nightlife

Lum's Bar & Grill Corozal, tel 317-6303. Sports bar popular with Zonians; live music.

■ KUNA YALA

Festivals

Carnaval (4 days preceding Ash Wednesday), Río Azucar. Four days of music, dance, and drinking of *chicha* (fermented corn alcohol).

Nogagope (Oct. 10–17), Isla Tigre. Celebration of traditional *nogagope* dance, plus canoe races and games.

■ DARIÉN

Festivals

Emberá-Wounaan Cultural Festival (Oct.), Emberá Purú. Traditional music and dance.

CENTRAL PANAMA

Festivals

Carnaval Acuático (4 days preceding Ash Wednesday), Penonomé. Mardi Gras–style carnival, with the carnival queen and attendees floating on a raft.

Feria de las Orquídeas de Santa Fé (Aug.), Santa Fé de Veraguas. Orchid festival.

Festival del Toro Guapo (Oct.), Antón. Three-day fiesta with floats, beauty contests, and bullfighting.

Festival del Topon (Dec. 8 & 9), Penonomé. Christmas procession with participants bearing the figure of the patron saint.

AZUERO PENINSULA

Casinos

Casino Fiesta Hotel los Guayacanes, Vía Cicunvalación, Chitré, tel 996-9756, losguayacanes.com

Festivals

Fiesta de Los Reyes Magos (Jan. 6), Macaracas. Celebration of Epiphany with the three wise men on horseback.

Carnaval (4 days preceding Ash Wednesday), Las Tablas. Panama's most popular, crowded, and colorful Mardi Gras–style carnival.

Festival de Corpus Christi, (May/June), Villa de los Santos. Two weeks of elaborate devil dances, parades, and fireworks.

Festival de la Pollera (July), Las Tablas. Young women model the national costume, vying to become the National Queen.

Fiestas Patronales de Santa Librada (July 20), Las Tablas. Religious procession, irreligious revelry.

Festival Nacional de la Mejorana (Sept.), Guararé. The nation's prime folkloric festival, with oxcart parade and villages queens in *polleras*, plus folkoric music and dance.

El Grito de la Villa de los Santos (Nov. 10), Villa de los Santos. Parade celebrates the first call for independence.

Nightlife

Centro Turístico Los Guayacanes, Chitré, tel 996-9758. Two bars plus nightclub adjoin a hotel.

CHIRIQUÍ & THE CORDILLERA

The Arts

Chiriquí Eventos Cultural chiriqui eventos.blogspot.com. Excellent resource for events. Spanish only.

Casinos

Fiesta Casino Hotel Gran Nacional, Calle Pérez Balladares, David, tel 775-2222, hotelnacional panama.com

Money Casino David David, tel 774-8887

Festivals

Feria de las Flores y Café (mid-Jan.), Boquete. Hugely popular flower festival.

Boquete Jazz & Blues Festival (Feb.). Regional towns come alive.

Feria Internacional de David (mid-March), David. Agricultural fair, with livestock, rodeo, and folkloric performances, plus live music.

Fiesta Patronal de San José (week of March 19), David. Celebrates the town's patron saint.

Independencia de Panamá de España (Nov. 28), Boquete. Independence Day celebration.

Festival del Tambor (Nov. 28), David. Folkloric presentations honor Panama's independence.

Nightlife

La Cabaña Calle, de la Feria, Boquete. Riverside disco on the fairground draws youth for everything from reggaeton to salsa.

Zanzibar Ave Central, Boquete, no tel. Hip low-key jazz bar; live music weekends.

BOCAS DEL TORO

Festivals

Carnaval (last week in Feb.), Bocas Town. Party Brazilian-style, with floats, beauty contests, and nonstop music and dance.

Fiestas Patronales de la Virgen del Carmen (3rd Sun. in July), La Colonia Santeña, Isla Colón. Religious pilgrimage.

Feria del Mar (Sept.), Bocas Town. Four days of dancing, feasting, and fun on the beach.

Fundación de la Provincia de Bocas del Toro (Nov. 16), Bocas Town. Parades and street parties celebrating the founding of Bocas del Toro Province.

Nightlife

Aqua Lounge Isla Carinero, bocasaqualounge.info. Waterfront dancing with a diving board.

Barco Hundido Calle 1, Bocas Town. Party-hearty bar with dancing on floating docks.

Mondo Taitú Calle 5 & Ave. G, Bocas del Toro, tel 757-9425, mondotaitu.com. Beachfront party central hosting frequent special events. Hookahs.

Pickled Parrot Isla Carinero, tel 757-9093. Karaoke on Wednesday nights.

Roots Old Bank, Isla Bastimentos, tel 6662-1442. Colorful reggae bar.

La Rumba Big Creek, Bocas Town, tel 757-9181. Open-air sports bar with satellite TVs.

El Toro Loco Ave. Central, Bocas del Torro. Hooters-style expat-run sports bar serving draft beer; live music.

Riptide Calle Norte, Bocas del Toro, tel 6948-3762. A beaten-up boat converted into a bar.

Wine Bar Calle 3, Bocas del Torro, tel 6606-1736. Sink into a lounge chair in this rickety upstairs bar serving tapas.

Activities

The nation supplements its entertainment scene with activities that make the most of the natural diversity. Below you'll find a general primer on activities and various outfitters throughout Panama, followed by a listing of region-specific ones. Note that the companies described may cover additional activities and areas than the ones featured here.

GENERAL

Adventure Trips

Ancon Expeditions tel 269-9415, anconexpeditions.com. A variety of adventures offered throughout Panama, including exploring Darién by dugout canoe, a trek along the Camino Real, and family trips to Panama's best places.

Expediciones Tropicales tel & fax 317-1279, xtrop.com. Adventure travel stressing conservationism. Custom itineraries are offered.

Panama Explorer Tours tel 215-2330, pexclub.com. Adventure trips in Chiriquí, Cocle, and Panamá Provinces.

Birding

Observing birds and wildlife is best done with a guide.

Ancon Expeditions tel 269-9415, anconexpeditions.com. This outfitter has some of the best guides in the country.

Birdingpal birdingpal.org /Panama.htm has a list of freelance birding guides.

Birding Pipeline Panama tel 6997-1935, birdingpipelinepanama .com. Birding trips in Central Panama and the Canal Zone with local ornithologist Kent Livezey

Fundación Avifauna Eugene Eisenmann, tel 264-6266, avifauna .org.pa. Nonprofit society to protect Panama's birds.

Just Adventures Panama tel 6446-0466, justadventurespanama .com. One-to-four-day birding trips through Panama, including Darién, Chiriquí, and Bocas del Toro.

Fishing

Sportfishing focuses on the Hannibal Bank in the Pacific. Fishing excursions are also offered from Panama City. Lake Gatún is world-class for peacock bass.

Panama Fishing & Catching tel 6622-0212 or 6505-9553, panamafishingandcatching.com. Fishing trips throughout Panama, including Lake Gatún, Bayano River, and Tuna Coast.

Golf

Panama has about a dozen 9- and 18-hole courses. Premier golf courses are concentrated around Panama City and the Pacific beach resorts of central Panama.

Hiking & Mountain Biking

Mountain bikes can be rented in popular tourist spots such as Bocas del Toro, Boquete, and El Valle de Antón.

Backroads tel 510/527-1555 or 800/462-2848, backroads .com. Its multi-activity family trip in Panama includes hiking.

Nature Cruising

Cruise boats travel mostly at night, with days spent at wilderness sites, at indigenous communities, and in passage through the Panama Canal. Wildlife guides lead hikes and excursions by boat. Snorkeling at prime coral reefs.

Nature-focused cruises on small ships, including on the Panama Canal.

National Geographic Expeditions tel 888/966-8687, nationalgeographicexpeditions.com. Nature-oriented small-ship cruises of Costa Rica and Panama using the best naturalist guides in the region.

Windstar Cruises tel 866/643-3105, windstarcruises.com. Nature-focused cruises on luxury masted ships, including through the Panama Canal.

Nature Tours

Panama abounds in opportunities for enjoying nature, which is best done with a licensed naturalist guide. The following companies specialize in nature trips.

Ancon Expeditions tel 269-9415, fax 264-3713, anconexpeditions.com

International Expeditions tel 855/230-6751, ietravel.com. Its nine-day "Panama: Wildlife Bridge of the Americas" trip is led by a renowned Panamanian naturalist.

Panama Travel Experts, tel 6671-7923 or 213/455-2314, panamatravelexperts.com

Reef & Rainforest, tel 01803/866-985, reefandrainforest .co.uk. UK-based nature company with group tours and tailored itineraries.

Sailing & Cruising

There are splendid anchorages on both Caribbean and Pacific shores, plus a wide range of marina facilities cater to private yachters. Several companies offer daylong to ten-day boating adventures, and sunset cruises are available at some locales.

Panama Sailing Adventures tel 6804-8484, panamasailing adventures.com

Panama Sailing & Diving Adventures tel 6668-6849, panamasailing.com

San Blas Sailing, tel 314-1800, panamayachttours.com

Scuba Diving

On the Pacific side, the waters around Isla Coiba and Archipiélago de las Perlas offer the best opportunities. On the Caribbean side, Bocas del Toro has great reef diving, and Spanish galleons litter the ocean floor around Portobelo.

Scuba Panama tel 261-4064 or 6673-3173, scubapanama.com. Dive in some of the best places in Panama, including the canal. Offers scuba trips, a dive resort near the town of Portobelo, and courses.

Surfing

The Pacific coast has superb surfing spots good enough to host international competitions. Playa Venado and Santa Catalina are especially good. On the Caribbean side, Bocas del Toro and Isla Grande offer worthy challenges.

Panama Surf Tours, tel 6671-7777, panamasurftours.com. Surfing trips to all major surf sites in Panama, including Catalina, Isla Grande, Punta Burica, and Bocas.

▓ PANAMA CITY

Miscellaneous

HeliAncon tel 315-1840, heli-ancon.com. Helicopter tours.

Panama Marine Adventures tel 226-8917, pmatours.net. Segway tours of Panama City.

Sportfishing

Panama Fishing & Fun Time tel 203-3363, letsfishpanama.com

Water Sports

Balboa Yacht Club Fort Amador, tel 228-5196, balboayachtclub .com.pa. In Balboa Harbor, with haul-out service for yachts.

Flamenco Yacht Club & Marina tel 314-1980. Modern marina.

Panama Yacht Tours tel 263-5044, panamayachttours.com. Fishing and motorized sailing tours.

▓ CENTRAL CARIBBEAN & THE CANAL

Birding

Canopy Tower Parque Nacional Soberanía, tel 214-9714 or 264-5720, canopytower.com. Renowned birders' hotel with lookouts.

Panama Rainforest Discovery Center, Paque Nacional Soberanía, tel 6588-0697, pipelineroad.org. Good birding venue.

Boat Tours

Canal & Bay Tours tel 209-2002, canalandbaytours.com. Guided transits of the canal.

Panama Marine Adventures tel 226-8917, pmatours.net. Partial and full transits of the Canal.

Golf

Summit Golf & Resort tel 232-4653, summitgolfpanama.com. 18-hole championship course.

Rafting

Aventuras Panamá tel 260-0044 or 6679-4404, aventuraspanama .com. White-water trips on the Chagres and Mamoní Rivers.

Scuba Diving

Coco Plum Eco-Lodge 3 miles (4.8 km) W of Portobelo, tel 448-2102, cocoplum-panama .com. Dive shop runs trips to the nearby reefs.

Coral Dreams Isla Contadora, tel 6536-1776, coral-dreams.com. Diving in the Islas de las Perlas.

Panama Divers tel 448-2293, panamadivers.com. Specializes in dives at Portobelo.

Scuba Panama tel 261-4064 or 6673-3173, scubapanama.com. Dive trips at Portobelo.

▓ KUNA YALA

Birding & Hiking

Burbayar Lodge, Nusugandí, tel 236-6061 or 6949-5700, burbayar.net. Guided excursions.

Ecocircuitos tel 315-1305, ecocircuitos.com. Kayaking excursions, plus snorkeling and dugout canoe trip in a ten-day tour.

Exotic Adventures tel 6673-5381, panamaexotic adventures.com. Hiking and kayaking adventures.

Sailing

San Blas Sailing tel 314-1288 or 314-1800, sanblassailing.com. Four- to 21-day itineraries in the San Blas Islands.

Scuba Diving

Coral Lodge Costa Arriba, tel 838-9988, corallodge.com. Also arranges sea kayaking and horseback riding.

Sea Kayaking

Expediciones Tropicales tel 317-1279, xtrop.com. Sea kayaking in the San Blas.

▓ DARIÉN

Adventure Trips

Ancon Expeditions tel 269-9415, anconexpeditions.com. Specializes in birding, hiking, and other nature programs in Darién.

Ecocircuitos tel 315-1305, ecocircuitos.com. Various ecotours and adventures.

Exotic Adventures tel 6673-5381 or 6747-6096, panamaexotic adventures.com. Three-day hiking, kayaking, and horseback adventure.

Sportfishing

Tropic Star Lodge tel 407/423-9931 or 800/682-3424, tropic star.com. World-class sportfishing.

▓ CENTRAL PANAMA

Adventure Trips

Crater Valley Adventure Center El Valle de Antón, tel 215-2328, crater-valley.com. Rock climbing, canyoneering, and more.

Panama Explorer Tours tel 215-2330, pexclub.com. From hiking, kayaking, and biking to corporate and kids' adventure retreats.

Boating

Santa Catalina Boat Tours tel 6767-0749, santacatalinaboat tours.com. Boat and surfing tours to remote beaches and islands.

Canopy Tours

Canopy Adventure El Valle de Antón, tel 264-5720, canopy tower.com. Zipline tours.

Golf

Buenaventura Panama Golf Course Río Hato, Coclé, tel 908-3333, buenaventurapanamagolf .com. Par-72 Nicklaus-designed oceanfront course.

Coronado Golf Course Coronado Golf & Beach Resort, tel 264-3164. Tom Fazio–designed course.

Vista Mar Resort Playa San Carlos, tel 340-3888, vistamar resort.com. New 18-hole championship course.

Horseback Riding

Alquiler de Caballos El Valle de Antón, tel 6646-5813. Horseback trips from one hour to half day.

Club Equestre Coronado tel 264-3164. Resort equestrian club.

Kiteboarding

MacheteKites, Punta Chame, tel 264-7560 or 6674-7772, machete kites.com. Kite-surfing school Nov.–April.

Nitro City Panama Punta Chame, tel 202-6875, nitrocity panama.com. Also wake-boarding, ATVs, and MotoX.

Scuba Diving

Coiba Dive Center Playa Santa Catalina, tel 6774 0808, coibadivecenter.com. Snorkeling

and scuba trips to Isla Coiba.

Scuba Coiba Playa Santa Catalina, tel 6980-7122, scubacoiba .com. Dive trips twice daily, plus multiday trips with overnights.

Sportfishing.

Pesca Panama tel 6614-5850 or 800/946-3474, pescapanama.com. Fabulous fishing adventures around Isla Coiba.

Water Sports

Fluid Adventures Panama Playa Santa Catalina, tel 6560-6558, fluidadventurespanama.com. Kayaking trips to Isla Coiba.

▓ AZUERO PENINSULA

Scuba Diving & Sportfishing

Pedasi Sports Club Pedasí, tel 995-2894, pedasisportsclub.biz. Diving, including PADI training, plus sportfishing.

▓ CHIRIQUÍ & THE CORDILLERA

Canopy Tours

Boquete Tree Trek Boquete, tel 202-6843, aventurist.com. Glide between treetops.

Fishing

Gone Fishing Panama Resort Hotel tel 6480-5296, gonefishing panama.com. A family-friendly secluded vacation eco-resort in Gulf of Chiriqui National Marine Park.

Golf

Valle Escondido Resort, Golf & Spa tel 720-2454, veresort.com. An18-hole championship golf course with spectacular views.

Rafting

Chiriqui River Rafting tel 6879-4382, panama-rafting.com. Half-day rafting trips on seven rivers.

Scuba Diving

Golden Frog Scuba Boca Chica, tel 6586-4838, goldenfrogscuba .com. Diving at Islas Secas and Isla Coiba.

Sportfishing

Panama Big Game Fishing Club tel 6627-5431, panama biggamefishingclub.com. All-inclusive three-, four-, five-, and six-day fishing packages.

Paradise Fishing Lodge Quebrada de Piedra, Chiriquí, tel 6029-1104, paradisefishinglodge.com

▓ BOCAS DEL TORO

Cultural Tours

ODESEN tel 6569-3869, odesen.bocasdeltoro.org. Immersions in Naso-Teribe culture.

Fishing

Boteros Bocatoreños Bocas Town, tel 757-9760, e-mail: boterosbocas@yahoo.com. A local boatmen's cooperative offering custom tours.

Scuba Diving

Starfleet Scuba Bocas Town, tel 757-9630, starfleetscuba .com. Reputable dive resort and operator with a full complement of PADI programs and trips.

Surfing

Del Toro Surfing Bocas Town, tel 6570-8277, e-mail: deltorosurf@ yahoo.com.ar. Offers surfing lessons and trips.

Panama Surf Tours Boca Chica, tel 6671-7777, panamasurftours .com. Surf lessons plus trips to the best surf breaks.

INDEX

ILLUSTRATIONS CREDITS

All photos by Gilles Mingasson/Reportage by Getty Images, unless otherwise noted.
Front Cover, Danielho/iStockphoto; Spine, J Marshall - Tribaleye Images/Alamy; 9, Eleana/Shutterstock; 11, Stephen St. John/National Geographic Creative; 12, Amy Pinoargote/Bigstock.com; 14–15, Jon Hicks/Corbis; 21, Jim Lipschutz/Shutterstock; 22, Humberto Olarte Cupas/Alamy; 26, Hulton Archive/Getty Images; 28-29, Hulton Archive/Getty Images; 33, Hulton Archive/Getty Images; 35, Stephen Ferry/Liaison/Getty Images; 37, Rodrigo Arangua/AFP/Getty Images; 40, Vilainecrevette/Shutterstock; 47, WorldsWildlifeWonders/Shutterstock; 51, WorldsWildlifeWonders/Shutterstock; 56, Paul Hawthorne/Getty Images; 60, Holger Mette/Shutterstock; 75, Humberto Olarte Cupas/Alamy; 80, Courtesy © Biomuseo/photo: Victoria Murillo, Istmophoto.com; 94, AP Photo/Heinz Krimmer/picture-alliance/dpa; 97, AP Photo/ Arnulfo Franco; 98, George F. Mobley/National Geographic Stock; 104, Mattias Klum/National Geographic/Getty Images; 106, Hulton Archive/Getty Images; 113, Danny Lehman/Corbis; 121, Diana Walker/Time & Life Images/Getty Images; 136, WorldsWildlifeWonders/Shutterstock; 137, George Grall/National Geographic/Getty Images; 164, Wolcott Henry/National Geographic/Getty Images; 170, Daniel Ho/Istmophoto.com; 184, Tim Graham/Getty Images; 187, John Warburton Lee/SuperStock; 188, Alberto Lowe/Reuters/Corbis; 191, Dave G. Houser/Corbis; 193, Peter Knif/Shutterstock; 194, jcarillet/iStockphoto.com; 214, Scott B. Rosen/Alamy; 218, Alexey Stiop/Shutterstock.

National Geographic
TRAVELER
Panama

Published by the National Geographic Society
Gary E. Knell, *President and Chief Executive Officer*
John M. Fahey, *Chairman of the Board*
Declan Moore, *Executive Vice President; President, Publishing and Travel*
Melina Gerosa Bellows, *Executive Vice President; Publisher and Chief Creative Officer, Books, Kids, and Family*
Lynn Cutter, *Executive Vice President, Travel*
Keith Bellows, *Senior Vice President and Editor in Chief, National Geographic Travel Media*

Prepared by the Book Division
Hector Sierra, *Senior Vice President and General Manager*
Janet Goldstein, *Senior Vice President and Editorial Director*
Jonathan Halling, *Creative Director*
Marianne R. Koszorus, *Design Director*
Barbara A. Noe, *Senior Editor, National Geographic Travel Books*
R. Gary Colbert, *Production Director*
Jennifer A. Thornton, *Director of Managing Editorial*
Susan S. Blair, *Director of Photography*
Meredith C. Wilcox, *Director, Administration and Rights Clearance*

Staff for This Book
Justin Kavanagh, *Project Editor*
Elisa Gibson, *Art Director*
Ruth Ann Thompson, *Designer*
Carl Mehler, *Director of Maps*
Mike McNey & Mapping Specialists, *Map Production*
Marshall Kiker, *Associate Managing Editor*
Michael O'Connor, *Production Editor*
Galen Young, *Rights Clearance Specialist*
Katie Olsen, *Production Design Assistant*
Hannah Lauterback and Marlena Serviss, *Contributors*

Production Services
Phillip L. Schlosser, *Senior Vice President*
Chris Brown, *Vice President, NG Book Manufacturing*
Nicole Elliott, *Director of Production*
George Bounelis, *Senior Production Manager*
Rachel Faulise, *Manager*
Robert L. Barr, *Manager*

Map illustrations drawn by Chris Orr Associates, Southampton, England.
Cutaway illustrations drawn by Maltings Partnership, Derby, England.

The information in this book has been carefully checked and to the best of our knowledge is accurate. However, details are subject to change, and the National Geographic Society cannot be responsible for such changes, or for errors or omissions. Assessments of sites, hotels, and restaurants are based on the author's subjective opinions, which do not necessarily reflect the publisher's opinion.

The National Geographic Society is one of the world's largest nonprofit scientific and educational organizations. Founded in 1888 to "increase and diffuse geographic knowledge," the member-supported Society works to inspire people to care about the planet. Through its online community, members can get closer to explorers and photographers, connect with other members around the world, and help make a difference. National Geographic reflects the world through its magazines, television programs, films, music and radio, books, DVDs, maps, exhibitions, live events, school publishing programs, interactive media, and merchandise. *National Geographic* magazine, the Society's official journal, published in English and 38 local-language editions, is read by more than 60 million people each month. The National Geographic Channel reaches 440 million households in 171 countries in 38 languages. National Geographic Digital Media receives more than 25 million visitors a month. National Geographic has funded more than 10,000 scientific research, conservation, and exploration projects and supports an education program promoting geography literacy. For more information, visit nationalgeographic.com.

For more information, please call 1-800-NGS LINE (647-5463) or write to the following address:

National Geographic Society
1145 17th Street N.W.
Washington, D.C. 20036-4688 U.S.A.

For information about special discounts for bulk purchases, please contact National Geographic Books Special Sales: ngspecsales@ngs.org

For rights or permissions inquiries, please contact National Geographic Books Subsidiary Rights: ngbookrights@ngs.org

National Geographic Traveler: Panama
(Third Edition)
ISBN: 978-1-4262-1401-1

Printed in Hong Kong
14/THK/1